City of Dreams

City of Dreams

Illustrations by Robert Biffle

A GUIDE TO

Port Townsend

Edited by Peter Simpson

with contributions by

Robin Biffle

Jim Heynen

Nora Porter

Mark Welch

BAY PRESS / PORT TOWNSEND / WASHINGTON

The illustrations on pages 13 and 34 are by Hillary Stewart from her book *Cedar: Tree of Life to the Northwest Coast Indians*. University of Washington Press, 1984.

The illustration on page 268 is by Rod Freeman from *Wale*.

The photos on pages 44, 70, 71 & 307 are from the Jefferson County Historical Society.

Printed in the United States of America

92 91 90 89 87 86   5 4 3 2 1

BAY PRESS

3710 Discovery Road North

Port Townsend, Washington 98368

Library of Congress Cataloging-in-Publication Data

City of dreams.

Bibliography: p.

Includes index.

1. Port Townsend (Wash.) – Dictionaries and encyclopedias.

2. Port Townsend Region (Wash.) – Dictionaries and encyclopedias.

I. Biffle, Robin.

II. Simpson, Peter, 1934-

F899.P85C57   1986   979.7'98   85-72730

ISBN 0-941920-06-2

ISBN 0-941920-05-4 (pbk.)

To Richard F. McCurdy, Sr.

Each of the contributors wishes to acknowledge the ACKNOWLEDGMENTS friendly assistance and the daily welcome offered by Dixie Romadka, Cecelia Casprowitz, and volunteers at the Jefferson County Historical Society's museum, and Illma Mund and other volunteers of the Jefferson County Genealogical Society. A major part of the research was conducted in the volumes of the nearly one-hundred-year-old *Port Townsend Leader*, which the newspaper contributed to the museum's library in the early 1980s. Thanks are offered to publisher Frank Garred for making them so readily available for research.

In addition to these shared acknowledgments, each contributor was assisted and inspired by numerous others.

Robin Biffle offers thanks to Sally Weinschrott, chair of the Jefferson County office of the Washington State University Co-operative Extension Service, and to the Eels Northwest Collection at the Whitman College Library. She also offers special acknowledgment to Josephine Howell, Chauncy Park Biffle, Evelyn Monger, and Allen Crenshaw Taylor – "my grandparents who taught me that history is really just a bunch of good stories."

Jim Heynen acknowledges the assistance of Carol Bangs, Jeremiah Gorsline, and Liz Smith.

Nora Porter thanks Marge Abraham, Noreen Hobbs, Bob Porter, Linda Okazaki, Tom Wilson, and Wendy Sternshein.

Peter Simpson acknowledges Paul and Sally Boyer, B. G. Brown, Frank Green, Marilou Green, David and Judy Hartman, Paddy Hernan, Anne Hirondelle, Tony King, Robert J. Osborne, Mark Rasmussen, and Dennis Sullivan, Jr. He wishes to give special thanks to Thatcher Bailey who eagerly agreed to publish this book before ever seeing one page of copy and who never wavered in his support, Don Keenan who continually offered encouragement, Cathy Johnson who provided meticulous copy editing and cogent editorial suggestions, Pat Simpson who was always there, Tree

Swenson who sat through innumerable editorial meetings in order to develop the book's elegant design, and to each of the other contributors who so quickly got into the spirit of the thing and "who kept their humor in the face of my frequent nagging."

Mark Welch acknowledges the assistance of Jeffery McDonald, Margaret Wilson, and Marjorie Welch. He gives special thanks to Connie Welch, and to the memories of Joe Welch, Walt Herstrom and Bill Daly, "who instilled in me a love of history and the language."

At times I am certain that Water Street is part of a stage set, and that I never walked down it past the handsomely restored brick buildings of another century. Within the length and breadth of reality, I could never have entered bookshops where I was invited to linger and read, or eaten in restaurants where shellfish were prepared as they are in Paris, or hovered in antique shops where my heritage and my youth were restored to me in mariners' compasses, feathered weather vanes, and polished mahogany and brass.

Above the town there were green cliffs, and I sat on the grass of the highest one and listened to the cries of circling gulls. In the hollow of the land behind me, poets . . . sang aloud of a printing press for the publication of books of those who remembered their dreams.

At night, I watched from the cliff the illuminated palaces of distant ferry boats floating into the harbors far below. I want to remember this dream.

That is how short-story writer Kay Boyle remembers Port Townsend after a summer spent teaching at a writers' conference. Seattle-based magazine editor Rob Carson experienced a different dream after two years' residence in Port Townsend as a newspaper reporter. In a 1984 *Pacific Northwest* magazine article entitled "City of Dreams," Carson reported that when he first saw Port Townsend in 1976 he felt as if he "could lift off and fly . . . start [his life] all over. I liked the people I saw walking up and down Water Street, and I liked the books in the bookstores. I liked the idea of walking on empty beaches and watching the sun rise over the Cascades." Yet, two years later, he "moved away, full of doubts . . . part of a steady flow of dreamers who wash up in Port Townsend for a year or two or five and then move on. They drive through town on summer vacations . . . and they are entranced. The old Victorians get them, or the view, or the isolated *integrity* of the place. They give up good jobs in Santa Fe, Sausalito, Columbus, and Omaha to pack up and move here – almost always without work – trusting to their ingenuity to make ends meet. Like I was, they are fooled by the Victorian architecture into thinking they can step back in time. A few stay. Most, like me, do not. Making the dream work is harder than it looks.''

The disparity of opinion about Port Townsend has always been evident. In 1966, Northwest historian and editor of the *Seattle Post-Intelligencer* Nard Jones wrote this writer: ''I am not a Seattleite, although born one. I wake in the night longing for two places on earth, one is Manhattan, the other Port Townsend.'' He never explained why. Two generations earlier, Spokane attorney Patrick Henry Winston reminisced about his days in Port Townsend during its 1890 boom: ''Suh, when I first knew Port Townsend, it had three classes of people – Indians, sailors, and sonsabitches. But by now, suh, the Indians have all died and the sailors have all sailed away.''

It is curious how one town of six thousand people can evoke such contradictory responses. And it is curious that the differences can emerge with such unremitting regularity over a span of eighty years. It is even more curious that the opinions can be felt so intensely, sometimes cryptically, yet ever so freely. Invariably Port Townsend leaves a distinctive mark, unlike that of any other small town. Port Townsend hasn't the glitz of Vail or Aspen, the elegance of La Jolla, the intellect of Amherst, the history and restoration of Williamsburg, the money of Carmel, or the spirited zaniness of Key West. Instead, Port Townsend offers the image of the frontier, even a century after that frontier was geographically closed. Although the frontier is now metaphorical, it nevertheless helps to define the Port Townsend character. Never fully settled or entrenched, always with room for one or a dozen more, sensually one of the most enchanting places in one of the most enchanting regions of the world, Port Townsend offers the promise of the old frontier by inciting the dreams of its beholders. As Carson noted, it seems a place ''where people come . . . to be healed,'' a place where ''people are given a lot of room to go their own way,'' ''a place where one [can] have an impact.'' These dreamers see Port Townsend as a land of promise, when, in fact, it is only their desires that are released by the site. Expectations held for Port Townsend are seldom more than transubstantiated dreams. One's hope becomes the city's promise. Inevitably, as with a child who is to become an adult, disappointment must ensue, and a dreamer leaves only to have another take his place. It has gone on for more than 130 years in Port Townsend, and unless there is some drastic change, it will likely continue.

This book seeks to examine the promise that the city has evoked and to identify some of the triggers of those dreams. It is neither exhaustive nor inclusive. It is, rather, the separate and collective viewpoints of five residents of Port Townsend, men and women who share some of the dreams and some of the disappointments. Each of us, I suppose, has come to recognize and accept that Port Townsend is not simply our city of dreams, but also the rumpled bed in which we awaken from those dreams.

PETER SIMPSON
Port Townsend, Washington

All entries are listed alphabetically. EDITORIAL NOTES

An index is provided for locating names of historical and living persons.

Maps are located on pages 309–315.

CROSS REFERENCES THAT APPEAR WITHIN THE TEXT ARE GIVEN IN SMALL CAPITALS; cross references not incorporated into the text are listed in italics and parentheses.

Because of the numerous references to the *Port Townsend Leader*, the name has been shortened to the more familiar *Leader*. All other newspapers, magazines, and periodicals are referred to by their full and proper names.

The contributors have signed certain entries. Their initials appear in brackets at the end of each entry so attributed.

City of Dreams

"Port Townsend is a seed community, a mystical place ... a place where one can find people on the leading edge in many fields," said Forest Shomer, director of the Abundant Life Seed Foundation, which is as much a philosophy of life as it is a small Port Townsend business.

The foundation's concerns are holistic and include agriculture, lifestyle, environment, health and healing, and nonviolence. The name is based on the parable of the Good Shepherd – "that they might have life and ... have it more abundantly" – and the business operates on the "new age" motto, "Act locally, think globally."

Its activities include a successful retail and mail-order seed business, a bookstore with books on Northwest gardening, and an educational and informational network that sponsors workshops for gardeners and publishes a newsletter for its 9,000 members. Many local members test the foundation's seeds in their personal gardens.

Established in 1976, the Abundant Life Seed Foundation moved its offices from SEATTLE to GARDINER in 1977, then to BLYN, and on to Port Townsend in 1980. Shomer sees the foundation's work in gardening as a means to create a community of people who care for the earth through organic gardening and who care for one another by working together. He finds Port Townsend an appropriate place for local activation of global issues. Port Townsend's original Indian name, KAH TAI, referred to its function as a portage between the rough Strait of Juan de Fuca to the calm Port Townsend Bay. The foundation redefines the name as a metaphor, seeing Port Townsend as a place in which to move between different cultural environments. [J.H.]

Beginning at Point Wilson and extending to the southern tip of Marrowstone Island, Admiralty Inlet connects the Strait of Juan de Fuca and Puget Sound. It was named by Captain George Vancouver in 1792 to honor his commanders, the Board of Admiralty, supervisors of England's Royal Navy. Earlier attempts by Spanish explorers to name the inlet "Bocode Camano" failed because they neglected to publish charts proclaiming their discoveries. The inlet is well known to mariners for the colliding currents of the strait and the sound, which create some of the more impressive and hazardous RIPTIDES in the Northwest.

AGRICULTURE "Port Townsend is immediately surrounded by a country that is exceedingly rich for agricultural purposes. The soil is absolutely inexhaustible and like the fields of Italy may be cultivated for thousands of years without causing perceptible diminution of crops. Compost is unnecessary and growing crops requires only ordinary care. There are thousands upon thousands of acres of such land within easy reach of P.T. and the product of the farms will always find a ready market." So said the Port Townsend Chamber of Commerce in 1891. This optimistic evaluation of the area's agricultural potential was generally accepted for years. Farming, maritime interests, and the wood products industry were of equal importance in the area's early economic development.

Among the earliest and eventually most prominent farmers were William Bishop and William Eldridge, who took up claims in CHIMACUM in 1854 and were partners for more than twenty years. Bishop concentrated on dairy farming, and his butter and cheese were highly regarded even in Seattle. In 1877, he produced 6,881 pounds of butter, which netted him, he recorded, exactly $2,619.24½. He was also a noted Holstein breeder and won several state awards for his cattle. Bishop sold his farm to Portland investors during the boom in 1889 and moved to Port Townsend. Bishop's and a neighboring farm were consolidated as the Glendale Creamery in 1909, which introduced the county's first irrigation system in 1910, operated by a pump powered by a wood-burning steam engine.

Another rich farming area centered around Nordland on Marrowstone Island. Known for many years for its fine turkey crop, it is still a strawberry-producing area and celebrates an annual Strawberry Festival.

Until World War II, the Port Townsend vegetable market was controlled by Chinese truck gardeners. The names and faces of Hop Yuen, Charley Tuey, Charley Foo, and Yip Suey were recognized by every housewife in Port Townsend in those years, for the Chinese not only grew the vegetables but also delivered them to the door, attractively arrayed in horse-drawn wagons. (The last of these gardeners, Ah Tom, died while working his farm in the mid-1960s). Much of their produce was grown on land that is now a drainage pond near North Beach (see *Chinese Gardens*). These farmers developed a tide gate that allowed excess water from underground sources to run off at low tide yet shut out the potentially flooding seawater at high tide. For many years, spanning the nineteenth and twentieth centuries, the Chinese also cultivated land at Station Prairie, which has since become the Jefferson County International AIRPORT.

In 1910, Jefferson County exceeded the state average in the value of farmland and buildings. In 1914, it was classified as a "general agricultural county" (as opposed to lumber, urban, shipping, or fishing). In 1928, 12,000 to 14,000 of Jefferson County's 1,805,000 acres were cultivated. The county extension agent had a column in the *Leader* for years, and agricultural news took up more inches of news reporting than did sports or social activities. To encourage farming, local canneries offered incentives: in 1920, the Olympic Canning and Packing Company offered a fifty-dollar prize for the best acre of beets and beans.

In recent decades, however, fewer and fewer small farmers could be guaranteed a livelihood. In 1940, there were 513 farms in Jefferson County. In 1978, there were twenty-five. In 1982 the average assessed value of agricultural land in Jefferson County was approximately six hundred dollars per acre, its market value between fifteen hundred and three thousand dollars. By comparison, residential property was selling for twenty-five hundred to four thousand dollars per lot or between thirty-four thousand to fifty thousand dollars an acre.   [R.B.]

In November 1946, Jefferson County became the proud owner of an airfield known by some as "Jefferson County International Cow Pasture," by others as "the shortest international airport in the country," and by everybody in the county as "the issue that won't die." Regardless of local sentiment, the Jefferson County International Airport is one of only forty-nine designated point-of-entry airports in the United

A comparison of the number of acres planted in each crop:

	1928	1982
Oats	258	0
Apples	160	36
Wheat	155	0
Potatoes	100	0
Barley	39	0
Strawberries	28	0
Corn	8	0
Cabbage	5	0
Lettuce	4	0

A comparison of the county's animal census revealed the following:

	1928	1982
Poultry	32,378	723
Cows	3,544	4,757
Hogs	914	137
Horses	436	178
Sheep	353	102

AIRPORT

States; customs service is available twenty-four hours a day.

In 1929, in an effort to win international status (awarded first-come first-served based on facilities offered), the aviation committee of the Port Townsend Chamber of Commerce enticed Gorst Air Transport to include Port Townsend in its sphere of proposed service. The first airplane to clear customs in Port Townsend did so that year. In 1930, Port Townsend was briefly a seaplane "flag stop" between Seattle and Victoria and received its coveted point-of-entry status.

A proposed airport site at Point Hudson was all but abandoned in 1931 when the Army established its emergency flying field at Station Prairie, four miles from Port Townsend on part of the old Fort Townsend reservation. The field was also used in training coast artillery and air corpsmen and was accessible to civilians, who were issued "revocable permits to land and take off" but who had to store their airplanes elsewhere. Because Port Townsend was still not regularly served by any airline, its chamber of commerce submitted a proposal in 1936 for a Works Progress Administration project, a seaplane landing in what is presently the boat basin at Point Hudson. The project was never approved.

During World War II, civilian aviation interests took a backseat to military needs, but in early 1946, Station Prairie Field came under local control. In the summer of 1946, West Coast Airlines proposed including Port Townsend as a stop in its network, but airline officials ruled that the airport facilities were too limited. The local populace plunged headlong into a controversy over the adequacy and location of the airport, an issue that is resurrected every few years.

Amid endless debate, Jefferson County International Airport serves the county year-round – except on a few wet winter days when the east end of the turf field is covered with surface water.

ALCOHOL PLANT   After the 1907 closure of the Washington Mill Company, its president, W. J. Adams, remained interested in the area and in 1911 spearheaded the development of Classen Chemical Company at the south end of Port Townsend Bay, below HADLOCK. He imported distillery equipment from France to convert sawdust into alcohol and bastol, a farm product made of leftover pulp mixed with cattle feed. The company was never successful. The bastol mildewed in its San Francisco warehouse, and alcohol from other distilleries could be transported by rail at half the price of local shipping costs. By 1913 production ceased and the plant closed. It remained vacant until recent years, when it was purchased for a resort that was still under development six years later.

(*Alnus rubra*) The most abundant deciduous tree in **ALDER**
the Puget Sound region, alder is used primarily as firewood because of its availability and lack of spark. It burns quickly, but airtight stoves retard combustion enough to hold a fire overnight. Cold, still mornings in the spring and fall reveal streaks of alder smoke over Happy Valley and other low-lying areas. A species of lichen attaches to the alder bark, giving it a whitish cast that resembles birch, for which the tree is often mistaken.

Some tribes used red alder bark to make a dye in which nets were boiled rendering them invisible to fish.

Alder serves a key function in the natural reforestation of evergreens. When an evergreen, or coniferous, forest burns or is CLEAR-CUT, alder immediately takes over, growing several feet in a season and serving as protector to slower-growing, more sensitive evergreens. Within twenty years or so, the alder becomes old and brittle, blowing down in winter storms and leaving the young conifers to reestablish the forest.

To the Indians, alder was – next to cedar – the most widely used wood for tools and implements, among them dishes, spoons, platters, canoe paddles, and baby cradles. Alder buds were eaten by some tribes to cure colds and biliousness. Alder was and still is the preferred wood for smoking salmon, one of the few Indian traditions adopted by whites. The flavor created by the slow infusion of alder smoke into the moist flesh of the salmon is among the unique tastes of the Northwest.

Salmon, butterflied . . .

(*Lawrence and Tyler Streets*) In 1865, Clark Aldrich **ALDRICH'S**
opened the doors of his "racket" shop to Port Townsend's uptown citizenry. The shop stood cater-corner from Aldrich's present location and was chock-full of toys, tobacco, candy, musical instruments, notions, patterns, school supplies, books, and apparently boundless omnium-gatherum.

Upon Clark's death, his son Ben assumed proprietorship, bought the Good Templar's lodge, and moved the business into the ground floor, expanding the stock to include a full line of grocery items. Brother Fred joined Ben during the Depression, and under their direction, the enterprise thrived. Aldrich's was the first grocery in town to offer free home-delivery (a service that continued until the store was sold in 1983). Clark, Jr., ran a "modern electric and furniture store" across the street in the Katz Building until his death in 1954, whereupon the stock was moved to the second floor of his brothers' business.

Aldrich's, in keeping with its image as a family store, featured "Happy Home" canned goods, grown and packaged in Washington. The Aldrich's were tee-totalers and never sold alcoholic beverages. In January 1940, Aldrich's claimed the distinction of possessing one of two operating elevators in Port Townsend (St. John's Hospital had the other), when a freight elevator was installed to travel between the basement and the second floor. The brothers ran the store with the help of their children and grandchildren until Ben's death in 1980. Fred did the books until he was over ninety years old. Over the years, the store amassed an inventory of such proportions that in 1960 it was still possible to find high-button shoes, and during the 1983 close-out sale, "V-mail" stationary from World War II was available by the box.

When the family sold the store, it could not have been to a more appropriate buyer than John Clise, who ran Seattle's Pike Place Market for several years. From the quintessential farmers' market, Clise moved to the quintessential neighborhood grocery, retaining several members of the Aldrich family as employees and keeping the store name. "People would call it Aldrich's no matter what I did, so why change it," he said.   [R.B.]

ALEXANDER'S CASTLE   A two-story residence built by the Reverend John B. Alexander at FORT WORDEN for his fiancée who married another. (see *Castles*.)

ANTIQUES   Formerly thought to refer only to remains of the classical cultures of Greece and Rome, antiques are currently defined as objects of artistic and historical significance that are at least one hundred years old. Antiques are sometimes found in antique stores, but more often in

Port Townsend, they are found in second-hand and used-furniture stores or combing the want ads of newspapers for garage sales, auctions, moving sales, and estate sales. A few ghouls watch the obituaries; they have superior collections. Actually discussing the origin of anyone's antiques may be a bit like trying to get directions to his or her favorite wild blackberry patch or clam bed.

Oddly, little interest is shown in Victoriana, in spite of the availability of many good pieces and the ever-present reminder of Port Townsend's architectural heritage. No doubt the cost, scale (people are bigger in the twentieth century), formality, and excessive detail of much Victorian furniture makes it an impractical choice for many. Oriental and Northwest Indian pieces are popular and prized, but the real volume is in good, sturdy utilitarian oak furniture of American or, more likely, English origin.

Most Port Townsend residents who restore antiques limit themselves to stripping a table or recaning a chair. In 1979, however, a celebrated antiquary settled in their midst. A self-taught artist and craftsman and one of only a handful of specialists in the restoration of broken and damaged art treasures, David Etheridge's formal training was confined to public-school art classes. While working in an auction house, he began taking home pieces considered beyond repair and mending them in his spare time. His work was so gifted that his employers urged Etheridge to consider making restoration his career. The invisible mending of museum-quality porcelain, bisque, chalk, alabaster, bronze, spelter, and pewter is a delicate and painstaking process. From palace urns to oriental temple vases, the artifacts of nearly every era and dynasty have been sent to Etheridge by museums, art dealers, and private collectors all over the world.   [N.P.]

JAMES G. SWAN, Port Townsend's foremost visionary, is responsible for many "firsts" in the city's history, including the first attempt at aquaculture. In January 1890, Swan planted 200 live lobsters and 640,000 eggs on Port Townsend's shoreline. The lobsters and eggs had been shipped by rail from Maine to Portland, Oregon, and then overland to Olympia with 170 gallons of sea water to sprinkle on them. The journey took more than two weeks, and the crustaceans

AQUACULTURE

and ova were doubtless a bit travel-weary when at last they reached Port Townsend. Swan maintained that he saw lobsters feeding on offal in Scow Bay in the months that followed, but none were ever reported by anyone else and none were ever harvested.

Aquaculture and fisheries were encouraged in June 1896 when a visiting Columbia University professor said, after taking samples from Port Townsend Bay, that he had not seen a place "so phenomenally rich with marine life except the Bay of Naples, Italy." Early oyster farms were successful, and in April 1890, the Port Townsend Bay Oyster Company was established, marking the first of several such ventures in local waters that continue to the present. Japanese oysters and spat were introduced into Tarboo Bay in 1914. Today, DABOB BAY and adjoining QUILCENE BAY are the heart of the state's oyster industry. Ninety to 95 percent of all West Coast oysters are produced in Washington, and although they are cultivated up and down the coast, at least 60 percent of the seed comes from Dabob and Quilcene Bays. Dabob Bay is home to the Quilcene oyster and one of only three bays on the West Coast to produce oyster seed in commercial quantities. Quilcene Bay's commercial oyster operations include what is reputed to be the world's largest oyster hatchery in addition to providing a home for the famous Canterbury oyster.

Kelp was another marine product to catch the attention of local entrepreneurs. Kelp had been used as fertilizer, and some proposed that it might be distilled into liquor. Alaskan Indians had produced such a beverage, called "Hoochinoo," but when sampled by local residents, it was found to be the "vilest liquor ever used by man or savage." Businessmen decided to concentrate on fertilizer development, and in 1913, four corporations were formed to make potash fertilizer from kelp. According to a University of Washington study the previous year, from three hundred thousand to four hundred thousand tons of kelp could be harvested annually from Puget Sound and processed into seventy thousand tons of potash worth seventy-five dollars a ton. Local seaweed, most of it "nori," is nutritious, rich in vitamins A, B, and C, minerals, carbohydrates, and protein. It is also harvested by local organic farmers for enriching soils. In Japan, its harvest and sale is a billion dollar industry with commercial sales that surpass any other marine item. Puget Sound is probably the only place in the United States that can sustain a commercial quality and quantity nori industry.

CLAMS are also grown in abundance in local waters. Littleneck clams are found on Discovery Bay, one of the few remaining strongholds of this rare clam in the state. Ivar's restaurant chain operates clam leases in KILISUT HARBOR and other local points.

In the 1970s, the largest independent business employer in Port Townsend was Maruishi Sea Foods, a company that harvested twenty-one tons of sea urchins per week, from which eggs and sperm were extracted for export to Japan, where they are considered a delicacy. Maruishi was forced to cease production and lay off its sixty employees when it was determined that the company was overharvesting.

In recent years, salmon and trout pens have been placed in waters off INDIAN ISLAND to raise fish for restaurants across the nation. Scallop seed harvesting in Bywater Bay, north of Hood Canal, and tube worm harvesting on the edge of Kilisut Harbor have also been attempted with varying degrees of success. (Tube worms are used as bait for bottom fish.) Kilisut Harbor is the proposed site for proposed GEODUCK cultivation. The Jefferson County Planning Department estimates that aquaculture may account for between 5 and 15 percent of the county's economic production. Seasonally, it employs up to 10 percent of the county work force. However, in the minds of many, aquaculture remains an unproven industry. Venture capital and loans are difficult to procure. Shoreline dwellers are concerned that aquaculture operations will decrease their property values and diminish the quality of waterfront living. Yet, just as timber harvesters of the Northwest learned to sow trees as well as reap them, so have far-sighted marine harvesters come to learn that the natural supply of seafood is finite and that what is taken from the sea must be returned to it.

[R.B.]

Port Townsend is one of this nation's four remaining Victorian seaports to have preserved its architectural heritage, the others being Mendocino on the California coast, Galveston on the Gulf of Mexico, and Cape May on the southern New Jersey shore. Port Town- **ARCHITECTURE**

Example of second empire style
(Bartlett House)

send architecture is distinguished not by the individual structures, for there are only two or three of truly national importance, but rather by the collection itself – the number and proximity of so many fine examples that were frozen in place when the town's economic dreams of becoming the major metropolis on Puget Sound were permanently dashed by the success of SEATTLE and Tacoma in the 1890s. (Those Puget Sound competitors had many more and even grander Victorian structures, but the evolution of the urban landscape is brutal and offers little opportunity for preserving the past. Except for Seattle's Pioneer Square, only a few Victorian buildings remain, and they are isolated.) The preservation of Port Townsend's commercial core and supporting residential community presents a remarkable picture of life in the 1890s.

Three major periods of American architecture are represented: folk houses, which were common to the initial development of any frontier town; romantic houses, which were popular nationally from 1820 to 1880 but in Port Townsend until the 1890s; and Victorian houses, which were built in the United States from the time of the Civil War through the turn of the century. Due to its isolation, Port Townsend's adoption of national styles always was later than that of the rest of the country. Until the late 1870s, information traveled with wagon trains across the plains or on ships around Cape Horn.

During its first twenty-five years, between 1851 and 1876, Port Townsend, with a population of about three hundred, was little more than an outpost that provided lumber for San Francisco and other distant ports. Folk houses of that era were simple structures, usually rectangular, built to provide shelter, with little attempt at fashion. However, they were a considerable step forward from the dark and drafty log cabins that were first built on the beach. Examples that remain show the influence of the Greek revival period but are basic structures limited by the capacities of early sawmills. All were built in the 1860s. (See *Fowler House, Rothschild House.*)

In the romantic period, the Italianate style was best distinguished by a low-pitched roof line; overhanging eaves with decorative brackets; tall, narrow windows, often with elaborate crowns; and bay windows of one or two stories. (See *DeLion House, Downs House, Grant*

House, Clapp Building.) The Second Empire, or French mansard, style featured concave roofs with dormers to allow light into the second floor, bay windows, and decorative brackets. (See *Bartlett House.*)

In the Victorian period, the Queen Anne style was by far the most popular among Port Townsend's affluent. With steeply pitched roofs of irregular shape, asymmetrical facades, towers, full-width or wraparound porches, patterned shingles, bay windows, and an almost neurotic abhorrence of smooth exterior walls, this style gave Victorian architecture its deserved reputation as cluttered. Port Townsend versions are no exception. (See *Frank Hastings House, Devoe House, Lucinda Hastings House, James House, Mutty House, Pettygrove House.*)

Example of Queen Anne style mixed with stick style (Starrett House)

Many houses represent mixtures of Victorian features, not an uncommon occurrence since the characteristic details were often shared by more than one style. Almost all Victorian styles featured steeply pitched roofs and textured walls with many interruptions of surfaces. The STARRETT HOUSE – Port Townsend's most significant structure – includes characteristics of Queen Anne and stick styles, and the SAUNDERS HOUSE adds elements of the shingle style to Queen Anne.

In the modern period, conversion to the craftsman style was accomplished when the Sims House was remodeled in 1909. Few examples of pure craftsman style exist because Port Townsend was in the midst of its thirty-five-year decline during the reign of this style.

Boston architect Henry Hobson Richardson (1838–1886) was dead before his innovations, which became known as Richardson Romanesque, were seen in Port Townsend. After 1886, the architecture of downtown buildings was deeply influenced by Richardson's sculptural vision. Use of carved stone, decorative plaques, and large arches with deeply recessed windows characterize the CUSTOMS HOUSE AND POST OFFICE and the JEFFERSON COUNTY COURTHOUSE, which are among the prime examples of public buildings reflecting his influence. Many downtown commercial buildings, notably the PIONEER BLOCK, borrow elements from his style.

At the height of the building boom in 1889–1891, Port Townsend had no less than six resident architects.

*Example of Queen Anne style
(Frank Hastings House)*

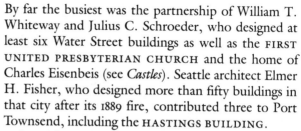

By far the busiest was the partnership of William T. Whiteway and Julius C. Schroeder, who designed at least six Water Street buildings as well as the FIRST UNITED PRESBYTERIAN CHURCH and the home of Charles Eisenbeis (see *Castles*). Seattle architect Elmer H. Fisher, who designed more than fifty buildings in that city after its 1889 fire, contributed three to Port Townsend, including the HASTINGS BUILDING.

As with today's homes, however, most of Port Townsend's Victorians were built without the benefit of architects, relying instead on pattern books, the owner's sensibilities, and the skills of the contractors. Like those homes of mixed styles, many of these were updates – older, simple houses festooned with Victorian embellishments to give them a fashionable look (see *McIntyre House*). Two contractors were dominant, each in different periods of the town's development, though both provided design as well as carpentry skills. A. Horace Tucker (1839–1938) was typical of the early pioneer – a jack-of-all-trades and the master of most. As a carpenter and contractor, he built not only his own home but also "Baron" Rothschild's and ST. PAUL'S EPISCOPAL CHURCH, in which he and his bride were the first to be married. Coming to Port Townsend in 1862, Tucker's wherewithal came from many sources (carpenter, contractor, coffin maker, manufacturer of house-finishing products and bricks), and he served in many capacities (city councilman, mayor, state legislator). Versatility was necessary for success in Port Townsend. In 1885 – perhaps the height of Port Townsend's actual prominence in the Puget Sound area, though only the beginning of its grandiose dreams – thirty-year-old George Starrett came to town and began building houses at a rate he estimated to be one a week for several years. His major design achievement – and the town's – was his own home, the Starrett House.

Contemporary architecture in Port Townsend includes many examples of "hand-built houses" (new homes or, in some cases, remodels), designed and built by owner-craftsmen who incorporate various features, old and new. Some of the houses are octagonal, many use patterned shingles of native cedar, and almost all have passive solar heating features worked into their design. Unlike the folk Victorian homes, which were integral to the urban scene of the late nineteenth cen-

*Example of Italianate style
(Downs House)*

tury, the new folk designs are invariably in the country, most frequently situated on five-acre short-plats that hide them from easy view, which perhaps reflects the Port Townsend life-styles in the 1970s and 1980s just as the proud, visible Victorians did at the end of the last century. [P.S.]

ARTILLERY HILL

Named for its many gun emplacements, or batteries, installed in the early part of the twentieth century to protect Puget Sound from foreign invasion, Artillery Hill at FORT WORDEN became a favorite hiking spot for visitors and residents after the Fort's transformation into a state park. The hill is home to massive concrete structures and underground ammunition storage vaults that echo a mere footstep; panoramic views of Point Wilson, Mount Baker, and the San Juan Islands; groves of fir and CEDAR; wildlife that includes deer, red and silver fox, raccoons, and, some would add, human road runners. It is traversed by a maze of paved roads and dirt paths that are off-limits to wheeled vehicles.

ARTS

Port Townsend's reputation as an arts colony is not a recent phenomenon. In 1862, the Territorial University's first art instructor was forced to move to Port Townsend to find a job. Sarah Cheney was a "Mercer Girl," one of many single women recruited by the university's first president and lone teacher, Asa Mercer, to come west to settle in the largely male logging community. An adventuresome twenty-one-year-old from Massachusetts, Cheney sailed into Seattle in 1862 with ten other instructors hired for the university. On arrival she discovered that no students had enrolled in her art classes and that she had been reassigned, with three pupils, to the music department. Greatly discouraged, she sought a teaching job in Port Townsend – then larger than Seattle – and was hired at once. In the fall of 1865, she married widower Charles Willoughby, whom she had met at a dance at FORT TOWNSEND. Captain of a coastal survey ship, Willoughby took jobs at Neah Bay and Quinault to stay on shore with his new, growing family. While living in the wilds of the peninsula, Sarah Willoughby sent away for a set of colored wax crayons to sketch her primitive surroundings. Eleven of these drawings now occupy a case in the Northwest Room of the University of Washington Library. Other drawings by Willoughby of life among the Indians were sent to the Smithsonian Institution and were published in its leaflets.

Sarah Willoughby's daughter, Adeline McCormick, was also an artist and studied with Port Townsend's best known and most accomplished artist and teacher, Harriet Foster Beecher. Born in Indiana in 1854, Foster came west in the 1870s where she studied art at the San Francisco School of Design, then moved to Seattle in 1880 to marry Captain Herbert Foote Beecher, son of famed evangelist Henry Ward Beecher and nephew of abolitionist author Harriet Beecher Stowe. In Seattle she opened what was reputed to be the city's first art studio, giving lessons to the wives and daughters of many of the area's prominent citizens. She also taught in the art department of the Territorial University in 1882, but once again the University lost its art instructor to Port Townsend. In late 1883, Captain Beecher bought the mail route between Port Townsend and the San Juan Islands, and Hattie and Herbert took up residence on Walker Street. A large studio was added to their home, opening in 1891 with an exhibit of her students' work. They were a talented and productive group. Nearly one-fourth of the 150 paintings exhibited by the State of Washington at the 1893 Chicago World's Fair were from Beecher and her Port Townsend students.

In Port Townsend, clubs and societies were formed to give support to the cultural enthusiasms. The Tuesday Musical Club – not unlike the later-organized and still-active Science, Literature, and Art Club – was primarily social and educational, whereas the Histrionic Club staged public performances and charged admissions.

Learned's Opera House, constructed in 1887, regularly hosted touring shows from New York and San Francisco whose "characters [were] as natural as could be expected upon the stage." When the economic boom went bust, the arts weren't far behind. Learned's became a gymnasium "before firebugs burned it down in the early 1920s," and culture came to town through the national Community Concert Series when it came at all.

Then, in 1957, Grant Redford, a University of Washington English professor, proposed to the trustees of the Port Townsend Chamber of Commerce that the town sponsor a summer arts festival. He came again a year later repeating his suggestion, and this time the idea took hold. The chamber of commerce appointed a "temporary committee," but declined to donate fifteen dollars for mailing costs. Meanwhile, a group of Port Townsend women who painted together on Sunday afternoons formed an art league and held an exhibition featuring prominent Northwest painters. "They caught the first ferry to Seattle and begged, borrowed, and almost stole paintings from individuals, galleries, museums, and anyone else willing to part with their objets d'art." In short order, they put together the area's first annual arts festival with music, drama, creative writing, and displays of local artists' work in the windows of business firms up and down Water Street. Art was everywhere one looked, but the talk of the town was the exhibition of paintings by artists of national and international fame, among them Mark Tobey, Paul Horiuchi, Morris Graves, and Guy Anderson, all members of the "Northwest School." At the same time, the Pacific Northwest Music Camp made FORT FLAGLER on MARROWSTONE ISLAND its permanent location, and the camp's musical director Vilem Sokol celebrated the occasion with a concert in Port Townsend in conjunction with the arts festival.

The timing was perfect. FORT WORDEN had just that summer reinvigorated the town's depressed economy by reopening as a juvenile correction institution, bringing new people with new ideas and energy. People who had been here all along had recently elected the town's first woman mayor, an arts enthusiast. The *Leader* noted that the Seattle Municipal Art Commission had voted unanimously "to begin studies of possible sites for a permanent festival city to be operated on Puget Sound by the state as a tourist haven." The idea that Port Townsend should become that festival city was immediately taken up by Grant Redford and others. In *Seattle, Past to Present*, Roger Sale describes how good things happened in Seattle; he might have been describing Port Townsend: " ... these are public actions of private citizens either ignoring government or making it suit their immediate needs ... the result of people working from a sense of possibility, or occasionally alarm, generated by their sense of satisfaction with what they already have.

"This is the town where all those people who think they're artists live."
– anonymous ferry passenger arriving in Port Townsend

23

Hope seems liveliest . . . when based on people feeling, first individually and then collectively, the riches and content of their past.'' Port Townsend's past became prologue.

In 1961, the Port Townsend Art League and the Port Townsend Chamber of Commerce sponsored a lecture on the city's historic architecture by Seattle preservationist Victor Steinbrueck, who told the gathering that ''Port Townsend is a museum and you're the caretakers.'' He was preaching to the already converted in at least one case: Mary Johnson and her husband, Harry, had completed restoration of the historic Frank Bartlett house on the bluff, and Mary Johnson had long before been dreaming and scheming about an arts school, which she established that year. The *Leader* once described Mary Johnson as ''the prime mover in cultural, community development, and restoration activities.'' When she was not restoring old buildings, running a gallery, founding and running an arts school, or raising funds to support these projects, Mary Johnson was also a city councilwoman concerned with the city's future growth, a charter member and first secretary of the Washington State Arts Commission; author of a children's book published when she was seventy-eight; a poet, an artist, a farmer and cattlewoman, a puppeteer, a wife and mother of four children, a hostess, and an all-around community spark plug. Gifted with ferocious determination and energy (she was sixty-six when she founded her school), she was a woman of impeccable personal taste with a genius for tolerance of the tastes of others. While always calling for – indeed hoping for, sometimes pleading for – excellence from faculty and students in her school, even the most imperfect result was accepted with her unforgetable blessing: ''Well . . . it was good of its kind.'' The University of Washington had taken notice of her interest in the arts and staged a symposium on the arts in Port Townsend in May of 1961.

That year's summer arts festival was a whirlwind of impressive events. Three important art exhibits (one organized by the Seattle Art Museum), an invitational craft show, a jazz concert, foreign films, a new music performance, demonstrations of pottery and weaving techniques, and symposia on filmmaking and poetry were offered.

The 1961 festival was planned and organized by an artist who was to have a major impact on Port Townsend. Tom Wilson had come to town in 1960 and was taken in hand by Mary Johnson the very day he arrived. A painter schooled in Illinois and Oregon, Tom Wilson's skills and knowledge together with his engaging personality and eclectic tastes were the perfect foil for Mary Johnson. The combination was irresistible, and their energies established the Port Townsend Summer School of the Arts in cooperation with the University of Washington. Mary became director of the school whose purposes were "to provide the best possible instruction in the arts; to provide absorbing goals for greater understanding of the arts; to explore the relationship of the arts to each other for creative accomplishment; to provide direct involvement in the arts for people of all ages; and to broaden interest in the arts in Port Townsend and the Olympic Peninsula." It was the Summer School that staged a contemporary prose version of "Julius Caesar" in CHETZEMOKA PARK with a local attorney heading the cast of more than fifty citizens. It was the Summer School that sponsored local productions of avant-garde theater, inspiring a local lab technician to write two plays ("Put the Baby in a Plastic Bag, Mustn't Spoil the Little Darling" and "Stay Home and Watch Sunday") performed in 1968 and later in Seattle. It was the Summer School that encouraged everyone to get involved, no matter how nutsy or extravagant the idea, and proved it by receiving substantial private and federal support to produce an experimental theatre workshop with painter Robert Rauschenberg. Said the *Seattle Times*: "[This] could make the creative energy generated in Port Townsend felt throughout the entire U.S. arts world." Rauschenberg's "combines" of found objects and paintings prepared the way for "happenings" and performance art. For his experiments in Port Townsend, Mary Johnson's farm at MIDDLEPOINT was the studio, or stage, but because of its experiential approach in which the audience and the eight students were one in the same, few people in town even knew that an international celebrity was developing a new approach to art in their midst.

That same year, the Johnsons bought the CLAPP BUILDING on Water Street, restored it, and moved into it the Summer School offices and the commercial

"It's almost as if, if you wanted something to happen in Port Townsend, all you had to do was think about it hard enough for a while, and it would happen..."
– Linda Okazaki, Port Townsend painter

art gallery she had run in her home for the previous four years. The following year – 1967 – began a discouraging period. Three Summer School classes were canceled for lack of enrollment and the season ended with a deficit of seven hundred dollars. Mary was seventy-three and her energies were lapsing. Bills mounted. Spirits flagged, and the school, no longer affiliated with the University of Washington, offered credit through a two-year community college. A number of key supporters and Summer School activists moved away, including Tom Wilson in 1972. The following year an exhibition of fifty-six of his portraits, many of Port Townsend friends, was presented at the Henry Gallery at the University of Washington. It was an accidental and a bittersweet final communion between Port Townsend's Summer School supporters and the university. The Henry Gallery had donated exhibition space to an annual Seattle arts auction, and the space was purchased by Jeannette Rockefeller, widow of Winthrop Rockefeller, to showcase her recently completed portrait by Wilson. The opening was a significant Seattle social event. For Wilson's many Port Townsend friends who attended and whose portraits were on exhibit it was not a celebration, it was a wake.

The Summer School struggled on in a troubled search for stability and continuity, unwilling to wake up from Mary's dream. Finally her vision and determination melded the Summer School of the Arts with the CENTRUM FOUNDATION, a multipurpose cultural center established by the state arts commission, of which Mary Johnson was a charter member. The transition was highlighted by master painting classes taught at Centrum by Elaine de Kooning, Kenneth Calahan, Carl Morris, Jack Tworkov, and Nathan Oliveira. It was a fitting end to Mary's Summer School; the best had once again come to Port Townsend. [N.P.]

BANNERS   In 1979, when banners of a decidedly artistic design suddenly appeared on the unused flagpole at the Carnegie Library, they served to signal an approaching storm. The pole was unused because the library flew the U.S. flag from a bracket on the building. To some folks an empty pole was one thing, but an official flagpole flying something other than the national ensign was a threat. Always quick to join a fracas, Mayor Joe Steve forbade the flying of anything but U.S. flags on city poles. Artist Peter Gritt had been counting on city poles to display his newfound art form. A solution was found through installation of two more poles at the library (since removed). Subsequently, banners of all shapes, colors, and sizes have adorned the town with unflagging spirit. Banners range from two feet to twenty feet or more. "It just happens," says Wendy Sternshein, Port Townsend bannermaker. "The banners tell me how big they want to be. I'm just playing with the wind."

Captain of the vessel *Imperial Eagle*, Charles Barkley (1760–1832) was an English fur trader generally given credit for the discovery of the STRAIT OF JUAN DE FUCA in July of 1787. Barkley's teenage bride, Frances Hornby Trevor, accompanied him on that voyage, becoming the first European woman to visit the Northwest coast. (See *George Vancouver*.)

BARKLEY, CHARLES

As a frontier community, the basis of Port Townsend's initial economy was barter. Local Indians did not use a cash system. When Captain Vancouver and his men visited the area, they traded knives and "trinkets" for venison and fish. Early settlers traded amongst themselves: eggs for laundry, sewing for building, or labor for labor ("You help build my house, I'll help build yours"). They traded with outsiders: logs for staples, or meat to a ship's captain for passage upsound. And trade with local Indians continued. May Smith, a turn-of-the-century resident, recorded: "Trading with the Indians always took plenty of time and the more casual one appeared, the more likely one was to secure a real treasure. Sometimes an Indian woman wandered about through the town, carrying a basket of clams for sale; and if one had time to talk with her, she might pull out from under her shawl a small basket and offer it for trade. The proper procedure then, was to bring out an old garment and dicker for an exchange. The garment might be a generation old, but if it had no holes, some kind of trade was sure to be made."

BARTER

Indeed, until the boom years of the 1880s and the establishment of the first bank in 1883, cash was not a common commodity in Port Townsend. And it is safe to say, among certain segments of the 1980's Port

Townsend society, barter is still an important economic force. Skilled workers have an advantage in the trading community – be they mechanics, plumbers, or electricians – because their talents are often needed in an emergency when they can request just about *anything* in exchange. But almost anyone with a talent or a desire to work can find employ for barter: counseling for house cleaning, dentistry for cordwood, house painting for music lessons. In 1980, a "skills exchange bank" was established at the public library, funded by a federal grant. One could register one's skill and one's need and, by performing a service, earn points that were applied toward "hiring" another service. So, for example, a masseuse might earn points by giving a massage to an injured carpenter, who would repair a porch for a musician, who then performed at a wedding, after which the groom used his mechanic's skills to service the masseuse's second-hand Saab. The grant expired with the advent of the Reagan administration, and the service ended in 1982, but bartering continues in the private economy from which it sprang. [R.B.]

BARTLETT HOUSE (*Polk and Jefferson Streets*) Built at a cost of $6,000 in 1883, the Bartlett House, with its distinctive mansard roof, represents an architectural style known as Second Empire which was popular in the United States from 1855 to 1885. Most examples were three- and four-story, but the Bartlett House and two other Port Townsend models are two-story, creating a design problem of a roof structure appearing too heavy for its base. Architectural historian Allen T. Denison attributes the success of the Bartlett design to its "intentionally wide proportions" and "substantial [bay windows] with Italianate detailing." He calls the house "a tribute to how stylishly the Victorians were capable of building."

It was built by Frank Bartlett, the son and partner of Charles C. Bartlett, Port Townsend merchant and descendant of Josiah Bartlett, the first governor of New Hampshire and a signer of the Declaration of Independence. Born in 1859 in Massachusetts, Frank Bartlett came to Port Townsend at the age of five. He entered his father's business as a clerk when he was eighteen, and three years later he was general manager. Bartlett served several elected positions and was an officer in several corporations, including president of the short-lived Port Townsend Steel, Wire, and Nail Company. Upon his father's death in 1893, at the height of the national depression that ruined Port Townsend's speculative economy, C. C. Bartlett and Company was dissolved, and Bartlett moved to "a less auspicious house and became a 'gentlemen's furnisher.'"

The house gained new prominence in the late 1950s when it was restored by Harry E. and Mary P. Johnson, heralding the Port Townsend Victorian renaissance. The Johnsons, from Tacoma, turned the house into a Victorian showpiece, using it for social occasions and art and educational events. They advocated historic restoration and were instrumental in the development of the Port Townsend Summer School of the Arts, forerunner to the Centrum Foundation (see *Arts*). The Johnsons entertained perhaps thousands during their years of ownership, bringing together Port Townsend residents with such people as Governor Albert Rosellini, artist Robert Rauschenberg, and gourmand James Beard. The Johnsons sold the house in the early 1970s, then purchased and restored the FOWLER-CAINES BUILDING on Water Street. The Bartlett House was among the first Port Townsend residences to be placed on the National Register of Historic Places.

Bartlett House features the mansard roof typical of the second empire style

In his obituary in the *Leader*, Albert Bash (1848–1926) was praised for "grasping the mysteries of the Oriental process of thought." As collector of customs for the District of Puget Sound, he was credited with the "amicable adjustment" of many race riots against CHINESE immigrants. Bash was active in several financial transactions between the U.S. and China. His successful relationships with officials in China brought him the first railway franchise given to a foreigner. The route connected Canton with the Yangtze River port of Hankow.

Born in Indiana, Bash was a boyhood friend of Benjamin Harrison who, while a U.S. senator, visited the Bash family in Port Townsend. When he later became president, Harrison supported the establishment of Forts Worden, Casey and Flagler as the primary protection of Puget Sound. Bash's daughter, Clementine, continued her father's interest in China when she became a physician in Peking.

BASH, ALBERT

BASKETRY   Basket-making among Port Townsend area Indians
was the exclusive province of women and girls. Since
pottery did not exist on the Northwest coast, baskets
were mostly practical, made specifically for gathering,
cooking, and storage.

The KLALLAM INDIANS of the Port Townsend area
made two kinds of baskets: watertight and openwork.
Watertight baskets were made of long, straight roots
taken from large CEDAR trees. The better roots were
used for the weft and the others for the bundle foundation. Coiling was done with an awl made of bone.
Handles of buckskin were attached on each of the long
sides of the basket.

The openwork basket was made from split cedar
twigs, usually gathered in the spring when the fresh
sap was running. Strips were soaked in water overnight
and then split. The woman held the inner part of the
strip in her teeth and tore off thin layers. She then used
the inner part for the weft and the outer part with the
bark on it for the warp. A handle was made from two
or three young cedar limbs twisted together.

Early baskets were nondecorative; baskets showing a
concern for ornamentation, including designs of over-
laid grass, became more prevalent toward the end of
the nineteenth century, probably in response to the
interests of white buyers.   [J.H.]

BAYSHORE ENTERPRISES   Bayshore Enterprises was incorporated in 1973 to provide community residence, job training, and real work
with realistic pay for developmentally disabled adults
whose handicaps include mental retardation, epilepsy,
autism, cerebral palsy, and organic brain syndrome.
With small initial grants, Bayshore created its own
funding by developing two private business ventures.

Established in 1977, the Jefferson Recycling Project
was the first of its kind in the state. In 1980, when it
moved to the Jefferson County Landfill, it was the first
recycling project to be situated at a dump (and probably the first to greet its customers with the sign:
"Prepare to meet your Recycler"). Between 1979 and
1984, money paid to the handicapped employees
increased from $1,644 to $15,800, and income generated from recycling increased from $6,000 to $89,000.

In 1981, under the training and guidance of a master-
baker, Bayshore Enterprises restored baking facilities at
FORT WORDEN State Park. Doing business as the Port

Townsend Baking Company, Bayshore produced a variety of bread products that quickly became Olympia Peninsula favorites. Its recognition of the evolving demand for whole-grain, nonchemical bread was rewarded by revenues that tripled in three years (from $62,000 in 1981 to $260,000 in 1983). Bayshore Enterprises has served as a model for many other Northwest social service programs.

BEACH OF THE DEAD Two shipwrecks four miles north of LA PUSH have given this somber name to this beach at Cape Johnson. The first disaster took six lives in 1891 when gale-force winds forced a Chilean bark onto the rocks. In 1920, ninety-mile-per-hour winds drove another Chilean ship ashore, killing twenty. A concrete monument known as the Chilean Memorial marks the graves of the victims of the first wreck.

BECKETT POINT A triangular point of sedimentary deposit on the east side of DISCOVERY BAY, approximately six miles west of Port Townsend, Beckett Point was formed by a sand spit that curved back to shore and enclosed a lagoon, which has since become a marsh. Its shores are lined with weekend and summer homes. Named by British captain Henry Kellett in 1846, it was known locally for years as Contractors' Point. Beckett Point is the site for one of the largest family salmon derbies in the nation. Each year over one hundred descendants of Italian immigrant Michael DeLeo, who came to Port Townsend to work the railroads in 1888, return to their American homeland to see who can catch the largest fish.

BELL TOWER (*Jefferson and Tyler Streets*) Built in 1890, the Bell Tower was erected on the bluff above Port Townsend Bay to alert downtown volunteers of fires in the uptown district. It also housed a new $900 fire engine that volunteers engaged upon reaching the tower after their climb up from Water Street. An example of the architectural adage that "form follows function," the towers's pyramidal shape helped to deflect strong southeast winds in winter.

In the early 1970s the tower was found to be seriously deteriorated and in danger of collapse. The Jefferson County Historical Society took it on as a project, raising several thousand dollars for its restoration; the society continues the annual maintenance.

Four conifers dominate the forests of the Olympic Peninsula. The Douglas fir (*Pseudotsuga menziesii*) is the most numerous species in the West, after the California redwood, and is the major source of lumber in western Washington. Its red bark is deeply furrowed, and its needles stick out in all directions. A young uncrowded tree tends to be triangular in shape, but maturity brings an irregular shape sculpted by wind and disease. The United State's largest fir (14' 6'' in diameter) is located in the Queets Rain Forest. The western red CEDAR (*Thuja plicata*) is a member of the cypress family and is identified by its lighter color, fibrous bark, and scale-like foliage. The world's largest (21' 4'' diameter) can be found off Highway 101 near KALALOCH. The top of the western hemlock (*Tsuga heterophyllia*) droops, giving it a distinctive shape; the needles are both long and short, intermixed, and the bark is relatively smooth. The largest (8' 7'' diameter) grows in the Upper Quinault Rain Forest. The Sitka spruce (*Picea sitchensis*) is found almost only in coastal areas and is noted for its sharp needles and drooping branches that give it a weeping appearance. The largest is in Oregon, but the second largest (17' 9'' diameter) can be found along the HOH RIVER.

BLACKBERRIES Four types of blackberry vines are common around Port Townsend. The native dewberry (*rubus ursinus*) creeps close to the ground, preferring dry areas covered by small trees and shrubs. The black cap (*rubus leucodermis*) is similar, but its berry is more the shape of a red raspberry. INDIANS used both for a variety of purposes. Several tribes ate them fresh or dried them in the sun or over a fire, storing them in baskets for winter use. In spring, KLALLAM INDIANS ate the sprouts and young leaves, while other tribes brewed them for tea to aid stomach trouble or colds or simply to drink as a beverage. The most visible of blackberries, those that thrive on roadsides and vacant plots, are not indigenous but, rather, Old World varieties, the evergreen (*rubus laciniatus*) and the Himalayan (*rubus discolor*). The distinction is primarily in the leaves. Finding native blackberries requires patience and knowledge of the local terrain; the ubiquitous domestic blackberry, however, took to the land so well when introduced that it is easy to find. Blackberries ripen in stages, and a single patch will have many harvests over several weeks, starting in July and extending into September. Only the ripest should be picked. A fully ripe berry is plump, about to lose its sheen, and almost ready to fall off its stem when picked. Any berry less than ripe is so tart it will cause the mouth to pucker, and while it can be sweetened with sugar it lacks the heady liquor of the fully ripe. Berries are more easily picked from underneath, thus avoiding most if not all of the thorns.

A person of indeterminate ideological or religious orientation characterized by a joyful facial expression at all times, often for no apparent reason.   [J.H.]
BLISS NINNY

A small community twenty-five miles west of Port Townsend at the head of Sequim Bay on Highway 101, Blyn was once a full-fledged town with a mayor, a justice of the peace, and a three-story hotel. Logging operations, a sawmill, and a shingle mill were its economic mainstays, the last of which closed in 1926. All that remains is a tavern and a few scattered houses. Two accounts offer the origin of the town's name. One says that it was named for mill operator Marshall Blyn. Local sources give credit to mispronunciation of the name Orville Dean, the son of B. F. Dean, who settled there in 1881. The area was settled also by members of the same immigrant Portuguese families that gathered in Port Townsend on what became known as POR-TUGEE HILL.
BLYN

Large-scale marine construction, especially before the twentieth century, required easy access to water and to materials. It was generally more convenient to take the boat yard to the woods than vice versa. Being surrounded on three sides by water, Port Townsend quickly exhausted the readily available local timber suitable for shipbuilding. Consequently, while Port Townsend's early reputation was made as a seaport, its prowess as a boat-building center has been relatively modest until recent years.

The first local boat builders were the aboriginal tribes that made their home along the shores of the peninsula. The KLALLAM like many Northwest Indians, were a nomadic tribe, ranging from the Hoko River east to the shores of Port Townsend Bay. Although manufactured with only the most rudimen-
BOAT BUILDING

tary technology, their craft were capable of hunting whales or hauling people and cargo over the often treacherous waters of the Northwest.

Canoe-building was practiced by only a few men in each tribe. A tree of appropriate size and quality was selected and felled usually by slaves with stone hatchets. Because of its light weight, rot resistance, and easy working characteristics, CEDAR was used almost exclusively. After the log was split with wedges, the builder could begin the arduous task of shaping the craft using fire, a stone adze, and chisels made from shells. The general form of the canoe was created by splitting out the wood and by selectively burning the log and then chopping away the charred material. Once the exterior form was approximated, the interior was hollowed out in the same manner. Further shaping was accomplished by a steaming method. The canoe was partially filled with water and heated near a slow fire. Red-hot rocks were added to the canoe's interior. The water was boiled until the wood was well steamed and pliable. Thwarts were pressed into the hull to spread the gunwhales to shape the craft and give it added strength. Fine finish work was accomplished using a pitch-stick torch and then dogfish skin as sandpaper. Elongated sections were scarfed onto the bow and stern of the craft, giving it the appearance of a living creature. As a final touch, the interior was painted with red ochre and the exterior rubbed with oil.

Canoe typical of the inland water tribes such as the Klallam

Over the years both design and production of local canoes were extensively modified. With the arrival of the first Europeans, Indians added sails to their canoes. At first they were square-rigged, using cedar-bark mats as sails. As canvas became available, jibs were sometimes added. By the 1930s the traditional stern piece had given way to an outboard motor bracket. Today, the few traditional canoes that are built are shaped with a chainsaw.

As European influence expanded northward in the early nineteenth century, more sailing ships joined the West Coast trade. Until the late 1800s, most ships were built on the East Coast or imported from Europe. Smaller craft were either disassembled and brought around Cape Horn as cargo or shipped overland through Central America. With increased demand for vessels, it was inevitable that a West Coast shipbuilding industry would evolve. Considering the abundant supply of raw materials, it was equally obvious that Puget Sound would play a major role. Locally, boat building began almost as soon as the first settlers arrived. A forty-six-foot trading packet, the *A. Y. Trask*, was built at Port Discovery in 1850 by Captain John E. Burns. It later became the first boat to travel up the Snohomish River. In Port Townsend, L. B. Hastings constructed a twenty-ton, forty-foot vessel, the *Colonel Ebey*, in 1854, only two years after the settlement began. Five years later, Port Ludlow Shipbuilding completed the *John T. Wright*, a 174–foot side-wheeler. It was the first oceangoing steam vessel built on the West Coast. In 1863 they followed with the 116–foot *George Wright*. It spent ten years in arctic waters before disappearing on a run from Sitka to Portland. In 1892 Perrot's Boat Factory of Port Townsend launched the first racing yacht built on Puget Sound. The flush-decked sloop had a waterline length of twenty-five feet and an overall length of thirty-six feet; it carried 3,631 square feet of sail and by all accounts thrashed its competition.

While sailing ships dominated the oceans in the mid-1800s, coastal traffic was becoming increasingly dependent on steam-powered craft. Even the great schooners and barkentines usually required a motorized tow into or out of Puget Sound. The topography and weather patterns of the Northwest are such that, as the flow of a river is contained by its banks, the winds of Puget Sound tend to be channeled parallel to its shoreline. Vessels rounding Point Wilson would invariably have a westerly on their stern or a southerly in their teeth. To a square-rigged ship, designed for trade-wind reaching, voyaging the length of Puget Sound against a head wind was an object lesson in futility. It was this quirk of geography, along with a fine harbor, that made Port Townsend a successful seaport in the late nineteenth century.

These characteristics made the city the tugboat capital of the Northwest. Between 1880 and 1900, much of the marine construction taking place in Port Townsend was associated with the towboat industry. The first tug to be built locally was the 130–foot *Mastic*. Built at Port Discovery in 1869, it spent its first ten years in San Francisco, returning to the sound after being purchased by L. B. Hastings and Henry Morgan for the American Tugboat Company. Over the years Hastings built several boats in Port Townsend, including the ill-fated *Discovery* in 1889 (see *Shipwrecks*). During the KLONDIKE gold rush, reporters from several of the major western newspapers kept local tugs on retainer. When steamers returning from the Yukon were sighted, the reporters would race in the tugs to get the first news of the gold being brought back.

By 1900 steam had all but replaced sail power. Most of the commercial traffic was passing Port Townsend for ports farther upsound, as was nearly all of the shipbuilding. In 1899, more than 550 vessels were built on Puget Sound; only a couple of those were constructed in the Port Townsend area. Although the occasional fishing boat or pleasure craft was lofted, for the next forty years boat builders survived primarily on repair and refit work. During World War II, the shipwrights' craft made a modest if short-lived comeback when the Cotton Corporation was contracted to build thirty-five barges for the U.S. Army.

It was not until the late 1960s that Port Townsend's boat-building heritage underwent a renaissance. It began modestly: H. J. McCool, Sr., set up a small shop in CHIMACUM specializing in the repair and construction of small pleasure-craft. He was followed by Skookum Marine at the Port of Port Townsend. Skookum's combination of sail power and work boat capabilities made its ruggedly built hulls an early favorite with an emerging generation of offshore sailors. With the gas shortage in the 1970s, they found an increasing popularity with cost-conscious fishermen as well. Radon Boats came to Port Townsend in 1972. Compromising nothing to traditional aesthetics, their fast, fiberglass bow picker was an ugly craft, yet it became a standard for performance among the gillnetters of the Northwest.

In the mid-1970s, a renewed interest in traditional techniques and materials manifested itself locally with a return to classic design and wood construction. Sam Connor's shop at the old armory at POINT HUDSON restored and built classic wood boats, while Carol Hasse and Nora Petrich working in an expansive loft upstairs established a reputation for building high-quality cruising sails. Their emphasis on craft and fine hand work made their products a perennial favorite among world cruisers. In 1976 the Port Townsend Boat

Works quickly established a solid reputation among wooden boat owners, especially with Alaska-based fishermen. The renewed interest in the shipwrights' craft gave impetus to the first Wooden Boat Festival in 1977. Conceived by Sam Connor and Marybell Kern and *Wooden Boat Magazine* writer Tim Snyder, it provided a forum where people enamored of wood boats could share an enthusiasm that borders on dementia. Additionally, the festival attracted specialists, including designers, builders, foundry men, and riggers. Many of those who attended the annual festival stayed to pursue their affliction. Currently, more than a dozen firms are actively engaged in boat building in Port Townsend. Almost every peripheral service is available, including sail making, custom foundry work, and all types of engine repair. For the budding enthusiast, there is the Northwest School of Wooden Boat Building founded by the well-known Seattle boat builder Robert Prothero. In six-months time, the school can provide all the training required to turn a stack of lumber into a life's obsession. [M.W.]

"There is nothing – absolutely nothing – half so much worth doing as simply messing about in boats." – Kenneth Grahame, *The Wind in the Willows*

Popular CHINESE expression (circa 1880) for members of the predominant culture. Literally "white devil."

BOK KWEI

"Boston Men," or the "Bostons," was the term widely used by INDIANS to distinguish American settlers and pioneers from "King George's Men," who were English, originally representing HUDSON'S BAY COMPANY. For many Indians of the area, the Bostons were synonymous with whiskey, which the Americans were known to trade or sell. The English did not engage in this trade. Boston Men were often called *cultus tillicums*, "the common crude people," while King George's Men were termed the *hyas tyee*, "the great chief people," and were considered much more worthy of respect.

BOSTON MEN

Located thirty-three miles south of Port Townsend on Highway 101, Brinnon is the southernmost community in eastern Jefferson County. The population is approximately twelve hundred, 60 percent of whom are over the age of sixty. In the 1860s, Elwell P. Brinnon staked a claim at the mouth of the Duckabush River, which he later sold. He moved with his wife, a sister to Klallam Indian chief CHET-ZE-MOKA, to another

BRINNON

claim on the DOSEWALLIPS, the present site of the town.

Settled by homesteaders and loggers, Brinnon is now an odd assortment of old houses, prefabs, and mobile homes occupied largely by a retirement community and a few remaining old-timers and loggers. There is also a cadre of marine biologists and fisherfolk devoted each in their own way to the harvest of the canal waters – a growing AQUACULTURE business of oysters and their spat and a dwindling shrimp catch that has only a six-week season each summer. Nevertheless, Brinnon hangs tenaciously onto its school, grades one through eight with less than fifty pupils; one new industrial hope – a sports equipment manufacturer; a booster-club community building and a volunteer fire hall; and a well-articulated civic pride. In an early 1980's flap with an insensitive State Department of Transportation, the community declared itself in secession from the state and stopped traffic on Highway 101. As a result of the attendant media coverage, its complaints were heard and heeded by the state bureaucracy. Many towns as obscure and removed as Brinnon attempt to publicize themselves with bumper stickers reading, "Where the hell is .... ." Not this community. Its bumper sticker reads "Think Brinnon." (See *Whitney's Rhododendrons*.)

CANDLEFISH   (*Eulachon. Thaleichthys pacificus*) The candlefish – so called because when dried its flesh burns readily – is a smelt, harvested at three to four years of age while spawning in coastal streams and rivers. Historically, the rendered oil of the candlefish was prized as a condiment by the Indians. Large quantities of the fish were netted each year and allowed to partially decompose in leaf-lined pits. The fermented residue was placed in large bentwood boxes or in interiors of canoes for processing. Hot rocks were added to cook the mixture, and the resultant "grease" was ladled off and stored. The oil was so valuable that it was carried over mountain trails to eastern tribes.

CAPE ALAVA   The westernmost point in the contiguous United States, Cape Alava is reached by a three-mile boardwalk trail from the north end of LAKE OZETTE. Until abandoned in the 1930s, the Cape was home to the southernmost village of the MAKAH INDIANS.

Artifacts from recent archaeological digs are on display at the MAKAH MUSEUM in Neah Bay. The cape was named by explorer MANUEL QUIMPER for José Manuel de Alava, commissioner for Spain at the Nootka Convention in 1790.

CAPE FLATTERY

The northwesternmost projection of land in the contiguous United States was discovered and indirectly named in 1778 by Captain James Cook. Sighting the promontory, he wrote of "a small opening that flattered us with hopes of finding a harbor there." Cook missed this southern entrance to the fabled STRAIT OF JUAN DE FUCA, and it was nine years before Captain CHARLES WILLIAM BARKLEY identified the passageway. Captain GEORGE VANCOUVER, who had been with Cook in 1778, charted the cape in 1792 and used Cook's journal reference for the name.

CAPE GEORGE

The eastern point of entrance to Discovery Bay was named by British explorer Henry Kellet in 1846, probably in honor of Captain George Vancouver. Nevertheless, early local maps and common usage referred to it as Dead Man's Point, although the reason has since been lost. The cape became a Civilian Conservation Corps camp during the Great Depression. In the early 1960s, a wealthy midwesterner, J. Frederick Palmer, turned the cape into a residential development, the first major real estate project after the boom period of the 1890s.

CASTLES

More by visual suggestion than in fact, two Port Townsend structures are known locally as castles: Alexander's Castle at FORT WORDEN and Manresa Castle on the town's western slopes.

Alexander's Castle was built in 1883 by the Reverend John B. Alexander, rector of ST. PAUL'S EPISCOPAL CHURCH. The fortress-like tower, built to collect rainwater, is reminiscent of the Gothic revival period of 1840 to 1880, but possibly Alexander designed the structure to remind him of his native England. Its modest scale was appropriate to his vicar's income. Alexander originally intended the castle to be the future home of his Scottish sweetheart, but when he went back to fetch her, she had married another. Subsequently, the disappointed suitor occupied the building only occasionally as a solitary retreat.

John B. Alexander's castle, built for a sweetheart who married another

When Queen Victoria's Foreign Office named him British vice-consul, the Reverend Alexander resigned his rectorate to devote his duties to Her Majesty, flying the British flag from the castle, which became his consular residence. He was transferred to the British consular service in Tacoma in 1892. The castle and its ten-acre plot were purchased in the late 1890s by the United States Army and incorporated into Fort Worden. Alexander died in his native England in 1930 at the age of 81.

Manresa Castle is a recent name. Known informally for years as Eisenbeis's Castle in recognition of CHARLES EISENBEIS's rags-to-riches success in Port Townsend, the residence was designed by local architect A. S. Whiteway and built with brick from Eisenbeis's own brickyard to resemble a castle from his native Prussia. Architecturally, it falls within an eclectic period that drew from authentic European sources.

In 1925, twenty-three years after Eisenbeis's death, the property was purchased by the Society of Jesus as a school and retreat center. Renaming it Manresa after the city in Spain where Jesuit founder Ignatius of Loyola wrote *Exercitia Spiritualia* in 1522, the local order added a wing that included a chapel and sleeping rooms for students and covered the deteriorating brick with stucco.

The Jesuits sold the facility in 1968 and it was turned into an inn with the chapel converted into a dance hall. A later owner, concerned about vandalism, erected a chain-link fence topped with barbed wire around the southern parking lot, prompting local wags to give it a third name: Stalag Manresa.

CEDAR   A legend of a Coast Salish tribe tells of a generous man who met the needs of others almost on demand; whatever they needed, he would supply. When the Great Spirit observed the man's good works, he determined that when the man died a cedar tree would grow on his grave and be useful to the people.

The western red cedar (*Thuja plicata*) – along with its less abundant relative, the yellow cedar (*Chamaecyparis nootkatensis*) – served the Pacific Northwest Coast Indian with a versatility unsurpassed by any other raw material. It was used for house planks, house posts, roof boards, and canoes; and for boxes, cradles, arrow shafts, and mats for sails on the cedar canoes. From cedar, Indians fashioned a spindle to spin wool of the mountain goat. Its bark was shredded for padding, towels, and sanitary napkins. It was shredded and twined into skirts and capes, and plaited into headbands, mats, and rainhats. By shredding the bark, it was turned into tinder for fire and slow-burning matches. Its limbs were soaked and twisted into rope used for making baskets and towing whales. Cedar buds were chewed to cure sore lungs and tooth-ache; infused with water it became a gargle that reme-died coughs and colds and – for the Klallams – tuberculosis. It could bring about menstruation and break fever.

The spirit of the cedar was known to many as Long Life Maker, and Indians returned the favor with a conservation philosophy that prevented them from ever pulling more bark from a tree than would allow it to survive. Today Indian use in this area is limited mostly to occasional totems and dugout canoes; whites use it for shingles, shakes, and siding.   [P.S.]

cedarbark clothing made of twined rain cape and fringed skirt

Rather than consigning the corpse of a loved one to a damp, dark hole in the ground, local INDIANS before the arrival of the whites, practiced a more picturesque disposal of their dead. An adult who died was depos-ited in a sitting posture in a large canoe and covered by a smaller canoe. Sometimes the canoe was elevated into the branches of a strong tree and left uncovered. In either case the body was surrounded by bows, boxes, fishing gear, and other useful and decorative items. Clamshells were strung along the sides of the canoe or in surrounding shrubbery or branches so that the continuous rattling would keep malicious spirits at a distance. A dead child was placed in a basket woven by its mother, and the basket suspended from the branches of a tree to gently rock on the wind. In later years, after the whites arrived, the Indians placed their dead in shallow graves with principal belongings. If the deceased was a person of importance, a small "death house" was built over the grave. Long streamers were fastened to the structure to frighten off evil spirits.

The first cemetery in Port Townsend was at the corner of Jefferson and Van Buren. As the uptown bluff became more densely settled, it was moved to a plot of ground where Tyler curves into "F" Street. Then, in 1871, the local lodge of the Free and Accepted

CEMETERIES

Burial was often a public busi-ness. In 1931, the county com-missioners approved an appropriation for the "burial of the indigent poor." It set aside forty-five dollars for a covered casket, five dollars for a burial robe "when necessary," and a mileage allotment of ten cents per mile if the body had to be moved from outside Port Townsend.

41

Masons purchased eleven acres on Discovery Road near Twenty-second Avenue and established the present Laurel Grove Cemetery. Remains from other cemeteries were interred in the new grounds.

Ceremonies at the cemetery have reflected the varied customs of the cultures it serves. At the funeral of On Tai in 1900, the *Leader* reported: "As the procession proceeded numerous pieces of yellow paper with little holes punched in them were scattered along the road for the purpose of attracting the attention of the Devil and it is claimed that his Satanic majesty is a curious personage and that he will pick up the pieces of paper and count the holes therein, which takes up so much time that the corpse can be buried before the Devil arrives at the cemetery and then will be safe out of his reach." In 1901, the *Leader* described Laurel Grove on Memorial Day: "The cemetery presented a striking appearance and an abundance of flowers were scattered on all the graves. The day before many people ... bedecked the graves with choice flowers until it resembled a flower garden more than it did a city of the dead."

Redmen's Cemetery was established in 1902 by the International Order of Redmen, a popular fraternal organization of the day. Redmen's Cemetery made the news in 1913 with several reports of ghosts and other ghoulish characters roaming the grounds. After five months of reports and investigations, it was determined that the spectral visitors were no more than the reflection on gravestones of newly installed street lights.

Two other cemeteries are operated in Port Townsend: St. Mary's Star of the Sea Cemetery, a four-acre Roman Catholic burial ground on San Juan Avenue, and the military cemetery on the grounds of FORT WORDEN at the corner of W and Spruce. Two "unknowns" are buried at the Fort cemetery. One is a civilian who died in the construction of the Fort at the turn of the century. The other is believed to have been a soldier, as brass buttons were found on shreds of cloth with the skeletal remains that washed up on the beach below the CROW'S NEST. Originally in the center of the Fort Worden cemetery, there had been a "muzzle-loading parrott," a cannon said to have been used to quell Indian uprisings on Puget Sound in the 1850s. The big gun was eventually scrapped and replaced. The story goes that the caretaker wanted shells to display on the ground near the cannon, but no one knew what kind of shells fit the gun, so the enterprising gentleman painted several bowling balls flat black and arranged them beneath the muzzle. "I hope they don't look too bad from the road," he said.

[R.B.]

CENTER

A small settlement approximately halfway between Port Townsend and Quilcene, Center consists of a grocery store/gas station that serves as a transfer point for JEFFERSON TRANSIT and Greyhound in its Seattle – Port Angeles run.

CENTIPEDES

The Port Townsend Centipedes were a ten-man team who, on July 27, 1977, thrilled some ten thousand Seattle Kingdome spectators by winning the Seafair World Championship Tug-of-War. They not only brought home the laurels but also a winner-take-all check for ten thousand dollars. The Port Townsend Centipedes' success story was an object lesson in strategy. By adding art, ratiocination, strategy, and what might best be called a strange brand of Port Townsend spirit, they essentially redefined the sport. One reporter described their tactics as a "gumbo of hatha yoga, martial arts, intense dedication, and communal discipline." They proved that tug-of-war can be a little man's sport. Their average weight was less than 150 pounds. On the evening of their victorious tug in the Kingdome against the Montgomery Loggers of Cle Elum, Washington, authoritative bystanders noted how much more muscular the opposition was and predicted an easy victory for the Centipedes' opponents. But, as one of the Centipedes said, "We are one being when on the end of a rope." They chose their name as one indication of their strategy: traction. They reasoned that if they could get ten sets of arms and legs working in perfect unison, they would have an advantage over those who tugged with fewer, larger bodies. They were right. They also practiced rhythm, which included not only coordinating their breathing, but also pacing, the use of the "standing arch," and allowing some members to rest at given times during the tug-of-war. The Centipedes developed their own mythology and terminology: their "house of pain" was a technique of prolonging the tug-of-war in order

Team members included two members of a marine-hardware manufacturing operation, a butcher, an oyster farmer, a boxing coach, a wrestling coach, a sailor and sail-maker, a fisherman, a boat builder, a pattern-maker, and a businessman.

to exhaust the opposition before administering the coup de grace. [J.H.]

Centrum is sometimes called "Port Townsend's Number One Nonpolluting Industry." Located at FORT WORDEN, it produces a variety of programs in the arts and education – workshops, residencies, performances, festivals, symposia, and conferences – and, in many people's eyes, is the main reason Port Townsend has an unusually large and active artists' community. Established in 1973, Centrum provides workshops for preprofessional artists in the fields of dance, drama, literature, visual arts, jazz, and folk arts; a schedule of public performances featuring an impressive array of internationally respected artists; and problem-solving programs and week-long workshops in the arts and sciences for Washington's gifted elementary and secondary school students. Centrum also sponsors several long- and short-term residencies for artists in all disciplines.

CHEAPSKATE HILL (Also known as "Tightwad Hill.") Overlooking the downtown Jefferson County Memorial Field is a high bluff that affords a fine view of football games and other events and attracts spectators unwilling or unable to pay the price of admission as well as those who simply prefer this vantage point. Since no effective controls have been devised, the "cheapskates" are usually indulged.

CHET-ZE-MOKA Klallam Indian chief Chet-ze-moka (circa 1808–1888) was about forty years old when the first white settlers came to Port Townsend. He seems to have adjusted quickly to the presence of the white man and in the early 1850s journeyed to San Francisco, where he first met JAMES G. SWAN. Swan showed him around the city and forever impressed the chief with the number and strength of the white man. Chet-ze-moka sent Swan a gift of appreciation and invited him to Port Townsend. In 1859 when Swan visited the area, the two met again and became firmer friends. Swan seems to have been duly impressed with the Klallam chief. In 1859 he wrote in the *San Francisco Evening Bulletin* that Chet-ze-moka, nicknamed DUKE OF YORK by the early white settlers, was "an intelligent and very reliable Indian, formerly much addicted to whiskey drink-

Indian chief Chet-ze-moka dressed in Boston Man's garb

44

ing; . . . he has been very sober."

Though he was to get his good and bad press, Chet-ze-moka was much respected by the whites for adjusting to the changing times. Today all that remains of him are some often published photographs showing him in rather ludicrous BOSTON MAN garb, a collection of conflicting historical records, and a wonderful park named in his honor. (See *Chimakum Indians, Customs House and Post Office.*)

In a county where almost three-fourths of the total land is in public ownership, it might seem surprising to find much emphasis placed on city parks. Yet within the boundaries of Port Townsend, nearly 500 acres (or 3,000 square feet per resident) are dedicated as public open space. While more than 70 percent is state-owned and directed toward regional use, the city itself maintains 102 acres of park on thirteen sites. The oldest, and to many the most beautiful, is Chetzemoka Park. Established in 1904, it was the first undertaking of the recently formed Civic Club, an offshoot of the Native Daughters of Washington.

Almost eight acres overlooking Admiralty Inlet were donated by the city council for the project. To build interest and to make the property usable, a community Park Day was planned. On the appointed day in June, nearly two hundred people gathered at the site to help. Working their way in from the old brewery on the park's south side, they managed to cut a swath through the underbrush as well as through food provided by the Civic Club. In spite of the progress, it was decided that it might be less expensive in the future to hire workers than to feed volunteers. By August the impenetrable forest had yielded to civilization. But it was discovered that the park had no entrances. When asked by the city council for a solution, one member of the Civic Club suggested that they buy a flying machine. Eventually it was determined that a more practical solution would be to purchase adjoining property.

A number of names were considered for the new park. Kulshan, the Indian word for Mount Baker, was the most popular. Ultimately it was decided that CHET-ZE-MOKA, the name of the well-known KLALLAM chief, had more local significance. Some people apparently had difficulty pronouncing the name, which means "fine young man." But the *Leader* effused "... after the word has fallen from your lips the music of its syllables will appeal to you to such an extent that, like the time honored Castoria, 'You will sigh for it, and cry for it, and would not be without it in the home'." That the Native Daughters would name a public park after Chet-ze-moka holds a certain irony: It was not until the late 1960s that the club admitted nonwhite members.

CHEVY CHASE Disappointed in his quest for California gold, John Tukey, a "state of Mainer," headed north on a tramp lumber schooner. Life aboard ship was unpleasant at best and when the vessel anchored in DISCOVERY BAY in the early 1850s, Tukey jumped ship and became the first permanent white resident in the area. Tukey first settled on a timber claim near Mount Chatham (see *Crybaby Mountain*), west of Discovery Bay, but in 1852 took a donation claim on the eastern shore of the bay. During the 1880s boom, he sold about half of his five hundred acres and with the profits built a picturesque, white, Italianate style home on the bluff overlooking the bay. Boom turned to bust, and in 1897, he and his wife opened the gates of the splendidly situated farm to paying guests. They named the vacation hideaway Saint's Rest. The venture was a success; small cabins were built, and the main house or inn was expanded to include ten bedrooms.

While Mr. Tukey concentrated his energies on the remaining acreage, tending five hundred sheep, thirty cows, horses, and poultry, Mrs. Tukey served as a hostess in the house. The bucolic "working farm" provided the ideal retreat for well-to-do vacationers from Victoria, Portland, Seattle, San Francisco, and Spokane who longed for a bit of rural charm and relaxation. During "the season," the resort spilled over with visitors. Sometimes children would be sent alone to the healthful climate of the haven (a combination of summer camp and "grandfather's farm"), to be followed later by mother and father. In many cases, families would stay for weeks or months.

In 1913, following the deaths of her mother and step-father, Mary Chase, a born hostess, modernized the facility and changed the resort's name to Chevy Chase (after the Cheviot Hills in England where the family originated). A nine-hole golf course was carved out of

Tukey's pasture (the split-rail fence he hewed can still be seen along the road), and a cement tennis court was laid. But Miss Chase maintained the rural atmosphere. Children thrived in the pastoral setting with its rustic pleasures; hayriding, horseback riding, beachcombing, and clam-digging put roses in their cheeks. Boys built and raced rafts; the adventurous would take beach walks at low tide to Fort Worden or Port Townsend. A miniature golf course was erected for their amusement. At sundown, the boys would dress up like cowboys and help drive the docile cows to the barn.

Adults entertained themselves with croquet, golf, and tennis (sometimes making it a "costume" event with prizes for the most outlandish), or on rainy days with whist or bridge around flower-bedecked tables. If things got too quiet, there were automobile outings to Gardiner, Blyn, or Sequim and speedboat "shopping tours" to Seattle (a distance covered in 1930 in William O. McKay's Dodge speedboat in two hours and twenty minutes).

But it was the comfortable atmosphere that brought the guests back year after year, generation after generation. "A note of informality prevails which makes it seem like one big family," wrote a guest in 1932, "with the center of attraction the beloved Miss Chase .... Everyone gathers in the living room around the fireplace in the evening." Sometimes, the children entertained with a recital of songs or poems, or a tableau directed by Miss Chase. Miss Chase made certain to have the very latest *Vanity Fair* or *Vogue* for the women to thumb through and an assortment of conservative, Republican newspapers in the parlor for the men to peruse.

In August 1930, in the midst of a drought gripping the region, the barn caught fire and burned to the ground, threatening the inn itself. The Port Townsend Fire Department was extinguishing a blaze in town, so the fire was at last bested by a bucket brigade of guests assisted by campers from a nearby church retreat. Burning barns notwithstanding, Miss Chase saw to it that "a delicious dinner was served to the guests at the usual hour," recorded guest Harriet Conner, "and the fire was almost forgotten in the normalcy of things ... Everyone extends sympathy to Miss Chase ... in the great inconvenience caused by the fire at the height of the season.'' Two weeks after the fire, Mrs. Conner noted that as a result of the barn fire there was now ''a nice view of the golf course from the house.''

Life went on. Yachts anchored in the harbor off Tukey's landing. Sunset after sunset faded from crimson to gray while festive groups made merry around a roaring driftwood bonfire. At the appropriate hour, adults in summer linen sipped beverages on the lawn. Enthusiastic children pitched tents on the sand and camped out at night; the most daring braved the chilly waters for a midnight ''skinny dip.''

After the Second World War had disrupted the flow of visitors and age had quenched her energy, Miss Chase decided to retire. She sold Chevy Chase in 1946 to a Seattle newspaper publisher, a frequent guest with great affection for the inn and the wherewithal to continue its operation. He added a heated swimming pool, resurfaced the tennis court, planted hundreds of trees along the golf course fairways, and for seventeen years maintained Chevy Chase as the favored retreat of Seattle's ''smart set.'' But his dream was to live at Chevy Chase, and in 1963, after three-quarters of a century of regular seasonal operation, he closed the inn to refurbish it as a year-round family home. Today the grounds are well tended but quiet. Many of the vacation cabins have been pulled down. A single eagle rises from its treetop aerie and plunges into the water. The cackle of crows echoes in the silence through the memory of a way of life, long lost.   [R.B.]

CHICKEN COOP ROAD   In 1929, Joe Reposa, a member of the Olympic Peninsula's Portuguese community, built a chicken coop on Burlington Road near Blyn. To celebrate its completion, he held a party of such success that he decided to turn the building into a dance hall. Chickens never saw the inside of the coop, and Burlington, whoever he was, was never again associated with the road. Reposa died in 1967 and the coop is closed, but the memory lingers on.

CHIMACUM   A farming community ten miles south of Port Townsend, Chimacum is the agricultural base of three communities known collectively as the TRI-AREA. Chimacum also hosts the school district and a bustling community center. (See *Hadlock, Irondale*.)

Two valleys extend from the town, one – roughly

westward – called Center Valley and another – to the east – known as East Valley, which extends into Beaver Valley. (Although the term "Chimacum Valley" is frequently used, it is a generic reference to the area rather than a specific geographical site.) Carved by glaciers more than twelve thousand years ago, the valleys were lakes that eventually were taken over by lush vegetation. Today the valleys are filled with peat up to sixty feet deep. Trucks rumbling by can cause the land to shake, and an earthquake is more keenly felt there. Piling would be required to make the valleys viable residential property. They serve as decent pasture, but poor drainage limits their value as croplands.

Settled first by Reuben S. Robinson, Chimacum established its community base in 1853 when seven sailors abandoned a British man-of-war, *The Monarch*, anchored near Victoria. Hiring an Indian guide to canoe them to U.S. waters, they landed at NORTH BEACH in Port Townsend. Two of the men, William Bishop and William Eldridge, eventually took up claims along Chimacum Creek in what is now Center Valley and for decades were partners in several agricultural businesses. According to family records, the partnership was always profitable, although one week the two men had to split a lowly surplus of $3.75. Descendents of both families (which became interrelated when Eldridge married Bishop's niece) still reside in the area. (See *Agriculture, Egg & I Road*.)

CHIMAKUM INDIANS

The history of the Chimakum is, to say the least, muddled. They were a remnant of the QUILEUTE band from the coastal town of LA PUSH who, according to one legend, fled the coast in boats at the time of a great flood and many days later beached near Port Townsend, several hundred miles and a mountain range away.

According to popular lore, they were a particularly warlike, aggressive, unclean, and disagreeable lot and were reported to have suffered near or total extinction at the hands of their enemies. According to one account, the Chimakum were attacked by neighboring tribes as early as 1790. There are also records of a second massacre between 1815 and 1850, committed by any of the following: the Suquamish, the Klallam, the Skagit, or the Haida. Census records show a dramatic decline from a population of four hundred in 1870 to three in 1910.

Just what did happen to the Chimakum? According to a seldom-cited work by J. C. Costello (1895), around 1869 Port Townsend residents found vast quantities of human bones on the beach near KUHN SPIT, not far from today's KALA POINT beach. Indians of the area refused to talk about this evidence of an apparent killing field – or, more accurately – killing beach. In Costello's account, Joe Kuhn tried to get the story from CHET-ZE-MOKA, who refused to talk until Kuhn applied a bit of Yankee trickery. He invited the chief to call at his house on the day of a solar eclipse. He foretold the approaching darkness and, supposedly, so impressed the Indian chief with his apparent connection to the spirit world that Chet-ze-moka confessed that he had plotted the extermination of the Chimakum. In this story, Chet-ze-moka induced the Skagit tribe to go to war with him. While the Chimakum were encamped on the beach, the Skagit came by boat, whooping and hollering. Chet-ze-moka and his men burst from the woods and "soon there was not a Quileute [Chimakum] left."

So where is the truth about the Chimakum? There may never have been a Chimakum massacre. The records are too contradictory. Did Chet-ze-moka really confess to leading an assault on the Chimakum? Costello's story sounds fishy. Even if he is reporting accurately, we would still be dependent upon the veracity of Kuhn, a notably colorful character who was certainly capable of a tall tale or two. (See *Clambake*.) His story of luring a confession with the old "sun-eclipse trick" sounds more like a good bar room tale than factual history.

There is a more plausible explanation for the demise of the Chimakum. Smallpox came to Puget Sound in the early 1780s, a date close to the first reported "massacre." In 1792, GEORGE VANCOUVER noted the telltale pockmarks on the faces of smallpox survivors among Indians in the area. But what about all those bones on the beach? There are, in fact, accounts of other Northwest Indians (the Chinook, for example) breaking traditional burial practices under the onslaught of high-fatality diseases brought by the white man. Native survivors simply heaped the dead bodies on the beaches. Today we tend to ignore the extent to which foreign diseases devastated the native populations of North America. By the nineteenth century, anywhere from one-half to nine-tenths of the Indians in the Northwest had been exterminated by white man's diseases. The Chimakum may have been among the most unfortunate. They were indeed an unpopular people, and other tribes may have had a stake in perpetuating the myth of their massacre.

[J.H.]

Of all the immigrant pioneer groups to have settled in the West, none has had its contributions more widely overlooked than the Chinese. The popular mythology that surrounds the period generally relegates them to footnote status at best. Yet, without them, much that was accomplished to make the territories habitable would have taken years, perhaps decades, longer.

CHINESE

The first Chinese to arrive in Port Townsend were probably laborers hired to clear land and to work the cook houses. Their dependability, honesty, and willingness to work under terrible conditions for low wages kept them in great demand. They were an almost exclusively male group, having come east to support families in China. Most arrived with hopes of eventually returning home in wealth.

By the early 1880s, the local Chinese population had grown to at least five hundred, many of whom were employed as domestics and cooks in local homes or as workers in the lumber and shipping industries. A thriving Chinese business community was established that covered a four-block area of downtown. It was during this time that the first of the Chinese Exclusion Acts was passed and, in most areas of Washington Territory, pursued with a vengeance. Ironically, the qualities that had made the Chinese desirable as laborers earlier made them pariahs twenty years later. White laborers and businessmen, fearful that the Chinese, willing to work for less pay, would usurp their positions, fueled a racist fire that burned for generations.

The Exclusion Acts, first passed by Congress in 1882 and rewritten three times over the following decade, were intended to restrict the immigration of Chinese laborers into America. In many municipalities, these ordinances were amended to prohibit Chinese from doing business or, in some cases, even living within the boundaries of the city. Because the federal acts were specific to laborers, and not to merchants, and because

51

after 1888 they also restricted the readmittance of any Chinese laborer who would leave the country, the Chinese went to great lengths to establish merchant status. In Port Townsend where the Chinese community was ultimately tolerated, there were shops opened with as little as $300 worth of merchandise and twenty partners. Each partner could then claim the treasured merchant classification on his "Section Six Certificate," as the identification papers were called.

Although not physically driven from their homes, the Chinese did not always have an easy time in Port Townsend. As early as 1879, the editor of the *Puget Sound Argus* began calling for limits to Chinese immigration. By the mid 1800s acts of violence against local Chinese citizens had become common. Gangs of white "toughs" made a sport of cutting the traditional queues off the heads of their unfortunate victims. The Chinese fought back. Many whites and Chinese were injured. Fortunately, calmer heads prevailed over the hysteria. The Chinese had achieved a level of respect in Port Townsend that they held in few other communities. This was due in large measure to the acumen of the local merchant class and the economic interdependency that they had fostered with the white community. Wisely, the Chinese had seen fit to invest much of their considerable wealth in local enterprises. Companies such as Zee Tai, Wing Sing, and Yee Sing Wo Kee provided not only goods to the white citizenry but also a solid tax base that could not be ignored.

Because of the general tolerance of the Chinese that prevailed in Port Townsend, many who had fled from other Washington communities eventually came to reside here. By 1890 the Chinese population is estimated to have been as high as fifteen hundred people or about one-fifth of the total population. After the Depression of 1893, the Chinese community began to decline with the local economy. By the 1930s most had moved on to other, more prosperous areas. (See *Zee Tai Company, Smuggling, Shipwrecks.*)   [M.W.]

CHINESE GARDENS   The lagoon at the north end of KAH TAI Valley near the Strait of San Juan de Fuca was named for a large garden tended by Chinese in the 1880s. (See *Agriculture.*) The garden was used as an underground railroad for Chinese laborers smuggled from Canada to jobs in the United States. Historian James McCurdy writes: "After a Chinaman had been on the farm long enough to get somewhat domesticated, he was brought into town and another worker, imported by the 'grapevine route,' soon filled the vacancy."

CHINOOK JARGON

The undated *Dictionary of Chinook Jargon* lists a vocabulary of less than five hundred words. Still, for many years Chinook Jargon was widely used as a trade language between Northwest coastal Indians and European traders. Although it may only be an extension of a language that had already been evolving among Indian peoples before the arrival of white traders, the Chinook Jargon that the traders came to know was made up of English, French, Chehalis, Nootkan, and, of course, Chinook, which was spoken around the mouth of the Columbia River and which comprises about one-half of the Chinook Jargon vocabulary. Although some Indians can still speak Chinook Jargon, particularly the Quileute, the language went out of general use by 1920.

Samples of Chinook Jargon:

Boston illahie: the United States
Glease: grease
Kah-kah: a crow
King George: English
Puss-puss: a cat
Skoo-kum: a ghost; strong
Tum-tum: the heart; will
Tyee: chief

CHURCHES

(See *First United Presbyterian Church, St. Paul's Episcopal Church, and St. Mary's Star of the Sea Catholic Church*.)

CITY HALL

(*Water and Madison Streets*) Although the decision in 1891 to build the Port Townsend City Hall was not made until after construction was already underway on the CUSTOMS HOUSE AND POST OFFICE and the JEFFERSON COUNTY COURTHOUSE, it was the first of the three to be completed. Modest in size and scale, the city hall cost only $30,000, as compared to $241,000 for the federal building and $100,000 for the courthouse. Nevertheless, it was a sizable investment for the citizens of Port Townsend, and it spoke to the dreams they tenaciously held for their town. The Oregon Improvement Company, the subsidiary of Union Pacific that was to have connected Port Townsend with a railway terminus in Portland, had gone into receivership, the building boom had halted, mortgages were being foreclosed, and still the voters approved the commitment of funds. (See *Railroad*.)

The designers, local architects Edward A. Batwell and Andrew G. Patrick, drew upon the Richardson Romanesque style with their use of carved sandstone for the foundations, sills, lintels, and capitals. Their use of sheet metal for purely decorative sunbursts was unique. Applications of the rolled and pressed metal in bracketed shapes on other buildings had at least given the semblance of structural support. Unlike the Jefferson County Courthouse, the city hall was built of soft local brick, and deterioration is evident today. Although its cost was small in comparison to other public buildings, it took half a century to retire the bonds. Just as the city was to make its final payment, a windstorm caused severe damage to the city hall's gabled roof and tower. With the dreams long since past, the city council of the early 1940s chose to remove the top floor rather than spend the extra money to restore it.

Port Townsend City Hall before the top floor was removed

CLALLAM BAY

A small community thirty-five miles west of Port Angeles on the Strait of Juan de Fuca, Clallam Bay served for many years as the only access to the WEST END. Before the arrival of white men, Clallam Bay and neighboring SEKIU to the west were the westernmost village sites of the Klallam Indian tribe. Since its settlement by whites in 1890, Clallam Bay's economy has depended almost entirely on timber. The character of the town is expected to alter radically with the opening of a five-hundred bed state maximum-security prison.

CLALLAM COUNTY

Created in 1854 by the bisection of Jefferson County, Clallam County was named for the KLALLAM INDIANS, who inhabited nearly the full stretch of the southern shore of the STRAIT OF JUAN DE FUCA. With 1,753 square miles, it ranks as the twentieth largest of the state's thirty-nine counties. Nearly 17,100 of the county's total population of 52,200 reside in Port Angeles, the seat of government. Twenty percent of the jobs in the county are manufacturing, and 25 percent are governmental; most are timber related. Nearly 20 percent of the county's population is over the age of sixty, due in large part to the retirement community of SEQUIM.

CLAMBAKE

The Joe Kuhn Clambake was perhaps the earliest of Port Townsend's community celebrations. Begun in 1866 and continuing episodically into this century, the festive, and often ribald, occasion was traditionally held at KUHN SPIT near Chimacum Creek. The date was flexible, but the invitation invariable:

NEAH!

*Nika Tiḷlicums, Klosh nanitch: Al-ki nika tickey manook
ict hyas Potlatch, caqua nesika mamook ahn kottie. Mesika
kiosh charco copa Port Townsend, kah Klallam Siwash
mitlite ahn kottie, wake syah Chimacum Creek, kah nesika
mamook hyu he-he; pe manook tin-tin, pe much a muck-hyu
Clams, pe clap klosh chuck. Spose nika nanitch pirechuck,
nika iskum delate sullox-klosh wake lo-lo. Klosh charco pe lo-lo
konaway tenas man pe tenas klootchman, pe tenas sap- olil
icktas. Spose mesika wake charco, nika iskum sick tum-tum.*

HELLO!

My friends please take notice: Soon I wish to make a
big clambake such as we made long ago. You please come
to Port Townsend where the Klallam Indians lived long
ago, not far from Chimacum Creek, where we will have
lots of amusements and music, and eat plenty of clams,
and fine good water. If I see any liquor I will be angry –
don't bring any. Please come and bring the little boys
and girls, and things made of flour. If you fail to come
I will be sorry.

Seven varieties of clams are commonly harvested and
eaten. The native littleneck (*Protothaca stamina*) or
"steamer" is the most popular. Tan-colored lit-
tlenecks live close to the surface of gravelly beaches
that are mixed with mud and sand. At one time, they
were so plentiful in some areas that several could be
found in one turn of a shovel, but those days are wan-
ing. The littleneck ranges in size from approximately a
quarter to a silver dollar. A thin-shelled variation (*Protothaca tenerrina*) has pronounced concentric ridges
and is as tasty as its cousin. The Japanese, or Manila,
littleneck (*Tapes japonica*) was imported to these shores
unintentionally with seed oysters earlier in this century; it has become well established and can be distinguished by a calico-like coloring.

CLAMS

The butter clam (*Saxidomus giganteus*) is nearly twice
as large as the littleneck and is used for chowder or
chopped for clam fritters or patties. The same is true
of the horse clam (*Treseus capux*), which is double the
size of a butter clam and, except for the GEODUCK
(*Panopea generosa*), is the largest bivalve. In a class of its
own is the razor clam (*Siliqua patula*), which may be
sauteed or used for chowder. A native of sandy coastal
beaches, it has a thin, polished shell in the shape of an

old-style razor (which, when broken, is just about as sharp). This clam is tricky to catch. A muscular "foot," which extends the length of the shell, can reach down five inches in the sand to form an anchor; the clam then pulls itself deeper, discharging water from its neck.

CLAPP BUILDING   (*725 Water Street*) Architectural historian Allen T. Denison calls this "one of the truly fine cast-iron facades in the Puget Sound area," noting that the work was cast in a Seattle foundry but with ore from nearby IRONDALE. (Subsequent Port Townsend buildings were built with cast iron manufactured locally.) The segmentally-arched windows with hooded crowns and the massive decorative brackets place the building in the Italianate style. The building was constructed in 1885 by Cyrus F. Clapp, who came to Port Townsend in 1869 to work for his uncle at the Cosmopolitan Hotel, an enterprise he purchased six years later. Known to his contemporaries as a "natural money-maker," Clapp owned a bank, which was housed in his building; was a DUNGENESS merchant who also shipped produce from the area to Victoria; and was one of the leading subscribers to the purchase of the Port Townsend Southern Railroad by the Union Pacific's Oregon Improvement Company (see *Railroads*).

After the economic depression of the 1890s, a series of taverns were the primary occupants of the building. In 1968, Harry E. and Mary P. Johnson purchased the building and turned it into an art gallery. It was the first of the Water Street commercial buildings to undergo restoration.

CLEAR-CUT   Clear-cutting is part of a forestry management practice known as "multiple use." Forest lands managed by federal and state agencies are divided into sections and designated for use as watersheds, wildlife habitations, recreational areas, or timber harvest areas. The guiding principle is that each use enhances or, at a minimum, does not interfere with the other. Lands set aside for logging are divided into parcels that, on a rotating basis, are cleared of all trees and then replanted. This gives a patchwork effect to Northwest forest lands. Critics of clear-cutting charge that the practice actually destroys watersheds and propose that selective logging be instituted. Timber companies, loggers, and forestry officials deny that claim, arguing that the concern of conservationists is more aesthetic than environmental and that selective logging is too expensive.

Port Townsend's climate is generally temperate, but a balmy summer's day in Port Townsend can be quickly chilled by a Pacific wind off the STRAIT OF JUAN DE FUCA or by encircling sea fog that snakes up the same channel. Camellia bushes nestled against the warmed bricks of Jefferson County Courthouse begin to bloom in late January, and the last rose may not be picked until Christmas. But the promise of spring in January is often the same promise in March, April, and May – a promise that has become a tease.

Summer sometimes comes in three- or four-day spurts followed by a cold front, followed by a few more days of warmth and sunshine. Sustained good weather is rare, and when it arrives it is worshipped, though not without suspicion. ("This won't last." Usually it does not, but sometimes there are "mother-of-pearl" summers of brilliant hue, endless warmth, and refreshing breezes. Recommitments to the Northwest are often made in such summers.)

Autumn with its thicker golds and deepened blues is reliably lovely unless the southwesterly storms of winter come early. Port Townsend may get only eighteen inches of rain a year, but 65 percent falls between October and March. By January, those who can afford it – even those who can't – head off to Hawaii or Mexico.

Port Townsend's climatological distinction is its wind. In winter, storms slam in from the southwest, and in summer, Eastern Washington heat rises, thins out, and sucks cold Pacific air up the STRAIT OF JUAN DE FUCA with vacuum force. In late afternoon, the temperature can quickly drop twenty degrees. The climate has created a fashion known as "layering," in which undergarments, shirts, blouses, pullover sweaters, cardigans, windbreakers, and coats are peeled off and layered back on as the weather demands.

But for all the fussing about the climate, the weather is wonderfully involving. The duotone winters are dramatic and brooding. In a good blow, there is excitement and danger and the smell and taste of salt spray in the air. The silence of a hot summer's day is as welcome as the heat. The weather is neither indifferent nor indifferently regarded. Inevitably it returns one to oneself. Regardless of season, one cannot go out into it without first considering one's purpose, one's intent, or one's need and desire to be in it.   [P.S.]

CONSERVATION   Environmental concerns, and the debates that they foster, are not new to Port Townsend. Richard Achilles Ballinger (1858–1922), a predecessor of James Watt, came to Port Townsend to practice law in 1889 at the height of the town's economic boom. When boom turned to bust, he moved to Seattle where he received an appointment from President Theodore Roosevelt to be Commissioner of the U.S. General Land Office. President William Taft elevated him to Secretary of the Interior, and his problems began. His forestry chief, Gifford Pinchot, publicly accused Ballinger of refusing to fulfill Roosevelt's conservation measures, which Taft ostensibly supported. The acrimonious debate reached Congress, which absolved Ballinger of wrong doing, and Pinchot was dismissed. History, however, reversed the judgment. Pinchot is considered a founder of the conservation movement, and Ballinger is largely forgotten.

SRC bumper sticker during Northern Tier pipeline debate: 20,000 Leaks Under the Sea.

Area conservation and environmental concerns were more recently epitomized in Port Townsend's Save the Resources Committee (SRC), a nonprofit organization established in the 1970s with both local and regional concerns. Originally, SRC was organized to stop the Northern Tier pipeline that would have pumped Alaskan oil from tankers in PORT ANGELES to the Midwest via a pipeline laid in part on the bottom of the STRAIT OF JUAN DE FUCA and ADMIRALTY INLET. The committee was active in the research that revealed the potential environmental impact of the pipeline and made a major contribution to the testimony that resulted in the denial of Northern Tier's application for permits. After the pipeline victory, SRC's activities continued. Members worked with the Department of Ecology to monitor emissions from the local MILL; they engaged the Washington Shellfish Lab to test for toxic wastes at the old IRONDALE Foundry; they requested the Department of Energy to make a water-quality study of Port Townsend Bay and they joined the Department of Energy in a local acid-rain study.

The idea of cooperative production and cooperative distribution, or the "co-op," was a nineteenth-century development that waned in popularity in the urban twentieth century. In Port Townsend, however, the idea took hold in the 1970s. The guiding principles of the Port Townsend co-ops remain true to the original concept: a group of consumers or workers meets to discuss the rules and regulations for the enterprise and agree to furnish the necessary capital. Each shareholder receives an equitable part of the profits.

Organized in 1976 as a local tree-planting company, Olympic Reforestation, began with concerns and a commitment that were clearly ecological and political. Like many worker co-ops, the company was rooted in discontent. Its members started out as part of the local work force, employed mostly by Crown Zellerbach. From the beginning, they took a political stand against the use of Thiram, a white powder sprayed on tree seedlings to protect them from being eaten by deer, but which can have severe side effects on humans. When Crown Zellerbach refused to stop using Thiram, many workers who later became members of the co-op quit. The controversy eventually led the State Department of Natural Resources to stop using Thiram, although Crown Zellerbach continued.

Olympic Reforestation continued its activist stance and has been active in opposing to aerial and roadside spraying of herbicides. Olympic Reforestation also embraced an issue less clearly related to the timber industry, but indicative of a broader concern with preservation of all life forms, by doing volunteer tree-clearing at Ground Zero, the protest site adjacent to the TRIDENT nuclear submarine base at Bangor on HOOD CANAL. The felled trees were used as scaffolding to build makeshift residences for Japanese monks who held vigil throughout the protest.

In 1975, after several months in the woods living in tents, two tree-planters returned to Port Townsend and their primary interests – poetry and printing. In the middle of a press run, one turned to the other and asked, "What's the name of this press anyhow?" The answer, an apt symbol of their life-style, was "Empty Bowl." The press evolved into a regional cooperative of writers and publishers who support the idea that literature is the best representation of a region. Dedicated to promoting a regional consciousness, the press addresses such political concerns as women's issues, considerations of tree planting in the Northwest, and the Salvadoran refugees in the forest industry.

The men who incorporated the Port Townsend Shipwrights Co-op in 1982 did so clearly for economic reasons. Desiring independence as shipwrights, they lacked capital to start their own business. When a meeting was called to discuss a co-op, twenty shipwrights showed up. Eight emerged as founders of the worker-owned venture, each purchasing one share at $125. Within three years the value of their business had increased to $40,000. Each member sets his own hours; no one has to work full-time. A competitive hourly rate has secured them enough work to make a living and to establish a retirement fund and group health insurance plan. Their work is almost exclusively repair of wooden commercial vessels, with jobs ranging from $500 to $50,000.

Five Fingers is a partnership of seven women who manage a consignment shop on Water Street. Admittedly "almost nonprofit," the venture exists primarily to provide an outlet for local craftspeople. The number of partners is determined by the number of days the store is open. When established in the early 1970s, the store operated five days a week and had five partners. When the operation expanded to seven days, two partners were added. Several partners also make items sold in the store. Five Fingers merchandise includes knitted clothing, handcrafted Christmas ornaments, wooden toys, dolls, and kitchen items. Many of the products depict Port Townsend homes and buildings.

When the Blue Parrot restaurant closed in 1981, some people in Port Townsend started referring to it as the Dead Parrot. But like the dying Phoenix from whose ashes new life springs, the ashen feathers of the Blue Parrot rose into a fledgling offspring. Upon being released from the breakfast staff of the Parrot, two employees migrated to the Town Tavern Cafe and resolved never again to face sudden unemployment. Along with three other displaced members from the Parrot, they formed a corporation to serve breakfasts in cooperation with the Town Tavern. The receptivity of the Town Tavern family gave them the start they needed. The cooperative flourished and was eventually established at its own location as the Salal Cafe. All workers receive the same minimal hourly wage.

Upon purchasing stock at a nominal fee, they take part in running the business. Worker-owners have weekly meetings, and everyone is expected to attend. Decisions concerning management – down to the minutest details – are made by consensus. The group heralds no particular ideological dogmas other than a commitment to open communication and to group process.   [J.H.]

They stand as dark sentinels on the rocks, piers, and pilings of Puget Sound, their wings often outstretched and immobile as if frozen at the moment of takeoff. Three species of cormorant are common to the waters around Port Townsend. The pelagic (*pelagicus*) and double-crested (*auritius*) are permanent residents, while Brandt's cormorant (*penicillatus*) takes up winter residence only, preferring to breed on the coast.

Cormorants are diving birds. Propelled through the water by powerful webbed feet, they can reach depths in excess of fifty feet to feed upon herring, sticklebacks, cabezon, and sculpins. Unlike most diving birds, the cormorant's feathers are not water repellent; the birds must periodically leave the sea to dry out, which explains their peculiar wing display.

Early Chinese residents followed a homeland practice of using cormorants for fishing. Working from a boat, the fishermen would release the cormorants, each tethered by a length of string attached to a tightly fitted ring around the bird's long neck. The cormorant could catch its prey but was unable to swallow the fish past the collar. The fisherman would then retrieve the bird and remove the fish, letting the bird eat only enough for survival and for keeping its interest in the game. This technique remains common in China today.   [M.W.]

A small community at the tip of TOANDOS PENINSULA, Coyle was named by postal officials for George Coyle, the first postmaster, who, in August 1908, disappeared six months after his appointment.

(*Cancer magister*) Its habitat ranges from California to southeastern Alaska, but the Dungeness crab got its name from that stretch of the Strait of Juan de Fuca that reminded Captain George Vancouver of Dungeness in England. This local variety is several times the size of the more prolific Atlantic blue crab, though it is several times smaller than the Alaska king crab.

Catching the Dungeness crab requires either a trap or a rake, a flashlight, and hip boots. Traps are costly and require a boat to dispense and retrieve. Stalking the critters involves sloshing about in low winter tides, which always arrive at night. An experienced guide is recommended for the first time out.

Crabs sold in supermarkets have often been frozen; almost always they have been sitting in the case too long. If wrapped in plastic, the crab should be given no further thought. Fish markets sometimes carry live crabs, which is the best way to buy them, but they must then be dispatched. Two methods are touted as humane. Some advocate dropping the crab into a large pot of boiling water. If held correctly, the crab hits the broth claws down, capsizes, makes one scraping scramble to get out, emits a high hiss, and succumbs – all within a second or two. (A small pot of boiling water extends the process and the agony.) Others say it is best to start with the crab in cold water. As the heat rises, the crab – so adherents to this method claim – becomes anesthetized and drifts off into a sluggish but painless death.   [P.S.]

CRAFTS   Port Townsend's multimedia artists and craftspeople are engaged in bookbinding, papermaking, drawing, oil painting, watercolors, lithography, etched stonework, metalworking, silversmithing, woodworking, ceramics, fiber arts, weaving, quilting, and the design and fabrication of clothing, jewelry, posters, puppets and floor coverings. New artists arrive regularly, and many experiment in a variety of media. Port Townsend is also home to many hobbyists, who often have difficulty finding retail outlets for their work. Egalitarian COOPERATIVES have all but solved this problem. (See *Arts, Quilts*.)

CROW'S NEST   A residential area in Port Townsend on the high cliff between Points Hudson and Wilson, the Crow's Nest is the site of a THUNDERBIRD legend as told by Lahka-nim, son of Chet-ze-moka, to McCurdy, (1951). Thunderbird, the provider of rain, abandoned the Makah tribe when it chose the favors of his rival, Seagod. With three progeny, Thunderbird flew eastward, rounding Point Wilson, where he found a roost on a huge boulder atop the Crow's Nest bluff. There he could observe Kulshan (see *Mount Baker*). He brought needed rain to a village of the Chimakum tribe on the beach below. Jealous of this growing friendship, Sea-god, who controlled the waves, began to cut into the beach below Thunderbird's roost, causing the bluff to erode and exposing the boulder on which the great bird sat. Projecting over the edge of the cliff, the boulder was held in place only by Thunderbird's weight.

Fearing the damage and injury the boulder would cause if it fell on the village below, Thunderbird refused to leave, sending his three chicks to summon the rain the village needed. But they were unable to provide enough. Still Thunderbird remained on his perch in fear the boulder would fall if he flew to assist them. A delegation of braves climbed the cliff to dispatch Thunderbird to make rain. Water was scarce, food was no longer plentiful. Thunderbird explained his dilemma: If he flew away to summon rain, the boulder would fall. The young men were amused. Certainly ten of them could hold the boulder in place. Thunderbird demurred. Get to work, they demanded. Knowing the consequences, Thunderbird nevertheless was tired of the argument, and he flew to the heavens as ordered.

The young men took hold of the boulder, but it began to shudder and rock back and forth. A great storm gathered, dumping so much rain that the sea became swollen and lost its taste of salt. Despite great effort, the braves could no longer hold the boulder, and as Thunderbird had told them, it fell to the beach, killing many. Resentful of the Indians' disregard of his advice, Thunderbird flew back to the Makahs. The boulder remains today, partially submerged below continually sloughing cliffs that are eroded by the waves of a still-present Sea-god.   [P.S.]

CRYBABY MOUNTAIN

A low-lying foothill west of DISCOVERY BAY, Crybaby Mountain (Mount Chatham) is visible from Port Townsend, particularly on days when clouds obscure the Olympics. Indians chose the name because of their observation that one had only to point in the mountain's direction and it began to cry.

CUSTOMS HOUSE AND POST OFFICE

(*Washington and Harrison Streets*) The post office, as it is now commonly known, is one of Port Townsend's two best examples of the Richardson Romanesque style of the late Victorian period (see *Architecture, Jefferson County Courthouse*). The hipped roof, the rows of deeply recessed windows, the heavy posts and lintels, and the use of carved stone are characteristic features of the style made popular by Boston architect Henry Hobson Richardson.

Brought in at a cost of $241,000, the building required five separate congressional appropriations to complete. The exterior finish of sandstone covers the walls of brick, joists of riveted steel and clear twelve-by-twelve-foot cedar timbers, and subfloors of concrete. Walls at the base of the building are twenty-eight inches thick. Construction involved plumbers from Peoria, ironworkers from Chicago, and President Benjamin Harrison's brother-in-law as superintendent. The interior was just as grand: marble floors, polished redwood paneling that cost $34,500, brass cages with etched glass for postal windows, elaborate plaster mouldings, a federal courtroom with an eighteen-foot ceiling, and a whole floor for the customs house operation. It took five tons of bituminous coal and 150 cords of wood to heat each winter. The original plan had two towers flanking the Washington Street entrance – a circular tower on the west side from which the U.S. Signal Corps could raise flags and a taller rectangular tower to the east that would allow customs officials to observe incoming and outgoing vessels. But Congress was not forthcoming with a sixth appropriation, and Port Townsend in 1892 was happy to settle for one tower.

Begun in 1885, the building took eight years to complete, most of it in lag time as contractors waited for additional congressional action. Matters were hastened with the election of Benjamin Harrison as president in 1888. Harrison had visited ALBERT BASH (see *Presidents*) in 1884 and had become friendly to Port Townsend causes. Harrison sent his brother-in-law John Scott to superintend the effort, and construction moved forward. In 1892, N. E. Edbrook, supervising architect for the Treasury Department, visited the nearly completed building and pronounced that "for the money it cost it was the best constructed building, made of the best material throughout and finished in the most thoroughly workman-like style of any building in the United States owned by the government."

Many of the building's proponents were most proud of the carved capitals at the main entrance on Washington Street. Likenesses of Klallam chief CHET-ZE-MOKA; his two wives, See-hem-itza and Chill'lil; and his older brother, S'Hai-ak, were carved by stonemasons into the decorative capitals, making them as elaborate as their Greek Corinthian antecedents.

The Washington Street entrance was soon closed, however; architects, presumably stationed in Washington, D.C., were unaware of the force of the southwesterly winter winds of that made opening the massive doors extremely difficult. Southwest winds also caused damage to the copper roof, which by 1916 had to be replaced. Slate was the replacement choice. Local legend suggests that the copper was needed for fighting World War I, but research reveals that slate was used because copper was far more expensive. Earlier, with the removal of the port of entry to Seattle in 1911, the customs office needed only two rooms instead of a full floor to conduct its business, and the building has since served primarily as a post office. An attempt in the 1950s by a local developer to convince federal postal officials to move to smaller quarters that he owned downtown was thwarted by Postmaster Walt Herstrom, who knew the bureaucracy well enough to have funds committed for and spent on improvements by the Government Services Administration before the U.S. Post Office could come to an agreement with the developer.

Early plan for Customs House and Post Office include a massive east tower

On February 13, 1979, southwest winds that sank half the Hood Canal Bridge (see *Storms*) removed three hundred square feet of the slate roof. Faced with another roof replacement, postal officials compared costs, taking into account the building's position on the National Register of Historic Places, and chose to return to copper. Bid estimates were $261,000 for copper against $270,000 for slate. The actual bid came in at $198,000, about 82 percent of the original cost of the entire building. Additional funds were alloted to restore the first floor to its original condition, which involved stripping layers of paint that had been applied to the redwood paneling, thus returning the building almost to its original condition. [P.S.]

A ten-mile-long bay extending from TARBOO along the TOANDOS PENINSULA to HOOD CANAL, Dabob

DABOB BAY

Bay has been called Dabop, an Indian word of unknown meaning. At the northern end, Quilcene Bay fingers off to the west creating the Bolton Peninsula. Several oyster farms are situated along the shallow, relatively quiet waters of the two bays. (See *Aquaculture, Point Whitney*.)

DE LEO BROTHERS BUILDING

(*2468 Washington Street*) The only surviving example of nineteenth-century industrial architecture, the De Leo Brothers Building was built in 1892 to house the Port Townsend Steel, Wire, and Nail Company, an enterprise that held high hopes as machine-made nails began to replace handcrafted square nails. Though the machinery was laborsaving, the plant nevertheless employed two hundred people. The company, however, operated only a few years before the machinery was carted off to Everett, leaving Port Townsend's investors with another shattered dream. For a time the building, built on piling with a wharf that extended into Port Townsend Bay, was one of Ed Sims' fish canneries, but that too closed after a few years (see *Sims Way*). For several decades the structure housed a building supply firm run by Carl, James, and Michael DeLeo (see *Beckett Point*).

DE LION HOUSE

(*712 Clay Street*) Basically Italianate, the DeLion House is less ornate than most examples of the pre-Victorian romantic architectural style (see *Architecture*). The forty-by-forty-foot structure features a low-hipped roof, decorative brackets, and window crowns, but the square shape, with bay windows on the sides rather than the front, gives it a more formal appearance, typical of the earlier Greek revival and Adams (or federal) periods. The addition of small-paned windows and shingles on exterior walls further confuses the stylistic origins.

Built in 1883, the DeLion House was, along with the BARTLETT HOUSE, the grandest of its day. The house has no fireplaces, then considered unnecessary with the advent of central heating, which was first used in the DeLion residence. Unlike later Queen Anne–style houses, rooms in the Italianate DeLion house are on a grand scale. The dining room measures twenty-five by eighteen feet, and the east sitting (or morning) room is twenty-two by eighteen feet; ceilings are twelve feet high. Not counting bathrooms, halls, and pantry, the four thousand square feet provide only nine rooms. Its cost was said to be nine thousand dollars, the most anyone had spent on a house in Port Townsend until that time. Its owner, Rudolph W. DeLion (1838–1894), held hopes as grand as his house, and if a single life can epitomize the character of a time and place, his certainly represented late nineteenth-century Port Townsend. Born in Bavaria of French parents, DeLion came to Port Townsend in 1876 after twenty years in South America, an association he continued by representing the governments of Chile and Peru as their consul in Puget Sound. DeLion was involved in seafaring activities all his life, and as Port Townsend's economic hopes for a railroad terminus began to unravel, the town shifted its faith to DeLion's scheme to build the largest dry dock on Puget Sound. Without difficulty, fifty thousand dollars was subscribed by local investors, and building began on the 100-by-325 foot structure that required two million feet of lumber. An annual return was estimated at one million dollars.

DeLion appeared to be "sitting pretty." He was city councilman, then mayor. He presided over one of the town's most impressive residences, and he was father of a handsome family (one of his daughters married the son of a Port Townsend pioneer, another was betrothed to a U.S. congressman from Spokane). He enjoyed a summer residence in Quilcene, and he was owner of what was hoped to be the key instrument of marine repair in Puget Sound.

Then it all turned sour. He was unable to gather enough capital to complete his dry dock, and the mortgages came due without sufficient funds to redeem them. His local investors became impatient, and at one point he met their inquiries with a speech from the front balcony of his Clay Street home. His health failed. During gallbladder surgery a duct was accidentally severed, causing excruciating pain that he relieved with morphine, a common prescription of the day. He became an addict, and his behavior turned erratic and abusive. Finally, his family sought legal redress by charging him with insanity, seeking institutional commitment. After a week-long trial in November 1893, in which DeLion testified on his own behalf, the jury voted three times before declaring him sane. But two months later, in rooms he had taken in Seattle, he shot himself through the head. He left his wife distraught and without capital. Unable to maintain the family home, she turned it over to the county, which sold it in 1904 for less than two hundred dollars to satisfy back taxes.

DEVOE HOUSE   (*538 Lincoln Street*) What appears to be a rare example of residential use of brick in Port Townsend Victorian architecture turns out to have been a double deception. Elias Devoe was partner in the firm that contracted most of the masonry work during Port Townsend's boom years and chose, perhaps in tribute, to sheathe his wood-frame dwelling in brick. But as the local product was soft, he added another veneer, one of protecting red stucco that was tooled with raised ridges painted white to resemble mortar between bricks. The house was among the first of the Queen Anne style in Port Townsend (see *Architecture*). Devoe lost the house in 1893 in a mortgage foreclosure.

DERBY DAYS   It was the scandal of the year in 1981 when two out-of-towners brought in their thirty-pound catches of salmon to the Port Angeles Salmon Derby, collected the top prizes, and left town before suspicions were voiced that the winning fish looked as though they had been frozen. Investigation proved the suspicions correct, and the couple was returned to Port Angeles to stand trial; both were convicted. Held annually on Labor Day weekend, the event with fifty thousand dollars in prizes is the largest salmon derby in the nation and is a centerpiece of a ten-day celebration.

DESTRUCTION ISLAND   Spanish captain Juan Francisco de la Bodega y Quadra called it Isla de Dolores, the Island of Sorrows. On July 14, 1775, in the first recorded contact in Washington between white explorers and Native Americans, Quadra anchored near the island south of the HOH RIVER and sent ashore six men, with instructions to find water, chop firewood, and fell a mast. Equipped with muskets, cutlasses, pistols, cartridge boxes, and several hatchets, the men were attacked in the surf by – reports claimed – three hundred INDIANS, who required two hours to kill the half-dozen invaders. The Indians were observed carrying away parts of the bodies and salvaging iron. Another report told of the Indians canoeing out to the main ship, where Quadra dispersed them by firing a cannon, killing six.

Twelve years later English captain CHARLES W. BARKLEY sent another crew of six to explore the Hoh River; all were killed. Barkley named the river the Destruction. Later usage shifted the name to the island. One year later, at NOOTKA Sound on the west side of Vancouver Island, English captain John Meares reported seeing a dried hand and signet ring recognized as belonging to one of the slain Barkley party. The relics had worked their way north through trade.

The Makah Indians had a less bloody but bittersweet legend about the island's origin. Destruction Island was husband to Tatoosh Island. They lived together at the mouth of the Hoh. They had many children, who live now as rocks along the Washington coast. Destruction and Tatoosh were a quarrelsome pair. Finally, after one bitter argument, Tatoosh gathered her children and paddled north. The more she paddled, the angrier she became. Reaching the area now called POINT OF THE ARCHES, north of OZETTE, she said to her children in utter frustration, "You will all grow up to be just like your father," and she threw them all overboard, where they remain to this day. Tatoosh paddled farther north, rounded CAPE FLATTERY, and made her new home.

DIAMOND POINT

The western promontory marking the entrance to DISCOVERY BAY, Diamond Point was probably named for the shape of its projecting sedimentary deposits. Once the site of an Indian village, the point was first developed in 1893 as a quarantine station for Puget Sound. The station was active until 1934, when it was removed to POINT HUDSON. In recent years, Diamond Point has become a retirement community (see *Jefferson County*).

DISAPPEARANCE OF ISRAEL KATZ

Every town should have at least one good enigma, an incomplete puzzle into which succeeding generations can insert their own pieces and extract their own meaning. One of Port Townsend's most enduring mysteries has been the disappearance of Israel Katz (1851–circa 1917).

Born in Rotenberg, Germany, he immigrated to America at the age of fifteen and lived with an uncle in San Francisco while attending school. His father, Solomon Katz, along with a partner, Sigmund Waterman,

Israel Katz

had arrived in America several years earlier, establishing a ship's chandlery in Port Townsend. In 1868, Israel left California to join his father's business.

As Port Townsend's fortunes grew, so did those of Waterman and Katz. In 1871, they moved from modest downtown quarters to a new building in the expanding uptown district. Known colloquially as Solomon's Temple, it became a thriving center of retail activity. Upon Solomon's death in 1879, Israel and his older brother took over the firm's operation. In 1885 they reestablished the business downtown in a new brick structure on WATER STREET. In 1887, at age thirty-six, a prosperous Israel Katz returned to Germany to wed. Adele Maas, at seventeen years of age was charming, cultured, and strikingly beautiful. She was in love with a young soldier, and they hoped to marry. But he was of modest means, and Adele's family would not condone marriage beneath her station. Arrangements were made for a more appropriate union. When Adele's suitor heard of them, he shot himself. Israel and the heartbroken Adele met for the first time on the day before their wedding.

The newlyweds returned to Port Townsend, bringing with them Adele's brother Louis and a maid. If Adele was less than ecstatic about her marriage, she was despondent over the life she found waiting for her in territorial Washington. Although Israel was well-to-do, his home was little more than a shack. Its two rooms were not enough for her china, let alone her clothes, her maid, or her brother. Responding to his wife's distress, the generous Katz immediately summoned an architect. When asked what it was that he required, Katz replied with a phrase that would become his personal anthem: "Whatever my darling wants." Adele bore Israel four children, and he, in return, gave her one of the most elegant homes in the region with all the amenities of the day, including a hothouse, fourteen servants, and a cistern.

With the deaths of both his brother and Waterman in 1888, Israel became sole owner of Waterman and Katz. While he attended to his expanding business interests, Adele absorbed herself with her home and the town's meager social life. When their youngest son died of smallpox, Adele decided to take their daughter and return to Germany for a visit. Tragically, the young girl fell ill en route and died. Devastated and unwilling to return to Port Townsend, Adele moved to Mexico City, where she lived with another brother and acted as his hostess for two years. On her return she found Port Townsend a changed community. The addition of the military at Fort Worden had opened new social opportunity. Soon Adele claimed a position at the hub of society, entertaining lavishly at every opportunity. It was at one of these parties that she met a handsome officer named Herbert Millar. Their affair scandalized the town. In 1906, Adele asked for, and received, a divorce from her ever-acquiescent husband. Millar received a dishonorable discharge.

Adele Maas Katz

Leaving her two sons with Israel, Adele and Millar moved to San Francisco, where they were married. Millar had neither funds nor connections, so Adele turned to Israel for money. Perhaps with the hope that she might someday return, Israel once again complied. With Israel's financing, Adele opened a beauty salon catering to San Francisco's gentry. She installed steam baths and saunas and employed twelve Viennese beauties to pamper the city's dowagers with special techniques she had developed. It was a resounding success. Within a few years, Adele and Millar decided to expand their operation and open a New York branch. Adele gave her husband her power of attorney, and he and one of the Viennese girls left for New York to establish the new salon. Instead, he signed Adele's entire interest in the business over to himself and married the Viennese girl. Adele was left penniless, without even the right to use her own name in business. She suffered a nervous breakdown and had to be hospitalized.

Meanwhile, Israel had occupied himself with business and politics. After serving on the Port Townsend City Council, he was twice elected mayor, becoming one of the first Jewish mayors in the West. Adele was released from the hospital, and after two brief and unsuccessful marriages, she once again tried business. She marketed a turtle oil beauty cream. On the package she stated that "this product is so harmless it could be eaten by a baby." Unfortunately, a customer took her up on the claim. In addition to turtle oil, it also contained carbolic acid. Adele found herself in jail. Released on the condition that she refrain from ever going into business again, she spent her remaining years in relative poverty.

Israel's fate, however, remains a mystery. At 3:20 A.M., Sunday, January 14, 1917, twelve days after he had completed his final term as mayor, Israel rose early to say good-bye to his son Edwin, who was catching the 4:00 a.m. steamer to Friday Harbor. He was in good spirits as they exchanged morning pleasantries. An old friend had come to dinner the night before, and they had enjoyed one of the most pleasant evenings either had experienced in some time. When Edwin departed, Israel was in his own bedroom. At 7:00 A.M., a maid heard the family bulldog barking in Israel's room. On investigating she found his bed empty, but his glasses, watch, topcoat, and derby were still in their accustomed places. Knowing that Israel never went anywhere without these items, a search was launched. None of the employees in the store had seen him nor had anyone else downtown. Family, friends, police, and even the army searched the surrounding area, but no trace of Israel Katz was ever found. Theories abounded as to his fate; each had its flaw. Occasionally, someone would report seeing him alive in another city, but these claims were invariably disproved or discounted. Over time the sightings stopped, his sons moved away, and his home and the empty shell of the Waterman and Katz Building were all that remained to mark his passage.   [M.W.]

DISCOVERY BAY   MANUEL QUIMPER first entered Discovery Bay in 1790 and named it Porta de la Bodega y Quadra after the Spanish explorer Juan Francisco de la Bodega y Quadra. In 1792 it was renamed Port Discovery by English captain GEORGE VANCOUVER for HMS *Discovery*. The bay was actively used by INDIANS, and both Quimper and Vancouver reported having contact with them as well as observing grave sites on shore.

Sixty years later, S. B. Mastick established a lumber mill at the head of the bay, and by 1870 it supported a population of three hundred. But within thirty-nine years, the mill had come upon bad times and the Discovery Bay communities of MAYNARD, Fairmont, and UNCAS had become ghost towns. Some buildings remain, but only old-timers remember the community distinctions.

The shores of the bay offer major commercial clam beds, but its waters are seldom used by either fishermen or visiting sailors. Though winds are good, the bay's charms pale in comparison to the SAN JUAN ISLANDS, a few miles to the north, so few bother to venture in. PROTECTION ISLAND, which – as Vancouver observed – does protect Discovery Bay waters, also diverts large schools of fish, thus making the bay less interesting to fishermen. However, the waters are favored for springtime romps by seals and sea lions.

Built on the Thames in 1789 and commissioned as a sloop of war on January 1, 1790, the 337-ton *Discovery* was ninety-six feet on the gun deck and seventy-nine feet on the keel. It had a maximum beam of twenty-seven feet three inches and a hold depth of fourteen feet. The *Discovery* brought Captain GEORGE VANCOUVER to the northwest coast of America in 1792, covering some sixty-five thousand miles in four and one-half years.

DISCOVERY, HMS

The viscous, malodorous extract of the skin and liver of the dogfish was at the heart of the operation of the Port Townsend area's nineteenth-century lumber industry. Primarily, this rancid oil was used to grease the skid roads along which lumbermen transported their harvested timber. Hides tanned with dogfish oil were used as drive belts in sawmill machinery, and the oil was also used as a lubricant in the machinery. It was the source of nighttime illumination in the mills, which often operated twenty-four hours a day. The crude but effective lighting fixtures were tin kettles, similar to and sometimes adapted from a teakettle, with spouts on two sides. The kettles were filled with the foul fuel and wicks let down the spouts and lighted. The fetid odor was intensified by combustion.

DOGFISH OIL

Dogfish-oil extraction was revived in the war years when the usual source of fish oil used to supply vitamin D was either in enemy hands or was swimming in waters too dangerous to fish.

The KLALLAM and CHIMAKUM extracted the oil for use as a paint base and also as a seasoning and cooking agent, though not surprisingly the slightly less rank seal or whale oils were favored for edibles. Before extraction camps were established by whites, they traded with the Indians for the oil. Extraction was left to the Indian women, who collected the dogfish in discarded dugouts and crushed the carcasses by climbing into the canoes and trampling them. When the fish were sufficiently squashed, the women added saltwater and allowed the mixture to decompose for a period of days or weeks. The oil rose to the top of the noisome brew and was skimmed off. Whites did not much improve on this extraction procedure. They introduced iron-bottomed wooden troughs in place of the canoes so a fire could be kindled beneath to hasten the process.

Several factors in the mid-1880s marked the beginning of the end for the dogfish industry. Petroleum products, which cost less and were more efficient, became readily available. Skid roads were being phased out in favor of "lokies" (locomotives), steam donkeys, and logging carts on rails. And carbon arc lighting, a novelty ten years earlier, was common in sawmills by the end of the decade. Finally, rubberized belts were introduced into the more modern sawmills, replacing animal hides. Like the stench it created, however, the industry was tenacious, and as late as 1890, fifty thousand gallons of oil were produced in Washington plants. (See *Candlefish*.)　　　　[R.B.]

DOSEWALLIPS RIVER　The glacier-blue waters of the Dosewallips River are found thirty-four miles south of Port Townsend on Highway 101. Fourteen miles upriver is Dosewallips Falls, which cascades 125 feet over and around boulders in spectacular display. The road leads on to the only eastern entrance to OLYMPIC NATIONAL PARK that is accessible by automobile. Called the Dosie by local residents, the name Dosewallips comes from TWANA INDIAN mythology. "Dos-wail-opsh-wail-opsh" is a legendary man who turned into a mountain at the river's source. In a KLALLAM variation, the Great Changer transformed a Klallam chief into a mountain that forms the river's headwaters. (See *Brinnon*.)

DOWNS HOUSE　(*538 Filmore Street*) Built in 1886 when the Italianate style was still the preferred fashion in Port Townsend (see *Architecture*), the George W. Downs House typifies the period with its low-pitched hip roof and elaborate brackets in the eaves. The style was further delineated with a one-story, open, symmetrical porch and a cupola in the center of the roof. The cupola was later removed, and the original porch was enclosed, with a second story added to provide Mrs. Downs with a sunny sewing room. The existing porch to the side was installed at that time. The large detached garage and one-story addition at the rear of the house were built in the early 1970s. George Downs first settled at Discovery Bay in 1881 and worked at the sawmill there; he later

George Downs House, an example of the Italianate Style

74

operated the mill at Point Hudson for a number of years. The house remained in the family until the late 1950s.

DRY ROT

(*Merulius lachrymans* or wet rot: *Coniophora crebella*) Dry rot is a distinctive fungal infection of wood that may occur wherever the moisture content of wood exceeds 20 percent for an extended period. Particularly vulnerable are damp areas without sufficient ventilation, such as the enclosed areas of boats or the foundations of old houses. Rot tends to spread with the grain; under hot, moist conditions (which, fortunately, are rare), it can travel up to one centimeter a day, completely eliminating the structural viability of the wood as it goes.

Certain woods have more resistance to the fungi than others, which is why teak and cedar have found such favor with boat builders. Douglas fir, on the other hand, is a holiday camp for rot spores. It has almost no natural resistance to attack and should be viewed with suspicion if it has been used untreated in wet, unventilated areas. Locally – the claims of boat brokers and real estate agents aside – the condition is endemic to some degree in almost all wooden boats and older houses. It need not be a fatal flaw. Most rot, if detected early enough, can be treated successfully without totally dismembering the structure. It is not self-limiting, however, and without treatment it can do irreparable damage. Detection is largely a matter of careful observation. Areas of dark discoloration, paint bubbles, cracks across the grain of the wood, or a musty odor can all be signs of rot. Suspect areas should be tapped with a hammer or probed with an ice pick. In rotted areas, the ice pick will sink with almost no resistance into the wood. The affected wood will give a sickeningly dull thud when hit with a hammer. Treatment of rot consists of killing the fungus and restoring the structural integrity of the area. Additionally, measures should be taken to prevent the recurrence of the problem. It is well to remember – even when not heeded – that the only sure preventative of rot in the marine environment is fiberglass, and in home construction, concrete block. (See *Pests*.)

DUCKABUSH

Many travelers who pass the Duckabush signs thirty-six miles south of Port Townsend on Highway 101 are amused by the peculiar name. They imagine stories of people ducking under bushes to evade pursuers or envision some peculiar Indian game involving dodging and ducking to avoid bushes. Few can pass the signs without looking for the bushes. In fact, the small community and the river with the same name are called Duckabush after the Indian name "do-hi-a-boos," meaning "reddish face," a term which describes the appearance of the mountain bluffs in the region.

DUKE OF YORK   The first white men who came to Kah Tai, or Port Townsend, dubbed the local KLALLAM Indian chief CHET-ZE-MOKA "Duke of York." Renaming Indians after European aristocracy may have been a form of ridicule and a way of dealing with the difficulty white people often had pronouncing native names. Chet-ze-moka's brother was called King George, his two wives were known as Queen Victoria and Jenny Lind, and his son as the Prince of Wales. (See *Customs House and Post Office*.)

DUNGENESS   The first recorded settlement in Clallam County occurred at New Dungeness which had been named by Captain GEORGE VANCOUVER in 1790 for its resemblance to the southeastern coastline at Dungeness, England. "New" was dropped in common usage. Dungeness served as county seat for nearly forty years, losing that distinction to PORT ANGELES in 1890. It was the primary port for the SEQUIM Prairie until roads began to connect the peninsula communities. A convenience store, an attorney's office, the old schoolhouse that is now a community center, a restaurant, seafood plant, and a few historic residences are all that remain.

DUNGENESS RIVER   One of eighteen RIVERS flowing from the OLYMPIC MOUNTAINS, the Dungeness River provides irrigation water for the farms on the productive Sequim Prairie. Among Puget Sound area rivers, the Dungeness ranks last for annual runoff and sediment discharge.

DUNGENESS SPIT   Seven miles long, Dungeness Spit is the nation's largest natural sand spit, and it is still growing. With sediment from eroding western cliffs, Dungeness Spit can add fifteen feet or more to its sandy hook each year. Since 1855, when construction began on the lighthouse, the spit has extended sixteen hundred additional feet. Its intricate shape, which resembles an elaborate fishhook, is created by shifting seasonal wind patterns. A KLALLAM legend relates that the spit was once part of a longer EDIZ HOOK. Wearying of paddling around the hook to reach shore, a Klallam brave cut half the spit loose. It floated eastward where it snagged on the shores of the Dungeness River.

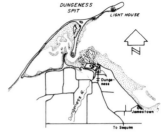

(*Haliaeetus leucocephalus*) With an estimated three hundred active nests in western Washington alone, the national bird is perhaps more abundant here than anywhere else in the contiguous states. Easily recognized by its white head and tail and a wing span reaching eight feet, the bald eagle scouts the shores of the Strait of Juan de Fuca, the San Juan Islands, and Puget Sound for food. Nests that are as large as eight feet wide and twelve feet high can be spotted atop old growth trees. Since nests are used year after year, frequent sighting of the same eagle is common. (See *Great Blue Heron*.)

EAGLE, BALD

Just north of FORT CASEY, along the windswept western shore of WHIDBEY ISLAND, is the former homestead of Colonel Isaac N. Ebey. Appointed by President Franklin Pierce as collector of customs for the Puget Sound region in 1853, Ebey lobbied successfully to change the customs department's district headquarters from Olympia to Port Townsend. He argued, as had his predecessor, that it was more sensible to have the port of entry closer to the border, where smuggling was occurring, than tucked away in the south Sound, where it was not. In bringing port-of-entry status to Port Townsend, Ebey gave the city its first taste of prosperity. Every ship entering Puget Sound was required to stop and clear customs. Crews were paid off and put ashore, and, ever-vigilant to opportunity, the town quickly established services requisite to seafaring men.

In November of 1856 a Tlingit raiding party from Kake, Alaska, made camp in Port Gamble. The demeanor of the Indians was such that workers at the Puget Mill Company took to their blockhouse and summoned help. The next day the USS *Massachusetts* arrived. When the Tlingits refused to leave, the warship opened fire, killing twenty-seven INDIANS. The

EBEY'S LANDING

survivors fled, swearing revenge.

On the night of August 11, 1857, Colonel Ebey and his wife, Emily, were awakened by the barking of their dog. As was his habit when trouble threatened, Ebey elected to spend the night outside. After a brief reconnoiter, he returned and woke up his house guests. On leaving his house again, he was confronted by a party of Indians. He asked what they wanted and was answered by two gunshots. As Emily Ebey yelled for him to come back inside, Colonel Ebey fled to the back of the house. He could be seen through the window holding his head, stunned. More shots were heard as Ebey disappeared into the night. While the Indians pursued Ebey, the occupants of the house escaped safely into nearby woods.

The next morning Ebey's brother found his body. "I came in the yard and beheld him in his gore. His headless trunk lay on its side near the end of the porch apparently where he had fallen. When I knelt by his side and took his rigid hands into mine there was no room for doubt as to identity. Although the head was not there I could have recognized him among a thousand. I have seen death often before and have seen the bodies of persons killed by savages but I never saw so horrible a sight as this."

Two years later, after long negotiations, Ebey's head was recovered from Kake by Captain Charles Dodd of the Hudson's Bay Company. [M.W.]

ECONOMY In the beginning, Port Townsend's economy was of necessity a BARTER economy based on fishing, beachside LOGGING, and AGRICULTURE. Settlers had to devise a means of acquiring food: either by growing, killing, or catching their own, or by trading among themselves or with the Indians. There was little cash and not much to buy with it anyway. The first business in Port Townsend was a fishery established and operated by the FOUNDERS of the community soon after they had settled themselves. A gold rush on the upper Fraser River in British Columbia in 1858 brought droves of adventurers and speculators, and their currency, to town as Victoria, British Columbia and Port Townsend were the best advertised ports north of San Francisco. D.C.H. Rothschild responded by opening The Kentucky Store, the community's first general mercantile store, and the town's RETAIL BUSINESS community was born.

The Civil War years were bleak, but after the war, commodity prices stabilized, shopping increased, and business activity picked up. Steamboat rate and fare wars in 1866 promoted trade and traffic. The seafaring business was increasing; half the ships that came into Puget Sound picked up their crews in Port Townsend, and there were simply not enough men who were willing to go to sea. Crimping and shanghaiing were considered necessary elements of a successful maritime community. Saloons, whorehouses, and gambling halls were likewise accepted as necessary, if regrettable, features of a thriving maritime economy. (See *Prostitutes*.) As the population increased (593 in 1870), Port Townsend promoter JAMES G. SWAN became an agent for Northern Pacific and worked to get the railroad routed from the Columbia River to Port Townsend, but Tacoma was chosen as the terminus, the first of the RAILROAD dreams to be broken. Nonetheless, in 1875, sixty-six entries were listed for Port Townsend in a regional business directory. In 1880 Port Townsend had 917 residents; a Washington Immigration Aid Society pamphlet published that year stated, "Port Townsend is the principal market and shipping point of the adjacent counties, and thousands of tons of grain, wool, potatoes, hides, cheese, and other products are exported from its wharves every year."

Then, in 1889, a speculation boom hit Port Townsend and hit it hard. It altered the way the community thought and dreamed of itself for at least a generation. Port Townsend developers formed a railroad company, optimistically expecting that its new line would be promptly snatched up by some larger railroad as its northern terminus. A mile of track was completed south from Port Townsend. And, indeed, in 1890, the Oregon Improvement Company, a subsidiary of the Union Pacific, agreed to build and operate a railroad from Port Townsend to Portland. The population of Port Townsend doubled. Property values skyrocketed. Businesses flourished. Fire had all but destroyed Seattle, and local residents felt sure Port Townsend's preeminence on the sound was now assured. The city boasted six banks, three street railways, and a new electric company. A New York newspaper proclaimed Port Townsend was "second only to New York City in marine crafts reported and cleared in the whole United

States." Consulates for Peru, Chile, Great Britain, Germany, the Hawaiian Islands, and France were established.

But building on the railroad had not progressed from the Portland end. In November, 1890, James Swan delivered the news that the Oregon Improvement Company was in receivership. Railroad work came to an abrupt halt. Residents were riding so high on the crest of prosperity that they simply refused to believe the end approached. Surely "eastern investors" would swoop to their rescue. Port Townsend clung desperately to its dream. The *Leader*, in the 1891 New Year edition, rhapsodized on the now familiar melody, "Today Port Townsend enters upon the happiest and most prosperous year of its existence . . . . On every hand are to be met evidences to establish the fact that Port Townsend is a pushing, active, go-ahead town, and that the men who would want to sleep twenty hours out of twenty-four would better hunt up some other location . . . ." But when a dry dock was built, it was towed away unused. A nail works was sold for scrap. Sawmills, canneries, and foundries came and went. The thousands of newcomers that had flocked to the community now deserted it. Original settlers died or moved to Seattle. Streets were empty and buildings boarded up. All but two banks closed. The streetcar lines pulled up their tracks.

The nationwide panic of 1893 worsened the already desperate situation. The shipping industry became so depressed that it was cheaper for shipowners to let vessels anchor idle than to sail them. A ghostly skeleton fleet silently floated in the Port Townsend Bay. Port Townsend probably suffered more from the collapse of the great land speculation and building boom than any other town its size in the Northwest. At its height, it had developed facilities for a city of twenty thousand. The sudden collapse meant that property owners lost everything. Suicides increased.

Finally, with congressional passage of the military fortification bill and the promise of construction of local coast artillery posts, things began to look up. Tireless James Swan was instrumental in this victory, and it was with great joy that he reported his success in the *Leader* in June of 1896: "The Israelites of old wandered forty years in the wilderness of the Sinai, before they saw the promised land. I, too, have been in the wilderness of the northwest coast for more than forty years and to me the promise of better times seems near; all these years, I never lost faith in Port Townsend ... and the passage of the fortifications bill is the first glimmer of a dawn in the East which will rise upon us to the perfect day.''

Although construction of FORTS WORDEN, CASEY, and FLAGLER brought an infusion of money into the community, they were not immediately fully activated, and once again Port Townsend feared its hopes for prosperity would come to naught. But vigilance in the war for prosperity must never falter, as the *Leader* editor reminded the citizenry, "If you don't want to pull, it would be better that you get out of the way, as you are likely to get run over. Port Townsend is going to the front, and it is going regardless of any man's pessimistic ideas or his jealousies as to the personnel of those in the van.'' The economy did pick up with the influx of soldiers during World War I. The community was giddy with joy and indulged in a spectacular whirl of dances, card parties, and light entertainments. Population again increased, but after the war, the city drifted into the doldrums. The sawmill failed. Fruit and vegetable canneries closed their doors. The WATER system, built just twenty years before, was in precarious condition, and there was no money to upgrade it. The day was saved by the Zellerbach Company which agreed to build a seven-million-dollar pulp and paper mill in Port Townsend and to pick up the tab for a new water system in the bargain. The MILL was welcomed with open arms, for it was seen as a stable industry, not susceptible to the vagaries of war or "eastern bankers.'' Its presence insulated Port Townsend somewhat during the Great Depression. "Port Townsend was a good place to be in the depression,'' say the old-timers, "if you had to be any place.''

In 1940, Port Townsend had 4,683 citizens. That number increased by 2,500 during the return of the military to Fort Worden for World War II. The war years were good for Port Townsend. The mill operated around the clock, and soldiers from the forts brought their paychecks to town. In 1950, the census count was 6,888. Just as the community was beginning to think maybe the military was here to stay, it pulled out for good, lowering the flag permanently on Fort Worden in 1953 (see *Dwight D. Eisenhower*). The town was devastated once again. More than 2,000 people left. Residents said they lived in a "doom town." The years that followed were almost as grim as the depression of 1893. In 1957, Fort Worden was purchased by the state as a juvenile diagnostic and treatment center. Once again, the community was rescued by outsiders. Once again, there was an influx of new residents. Once again, the economy stabilized for a time. Then, after fourteen years, the center was phased out.

Fort Worden was dedicated as a state park in 1973, and on the coattails of the HOMES TOURS begun ten years earlier, Port Townsend began to spiff itself up, emphasizing its Victoriana with an eye to luring tourist dollars. Small malls sprang up; boutiques, gift shops, and restaurants opened (and closed) with stunning briskness. Bed-and-breakfast establishments took over the larger mansions. As the nation began to focus on environmental concerns, Port Townsend offered something called "quality of life," which was apparently invisible to most natives who wished for a stable (i.e., industrial) economic base, but which was perfectly obvious to newcomers. Retirees and refugees from urban areas saw Port Townsend as a quiet haven. Retirees didn't need to earn a wage; and many of the young immigrants were willing to work for minimum wage in the "service industry," or they created jobs for themselves. After the HOOD CANAL BRIDGE sank in 1979, the ferry ran direct from Edmonds to Port Townsend, docking at the old Quincy Street ferry terminal and sending hundreds of visitors daily into downtown Port Townsend. Although local residents grumbled about traffic jams and parking difficulties, almost everyone welcomed the dollars. Port Townsend began to feel like a tourist town, an identity the city nurtures today. Regardless of economic vagaries, a certain optimism endures, echoing the sentiment expressed by the *Leader* in 1905, "Certainly prospects look cheerful for Port Townsend in this year of our Lord." [R.B.]

EDIZ HOOK   A three-mile-long sand spit that forms PORT ANGELES Harbor, Ediz Hook was frequently called – even charted – False Dungeness Spit. The name Ediz is believed to be a corruption of Yennis, the name of a village of KLALLAM INDIANS located nearby. The spit was formed by erosion of the Elwha River's delta several miles west and ceased significant growth five thousand years ago when the sea level rose as a result of melting glaciers. Damming the Elwha in the early 1900s reduced sediment even more, and wave action began to erode the spit until the U.S. Corps of Army Engineers placed tons of riprap on the spit's outer shore. They continue to periodically dump "beach feed" into the strait to offer the building material the Elwha River no longer provides.

Betty Heskett was a nineteen-year-old bride when she and her husband Bob moved to a Beaver Valley chicken farm in 1927. They left four years later and few, if any, heard or thought very much about them until 1945 when Betty (remarried as MacDonald) retold her experience in the national best-seller, *The Egg and I*. Two years later the story reached an even wider audience with the popular film starring Claudette Colbert and Fred MacMurray.

EGG AND I ROAD

For those acquainted with the area, it was not difficult to recognize CHIMACUM as "Crossroads" or Port Townsend as "a barren old maid of a place, aged and weathered by all the prevailing winds and shunned by prosperity . . . the world's only lighted cemetery." MacDonald's description was not far off the mark; she knew Port Townsend during those desolate days after the city lost its designation as port of entry for Puget Sound and before it regained prosperity with the establishment of its paper mill. But it was her characters – most notably Ma and Pa Kettle – (modeled after descendants of William Bishop and featured in a passel of successful spin-off movies) that caused rancor. Ultimately lawsuits brought even more publicity to the fuss. Surviving residents discount the accuracy of the novel's characters and cast a few aspersions of their own, suggesting that the Heskett's chicken farm was a ruse by which to buy grain for other purposes during those days of Prohibition. Whatever the truths or fantasies, the book sold more than four million copies and remained in print for nearly forty years. Betty MacDonald died in 1954, and was made a permanent part of local lore when the road that led to her farm was renamed after her popular book.

A Prussian émigré, Charles Eisenbeis (1833–1902) arrived in Port Townsend in 1858. Imbued with a strong

EISENBEIS, CHARLES

entrepreneurial drive, he was also infected with the popular delusion that Port Townsend would ultimately become the New York of the West. To this end he established and operated, among other enterprises, a cracker factory, a brickyard, and the first brewery in Washington Territory. During the boom years, he built several of Port Townsend's more prodigious structures, including the forty-thousand-square-foot MOUNT BAKER BLOCK.

Under the articles of incorporation, he became the city's first mayor. Eisenbeis, along with J. A. Kuhn, Robert C. Hill, Thomas Jackman, and Henry C. Landes, formed what was known as the "Big Five Syndicate." During the late nineteenth century, they were involved in almost every large-scale political and economic project in Port Townsend, including such star-crossed ventures as the Port Townsend Southern Railroad, Steel, Wire, and Nail Company, and the Eisenbeis Hotel. The latter, completed just weeks before the big bust, never served a single guest.

Although of relatively humble beginnings, Eisenbeis projected such an archetypical Prussian demeanor that he was often referred to as the "Baron." He had a penchant for the grand style and was never satisfied with anything but the biggest and the best. He modeled his home, called "The Castle" by townspeople, after the great estates of Bavaria. There, on the western slopes overlooking the town, he ensconced his family in appropriate Victorian splendor.

As did many of his contemporaries, Eisenbeis lost most of his wealth in the depression of 1890. Despite the economic reversals, he never conceded his pride or his dreams. When he died, twelve years later, he was buried, true to form, under the biggest tombstone in town.   [M.W.]

Charles Eisenbeis' castle

EISENHOWER, DWIGHT   Jean Foster (1912–1985) was a Port Townsend writer of the 1940s and 1950s who specialized in romantic fiction for "confession" magazines. Her titles included "And the Blind Shall See," "Must They Suffer for My Sins?" and "My Heart Has Wings," which was later dramatized for radio. Foster's stated ambition was to write for "slick" magazines, where she would be permitted a byline, but her fame resulted instead from a letter she wrote in 1954 to President Dwight D. Eisenhower. FORT WORDEN had been deactivated by the U.S. Army the year before, taking a six-million-dollar payroll with it. Several businesses failed, and community meetings were held to forge a new economic future while the military post sat idle. "Mr. President," Jean Foster began, "I cannot believe, I absolutely refuse to believe, that you have any inkling of what has befallen our small community due to your economic program . . . . I am firmly convinced that, if you are made aware of the situation, you will do something to help us."

In five single-spaced typed pages, Foster mustered her narrative skills to report to the president that she and her family and other Port Townsend residents faced the loss of their cars, their businesses, even their homes. Recognizing the president's need to bring the postwar economy into balance, Foster nevertheless asked: "How can you benefit something as a whole when you tear up and destroy parts within the whole?" She then noted that their next move would be to cash in their son's insurance policy to help meet the mortgage payments. "Give us something, anything, to bring back the people that we lost when Fort Worden was deactivated . . . . That is all we ask, for we will do the rest."

The result of Jean Foster's letter brought her and Port Townsend national attention. In a single-page reply, President Eisenhower responded: "I am deeply distressed by the situation in which you, your family and your neighbors find yourselves." He then dispatched an investigating team of federal and military officials to Port Townsend to see what they could do. The wire services picked up the story, making headlines around the country; Foster was interviewed on CBS radio, and the town readied itself for the Eisenhower delegation. Not everyone was impressed. In a letter to the editor the following week, one local critic, who was admittedly fully employed at the MILL, protested: "We are not a community of starving shopkeepers and landlords."

Within three years, Fort Worden was converted into a state juvenile correctional institution, and the Fosters kept their business and their home.   [P.S.]

The largest of the four remaining subspecies of North American elk, the Roosevelt elk (whose range extends from California to British Columbia) is prevalent on

ELK, ROOSEVELT

the Olympic Peninsula. Named for President Theodore Roosevelt because of his interest in wildlife, these elk are distinguished from other species by their greater size (bulls reach one thousand pounds) and their darker color. To the unpracticed eye, elk can be differentiated from deer by their light-colored rump patch. In summer, elk can be seen only in the high country; in winter, however, they come to graze in the Hoh, Queets, Elwha, Dosewallips, and Duckabush river basins and are frequently sighted by passing motorists.

FALSE DUNGENESS   An early name for EDIZ HOOK.

FLAMENCO   Certainly, it is a peculiar phenomenon that flamenco, an art whose geographic origins are so remote from Washington State, should find a home in Port Townsend. But it is probably a matter of fact that the city has the highest per capita population of aficionados and performers of any town or city in North America. Juergas – or flamenco "jam sessions" – are frequent events in several Port Townsend homes, and local dancers have taken part in performances and festivals throughout the Northwest. Performances in Port Townsend by such noted artists as Teo Morca, Dieguito, Gary Hayes, and Robert Zamora have contributed to the lively interest in this style of music and dance.   [J.H.]

FLORA, PRAIRIE   Just before one reaches the clubhouse on the small road in the Spring Valley Golf Course in Port Townsend, one will find a placard on a large rock, which reads as follows:

IN MEMORY OF CHETZEMOKA
CHIEF OF THE CLALLAM INDIANS
A FRIEND OF THE WHITE PEOPLE
FROM THIS ROCK
HE GAVE A WARNING OF DANGER
AND SAVED THEM
FROM MASSACRE IN 1856

ERECTED BY LUCINDA HASTINGS
PARLOR #1 – NATIVE DAUGHTERS
OF WASHINGTON
1938

CHET-ZE-MOKA's audience probably stood just beyond this spot, which, interestingly, is something of a miracle in the Olympic Peninsula flora. In 1985, Port Angeles botanist Nelsa M. Buckingham observed and cataloged this small area on the golf course. What survives here is a section of native prairie, the like of which the Indians may have maintained for twelve thousand years (from the retreat of the cordilleran glacier until the settlement of European Americans). Settlement, with its accompanying grazing, plowing, and building, has a greater impact on prairie flora than on almost any other group of plants. Thus, the Port Townsend plot stands out as a fortuitous accident, a living fossil that civilization somehow neglected to obliterate.

As Buckingham explains the prairie phenomenon, the first plants to colonize the bare lowlands after the retreat of the glaciers would logically be species that had survived above the glacier in the refuge provided by our northeast Olympic Mountains, or else ones that had moved in from unglaciated lowlands far to the south. Several subalpine species can still be found in the lowlands of the Olympic Peninsula, but there are some that can be found *only* on the golf course. They include old man's whiskers, grass widows, northern goldenrod, and showy fleabane.

Numerous other plants appear in other lowland areas and in high country as well. These include Menzies larkspur, field chickweed, woolly sunflower, Idaho, fescue, and bearded wheatgrass. Some of these plants can be proven to have survived glaciation in the higher Olympic Mountains. There are also several important Indian food plants still found at the golf course. These include riceroot fritillary, baldhip rose, shining Oregon grape, and one plant we know the Indians both cultivated and actually owned, camas.

Prairies were a special habitat that in drier areas such as Port Townsend provided growing room for plants that are otherwise found only farther east or south of the Cascades. Some of these exceptional species have also survived on the golf course, including Lemon's needlegrass and Scouler's hawkweed. Also, a hybrid buttercup suggests that perhaps once both its parents may have grown here. One, the western buttercup, is still here, but the other, the California buttercup, is not. Also, it is known that an unusual golden Indian paintbrush was collected here in 1890, but it can no longer be found anywhere on the Olympic Peninsula. Foothill sedge can only be found at the golf course, and purple sanicle is known to be in only three Olympic Peninsula locations. Other native species Buckingham has found on the golf course are common snowberry, pomo-celery, sickle-keeled lupine; dwarf owl-clover, naked broomrape, deadly zigadenus, early saxifrage, harvest brodiaea, Nuttall's fescue, and field woodrush. [J.H.]

FOGHORNS   Port Townsend's favorite foghorn story is about a bell. During the 1870s, the Reverend Peter Hylund used a school handbell to announce services at ST. PAUL'S EPISCOPAL CHURCH, then located near Point Hudson. One foggy October Sunday, he was called upon by Captain J. W. Seldon, who told Hylund that the bell ringing had prevented his revenue cutter, the *Wyanda*, from going aground earlier in the day. He later presented the church a bell for its steeple, with the provision that it be rung on foggy days. Some years later, Ira D. Sankey, an associate of evangelist Dwight L. Moody, was steaming from Victoria to Seattle, when fog enshrouded the ship. Nearing POINT HUDSON, the captain heard the bell and was able to avoid running aground. Sankey was so impressed with the incident that he wrote a hymn entitled "The Harbor Bell" while cruising to Seattle. The gospel song was a standard in hymnals for years.

Subsequent fog signals in the area were less romantic, high-pitched steam whistles, operated by lighthouse tenders who listened in thick weather for the whistle from passing vessels, then responded with a warning signal from shore. A whistle was installed at POINT WILSON in 1879. Often, though, ships' crews found them disorienting because they sounded too much like ships' whistles. Steam whistles weren't reliable either; for one reason or another, they would occasionally not operate, and ships would be left to flounder in a blanket of fog. According to the *Leader* in 1904, the Point Wilson signal failed with such regularity that the maritime community requested the acquisition of a second whistle to be used when the original failed. By 1913, steam whistles were being replaced with signals operating on compressed air, blasting in regular sequences of four-second hoots followed by twenty-six seconds of silence – a sequence that is still used. But according to the *Leader*, local residents did not like the newfangled whistle – its deep-toned trumpeting disturbed their sleep. Masters and pilots, however, welcomed the innovation because they no longer confused the shore whistle with the whistles of other steamers.

Another warning method was used as late as December 1913 at MARROWSTONE POINT and on Point Hudson where, according to the *Leader*, a big gun from Scotland provided a "distinctive signal when fired at stated intervals." This method of warning had its obvious drawbacks, dependent as it was upon human operation and persistence. The *Leader* reported that Joshua Green, owner of Puget Sound Navigation, endorsed a proposal in 1914 to get a new, more reliable fog signal at Point Hudson because boats from his company showed "such a marked affinity for the Point of late that they felt like the concern owned part of the sand bar." Military interests standardized fog signals by World War I. Under the supervision of the U.S. Coast Guard, three signals in the area operate to guide the fogbound ships: signals at Point Wilson, Point Hudson, and Marrowstone Point are linked to electronic sensors at Point Wilson that measure the density of water vapor in the air.

Forks, 103 miles from Port Townsend on Highway 101, is the westernmost incorporated town in the continental United States. About 117 inches of rain falls there each year. Its population density within the city limits – 3,060 people per square mile – approaches that of Seattle (at 3,445). Its population between 1970 and 1980 jumped 82 percent, then – three years later – dropped 7 percent. In 1981, at the height of a national recession, exacerbated in the WEST END of the Olympic Peninsula by the bottom dropping out of the logging and timber industries, unemployment reached an unofficial count of 70 percent. In 1980, the town's poverty percentage was a full point lower than the state total of 9.8 percent; by the end of 1981, nearly everyone in Forks, employed or not, was poor.

Located between the forks of the Calawah and Bogachiel rivers, Forks was originally known as Indian Prairie because the QUILEUTE Indians used the area as a hunting ground. Homesteaded by two bachelors in the 1870s, the community began to grow in 1878 when

FORKS

Luther Ford and his family joined them. Ford had first settled in Florida after the Civil War, but as a Yankee was not particularly welcomed, so he headed west. He is said to have spurned an offer of forty acres in what is now downtown Seattle to locate instead in the West End. The settlement grew apace, although farming eventually replaced logging and timber operations as the prime economic endeavor.

Forks was nearly consumed in 1951 when a forest fire spread throughout the prairie during a September dry spell. Fanned by forty-mile-per-hour winds, the blaze turned into an inferno that sped toward Forks at a rate of seventeen miles in eight hours. Most of the town fled in cars and trucks, colliding on smoke-choked roads with panicking deer and other wild animals. At age seventy-one, Ollie Ford, the first white child born in Forks, remained behind, stationed on his front porch with a garden hose to protect his property. He was successful, but scores of others who fled lost theirs. More than thirty-three thousand acres of good timber land burned, three times larger than any other recorded fire on the Olympic Peninsula.

FORKS TUXEDO   When dressing up for special occasions, such as the annual FOURTH OF JULY CELEBRATION, WEST END loggers and other woodsmen don shirts of blue and white pin-striped denim, red suspenders, and clean pants to spend a night on the town. The garb is known as a "Forks tuxedo"" and, except for weddings and funerals, is as dressy as the men get.

FORT CASEY   Located on Whidbey Island across Admiralty Inlet from Port Townsend, Fort Casey was one of three MILITARY FORTIFICATIONS designed to protect Puget Sound from invading navies. The first troops arrived in 1902, but after World War I, the post was placed on caretaker status – airplanes and submarines had made the harbor defense obsolete. An active training post during World War II, it was later deactivated and became a state park and an extension campus for Seattle Pacific University. (See *Fort Flagler, Fort Worden*.)

FORT FLAGLER   Along with FORT CASEY and FORT WORDEN, Fort Flagler, at the north end of MARROWSTONE ISLAND across the bay from Port Townsend, was among three harbor defense units established in the late 1890s to protect Puget Sound. Completed in 1907, the eight-hundred-acre post was obsolete by the end of World War I, at which time it was placed on caretaker status. During World War II it was reactivated as a training base. It was finally deactivated in 1954 and became a state park. For more than twenty years, it has been the summer home for the Seattle Youth Symphony, directed by Vilem Sokol.

FORT TOWNSEND

Fort Townsend was established in 1856 to protect Port Townsend from Indian raids but was sited four miles from the young town near the mouth of Chimacum Creek, the nearest available water. General William Tecumseh Sherman thought the fort too far away, and he remarked in 1877 that he "regard[ed] Fort Townsend as an obsolete establishment. Instead of the garrison protecting Port Townsend, the town is guarding Fort Townsend." It was abandoned finally in 1895 and, like all deactivated posts in the area, eventually became a state park.

FORT WORDEN

Until construction began on Fort Worden at the turn of the century, the area was populated only by black bear and timber wolves. Passing Indians usually avoided Point Wilson's swift currents and riptides, portaging instead from North Beach through KAH TAI tidal marshes to Port Townsend Bay. On a snowy winter solstice in the 1850s, a band of early white residents established a primitive "guard house" at Point Wilson as an early-warning outpost to protect them from northern Indians, who periodically stirred up trouble. The crude fortification was secreted among the grass and dunes on the point near where Battery Kinzie sprawls today. A lighthouse and a "deep toned whistle" to warn passing vessels in foggy weather were installed on the point in 1879. CHARLES EISENBEIS later built a kiln and brick factory on the beach, not far from the lighthouse. Using Eisenbeis's brick, the Reverend J. B. Alexander of St. Paul's Episcopal Church built the landmark tower now known as Alexander's Castle (see *Castles*). A few settlers occupied land above the point. Some of the acreage was platted and some changed hands during the boom of 1889, but the depression of the 1890s squelched any plans for residential development.

As early as 1889, General Nelson Miles had called for eleven million dollars worth of military protection on Puget Sound, but not until the Puget Sound Naval Shipyard was established at Bremerton did talk about possible downsound fortifications begin in earnest. The passage of the fortification bill in 1896 assured construction. Having suffered badly during the depression of the 1890s, Port Townsend welcomed the infusion of men and money (see *Economy*). Between 1897 and 1902, the government acquired more than three hundred acres around Point Wilson for $18,787, and much of the area had been logged by 1898. A dock and warehouse were built, and a tramway was rigged from the dock to the concrete mixing plant on the hill above. One thousand and sixty barrels of cement weighing four hundred pounds apiece were shipped around Cape Horn from Belgium. Concrete work on the battery emplacements was completed by March 1900. Sixteen guns (the two largest weighing sixty tons apiece) from Ohio foundries were inched up to the batteries more than one hundred vertical feet at a 52 percent grade. After this first phase of development, the government all but abandoned the reservation, and Port Townsend began to worry. The U. S. Harbor Defense System's first-line strength was a triangular fortification at the mouth of Puget Sound, comprising Forts Worden, Flagler (on Marrowstone Island) and Casey (on Whidbey Island), all to be constructed simultaneously. Flagler was the designated headquarters, which naturally irked Port Townsend in its persistent but elusive struggle to assert regional dominance. In 1902, to the relief of tenacious local boosters, Fort Worden was declared Coastal Defense Headquarters, and troops were slated to arrive, at last, in April. The *Leader* reported, with uncommon understatement, "The arrival of troops will be heralded with pleasure by the people of Port Townsend." When the glorious day came and word was received that the soldiers were on their way downsound, the locals, in their best bib and tucker, backed by a brass band and colorful bunting, crammed Union Wharf to greet the boys in blue. Then, in dismay, they watched as the steamer, instead of docking, puffed on past them, past Point Hudson, and on to Fort Worden, where she landed, presumably with no fanfare save the raucous greetings of gulls and the gentle drumming of waves. The troops numbered fewer than one hundred. Their days were spent in practice with the big guns, hurtling huge shells miles out into the strait, thrilling Port Townsend with the thunderous display. In 1903 more troops arrived and immediately set to work constructing additional buildings.

While the twentieth century was imposing the first of its special horrors on young soldiers in other parts of the world, troops at Fort Worden led a cloistered life. When constructed, the outpost was already something of an anachronism: a nineteenth-century seacoast artillery post retaining many romantic aspects of the old army. Officers and their wives calling on a fellow officer and finding him away placed engraved calling cards on a small silver salver in the hallway. An open mule-drawn wagon, with chairs in rows like bus seats, wound its way daily over seasonally dusty or muddy MORGAN HILL roads into Port Townsend for "post ladies" to do their shopping; officers' wives and wives of enlisted men went at different times. But life at the fort was not without peril. A bicycle path had been cut through the woods to town, but the forest was so thick that more than one soldier, a little worse for wear after a night's liberty, strayed from the path and was injured, only to be discovered dead or near death hours or days later. Some soldiers just disappeared; many an unidentified body washed up on the shore over the years. In 1913 alone, soldiers were involved in several fights (one of which resulted in the death of a policeman), a grocery store robbery, the theft of cigars from a racket store, the theft of a watch from "a prominent citizen," various incidents of "rough housing," drunk and disorderly conduct, "petit larceny," horse thievery, joy-riding, "dine and dash," the destruction of a downtown sidewalk with an axe, and the shoot-up of a theater.

By the spring of 1917, the entire Harbor Defense System was on war footing, but after the war, troop strength was reduced and many of the big cannons were dismantled and shipped away. In an effort to boost morale, General John Pershing visited the fort early in 1920. True to the old army traditions, he shook hands with only officers' children and ate luncheon only in the officers' mess. A balloon hangar was built in 1921, and an experimental balloon company of eighty men and two officers was installed to use balloons in

Primary fauna at Fort Worden:

Birds: *crow, mountain quail, purple martin, robin, Canada goose, gull, American osprey, ringtail pheasant, California quail, mourning dove, chucker partridge, and some bald eagles.*

Mammals: *cottontail rabbit, raccoon, skunk, red fox, and black-tailed deer.*

93

surveillance drills. Deemed unsuccessful, the company was reassigned within the year. Until World War II, staff at the fort was reduced and community focus was the MILL across town, but by the end of 1940, almost one thousand more men and officers had arrived at the fort. Additional housing was constructed in town, and businesses geared up for increased patronage. Greyhound added runs. Restaurants extended hours. Schools hired extra teachers.

The post was as isolated from the abominations of the second world war as it had been from the first. The fort newspaper, the *Salvo*, devoted much of its newsprint to gossip and sports. Official activities were, of course, secret, but to read the paper, life at the fort appears to have consisted of boxing, football, softball, volleyball, golf, skiing, skating, bowling, dancing, courting, attending variety shows or other on-base entertainment, and socializing with sympathetic "local" girls. Either the soldiers were better behaved in World War II or the local paper, in a public relations decision, was not inclined to publish news of their colorful escapades. The tone in the community was one of pleasant coexistence and relief at having the boys (and their bucks) back again. Three hundred people from the town were employed at the fort, and many of the young women from Port Townsend attended USO dances (to which they were extended free admission) and volunteered in the canteen. This time, the community hoped the occupation would be permanent; Port Townsend should have known better. The fort had become absurdly dated. The guns at Battery Benson were dismantled in 1943 and shipped away to be melted into mine anchors. Battery Kinzie's huge guns were stripped and scrapped. Battery Tolles was abandoned in 1945. The guns, never fired in anger, were forever silenced. The installation was more a holding station than a defense outpost. In 1950, nearly half of Port Townsend's population of 6,888 consisted of military personnel or dependents. The fort's annual payroll was close to six million dollars, twice that of the Crown Zellerbach mill.

An attempt to demolish some of the emplacements with an air hammer in 1953 failed because the concrete was so hard.

In March 1953, Port Townsend received a telegram from Senator Warren G. Magnuson: "Sorry to advise that the Army is today announcing the closing June 1" of Fort Worden, putting an end to fifty-one years of military jurisdiction at Point Wilson. According to the area's congressman, the closure would "cut the heart out" of Port Townsend. The chamber of commerce mounted a five thousand dollar campaign to retain the military installation, but the community, apparently resigned to its fate, could not muster more than about two thousand dollars (see *Dwight D. Eisenhower*). The flag was lowered by the army for the last time on June 1, 1953, with no fanfare or salvo to mark the occasion. The last troops left as the first had arrived, quietly, witnessed only by the gulls and the water. The week of the closure, a drive-in movie theater opened just outside Port Townsend. Its feature that week was *On the Sunny Side of the Street*. But the outlook for the community was anything but sunny. With stubborn Port Townsend optimism, the mayor voiced hope that the facility would be "resurrected in even greater glory in the years to come."

After several propositions for the property failed, Fort Worden was purchased by the state in 1957 for $127,533 for use as a diagnostic and treatment center for juveniles. The next year, the center opened and employed almost two hundred people, making it – after the mill – the largest employer in the county. During the early sixties, the fort was selected as an emergency shelter in case of atomic war. Stores of rations and medical supplies were deployed to the sepulchral subterranean vaults. For Christmas 1970, the state gave Port Townsend notice of the closure of the treatment center, which shut its doors officially in 1971. After months of indecision and uncertainty, ownership of the fort was transferred to the Washington State Parks and Recreation Commission, and the fort was dedicated as a state park in 1973. After studies on the feasibility of building condominiums in the mortar batteries and developing the site as a convention center, the state decided instead to maintain and upgrade existing facilities, opening ARTILLERY HILL to the public for the first time in three-quarters of a century.

Soon Fort Worden became the most heavily visited state park in Washington; in 1983, it hosted for the first time more than one million guests. In addition to its park facilities, the fort also became headquarters for CENTRUM FOUNDATION, MARINE SCIENCE CENTER, Copper Canyon Press, and Port Townsend Baking Company and host to varied community func-

Colonel Garland N. Whistler, commanding officer from 1908–1911, brother of James McNeill Whistler, had a portrait of their mother on the parlor wall of his Fort Worden home. Whether it was the famous Arrangement in Black and White *no one seems to know.*

95

tions, family reunions, weddings, and retreats. On a summer morning, no bugle musters the troops to the parade ground. Instead, a soccer team drills amid friendly banter and cajolery; a doubles match is waged on the tennis court; a runner circles the broad green field, now and then consulting her watch to monitor her pace; a bird-watcher with binoculars dangling around her neck, pedals a fat-tired coaster bike down to the beach; the queue at the mess hall is uniformed in sweats and leg warmers, jeans and bermuda shorts; a distant rooster trumpets. A child flying a small, bright kite suddenly cries out as the wind snatches it, lifts it out over the sparkling water, higher and higher. Offshore, the water parts as a TRIDENT SUBMARINE, the new weapon of war, slips soundlessly past the abandoned batteries on the bluff.   [R.B.]

FOUNDERS   When thirty-three-year-old Loren Brown Hastings left LaHarpe in Western Illinois on April 23, 1847, he wrote in his diary that his effects included, "2 wagons, 7 yokes of oxen, 2 cows, one very lazy driver by the name of Marshall Martin, a wife and a little boy, 13 months old, part [interest in] an Indian pony, clothing, provisions, &c, &c." It was a trip the wiry but muscular Hastings had been planning since 1838, when he had arrived in Illinois from his native Vermont. He even had named his son Oregon Columbus in anticipation of the new land and new life that he and his wife Lucinda Bingham were seeking. The Hastings were among the four thousand to travel the Oregon Trail that year, making them part of the first 5 percent to trek across the plains. The wagon train arrived in Oregon City on the third of December, 226 days after it had set out. Hastings soon became acquainted with Francis William Pettygrove, cofounder of PORTLAND, who had come to Oregon around Cape Horn in 1843. Hastings and Pettygrove became fast friends. In 1849 when the news of the California gold rush reached Oregon, the two men headed south to gain their stakes through trading. Both were successful. Returning to Portland where the climate was regarded as debilitating to Lucinda Hastings, the two friends decided to resettle their families in the Puget Sound region.

In October 1851, Hastings and Pettygrove set out by foot on the 120-mile trip to Steilacoom, where they hired canoes to find a site for homesteads. Landing at

POINT HUDSON, they found two men, Charles Bachelder and Alfred Augustus Plummer, who had come to Port Townsend Bay in April, attracted by the deep harbor for the purposes of logging. A native of Maine, Plummer had come to Puget Sound via Texas, traveling across northern Mexico to Mazatlan in 1849, just after the conclusion of the Mexican War of 1846–1848. Uninterested in prospecting, Plummer became a hotel keeper in SAN FRANCISCO. There he met Captain Lafayette Balch, who had made several trips to Puget Sound for piling and squared timbers. He had advised Plummer to head north. On the beach that is now WATER STREET, Bachelder and Plummer built a fifteen-by-thirty foot log cabin consisting of two rooms, with a fireplace built of clay and stone, and Plummer planted a small garden in the back of the cabin, using seeds he had brought from San Francisco.

Plummer, Bachelder, Pettygrove, and Hastings conferred that October day in 1851 and agreed to establish a partnership, create a town site, and begin a settlement. Pettygrove and Hastings staked claims and returned to Portland for their families. Hastings used some of his gold-rush earnings to purchase a two-masted, sixty-foot schooner named *Mary Taylor*, and he advertised passage to Port Townsend. One family and four men joined the Hastings and Pettygrove party, arriving in what was then called PORT TOWNSHEND on February 23, 1852. The boatload of emigrants was met by Plummer and Bachelder and a gathering of KLALLAM INDIANS in two canoes. Upon sighting six-year-old Oregon Columbus Hastings, the Indians became fascinated with his flaming red hair. As the adults stepped ashore, the Indians lifted the canoes still holding young Hastings and four other children and carried them to dry land. Later, in a conference between the two races, Oregon Columbus was seated to the right of S'Hai-ak, chief of the Klallams. The conference was called by the Indians, who wanted compensation for the land the settlers were claiming. Plummer assured them that the United States government would pay them, and Pettygrove gave substance to that promise by offering them needles, fish hooks, mirrors, and other items of trade.

Once an agreement had been reached, the settlers began developing their town. Hastings and Pettygrove each built log cabins, and Plummer soon took a wife.

Bachelder, however, had a falling out with his partners, as he frequently violated an early pact against inebriation. Pettygrove bought his claim for three hundred dollars, and Bachelder moved on to PORT LUDLOW, where he died not long after. The three remaining partners established their merchandising and fishing business, with Hastings putting up a two-story warehouse and trading post. Other settlers came, and the town grew apace. But times were not easy. Mostly it was a BARTER economy, and on those occasions when hard cash was needed, it was not always available. In November 1856, Pettygrove wrote his brother-in-law in Portland: "I am in great need of money at present and you will oblige me very much and send the amount due me by Wells Fargo Company Express which I am told is perfectly safe."

Life was no easier for Lucinda Hastings, Sophia Pettygrove, and Ann Plummer. According to Sallie Hill, granddaughter of another pioneer: "Their kitchen, usually a shed-like addition in the rear of the house, was likely to be the largest room and used as laundry room, dining room, and sitting room as well as kitchen. It was equipped with the small, rather low cook stove .... There was no running water in the house and no sink. Water that had been used for household purposes was thrown out-of-doors .... Bare unpainted floor and table tops were scrubbed with brush, soap, and sometimes with an abrasive such as sand. For laundering " ... heavy wooden bucket after bucket of water was drawn from a well or pumped from a cistern and carried into the kitchen to be heated on the wood-stoked stove. The boiling water was poured over the soiled clothes and household linens piled in heavy wooden tubs set on the conveniently low 'wash bench.' An excellent quality of homemade soft soap was freely used as the rubbing was done on a wash board. Step by step, in preordained order, the work proceeded. More water was fetched; white pieces were covered with cold water and boiled in a wash boiler on the stove. Every article was thoroughly rinsed, the white ones wrung out of bluing water. Finally those to be stiffened were dipped in liquid starch made from marble-sized lumps of starch in which form it was purchased. All wringing was done by hand at least in the first two decades. Nor was drying of the wash easy in this climate ...."

Although families had one another and new settlers were coming every week – and there was plenty enough to do – life was often lonely. A joyful reunion with old friends could often turn bittersweet with the disheartening news they might exchange. In 1856, an old friend of Pettygrove's stepped ashore in Port Townsend. It was the first time they had seen one another in twenty years. "I knew him at the first glance," Pettygrove recounted to his brother-in-law. "He tells me mother died last October a year ago which was sad news to me. I had intended to have gone home to the States next year when I should have had the pleasure of seeing her once more before she departed this life. I have no desire to go home now." The loneliness was felt also at the other end. Plummer's mother wrote from Maine in October 1851, "I want you to write and tell [me] why you went so far away and how long you think of staying there. What benefit can there ever be derived from your stay away at that remote place? You have but one life to live, and why deprive yourself of the peace and benefits of civilized life, for one so lonesome and heart sickening to think of, and still worse to endure? . . . Write to me and tell me what you are doing and how you fare; if the Indians are kind and you can talk with them and they with you."

What was it that kept these pioneers persevering? It is hard to know for certain more than a century later. In reconstructing those early years, descendant Sallie Hill credits their "homogeneity. The first wave of settlers on Puget Sound brought a considerable number of the progeny of the early Anglo-Saxon colonists on this continent. They spoke the same language; they embraced the same values; they were intelligent, not unlettered; thrifty, resourceful, versed in democratic procedures. They were usually not the sons and daughters of wealthy or socially prominent families, but they brought with them habits, attitudes, and manners that insured a simple grace in their private lives. Without conscious intention they established a community that basically had dignity and a distinctive sturdiness." Their endurance was created out of the virtues instilled in them by the mothers and fathers who now missed them desperately. All three founders succeeded and became prominent in Puget Sound affairs. Plummer became county auditor, an office that gave him the distinction of recording the first marriage license – his own. Pettygrove was the town's first postmaster and superintendent of schools. Loren Hastings became at various times sheriff, probate judge, and county commissioner; and he was a delegate to the Monticello Convention, which shaped Washington Territory out of the remains of Oregon statehood. None lived to see Port Townsend in its boom years. Hastings died in 1881, and Plummer followed two years later. Pettygrove died in 1887 just as the founders' sons and daughters were about to make a last futile bid to make Port Townsend the "NEW YORK OF THE WEST." (See *William Jarman*.) [P.S.]

FOURTH OF JULY
CELEBRATION

An annual community festival, the Fourth of July celebration helps to give the town of FORKS its rough-and-tumble reputation. During the week-long celebration, frontier life is given free rein. Events include frog jumping, a truck rodeo, truckers' "pay day," a log show with log rolling, chipping and axe throwing, a river-raft race, and a hanger dance at the airport that attracts between one thousand and fifteen hundred celebrants, many dressed in the garb known as a FORKS TUXEDO. Although July is one of the drier months of the year in the WEST END, rainfall still averages two and one-half inches in this midsummer month; thus the festival is often wet, but the spirit of celebration remains undampened.

FOWLER BUILDING

(*226 Adams Street*) In 1874 when Enoch S. Fowler erected his two-story office building, it was the largest structure of masonry in Port Townsend. Today, it has become the oldest two-story commercial building of masonry in the state of Washington. Its original facade was constructed of fine-cut ashlar, and its side and rear walls were built with rubble. A century of erosion has caused all that to be covered with stucco, but the new facade replicates the original pattern, though the color is grayer than the initial sandstone. The design is essentially folk architecture despite the use of segmented arches with keystones for window openings, which suggests the influence of the Adams, or federal, style. Downtown streets were originally six feet lower and were filled in during the 1880s to prevent frequent flooding at very high tides. Buildings of the period were forced to either raise their first floors or develop sidewalk "wells" as is the case with the Fowler Building. It is the last remaining example of the earlier ground level. The Fowler Building served first as a store, then a Masonic Temple, and from 1880 to 1892 as the JEFFERSON COUNTY COURTHOUSE. Since 1916 it has housed the *Port Townsend Leader*, the town's weekly newspaper.

(*630 Water Street*) Known originally as the Clarendon Hotel, the Fowler-Caines Building was built in 1889 by Mary Caines Fowler, widow of Enoch S. Fowler, and her son, Robert Caines. It was designed by Port Townsend architects Whiteway and Schroeder (see *Architecture*), and the exterior remains virtually unchanged from its original presentation. The building is notable for the facade extension over the alley shared with the Franklin Building and for the Bull Durham advertising sign on the west wall. For years it served as Lewis Emporium, an eccentric collection of hardware, appliances, and used furniture. It was renovated in the early 1970s by Harry E. and Mary P. Johnson as part of their personal campaign to restore the town's Victorian heritage.

FOWLER-CAINES BUILDING

(*Jefferson and Polk Streets*) Built circa 1860, the Enoch S. Fowler House is one of the two oldest surviving houses in Port Townsend (see *Tibbals Building*). As with most early houses built with milled lumber, the Fowler House displays the New England heritage of its owners. A linear plan with gabled front, the house shows evidence of the Greek revival style through the use of wide cornice boards that wrap partially around the gabled front. This was rare ornamentation for early Port Townsend houses. Enoch S. Fowler (1813–1876) was born in Maine, coming to Port Townsend in 1852, where he established an early mail route to various ports between Olympia, Washington and Victoria, British Columbia. He constructed the first dock in Port Townsend where vessels could safely land.

FOWLER HOUSE

Port Townsend's first "pocket park" was developed in 1983 by Tom and Lainie Johnson, who wanted to tie together their Franklin Building on Water Street and their wood-frame building around the corner on Quincy Street with a central courtyard. The Johnsons were confronted with two feet of ash and rubble, the

FRANKLIN COURT

legacy of numerous fires, and a jungle of junk. Tom Johnson transformed this backyard into a minipark, which he dubbed Franklin Court. Though privately owned and maintained, Johnson welcomes public use, most notably for free summer concerts produced by the CENTRUM FOUNDATION.

GALETEA   A Greek sea nymph whose name has become associated with HALLER FOUNTAIN.

GAMES, INDIAN   The bone game (*slaha'l*) was the most popular gambling game played by KLALLAM INDIANS around Port Townsend. Slaha'l was played with two cylindrical bones, each about three inches long and three-fourths of an inch in diameter – a size meant to fit comfortably into the hand. One was a plain bone, called the woman (*sla'ni*); the other had a narrow black band around the middle and was called the man (*swe'tka*). The object of the game was to correctly guess which bones were held in the opponent's hands. Players faced each other, alternating the roles of hider and guesser. Counting sticks about a foot long were stuck in the ground in front of each player – to win, a player had to get all the sticks, sometimes twice if stakes were high. The guesser followed the hider's movements pointing at the hand he thought the hider was using to conceal the bone. If correct he was awarded a counting stick. In early versions of the game, only one bone was used. In the 1800s, the Klallam began using two bones, with one marked to complicate the guessing. In big games, four bones were sometimes used, held by two hiders. Gambling songs and cheering sections accompanied the playing.

The disk game (*slaha'lem*) was a similar game that required greater skill at sleight of hand and attracted professional Indian gamblers. Eight to ten disks made of dogwood and somewhat larger than a silver dollar, all unpainted except for one, were mixed thoroughly in shredded cedar bark. The bark was pulled apart so that half the disks would be in each hand. As with the bone game, the object was to guess which hand held the painted disk.

The beaver-teeth game was a gambling game played only by women, who were neither professional gamblers nor players of the bone or disk games. The game used dice made either of beaver teeth or of bone carved into the shape of beaver teeth. Players sat across from each other on a mat. Points were made according to how the teeth fell on the mat. The game was played at potlatches, typically with mats, baskets, and dried fish offered as stakes.   [J.H.]

GARDINER

A small community on the west side of DISCOVERY BAY on Highway 101, Gardiner retains, along with BLYN, the visual charms of the era before World War II. Originally called Gardner after early resident Herbert Gardner, who settled there in 1906, it became Gardiner to help the pre-zip code U.S. Postal Service avoid confusion with another town of the same spelling.

GEODUCK

(*Panopea generosa*) To harvest the Godzilla of CLAMS, the enormous (some have been recorded at twenty pounds) and enormously ugly geoduck (pronounced "gooey-duck"), requires skill, muscle, an understanding of tides and marine habitat, and a bit of lunacy. If diggers are sighted at a minus low tide with their arms up to their shoulders in sand, they usually are groping for the elusive bivalve. Some restaurants serve it, but it is frozen and, like abalone, it toughens with the slightest handling. Novices to the sport should find someone experienced and willing to lead a geoduck hunt (for that is what it is), to demonstrate its slaughter (a stomach-strengthening exercise), and to quickly prepare it. Otherwise, they would do well to make it one of the tall tales of the peninsula; the look of it is a story in itself.

GLEN COVE

A sheltered beach on the west side of Port Townsend Bay, just outside the Port Townsend city limits, Glen Cove was homesteaded in 1852 by Albert Briggs (1813 –1888), one of the area's earliest pioneers (see *Scow Bay*). Briggs claimed 640 acres, which he farmed. His home was known as The Willows (see *Napoleon's Tomb*), and in the 1890s the cove became a popular resort area known as The Willows Country Club. In 1928, the land was sold to the Crown Zellerbach Corporation (see *The Mill*) as a site for a paper mill that helped Port Townsend through the Great Depression. There were no questions of the lost ambiance nor was concern expressed about the mill's impact on the environment. The origin of the name Glen Cove is unknown.

GRANT HOUSE (*731 Pierce Street*) Italianate in style, the Captain Thomas Grant House was built in 1887 and is typical of the local fashion for low-pitched, simple hipped roofs and elaborate brackets. It is distinguished from other Italianate residences such as the DE LION HOUSE and the DOWNS HOUSE in that its expansive bay windows are on the front rather than on the sides of the structure and are incorporated into the roof line through the use of impediments.

In the 1960s, the house was purchased by architect Victor Steinbrueck, who encouraged preservation of Port Townsend's Victoriana by restoring the house, teaching architectural history at the Port Townsend Summer School of the Arts, and by assigning his students projects in Port Townsend. His wife, Marjorie Nelson, one of the original Actors' Equity players with the Seattle Repertory Theatre, established the Port Townsend Festival Theatre, which played for several summers. In the late 1970s, the house was turned into a bed-and-breakfast inn called Lizzie's after Captain Grant's wealthy wife, who had been instrumental in its construction.

HADLOCK Hadlock, CHIMACUM, and IRONDALE – all approximately ten miles south of Port Townsend – are known collectively as the TRI-AREA. Hadlock is the commercial center. (See *Lower Hadlock*.)

HALLER FOUNTAIN (*Washington and Taylor Streets*) In 1906 Theodore N. Haller brought to Port Townsend a statue and fountain he had commissioned for the city in memory of pioneers. Most particularly, he wished to honor his father, Granville O. Haller, who had commanded FORT TOWNSEND from 1856 to 1860, and his brother, G. Morris Haller, who had drowned in an 1889 boating accident that also took the lives of his brother-in-law and THOMAS T. MINOR. After Haller's dedication speech, a poem about the Greek sea nymph Galatea was read to the assembled crowd of one thousand, and the statue has been so known ever since. Two legends involve Galatea. The better known was told by Ovid and concerns Pygmalion, a sculptor. Although a misogynist, Pygmalion was determined to sculpt the perfect female form. To his dismay – though ultimate redemption – he fell in love with his creation, but being marble, the statue was cold and unresponsive to the kisses and caresses he showered upon it. Finally, Venus, the goddess of love, turned his beloved figure into flesh, and Pygmalion and Galatea were united in earthly form. The myth led to the famous play *Pygmalion* by George Bernard Shaw and the subsequent musical *My Fair Lady* by Alan Jay Lerner and Frederick Loewe. In an earlier version of the legend by Homer, and perhaps the one more favored by Haller, Galatea was loved by the shaggy one-eyed giant Cyclops and by a young prince named Acis. Cyclops found Galatea and Acis playing on a beach and, enraged with jealousy, caused a portion from the cliff behind them to fall and crush Acis. Galatea, however, transformed Acis's blood into a spring of the purest water to run forever.

The waters of Haller Fountain, however, have frequently been interrupted. At quarter-century, jumping trout performed regularly in the basin of the fountain. Later, after passersby used it as a receptacle for garbage, it was filled in to serve as a flower bed. The fountain was restored in the early 1960s by the Kiwanis Club. Architectural historian Allen T. Denison notes that while the statue "may seem overly sentimental to a twentieth-century observer it is a mark of tolerance, sophistication, or resignation that such a display of unabashed voluptuousness would be acceptable to a Port Townsend audience in the 1906 Edwardian era." Nevertheless, in the early morning eighty years later, it is not unusual to observe the naked Galatea sporting a twentieth-century brassiere.   [P.S.]

HALLOWEEN

In Port Townsend Halloween begins early when store clerks arrive for work in costume and face makeup. By evening, especially at the TOWN TAVERN, the serious players have arrived. Their goal is to offer a spectacular appearance without being recognized. In an ever-watchful small town, assuming the cloak of a mysterious character has a certain appeal. A shy girl from the woods might emerge as a veiled Cleopatra, or a logger might waver through the room in the form of a geoduck. Disillusioned mothers dress their daughters as Orphan Annies, and the most gentle, beautiful woman in town may slap her way through a crowd dressed as a gorilla. Costumes provide the wearers with sex changes or species changes. Shadow figures and alter egos and fantasies roam the streets of Port Townsend on Halloween.

Costume events are held all year long, and they are always successful, especially those where the proceeds go towards buying more costumes. Talent shows engage many musical and dance performers, and for many, the performance is an excuse to wear a new costume or take on a new persona – a postal clerk becomes a belly dancer, a bookkeeper shows her Charleston routine with a man nearly half her age, a realtor convulses an audience with a passage from Gilbert and Sullivan. Decade birthday parties, summer solstice, anniversaries, a letter from an old friend in Ecuador have all been occasions to launch a costume party.

HAMMA HAMMA RIVER   The Hamma Hamma River in the northern part of Mason County flows into HOOD CANAL at Eldon. The name is of Indian origin, a corruption of the TWANA name of the place, "Du-hub-hub-du-hub-hub-bai", so named because a small rush called the "hub-hub" was found there. In the early 1900s, Eldon was a bustling town because of extensive logging operations on the upper Hamma Hamma River.

HAPPY VALLEY   A swale of land running north and south between the eastern and western halves of Port Townsend, Happy Valley was used by traveling Indian parties as portage to avoid the treacherous waters off Point Wilson. Indians called it KAH TAI, "to pass through." Loren B. Hastings, one of the town's FOUNDERS, staked his homestead claim in the area and christened it Happy Valley. It is also known as Spring Valley.

HARBOR DEFENSE SYSTEM   A defense concept of the late nineteenth century that led to the MILITARY FORTIFICATIONS of FORTS WORDEN, CASEY, and FLAGLER.

HARDPAN   A glacial till made up of unsorted clay, sand, and gravel, hardpan was packed by glaciers into impervious concrete-like layers that often overlap with similar remains from several glacial periods, sealing off the drainage of ground water and septic systems. Land development in much of Jefferson County is thwarted by either hardpan or its geological opposite, outwash, which is the accumulation of loose sand, gravel, or rock that was deposited by the runoff of melting glaciers. Outwash allows too fast an absorption of septic material, which can contaminate the water table by leeching into lower surface waters of rivers, lakes, and saltwater.

(*Southeast corner of Water and Tyler Streets*) Loren B. Hastings (1814–1881), one of Port Townsend's FOUNDERS, had been dead eight years before the first of four structures associated with his name appeared on the landscape. "Conceded by all [as reported by the *Leader*] to be the most elegant building in the City," the Hastings Building was built by the Hastings Estate Company, which had been established by the family with Loren's fortunes. Designed by Seattle architect Elmer H. Fisher in a combination of then-contemporary styles, the downtown building is distinguished by its use of Richardson Romanesque round arches and a conical roof on the tower (that has since been modified), Italianate brackets and paired windows, and the chateauesque tower that begins at the second story level. A two-story court with skylight was the first such approach to interior design in Port Townsend. The building cost forty-five thousand dollars, the most expensive commercial structure at that time. Unlike the James-Hastings Building, built the same year by Francis W. James and Lucinda Hastings, Loren's widow, the Hastings Building has remained in family ownership since it was built.

(*Washington and Walker Streets*) Riding high on the real estate speculation of the late 1880s, Frank W. Hastings, Port Townsend founder Loren B. Hasting's second son, planned to spend ten thousand dollars on his house, but an oncoming depression forced him to suspend construction in the summer of 1890 with only the exterior and a few rooms completed. It sat vacant with no windows for fourteen years, a symbol of Port Townsend's economic misfortune. In 1904, C. A. Olson purchased the shell for twenty-five hundred dollars, finishing the house without the original plans. With cross gables and steeply pitched roofs of irregular shape, classic detailing, and a porch that wraps around the front tower, the Hastings House is one of the more successful examples of the Queen Anne style. For all its fussiness, the house has a controlled unity that subdues the detail work; it is expertly sited on the lot, allowing the house to frame the Olympic Mountains

Frank Hastings House

107

from one direction and the JEFFERSON COUNTY COURTHOUSE from the other. The house became known as the German Consulate when boarder August Duddenhausen installed a brass German crest near the front door in response to a request from his native land to be its representative in Port Townsend. Duddenhausen's residence at the Hastings House was short, but the reference stuck.

HASTINGS (LUCINDA) HOUSE

(*514 Franklin Street*) Lucinda Hastings was the first white woman to set foot on Port Townsend's shores when she preceded Sophia Pettygrove off the schooner *Mary Taylor* on February 23, 1852. Thirty-eight years later, in 1890, she had the highest property tax assessment ($118,490) of anyone in Jefferson County. That year she put fourteen thousand dollars into her Queen Anne-style home overlooking Point Hudson, downtown Port Townsend, and the Cascade Mountains. Thus, she and her son (*see previous entry*) anchored both ends of the residential area with substantial houses. Though fairly typical of the style, with cross gables and asymmetrical design, Lucinda's residence is a timid presentation, according to architectural historian Allen T. Denison, who notes that the house contains more flat surfaces than usual. The later enclosure of the porch with windows, while thermally efficient given Port Townsend's southwesterly winter STORMS, gives the structure a visual heaviness. Inside, however, oak woodwork, milled by the family's sawyers, offers a graceful framework for well-proportioned rooms. The house was maintained by the family after Lucinda's death in 1894, but was later sold. In the 1970s, great grandchildren bought the house back for use as the Hastings family residence.

HASTINGS POND

Located in KAH TAI Valley at the intersection of San Juan Avenue and F Street, Hastings Pond was part of Loren B. Hasting's original claim. A favorite swimming hole among boys, the pond was enlarged in 1855 when William Bishop and William Eldridge, who later settled CHIMACUM, were hired to dig an adjacent well. At thirty feet the ground turned moist and the bottom fell out, revealing a spring that overflowed into and became part of Hastings Pond. It is a major obstruction on the second hole of the Spring Valley Golf Course and, as such, serves as a repository for wayward golf balls that are retrieved and resold by young children.

He gave new meaning to such words as melange and sandworm; because of him, the word dune became a proper noun. Writing six volumes – known as the *Dune* series – about a planet called Arrakis, author Frank Herbert (1920–1986) captured an audience of more than twelve million readers who became fascinated by the political, religious, and ecological issues that he projected into a fantastic future. He was considered among the great science fiction writers.

Herbert's success did not come early or easily. He began his career as a reporter for Seattle, San Francisco, and Oregon newspapers and was well into his forties before the first *Dune* book – rejected by twenty publishers – was finally accepted. Ultimately, his work was published in fourteen languages. In the early 1970s, Herbert moved to Port Townsend, which became his base for many years. He taught writing, became a familiar and friendly figure about town, and promulgated his concerns about alternate energy resources by building wind-driven and solar-collecting devices at his home. He was an anonymous benefactor to many people in unfortunate circumstances, a philanthropy not generally revealed until his death. After the death of his first wife, he moved to Mercer Island, near Seattle, using his Port Townsend property as a family retreat.

(*Ardea herodias*) Silhouetted against the shallow pools of an ebb tide, the great blue heron stalks with silent precision until it strikes its prey in a blur of deathly accuracy. With long legs, long neck, and long spear-like bill, the heron stands nearly four feet tall with a wing spread to seven feet. Though graceful in repose, it becomes a creature of heavy grace in the air, lumbering into flight like a Boeing 747. Yet it can stand on beds of floating kelp that serve as a platform in its constant search for food. Like the BALD EAGLE, its nests are frequently found in trees, often in colonies. A favorite nesting haven is INDIAN ISLAND.

(*Water and Quincy Streets*) The Hill Building is one of three downtown buildings designed by Elmer H. Fisher, a Seattle architect who was prominent in rebuilding that city after its fire in 1889. Built that same year, the Hill Building was the retirement project of Nathaniel D. Hill, who, at the age of 65, turned his pharmacy over to his sons and contracted with Fisher to design a building for their continuing enterprise.

Less spectacular than his HASTINGS BUILDING, the Hill project was designed by Fisher in an Italianate style, with grouped windows that are fully arched on the third floor but rectangular on the second, and with brackets that support arched pediments. The structure cost twenty-five thousand dollars, slightly more than half of the cost of the Hastings Building. In recent years, the building has best been known as the TOWN TAVERN.

HIPPIE HOLLOW   This residential hollow between the Port Townsend high school campus and MORGAN HILL was originally built by working men during the boom period of the late 1880s. The modest homes were neglected over the years, and by the 1970s their value was so low that many were purchased by members of a growing counter-culture. The neighborhood soon took the name Hippie Hollow, which has persisted although most of the settlers of the 1970s have moved on.

HOH INDIANS   The Hoh Indians have the smallest reservation on the Olympic Peninsula, occupying only one square mile at the mouth of the Hoh River. Fishing is, and traditionally has been, their mainstay. Historically, the Hoh are closely associated with the QUILEUTE of La Push: They speak the same language and are often considered part of the same tribe, which constitutes one division of the CHIMAKUM linguistic stock.

HOH RIVER   An historic fifty-mile-long river on the west side of Jefferson County, the Hoh River descends seven thousand feet from the slopes of MOUNT OLYMPUS to the Pacific Ocean. The name is an Indian word that may have several meanings: "fast white water," "snow water," "that place," "boundary," or "man quarreling with wives," the latter perhaps connected to Makah legends about DESTRUCTION ISLAND. Site of the disastrous first known contact between explorers and Native Americans, the river was among the first western peninsula sites settled by homesteaders. Most likely the first settler was John Huelsdonk, the IRON

MAN OF THE HOH; his farm remains in the family today. The mouth of the Hoh River became the site of the Hoh Indian Reservation in 1893, and, decades later, of OIL CITY. The Hoh River is best known now for the beauty of its RAIN FOREST in the Olympic National Park, some 25 miles upstream.

At the mouth of the Hoko River, fifteen miles east of NEAH BAY and a few miles west of the little resort town of SEKIU, is one of Washington's most productive "wet" archaeological sites. Discovered about the time of the OZETTE DIG, the Hoko site has revealed a fishing camp that dates back at least twenty-five hundred years. Mud at the site proved to be such an effective preservative that articles are found intact, giving much more extensive information about their use than the usual archaeological finds of "bits and pieces" of half-decayed artifacts. An angular chunk of unworked sandstone, for example, would give no indication of its use if found by itself. But at Hoko, the net to which it is still tied gives clear evidence that early Makah were netting fish.

HOKO DIG

Also found intact are small knives made with finger-nail-size flakes of quartz set in five-inch handles. Although these small blades, known as microliths, have been found throughout North America, the Hoko site is the first to show them still hafted. Replicas of the knives have proven how effective they would have been for filleting fish. Furthermore, microscopic wear patterns on the replicated blades from motions involved in filleting match those on the twenty-five-hundred-year-old blades. In a similar way, replicas of wooden fishhooks from the excavation are being tested for effectiveness in catching the kinds of fish that are suggested by the bone deposits at the site.

To excavate the site, archaeologists have been using water sprayed from garden hoses to gently free the fragile artifacts from riverbank deposits; conventional hard tools would have destroyed them. A rock shelter was also discovered nearby, one approximately one thousand years old and which once housed a salmon fishing camp.

"Open up your pocket books, Port Townsend, here comes Hollywood," led the *Leader*'s front page story in April 1981, announcing that Paramount Pictures had

HOLLYWOOD

selected Port Townsend to film a major theatrical movie, AN OFFICER AND A GENTLEMAN. The company said it would spend at least one million dollars in purchases and that the cast and crew – all on per diem – could be expected to drop twice that in Port Townsend coffers. "They'll live as they would in Los Angeles," a company spokesman said. Well, not quite. One of the first tasks required in securing Paramount's commitment to film in Port Townsend was to locate and upgrade enough lodging units for the one-hundred-member cast and crew – just as the summer tourist season was about to begin. Hollywood contracts call for certain amenities, and most local lodging was not up to L.A. standards. Paramount offered advance rent to three hostelries, which called out carpenters and decorators to give the glitterati just what they wanted.

For two months the money flowed. It was spent on props, on wages for local carpenters who were paid top dollar for constructing sets and then tearing them down, for automobiles and motorcycles, for salmon for Paramount's on-location catering truck, and for outsized tips at restaurants. One family received twenty-two hundred dollars for a week's use of its house while Paramount put them up – all expenses paid – at a local inn. The clam bisque at a local delicatessen became so popular that when location work took cast and crew to Seattle, they sent back to Port Townsend for a day's supply of the milk- and cream-laden stew. The *Leader* editorialized: "When you've got a million bucks to dangle at a community, almost anything can be bought." It was a giddy time, but it wasn't just the money. It was a chance to share the spotlight, however peripherally, an opportunity to be part of the Hollywood dream. When Paramount announced auditions for extras and small speaking roles, four hundred people – 8 percent of the town's population – turned out and were photographed and interviewed. Even for those citizens not involved there was excitement in the air. During shooting, one was never quite certain where the trucks, vans, and portable dressing rooms might turn up. There was a certain dash, a bit of élan, that distinguished the movie people from others on the street. It was not unusual to sit near one of the stars or featured players at a restaurant. Because the town was small, an easy interaction developed between many townspeople and the staff.

Not everyone was enamored, of course, and a bit of disquiet set in when the *Leader* revealed in a front page follow-up that Port Townsend had been chosen as the location only because the U.S. Navy had refused to let it be filmed at a naval air station in Pensacola, Florida. The navy chose not to cooperate because they felt the script did not "accurately reflect the Navy's mission." Said a navy public affairs officer, "To be brutally honest, I didn't think it was much of a story, rather trashy, a lot of violence, sex and filthy language in it. And the characters were not characteristic of Navy men." The story took place in an unattractive mill town called Port Rainier, where young girls, dreading a life with no opportunity, gave sexual favors to naval officer candidates in the hope of resulting marriage and a ticket out of town. It was indeed a trashy story, filled with violence, gratuitous sex, and four-letter words.

Some people complained of a parallel between the story line of girls prostituting themselves to entrap men into marriage and the real-life drama of local citizens seeking a place in the movie world with their brief jobs with Paramount. A few involved in the production became so caught up in the fantasy that they were lost to their families and friends for the two months of shooting. Cocaine was in great supply, and drug transactions were observed at local parties where cast, crew, and local residents mingled. The free-flowing money disturbed others. One wrote to the *Leader*: "Is it really necessary to convince townspeople to allow strangers in our midst for a mere eight weeks by approaching us through our wallets rather than our hearts?" A local artist was put off by how the town was caught up in the glamour and observed that if fine artists of comparable stature had come to Port Townsend, they would not have received as much attention. But for most townspeople, the two months were a vacation, a long recess from the daily routine.

When the production company left in late June, Paramount took out a full-page advertisement in the *Leader* thanking the community for its support and hospitality. "Port Townsend is a very special community. Thank you for letting us be a part of it." Immediately following were two more full-page ads from sixty-five businesses, individuals, and agencies in the community, thanking Paramount: "It's been fun having a little Hollywood excitement in town.''

A year later the movie was released and was, for all its raunchiness, enormously popular. Its gross box-office receipts that year were second only to Stephen Spielberg's *ET, the Extra-Terrestrial*, the highest grossing film of all time. It played in Port Townsend for a month, then moved to the drive-in theater for another few weeks. The film was even something of a critical success, largely because of the performances. In April 1983, two years after Paramount had come to town, the film had been nominated for several Oscars (it won two: Lou Gossett, Jr., as best supporting actor, and its musical theme, ''Up Where We Belong,'' as best song). Small Oscar parties were held throughout town, attended by Port Townsend's Hollywood extras.   [P.S.]

HOMES TOUR Two annual tours of historic homes and buildings showcase Port Townsend's fine collection of Victorian architecture and attract several thousand visitors from throughout the Puget Sound area. The first tour was held on a quiet Sunday afternoon in January 1963, and nearly two thousand people jockeyed for position on Sims Way to visit the SAUNDERS HOUSE. Both the city police and the highway patrol were called out to unsnarl the resulting traffic jam. Flabbergasted tour organizers, expecting to attract from two to three hundred visitors, scrambled to adjust for ten times that number by opening half an hour early and staying an hour late. Just as Victor Steinbrueck had told the townspeople two years earlier, the buildings had value, economic as well as historic. People would pay to see them. ''The town is a museum,'' he said, ''and you are the caretakers.''

Originally called the Victorian Homes Tour, it was later renamed to more accurately reflect the actual composition of the tours. Not all the homes were, strictly speaking, Victorian, yet all had a place in Port Townsend's history. The self-guided tours were fundraisers for the Parent-Teacher Association's student exchange and scholarship committees. In 1971, a fall tour was organized to benefit tourist promotion for the chamber of commerce, and a spring tour provided funding for TREES FOR PORT TOWNSEND. Subsequently, the tours continued to be held the third weekend in September and the first weekend in May.

In 1979, the spring-tour benefit was turned over to the Port Townsend High School Scholarship Foundation, whose tours both underwrote scholarships and established an endowment fund, which surpassed its goal of one hundred thousand dollars in 1985. The 1986 spring tour passed to a new organization, whose sole purpose is funding civic-improvement projects, such as street-end miniparks on the waterfront.

Now in its third incarnation as a body of water, Hood Canal was first a river, known by geologists as the Matlock Pathway, which carried melting glacier water to the Chehalis river basin and out of Grays Harbor to the Pacific Ocean. That was twelve thousand years ago. As the twelve-hundred-foot-deep glacier continued to retreat northward, the water level dropped, and the river became a lake. Eventually, as the Strait of Juan de Fuca was uncovered and opened to the Pacific by the retreat of the glacier, this fjord that extends eighty miles into the southern reaches of the Puget Sound lowlands finally became the tidal channel it is today.

Its first known residents were TWANA INDIANS, one of seven distinct Native American tribes that inhabit the Olympic Peninsula. Consisting of three bands, the Twanas occupied thirteen different villages, prompting anthropologists to speculate that a high population density forced the Skokomish band to settle upriver, an uncommon residential site for early peninsula inhabitants.

On May 13, 1792, GEORGE VANCOUVER sailed into the narrow waters and named it Hood's Channel for Lord Samuel Hood, an Englishman who fought in the revolutionary war. His name also graces Mount Hood and Hood River in Oregon. Livelihood on Hood Canal, as the name has since evolved, today depends primarily on a retirement economy, a few logging operations, and tourists attracted by the two eastern entrances to the Olympic National Park and a brief shrimp season in summer.

The Hood Canal Bridge is one of only four so-called permanent floating bridges in the world, all of them in Washington State, and it is the only one built over salt-water. It is also the only one to have been built twice.

The bridge was the 1950s brainchild of Governor

Albert D. Rosellini and his director of highways, William A. Bugge, a JEFFERSON COUNTY boy whose grandfather was CHIMACUM pioneer William Bishop, Sr. The 10,093-foot bridge contains a series of longitudinally linked concrete and steel pontoons, that are anchored to the bottom of the canal; it is covered with an asphalt and concrete surface with a movable center span.

The bridge was controversial from its inception. During its construction, two pontoons being towed from their construction site near Seattle sank in the Duwamish River in December 1958. State engineers reevaluated the bridge's overall design and determined that "it would be prudent to strengthen the pontoons and their connections." As a result, post-tension cables were installed within the pontoons, and a new grout was used to connect them. But on January 28, 1960, six pontoons were damaged by high winds. Repair for the damage cost the state half the eight-million-dollar total. When the state dipped into teachers' retirement fund money for repairs, tempers flared and Rosellini's popularity plummeted in certain sectors. A 1960 report by a consulting firm found the design inadequate. Said one of the authors later: "We felt maximum wind, wave and current conditions that could occur during the life of the bridge would produce forces exceeding those used as a basis for the original design." A study undertaken over a five-year period, although not released when completed, was revealed in 1972; it concluded that the bridge was "marginally designed."

Despite controversy and delay, the William A. Bugge Bridge was opened on August 12, 1961. The six thousand who attended the opening ceremonies celebrated the completion of the span with a certain humor: One family wore life jackets as they drove across; another car inched slowly across with a small boat strapped atop with a sign reading "Lifeboat #1." The first people to cross the bridge were in a sixty-car caravan from Port Townsend.

Judge A. C. Grady, speaker on opening day, said, " ... despite all the problems and delays that have plagued and beset this project, it stands today – rugged, solid and strong, a living memorial to the faith of the citizens of the State of Washington. Let it now be known, in the language of the astronauts, as the 'A-OK Bridge,' the 'O' in this case referring to the Olympic Peninsula, and the 'K' to the Kitsap Peninsula, as important in its way as are the satellites in the skies." On September 14, less than a month after its opening, a cable on one of the forty-two anchors snapped, once again raising questions about the bridge's adequacy.

Eighteen years later, in a rare confluence of high tides, high winds, and swift currents, the western half of the bridge sank on February 13, 1979. Winds up to one hundred miles per hour had forced the closure of the bridge at 2 A.M. The six-hundred-foot draw bridge was opened to ease pressure, but one of the twenty-seven pontoons broke loose, drifted, and sank. By 7:30 A.M. the western half of the bridge had separated and sunk. According to a witness quoted in the *Port Angeles Daily News*, "It made the awfullest racket you ever heard." The concrete and steel pontoons, broken and flooded, lay submerged, some in water more than three hundred feet deep. The span leading to the pontoons dropped into the canal and became a subterranean route to nowhere; three of the fifty-six-ton anchors had been dragged as much as one hundred fifty feet north of their original position.

A month after the sinking, Governor Dixy Lee Ray signed into law legislation authorizing reconstruction. Ray promised that "It will rise again, just like a phoenix." And a project manager during construction advised residents to not " ... worry about this new bridge. Puget Sound has never known a wind strong enough to harm it." Federal emergency relief monies funded most of the $96 million replacement; $41.5 million came from insurance and interest. The navy required a new drawbridge to accommodate the passage of its TRIDENT submarines. Twelve new pontoons, each longer than a football field, were anchored by twenty-six concrete cylinders, each fifty-six feet wide, twenty-nine feet tall, and each containing twenty-two hundred tons of rock and iron. These anchors were linked to the bridge with three-inch steel cable, twice the width of the original cable. The new pontoons were designed with individual watertight compartments and submarine-type screw-down hatch covers. Taller than a two-story building, the pontoons were topped by a two-lane highway with open railings to allow for the drainage of excess water. The second

William A. Bugge Bridge was dedicated on October 24, 1982. The first eastbound traffic on the span was a 1948 Harley-Davidson bearing Howard and Juanita Schmidt. They had waited at the western end of the bridge since 4 P.M. the day before. According to the *Daily News*, Howard said, "Once in a while you got to be first in line for something." [R.B.]

HOT SPRINGS Indian legend holds that the Soleduck and Elwha valleys in Clallam County were once home to two dragons who met on the ridge that separates those valleys and began a fight that lasted for years. Clearing timber from the high slopes and shedding skin that remains today as crusty growths or lichen on trees and rocks, neither dragon could prevail. Both withdrew to their caves, where they still cry in despair, their tears the source of the Soleduck Hot Springs and the Elwha Valley's Olympic Hot Springs.

The Soleduck Hot Springs became a major resort when, at the turn of the century, the flamboyant Michael Earles disregarded doctor's orders to seek a drier climate and chose instead to backpack for two days into the springs. When his health improved, he bought the place. His first investment was seventy-five thousand dollars to build a nineteen-mile wagon road from Fairholm at the west end of Lake Crescent to the springs. He then hauled in a sawmill piece by piece, putting three hundred men to work building a two-story hotel with 165 rooms and private baths, telephones in every room, private balconies, a bathhouse, a gymnasium, a hospital with an operating room, an electric plant, and a steam laundry. In its peak year, the resort drew nine thousand guests, who took a steamer from Seattle to Port Angeles, were driven to Lake Crescent in red Stanley Steamers, sailed a launch to Fairholm, and then were carried by stagecoach to the springs. The pomp lasted only four years. When the resort burned in 1916, insurance covered only seventy-five thousand dollars of the damage. Though later incorporated into the Olympic National Park, the rebuilt resort offers none of its former pretensions.

The first settler to see the Olympic Hot Springs in the neighboring Elwha Valley was Andrew Jacobsen, who told in 1892 of finding twenty-one pools with temperatures ranging from 116 degrees to 138 degrees Fahrenheit. When he failed to convince others of his discovery, he refused to disclose the location, which was not seen again until fifteen years later, when three men found the site and established a resort. Various lodges were built, expanded, burnt, and rebuilt, and finally, in 1966, closed for good. When a snowstorm caused the collapse of several buildings, Olympic National Park staff dismantled all structures, returning the area to its natural state. A half-dozen pools remain and are favored by a young crowd that, although discouraged by park officials, prefer to skinny dip.

The Hudson's Bay Company was first chartered by Charles II of England in 1669, giving it trade rights as well as the power to send ships to build fortifications in defense of its possessions and to make war or peace with the non-Christian inhabitants of the new world. The charter gave Hudson's Bay almost sovereign powers over the vast portion of North America drained by streams entering Hudson's Bay. The Indians in the northern regions had come to think of Hudson's Bay as an independent government. Known to the Indians of the Pacific Northwest as KING GEORGE'S MEN, the company had posts at Nisqually and Victoria and exchanged metal implements, blankets, and ornaments for furs. Though the Hudson's Bay traders brought some diseases to the Indians and intermarried with them, the negative impact of the Hudson's Bay people was not so pronounced as that of the Americans, or BOSTON MEN, who unscrupulously sold whiskey to the Indians and used its power as a heavy bartering item. At one point in the 1850s when Indian uprisings in the area seemed imminent, some Indians hoped that King George's Men would help to drive off the Bostons. In his book, *The Northwest Coast*, James G. Swan commented, "That the Company did furnish them [the Indians] with guns and ammunition is notorious to everyone." But it soon became apparent that the tide of American emigration was too great, and King George's Men withdrew without great incident into the agreed-upon territory to the north, leaving behind them a history of compatibility with the Indians that few Americans had ever known. (See *Klallam Indians*.)

HUDSON'S BAY COMPANY

Ranging in height from 5,757 to 6,450 feet, Hurricane Ridge obstructs one-hundred-mile-an-hour south-

HURRICANE RIDGE

westerly winter winds, lessening their impact on the northeast shores of the Olympic Peninsula. A favorite destination for Olympic National Park visitors, Hurricane Ridge – the only developed ski area in the Olympics – is just sixteen miles from Port Angeles and offers a view that Alaskans have compared to their own Brooks Range. During World War II, it served as a lookout against feared Japanese invasion.

INDIAN ISLAND It was said by ancient Indians that a prince dwelt on Tomanoas Mountain. Guarding the royal dwelling was a mammoth reptile whose back was revealed at low tide, hidden at high. Indians from the northern islands, who intermittently invaded Puget Sound, waited for high tide so they could paddle undetected over the submerged reptile's spine. Known later as Chimacum Portage, this land bridge connected – at low tide – Indian Island to the Quimper Peninsula near Port Hadlock. KLALLAM INDIANS and maybe the CHIMAKUM INDIANS used the island as a seasonal home. Klallam encamped at the mouth of KILISUT HARBOR, which separates Indian and MARROWSTONE ISLANDS.

Few white settlers came to the island in the early years of Port Townsend's founding, and the brutal and unsolved murders in 1879 of Dennis and Susannah Haight, early farmers on the island, did nothing to encourage further migration. The boom of the late 1880s, however, brought speculators, who developed a suburb on the southwest portion of the island, dubbed East Port Townsend. But only a few came, a handful of families and some reclusive bachelors who settled beyond the platted neighborhood and scratched a living from the island by raising chickens and garden crops and by digging clams. Industry came to the island in the form of a fish cannery and a boat yard, but the island remained rural. The "Prince of Wales," son of Chief CHET-ZE-MOKA, and his wife settled on the Klallam's traditional grounds on the northeast corner of the island. The prince was well liked by island residents, and he single-handedly effected several daring, lifesaving rescues in the waters off the point.

Indian Island was a popular hunting ground for sportsmen from the mainland. Raccoons, rabbits, and mink were trapped for their fur. Bears were hunted, but in decreasing numbers as land was logged by speculators. Upland birds such as grouse and Chinese pheasants were bagged in great numbers. Bluebills, sawbills, pintail ducks, and whistlers favored the island and fell victim to the hunter's prowess, as did seals.

Port Townsend shipping interests had agitated for the removal of Chimacum Portage since 1889 to shorten the upsound journey. Island residents opposed the action, which they feared would further isolate them, but their objection was ignored. In May 1915, claiming the interests of coastal defense, the U.S. Army Corps of Engineers undertook the task. Islanders were forced to row from the southern end of the island to Hadlock, until a ferry was established by the county on the same route – the shortest ferry route in the state. By the end of the 1920s, the population of Indian Island was estimated at fewer than fifty; twenty years later it was almost one hundred.

In 1936, the appearance on the island of two U.S. Navy appraisers ignited rumors that the navy was interested in the property. Speculation ran wild, and investors bought up island parcels. The rumors proved true in the summer of 1940, the navy announced plans to construct a $1,400,000 installation on the twenty-nine-hundred-acre island. It proposed a deep-sea dock for off-loading ammunition from ships destined for upsound ports. The munitions would be stored in small arsenals dotting the island. The navy also commissioned the Naval Net Depot in 1941. Nets were strung underwater across to Port Townsend as part of the coastal defense, ostensibly to snare enemy submarines, much as the Indians on the island had strung nettle nets between poles to snag ducks and birds. In November 1940, the navy condemned the island, offering owners of its thirty-two farms and homes a total of $50,858 or approximately $18 an acre. This represented about one-third the amount paid per acre for land acquired for Fort Worden more than forty years earlier. No reimbursement for buildings or other improvements was offered. Land owned by the state and county was to be acquired at no cost. Property owners were furious. Even Seattle newspapers took up the cause and rapped the navy for offering the same price for the island as it paid for "one small Navy boat." But no adjustments were made. The objections seemed unpatriotic in the face of war, and it was well known that some of the objectors were speculators

The island was so densely timbered that local boys made a game of climbing saplings to the height where they bent under their weight, then leaping to the next tree and so on. Some boys, said old-timers, managed to travel the length of the island this way.

who had bought the land in the hope of selling it to the navy at inflated prices.

By the time the war erupted in 1941, a pier provided five hundred feet of berthing space, and tucked into the island's timber were administration buildings, shops, and barracks. Fifty magazines were ready to store munitions, secreted under camouflage. Twenty-nine enlisted men and three civilians were on duty, and by 1945, their numbers had swelled to three hundred and thirty-four enlisted men and one hundred and fifty civilians. The facility reverted to prewar staffing at the end of the war. In 1952, the Portage Bridge was constructed to replace the ferry that had earlier provided connection to the mainland when the legendary tidal land bridge had been dredged away. By 1959, the Naval Net Depot had been phased out permanently, and the ammunition depot had been placed on reduced status; only a handful of men maintained the facility.

In 1976, the navy announced the transfer of its ordnance depot from Bangor on Hood Canal to Indian Island, necessitating the construction of a 1,660 –foot, eleven million dollar pier. Construction was begun in the bicentennial summer. The first vessel docked at the new facility in mid-May 1979. "Reduced activity status" was lifted. Indian Island is not a full-fledged ordnance station but is part of the Keyport Naval Undersea Warfare Engineering Station. It is the smallest ordnance station in the country, but the only one on the West Coast that can handle deep-draft ships. Its current function is the storage and shipment of ammunition; the maintenance, cleaning, and repainting of ammunition; and the replacement of components that are aged or defective. The facility handles only conventional weapons, no lethal chemical or nuclear weapons. The station employed approximately one hundred people in 1984. Approximately eight ammunition trucks per month, with up to twenty tons of explosives per truck, use state and county roads to bring munitions to the island.

In 1982, the naval facility on Indian Island won the coveted Secretary of Defense Natural Resources Award because of its "careful attention to environment, limited timber harvest, ban on herbicides, and protection of BALD EAGLE nests." Its BLUE HERON rookery is one of the largest in Puget Sound. Only one-quarter of the island's acreage has been cleared by the navy; the remainder is given to wildlife. During the 1979 storm that sank Hood Canal Bridge, more than one million board feet of timber blew down. The area was cleared and seedlings planted. Under a system developed in 1982, only an additional twenty-three acres a year may be clear-cut in parcels no larger than five acres. The navy and its munitions cohabit behind chain-link fences and barbed wire with more than three hundred deer, many raccoon, a dozen or more foxes, and several coyotes. Seals sport in the island's waters, and clams are making a comeback after being overharvested twenty years ago. Several bald eagles, symbols of America's vigilance and strength, call the island home.   [R.B.]

"When the tide is out, the table is set." This old adage   INDIANS
of the early inhabitants on the Olympic Peninsula coastlines is not far from the truth. Although the ease with which they gathered food was at the root of some of the prejudices against them, it in fact gave them time to develop a highly refined social and cultural life. Their boats, utensils, baskets, and fishing equipment were remarkably efficient, and their rituals were deeply linked both to their traditions and to their immediate lives. They were a highly mobile people, traveling in the summer to fish and gather provisions for the winter months, which were a time of art, craft, ceremony, and celebration. Although there are tribal distinctions in customs, the cultural similarities among the Northwest Indians of the Olympic Peninsula, and even among the Indians farther north to Vancouver Island and mainland British Columbia, are more striking than their differences. The fact that these were seafaring people meant they could trade with ease and exchange artifacts and stories, which drew them together. Intermarriage among tribes, especially royalty, was also common.

It would not be accurate to portray early Indians of this area as innocent and noble savages. They kept slaves, they had tribal feuds over such issues as fishing territory, and they were materialistic to the extent of granting social standing based on wealth. Ironically, in these regards, they had much in common with their civilized counterparts in America in the early 1800s. But the civilized counterparts gave them a lot of bad press. Early government reports, newspaper editorials, journals, and diaries abound in arrogant dismissals of the Indians as at best salvageable for Christianity and Westernism. Generalizing about all Puget Sound Indians, the respected Horace Greeley wrote some of the most devastating words of all: "Squalid and conceited, proud and worthless, lazy and lousy, they still strut out or drink out their miserable existence, and at length afford the world a sensible relief by dying out of it." Even JAMES G. SWAN, the famous nineteenth-century Port Townsend resident who made extensive collections of Indian artifacts and was befriended by many area Indians, assumed that they were probably the descendants of a "separate creation" from the white man and subjects whom white people should help raise to the level of civilization through cleanliness, English, and Christianity.

The ease and grace with which most coastal Indians accepted the white world cost them dearly. Some tribes lost nine out of ten of their members to small pox, measles, and other white man's diseases. All lost their nomadic freedom, and, for a time at least, they lost the right to carry on their traditional potlatch rituals. It was not until the 1970s that non-Indian residents felt the sting of Indian self-determination. In 1970, a coalition of fourteen tribes sued the state of Washington. Together with the Department of Justice, they charged that the state had violated their rights to fish usual and accustomed fishing grounds, a right guaranteed in perpetuity by treaties signed between tribal leaders and the state's first territorial governor, Isaac Stevens. On February 12, 1974, Federal District Court Judge George Boldt of Tacoma ruled that Indians were entitled to catch 50 percent of the harvestable salmon returning to off-reservation fishing areas in much of the state. The decision had profound effects upon non-Indian commercial and sports fishing and led to both racial and legal conflicts that continue. Nevertheless, in 1979, the U.S. Supreme Court upheld what had become known as the Boldt Decision.

Apart from the fishing controversy, attitudes toward Northwest Indian culture have become more favorable today than during the early days of white settlement. It seems to be a fact of human history that what is first despised eventually becomes romanticized. And so today, area Indian art and traditions are prized, not only as a tourist commodity but also for their inherent beauty and strength, and most resort areas and towns on the Olympic Peninsula sell Northwest Indian art. Many bookstores have Northwest Indian sections, including many reprints of early books about the Indians; and Indian museums, most notably the large Makah Cultural and Research Center in Neah Bay, have awakened general interest in the Olympic Peninsula's first inhabitants. This book in no way pretends to do justice to the historical subject of Olympic Peninsula Indians, nor is it a reference for contemporary Indian life and practices. It does provide separate entries with some historical data for the following tribes: Chimakum, Hoh, Quinault, Quileute, Twana, Suquamish, Quilcene, Kilsid, Makah, Queets, Nootka, and, especially, the Klallam, since they were the dominant tribe in the Port Townsend area. (See *Basketry, Boston Men, Chinook Jargon, Dosewallips River, Duckabush, Duke of York, Hoko Dig, Hudson's Bay Company, Indian Island, Kah Tai, King George's Men, La Push, Makah Days, Makah Museum, Neah Bay, Ozette Dig, Potlatch, Rainbow Decals, James G. Swan, Tamanous, Tamanous Rock,* and *Wool Dogs*.   [J.H.]

The Northwest of the 1860s seemed far removed from the bitter civil struggle that engulfed the United States. News of the great war filled the papers, but the daily lives of the people were more involved with taming the wilderness that surrounded them than in far-off causes, however vital. Information was weeks old; the sense of urgency was just as distant. In Port Townsend, port-of-entry status promised to bring civilization and prosperity, not civil strife. A sense of direction and economic destiny filled the pioneers.

INSURRECTION

Into this provincial environment came Victor Smith, who set off the great "Customs House Controversy." Born in Rhode Island in 1826, Smith moved with his parents to western New York State shortly after his birth. At the age of twenty, he moved to Chicago and studied law under James Collins, a prominent attorney involved in antislavery issues. Although he gave up law within the year, Smith retained the abolishionist fervor of his teacher. From law he turned to journalism, first as a clerk on a temperance paper, then in 1853, as a local editor for the *Cincinnati Gazette*. It was there he first came in contact with Salmon P.

Chase, a U.S. senator from Ohio and a perennial presidential candidate. Chase's brand of liberal republicanism appealed to the reform-minded Smith, and he was quick to serve the politician whenever he could.

During this period Smith and his fiancée, Caroline Rogers explored and were exposed to a wide variety of new ideas and beliefs. It was the age of the lecture circuit, and those like Smith, with a bent for the cerebral, could spend their evenings listening to Horace Greeley's thoughts on politics or a Lucy Stone treatise on women's rights. The 1850s and 1860s were, as their twentieth-century counterparts would be, a period of change and a time to test the limits of society. For his part, Smith approached new ideas with an intensity bordering on the fanatic. He was inspired to set up a utopian community. When that plan failed, largely because of his elitist attitudes, he became deeply involved in spiritualism, which was then seen as a way of bridging the gap between science and traditional religion.

While Smith probed new horizons, he continued to offer political aid to his acquaintance Salmon Chase. Chase became governor and when Lincoln was elected president, was appointed to the coveted position of secretary of the treasury. As was customary, rewards were allotted to those who had been of service. To Victor Smith went the position of collector of customs for the Puget Sound region. Smith arrived in Port Townsend on July 30, 1861, assuming his duties the next day. Determined to make Puget Sound the model customs district in the West, he approached his job with a zeal hitherto unknown to the office. His first order was to move the Marine Hospital from private operation in town to empty barracks at Fort Townsend, thereby saving the government the rental on vacant beds and the cost of private physicians. He then clamped down on the popular practice of importing Hudson's Bay Company whiskey without paying duty. While both actions undoubtedly saved money, they did not endear Smith to the townspeople, who appreciated cheap whiskey and the money the hospital brought to the community.

If the town was at first unsure of Smith, it rapidly became apparent how Smith viewed the town. In addition to his customs position, he had also taken over as editor of a local newspaper, the *North-West*.

The patronizing tone of his editorials offended nearly everyone. Even when he tried to be complimentary, he failed. He once told the host at a social event that he was surprised to find the people of Port Townsend as "intelligent as the country people back home." When he began to criticize the suitability of Port Townsend as the port of entry, battle lines were quickly drawn. Smith began an active campaign to move the port of entry to Port Angeles, telling his superiors in Washington D.C. that Port Townsend had a poor anchorage, bad water, and was out of the traffic path for ships heading to the San Juans. He also promoted the idea that should the British join the Civil War on the side of the Confederacy, Port Angeles would be an ideal location to protect the peninsula from invasion. While he was correct about the water supply, the anchorage in Port Townsend Bay was more than adequate and easily the equal of Port Angeles's harbor. Port Angeles had its own set of problems as well. It was basically undeveloped real estate. It had no roads, businesses, or any of the services needed to support a port of entry. This aspect was certainly seen as an advantage to Smith, who had quietly bought up twenty-five acres in the Port Angeles town site. In 1862 Smith returned to Washington D.C. to push the transfer and to defend himself against an increasing deluge of letters demanding his dismissal.

Not trusting anyone locally to serve as a deputy in his absence, Smith arranged for Lieutenant J. H. Merriman of the revenue cutter *Joe Lane* to serve as his replacement. Merriman was young, bright, and ambitious, and he immediately began scrutinizing the internal workings of Smith's empire. What he found delighted Smith's adversaries. Among the information in a letter from Lieutenant Merriman to Secretary Chase and President Abraham Lincoln was evidence indicating that Smith had never perfected his bond of office, a legal requirement of service. Additionally, as Smith's letters attested, he had lied about that fact to the Treasury Department. An examination of records had also revealed that Smith had asked for permission to sell an old revenue cutter and when permission was denied he had sold the vessel anyway. The funds received from that sale never appeared in the books. Before a reply was received to the complaints, news arrived that Smith had succeeded in securing the transfer. Angry townspeople hung him in effigy at the customs house.

On August 1, 1862, one year to the day after Smith had first assumed his duties, the revenue cutter *Shubrick* pulled into the bay. Victor Smith had returned. Merriman was quick to respond, locking the door to the customs house and denying Smith access. From behind the door, he told Smith that without a bond he was not legally entitled to act as a collector of customs, therefore he would not relinquish the customs records. Besides, he pointed out, complaints had been sent to the Treasury Department that would assure his dismissal. Smith maintained that the charges had arrived in Washington while he was there, and although he offered no proof, he claimed to have cleared himself on all counts. Merriman refused to yield. Angrily, Smith returned to the *Shubrick*. He next sent a contingent of armed crewmen to the wharf with a written request for the keys. Merriman again refused to comply. Smith ordered Lieutenant Wilson, the *Shubrick*'s commander to remove the solid shot from the ship's cannons and replace it with grapeshot. He trained the guns on the town and issued his ultimatum. Merriman had fifteen minutes to turn over the customs house to Smith or the town would be bombarded. A hurried conference between the town's leaders brought the only response possible. Within a few hours, Smith, the *Shubrick*, and the customs records were on their way to a new home in Port Angeles.

After examining the evidence, an arrest warrant was later issued by Territorial Governor Pickering, charging Smith with "assault with intent to kill." On pressure from Secretary Chase, that charge was eventually dropped. In September a grand jury was convened in Olympia. Smith arrived in the *Shubrick* and the Port Townsend contingent traveled on the chartered schooner *Potter*, rechristened "Revenue Ship #2" for the occasion. As they passed the anchored *Shubrick*, they fired a mock salute. After taking testimony from Smith, Lieutenant Wilson, and forty Port Townsend citizens, the jury indicted Smith on thirteen counts, including diverting federal monies for his own use and assaulting the people of Port Townsend. Chase sent a special treasury agent to examine those findings, and again charges were dropped. Smith returned to Port

Angeles to build his town, and the people of Port Townsend went back to writing President Lincoln about Smith. Anson Henry, Surveyor General of Washington and an old friend of the Lincolns, made a trip to the Washington D.C. to discuss the matter with the president. Lincoln called in Secretary Chase to hear Henry's story and dismissed Smith, telling Chase that although there wasn't evidence enough to convict Smith, "the degree of dissatisfaction with him there is too great for him to be retained."

Secretary Chase was allowed to give Smith another job. The secretary appointed him Special Treasury Agent for Puget Sound in 1863. He would remain in Port Angeles. That summer the small creek that ran past the new customs house dried up. No one bothered to investigate. If they had, they would have seen that a landslide in the valley above the town had created a natural dam, with a rapidly growing lake behind it. On December 16, while Smith was away, the dam gave way. A wall of water carried the customs house out to sea, drowning two agents. The next day Makah Indians found the customs house and towed it to shore. Most of the customs records became kindling in reservation fires. Smith's home was destroyed, and his family barely escaped.

In 1864 Smith was directed to transport three million dollars in payroll funds from Washington D.C. to San Francisco aboard the schooner *Golden Rule*. Off the coast of Panama, the ship hit a reef and sank. Smith remained in Panama to direct salvage operations while the rest of the passengers, including his family, continued north on another vessel. When the safe was finally removed from the ship, it was found to be empty. Smith accused the captain of theft, and when those charges proved to be unsupportable, he claimed that certain parties in Washington D.C. and Olympia were once again conspiring against him. With the end of the salvage operation, Smith made his way to San Francisco, where he booked passage on the steamer *Brother Jonathan* for Puget Sound. On July 31, while fighting heavy seas off Crescent City, the ship hit a reef and sank. Among the fatalities were Victor Smith and, ironically, Anson Henry, who had precipitated his removal as director of customs. Within weeks of Smith's death, the customs headquarters was returned to Port Townsend. [M.W.]

Legendary pioneer of the Hoh River Valley in the
WEST END, John Huelsdonk (1867–1946) was
acclaimed for a physical prowess beyond the capacity of
any mortal. As with most apocryphal stories, however,
there was truth within the tale. Huelsdonk measured
only five-feet, ten inches, but he weighed 225 pounds,
and his strenuous life as a homesteader assured that his
bulk was muscle, not fat. His varied activities were the
unintended result of a logging accident that mangled
his hands so badly that he resorted to jobs he could
manage with gross dexterity. He raised cattle and
sheep, gardened, trapped and hunted bounty, and
backpacked for hunters, geologists, loggers, and sur-
veyors. He was seen everywhere in the woods. An
average marksman, his reputation as a "deadeye"
came from a lucky shot before witnesses who carried
the tale. His most famous exploit – the one that gave
him his mythical title – was just as easily explained.
Seen packing a cookstove on his back one day in the
woods, Huelsdonk replied to a remark on the heavy
load: "Wouldn't be so bad but for the sack of flour in
the oven – it keeps shifting." What was meant as a
mild complaint was turned into an incredible feat. The
story grew as it spread. The stove was actually made of
sheet metal, but the retelling of the tale turned it to
cast iron. The flour became a hundred-pound sack; in
reality it weighed half that. But even when his so-called
exploits were explained, the man seemed larger than
life. Legends persisted and made their way into such
national publications as *Time* magazine and the *Satur-
day Evening Post*.

He was portrayed as a man to match mountains.
The Huelsdonk family had left their native Germany in
the late 1870s when John was a boy, out of sorts with
political unification of German states that would, they
feared, culturally deny their Dutch heritage. In his
later years, Huelsdonk opposed another state action
– the expansion of the Olympic National Park into the
Hoh Valley. He saw it as just another form of governmental tyranny. Driving to Olympia to meet with the
governor, he carried a placard declaring, "This Isn't
Russia! Secretary of the Interior [Harold] Ickes has no
right to take our homes from us." In the end, his
homestead was excluded from the extended park, but
state and national forestry and conservation policy put
an end to homesteading life in the West End, and the

Iron Man of the Hoh was left isolated to live out his remaining days.

The evidence of iron ore in the Chimacum area gave rise to another of Port Townsend's nineteenth-century industrial fantasies: Steel City of the West. Though six miles south of Port Townsend, Irondale's proximity was enough for Port Townsend to consider it part of its own. The Puget Sound Iron Company began operation in 1878 and had developed, according to an 1890 promotional pamphlet, into a daily thirty-five-ton capacity mill that employed 325 men producing pig iron. It was the only iron smelter in the state at the time. Another effort occurred when Homer H. Swaney, president of the Pacific Steel Company, began operating in Irondale, but his death in 1904 caused withdrawal of investments from eastern sources.

In 1909 SEATTLE developer James A. Moore, whose name remains on the Moore Hotel and Moore Theatre on that city's Second Avenue, formed the Western Steel Company, acquiring fifteen hundred acres that encompassed a mile of waterfront. Moore claimed assets of twenty million dollars and expanded the mill to include three blast furnaces and two rolling mills, producing three hundred tons of steel per day. Irondale boomed. Lots sold for a thousand dollars; on Moore Street they went for twice that much. A full community sprang forth, reaching a population of fifteen hundred; plans, however, were being filed to accommodate twenty thousand. With one of their city's own as principal investor, the *Seattle Post-Intelligencer* editorialized on April 7, 1909: "The making of steel on Puget Sound will bring about an industrial development of undreamed proportions, will mean more to Seattle and the state . . . than even the discovery of gold . . . it has every prospect of becoming the largest and most important manufacturing city in Western America."

But the dreams already had been dreamed; the rest was just hyperbole. The steel mill was a losing proposition. Chimacum ore was of poor quality, and it soon ran out; ore was expensively imported from British Columbia and China. Prices dropped. The mill closed in 1911, although it reopened for eighteen months during World War I. The facility that had employed six hundred men could not compete with its eastern rivals.

Over the years, fire and neglect took their toll on buildings, especially the industrial and commercial structures. All that is left are the roads and some old dwellings among newer ones. Irondale serves as a memory of another industrial dream in name only; today it is primarily a residential community for CHIMACUM and HADLOCK, the three of which comprise what is known as the TRI-AREA.

IRRIGATION FESTIVAL   The granddaddy of community celebrations on the Olympic Peninsula and certainly one of the oldest in the state, the Sequim Irrigation Festival was first celebrated as a picnic on May 1, 1896. The event served to witness the completion of the first ditch bringing water from the Dungeness River to the arid Sequim Prairie, the driest coastal area north of southern California. The festival is held annually in early May. (See *Sequim*, *Zucchini*.)

ISLAND COUNTY   Island County is the second smallest county in the state. Its 220 square miles consist of six islands: Ben Ure, Camano, Deception, Hackney, Smith, and WHIDBEY, located across ADMIRALTY INLET from Port Townsend. The demographics of the county are affected greatly by the naval air station located at Oak Harbor on Whidbey Island: Sixty-five percent of the county's employment is government-based, and forty-two percent of the population is below the age of twenty-five.

JACKSON SCULPTURE   Public art once meant WPA murals, bronze statues,
BEQUEST   and fountains – familiar images in comfortable surroundings like schools, parks, and post offices. For years public art was defined as art paid for with public funds and shown in public places. In recent decades public discussion has played an increasingly significant role.

Regina Hackett, art critic for the *Seattle Post-Intelligencer*, notes that "Many Americans are hostile to art, interpreting art that challenges them as art that is trying to insult them ... particularly irritating to some people is the notion that big sums are being spent for art they 'don't get' immediately. Art therefore becomes a focal point for public resentment." Perhaps, in fact, some people are upset because they do 'get it,' but dislike the messenger in proportion to their dislike of the message. That could account for the "cover-up" in Olympia wherein Michael Spafford's murals in the State Capitol Building, left partly finished, were voted out of sight if not out of mind by the state legislature. Or Stephen Antonakos's neon sculpture for the Tacoma Dome. After a three-to-one vote of no confidence on a city advisory ballot was ignored by the mayor and the city council, Tacomans returned to the voting booth to scrap the city's entire Percent-for-Art ordinance that had made the neon purchase possible in the first place. One of the first cities in the country to enact such an ordinance, Tacoma became the first to repeal it.

Brouhahas like Olympia's and Tacoma's are part of a national epidemic of public art furors. Other, bigger cities have unresolved, often bitter, ongoing disputes. If even New York City can engender massive opposition to Richard Serra's *Tilted Arc* in the city's federal plaza, less enlightened localities have every reason to be wary of public art projects.

Port Townsend didn't have a choice. When native daughter Ruth Margaret Seavey Jackson died in 1982, leaving the bulk of her estate of more than two hundred thousand dollars to the city for a "sculptured object or artistic monument" honoring her pioneer family, the town hit the big time in public art. Conditions and deadlines were tied to the bequest. The city, unused to arguing the merits of art, delegated the processing of the project to a joint committee of the arts and parks commissions. Ultimately, the joint commission, against some opposition, chose the former Quincy Street ferry terminal parking lot on the waterfront, near the city hall, as the site for the Seavey memorial.

Then, townspeople enthusiastically leapt into the fray, quarreling happily over each and every issue. Almost everyone had an opinion. Some citizens protested the idea of accepting the gift at all. The city didn't need the art, they insisted, and the money should go to Jackson's alternate choice, the Guide Dogs of the Desert. This objection enjoyed brief appeal until it was pointed out that the dogs for the blind were well funded and that the choice was not between "useless art and helpless blind people."

Ruth Margaret Seavey Jackson's grandfather, James Seavey, was an associate of Loren B. Hastings, became a representative to the territorial legislature, clerk of the district court, county auditor, county commissioner, and postmaster, and was one of the first teachers in Port Townsend. Her father was a public health doctor stationed at the old Marine Hospital during the early 1900s. Ruth (1906–1982) was elected president of the Jefferson County Historical Society in 1948 and was a founder of the society's museum.

133

The project remained quiet for about a year until the announcement of the jury selection, which became the focus of enraged protest, prompting one commissioner to comment bewilderedly, "but the fan isn't even on yet." The argument was that a jury composed of only outsiders would not be sensitive to Port Townsend and its qualities. The jurors included Arnold Jolles, director of the Seattle Art Museum; Richard Andrews, then coordinator of art in public places for the Seattle Arts Commission, since appointed visual arts director for the National Endowment for the Arts; Anne Focke, founder/director of the former and/or gallery and of a statewide foundation for individual artists; George Thomas, director of the Whatcom Museum of History and Art in Bellingham; and Dianne Vanderlip, curator of modern art at the Denver Art Museum. The jurors were seen as carpetbaggers who would undoubtedly import a "sculptor of the international style" or a member of the "New York conspiracy," who couldn't possibly know "what Port Townsend wanted." Conversely, one commissioner protested that the jury wasn't international enough, that its Northwest focus was too provincial. Fearful that local artists would be excluded in a national competition, as they ultimately were after nearly 400 artists responded, partisans were successful in getting the commission to amend its jury by adding Port Townsend ceramist Anne Hirondelle. Continuing to complain that the community was disempowered, yet denying that they required a local artist in the finals, some protesters knew all along that the local control issue was a paper tiger. Through its arts/parks commission, the town had been in control from beginning to end, and no matter what the jury decided, the city council was free to accept or reject their choice.

Of the 397 artists who entered the nationwide competition, finalists who submitted models were Mary Miss of New York; the teams of Buster Simpson, Seattle, and Lloyd Hamrol, Los Angeles; Charles Fahlen of Philadelphia and Doug Hollis of San Francisco; and Charles Greening of Seattle and Joan Brown of San Francisco. Interestingly, many had had previous experience in Port Townsend, either as visitors or teachers. Their models were displayed for two weeks. More than 800 residents viewed and discussed the possibilities, and 167 left detailed comments for the jurors' consideration.

In December 1984, in a marathon weekend, public meeting followed public meeting. The jurors' deliberations were "an Olympics of input;" everyone who had anything at all to say had a chance to say it. Everyone talked. Everyone listened. The open and thorough process wound down. And so did the critics. Acknowledging surprise at their own reactions to the artists' models and their relief at the artists' sensitivity to the site and the town, most of the early vocal critics joined the tide. They had little choice, really. It would have appeared contentious and grudging – even ignoble – to continue to insist on an all-local jury when the professionals had, in fact, unanimously chosen the public's favorite. The city council concurred with the choice of the team of Hollis and Fahlen, whose entry consisted of a tide clock and wave-gazing gallery. The tide clock is a shell-like chamber in which the tide can be seen to rise and fall, surrounded by curvilinear terraces of local basalt riprap. The wave-gazing gallery is a 180–foot, copper-roofed walkway of gradually stepped platforms connected to a large square pavilion, topped off by a wind harp. In their presentation to the public and the jury, the artists played a background recording of a similar wind harp, whose plaintive and mournful song set the stage for a touching communion among all assembled.

Following the jury's selection of the winning design, the room went silent, and for a satisfying few moments it seemed that all present were in agreement. They weren't, of course, but it was the next best thing: an unspoken commitment to agree to disagree and to accept the result of a long, tedious, and difficult public process. Juror Vanderlip, breaking the silence, noted that she had all but given up on public art a few years before but that her experience in Port Townsend with the Jackson bequest had changed her mind. The hard part was said to be over, but the difficulties were only beginning. Installation of the winning design stalled on a series of legal procedures, questions of bonding and licensing of the artists, issues of maintenance, and concerns about completion of the project within the budget. A year after their selection, the artists were still negotiating a contract with the City.　　　[N.P.]

"Well, art makes people mad."
– Linda Okazaki,
Port Townsend painter.

Because of a growing concern for United States – Nicaragua relations, Port Townsend peace activist Doug Milholland visited Nicaragua in 1983. The Port Townsend PEACE COALITION and the American Friends (Quakers), with whom Doug and his wife Nancy Milholland had been worshipping) provided the funding to send him. While in Nicaragua in December 1983, he chose Jalapa as a possible sister city for Port Townsend because it was known to have a well-organized city government. An inland city of about eight thousand people not far from the Honduras border, Jalapa is nestled in a verdant agricultural valley surrounded by mountains. Upon returning to Port Townsend, he met with Mayor Brent S. Shirley and the city council. Although some concern was expressed that sister-city designation might be viewed as political support for the Nicaraguan socialist government, on February 21, 1984, the city of Port Townsend passed a resolution adopting Jalapa as a sister city "to promote a relationship of understanding and friendship between the peoples of both cities," noting that the relationship was "not meant to be construed as an endorsement or condemnation of [the Nicaraguan] form of government."

After the adoption of the sister-city resolution, the Port Townsend committee sent a goodwill packet, which included a signed scroll from the people of Port Townsend, newspaper articles, and a letter from Mayor Brent Shirley. Later, sewing supplies and blueprint paper were sent, but the most significant contribution was in the form of a person – Chris Rhinehard – who volunteered to work in Jalapa as Port Townsend's representative of goodwill. Having done work in sewage and sanitation development in Port Townsend, she became a sanitation technician in Jalapa, working with the design stages of a sewer system. Port Townsend students have sent school supplies, and in January 1986, a delegation of Port Townsend government officials and merchants made a goodwill tour to the Nicaraguan city. In April, a delegation of officials from Jalapa visited Port Townsend.

JAMES HOUSE (*1238 Washington Street*) The first bed-and-breakfast inn in the Northwest, the James House is high Victorian both inside and out. Since its opening in 1973, it has served as the standard of the industry.

Built in 1891 by Francis W. James (1832–1920), the house is primarily Queen Anne in style with complex intersecting gables, few flat surfaces, chimneys of patterned masonry, and a tower. It also shows the influence of the shingle style with simple window surrounds, the polygonal dormer on the roof, and shingled walls without interruptions at the corners. Its interior design is noted for the superb detail in parquet flooring, detailed brass hardware, and wainscoting in oak, walnut, and cherry.

F. W. James is said to have made his fortune during the Civil War by converting gold into unsecured "greenbacks" at thirty-five cents to the dollar, which the U.S. government then redeemed in 1879 dollar for dollar. He then reinvested his gains in U.S. bonds at a 15 percent discount. Even more risky, though it must be acknowledged that there were no banks at the time in Port Townsend, was his means of storing extra cash. According to historian James G. McCurdy, James buried his money under a tree at the base of the Crow's Nest. During a storm, the tree was uprooted and the cache exposed. James recovered the money, but according to McCurdy, "the incident shot the faith of Mr. James in trees as treasure chests and thereafter he kept his surplus wealth hidden in a flour barrel in his store."

JAMESTOWN

Little remains today of the small settlement of Jamestown, which lies a few miles northeast of Sequim, close to the Three Crabs Restaurant. Jamestown, however, has an interesting claim to history. It is one of three sites (along with Lower Elwah and Port Gamble) where many KLALLAM INDIANS *chose* to settle after the 1855 POINT NO POINT TREATY. When whites asked them to leave Dungeness, the Klallam paid five hundred dollars for a 222–acre, one-mile strip of land back from the waterfront on the Strait of Juan de Fuca. Because the Indians bought it with their own money, it is technically not a reservation, though they have since received reservation benefits. The land was bought under Lord James Balch, a descendant of chiefs of the Dungeness band. When the town was founded in 1875, it was named after him – Lord James Balch's Jamestown.

Most people stay out of the history books by avoiding notable achievement. Some manage it by hiding their significant deeds. Then there are those few like William Jarman who lose their place in history by failing to file the proper paperwork. William Jarman (1819–circa 1904) arrived in North America as a seaman aboard the Australian brig *Platypus* in 1846. The intention of the merchants on board was to trade with the Indians of Vancouver Island's west coast. Unfortunately, the first tribe the hapless merchants encountered was more inclined toward robbery than fair bargaining. While Jarman was on shore, the *Platypus* was attacked and forced to flee, leaving the twenty-seven-year-old sailor to his fate. He managed to elude the Indians for several days, but ultimately was captured and made a slave. He remained in that unenviable situation for almost two years until the Hudson's Bay Company learned of his plight through a more amiable tribe. Using the friendly Indians as intermediaries, the company was able to secure Jarman's release in trade for several four-point blankets, a favorite Hudson's Bay product to this day.

In 1848, shortly after Jarman's arrival in Victoria, he set out alone in a canoe toward Port Townsend, then called KAH TAI by its inhabitants. There he became acquainted and friendly with the Klallam chiefs CHET-ZE-MOKA and S'Hai-ak. Eventually he shared their home and became the first white settler to inhabit Port Townsend. Jarman remained in Port Townsend for many years thereafter, never bothering to file homestead papers and for that matter never altering his lifestyle much, although he lived for a time with the Loren B. Hastings family. He did bow to convention somewhat by having Hastings perform a marriage ceremony for himself and his Indian wife. As the years passed, William Jarman was forgotten, and although his presence must have smoothed the way for the other white settlers, he never attained recognition as one of Port Townsend's founders. [M.W.]

Established on December 12, 1852, less than a year after homesteads were claimed in Port Townsend, Jefferson County was carved out of Thurston County in further division of the Oregon Territory. The name was chosen in recognition of the nation's third president, Thomas Jefferson, and his far-sighted policies, notably

the Louisiana Purchase in 1803 and the subsequent
Lewis and Clark expedition to the Pacific in 1804–1806.
Two years after it was formed, Jefferson County was
divided in two; the northern half, bordering the Strait
of Juan de Fuca, became CLALLAM COUNTY. In this
division, Jefferson County gained a portion of the
western side of Discovery Bay, a major port of that
time. The actual boundary was said to have been
determined by the fact that Jefferson County wished
to exclude an "undesirable" family located near DIA-
MOND POINT. In the late twentieth century, Jefferson
County is no longer in a position of power. With only
one incorporated town – Port Townsend – and the
bulk of its 1,805 square miles in the uninhabited
Olympic Mountains, the county has a population
density of only 9.3 people per square mile. Only nine
other counties in the state have less. With a population
of 16,900, it is 29th of 39 counties; its per capita income
of $9,739 is 24th. Most of its jobs are governmental (28
percent), with retail a close second (24 percent); manufacturing – the only one with high wage scales
– comes in third (18 percent). Demographic figures
show that only 27 percent of the population is under
the age of nineteen, the lowest among surrounding
counties, but in 1983 the marriage rate was twelve per
one thousand population, the highest among the same
counties. Fully 23 percent of Jefferson County citizens
are sixty years or older, almost 9 percent higher than
the state average.

(*Jefferson and Walker Streets*) In 1890 when twenty-six-
year-old Willis A. Ritchie was selected from among
eight competitors to design a new courthouse for
Jefferson County, the Ohio-born Seattle architect first
specified locally pressed brick as the primary building
material. But his review of the soft product made in
Port Townsend must have changed his mind for he
altered the specification, calling instead for a hard-fired
substitute from St. Louis. Criticism flew, both public
and private, but Ritchie held to his decision, and with
quiet alacrity, the county commissioners supported
him. The decision was practical. Four million bricks
were needed to construct a 75–by–140-foot three-
story house of government with a full basement and a
twenty-foot-square tower rising more than 124 feet.
After nearly one hundred years of exposure, the brick

JEFFERSON COUNTY
COURTHOUSE

and beaded mortar remain in almost original condition, while the local brick used in the commercial section of downtown has become porous and the mortar has crumbled.

Considered "absolutely fireproof" when completed in 1892, the only wood used as structural members in the courthouse were roof trusses, rafters, and tower floors. Attic rooms were protected with wire lath and plaster, and the roof of the main structure was made of tin shingles "so [according to the *Leader*] no fire could possibly reach the rafters to burn them." That the tower roof was covered with wood shingles, that heavily shellacked woodwork surrounded interior doors and windows and served as wainscoting on nearly all walls, that oak was the favored medium for clerks' cages, counters, and desks – none of this was seen as hazardous. Happily, the *Leader*'s enthusiasm has not been tested. Ritchie also received design awards for courthouses in Bellingham, Olympia, Seattle, Spokane, and Vancouver; only the Spokane and Port Townsend buildings remain.

Clock tower of the Jefferson County Courthouse

Largely self-taught, Ritchie was heavily influenced by Henry Hobson Richardson's Romanesque style (see *Architecture*). Ritchie went directly to Richardson's Allegheny County buildings in Pittsburgh for his Port Townsend inspiration. Smaller in scale (the Allegheny County buildings covered blocks, the Jefferson County building is contained in one), the local adaptation borrowed hipped roofs, towers, paired windows, and arched entryways from the now-demolished Pennsylvania model. Estimated at $100,000, the final construction bill came to $150,000.

The clock in the tower has served as the town's unofficial timekeeper since it began tolling in 1892. Built by the E. Howard Watch and Clock Company of Boston, the bell weighs thirty-five hundred pounds and is six inches thick at its crown. The weights and counterweights descend into the basement, and prior to its electrification in 1916, it took two men half a day to wind the clock. The hammer was cast at the ironworks across the bay in IRONDALE. With occasional shutdowns for necessary repairs, the clock has told the hour more than 810,000 times since 1892. During the 1950s when summer daylight time was determined by local option, the county commissioners, in deference

to farmers, maintained the clock at standard time, while Port Townsend city dwellers chose to move their watches ahead into daylight time. Since the bell can be heard only in town (and, with a good wind, across the bay), the result was mass confusion. The next summer, the commissioners set the clock to follow the city.

[P.S.]

Jefferson Transit is a small transit system based in Port Townsend that often adjusts its service to the special needs of its passengers. It features four-block deviations from scheduled routes for people who may be carrying groceries or who may not be dressed for the weather. It provides reports on road conditions. It has often been a finding service for parents whose children did not turn up as expected. Children who forget their fare are not denied bus service but are reminded to bring an extra quarter next time. If someone accidentally gets on the wrong bus, drivers have been known to radio the driver of the desired bus and to arrange a rendezvous. Drivers are friendly to tourists as well as their regular passengers, and a ride on a Jefferson Transit bus can be an experience in local color and gossip. Jefferson Transit both serves the city of Port Townsend and branches into the surrounding area as far as Brinnon thirty-five miles south and Sequim thirty-one miles west. Its ten transit vehicles and seven vans cover 1,050 scheduled miles per day. Its services include local freight delivery, charter service, a "dial-a-ride service" – primarily for the elderly – which picks people up at their door, car-pool matching (a free service for those with and those needing rides), and a van pool. In addition, it is the only public transit system in the country that acts as a Greyhound agency – for both ticketing and freight. Voters approved the system in 1980 with a 53 percent majority. Critics complained that buses were empty, that the equipment was oversized for the passenger load, and that the rates were too cheap. The transit authority, made up of local elected officials, put the issue to the voters again in 1985. Sixty-nine percent voted to retain the system.

JEFFERSON TRANSIT

A small community fourteen miles west of Port Angeles on Highway 112, Joyce was named in 1913 for postmaster J. M. Joyce.

JOYCE

JUAN DE FUCA   Fabled Greek sailor who, under a Spanish flag, claimed to have discovered the STRAIT OF JUAN DE FUCA in the sixteenth century.

JUNGIANS   Several practitioners of depth psychology, developed by Swiss psychologist Carl Jung, settled in the Port Townsend area in the early 1980s. Believing that dreams have intelligible meaning for both the individual and the culture, they focus on dream-work as a therapeutic tool, offering dream workshops for groups and Jungian analysis for individuals. Author and analyst Russell Lockhart was a central figure in Jungian psychology when he moved to Port Townsend with his family to practice and begin a small letterpress publishing venture focusing on literature related to dreams.

KAH TAI   Kah Tai is the name INDIANS used when referring to Port Townsend. It means "to carry" or "pass through." The original Indian inhabitants probably did not use Port Townsend as a permanent village because of the lack of running surface water. The meaning "to carry" suggests that Kah Tai was a place to haul in canoes from the strait and carry them on land to Port Townsend Bay in order to avoid the treacherous waters of Point Wilson. In recent years, area residents have come to associate the name with the Kah Tai Care Center for the aged and with the Kah Tai Lagoon, a haven for many types of marine life and waterfowl.

KAH TAI LAGOON PARK   Perhaps no piece of land has been so divisive in Port Townsend's history as Kah Tai Lagoon Park. When George Vancouver arrived in 1792, that division was purely physical. KAH TAI, which means "to pass through," was a broad salt marsh extending inland from Port Townsend Bay. Besides using the marsh and the valley to the north as a portage, the Klallam Indians also gathered an abundant supply of waterfowl native to the lagoon. Nets, woven from nettles and suspended from one-hundred-foot poles, were rigged across the mouth of the lagoon. Smokey fires were built underneath to obscure their presence. Flocks of birds would then be driven from their feeding grounds into the traps.

     With the white man's arrival, Kah Tai became a barrier to expansion. In 1891 a bridge was built from Law-

rence Street across to the developing residential area on the other side. An intersecting bridge linked San Juan Avenue. But because beach logs were often used instead of treated piling, the bridge rapidly deteriorated. By 1907 few drivers would chance a crossing. Those who did venture on the span usually carried garbage to the city dump in the lagoon's center. Construction of the paper MILL in 1928 provided the impetus to expand the roads out from the city. By 1930 SIMS WAY spanned the mouth of Kah Tai, sealing it off from direct tidal influences. The need for marine-oriented industrial property expanded the fill area south of the highway. The 1930s were a time of increased awareness of the lagoon's potential. The chamber of commerce planted poplar trees along Sims Way and lobbied to make Kah Tai a federal game reserve. Although denied, a nine-thousand-dollar WPA project was approved in 1938 to remove remnants of the old bridge, add a water control system, and divert city reservoir overflow to the lagoon. In 1939 wild rice was planted to attract waterfowl, and five thousand Montana black-spot trout were released to control mosquitoes. The trout vanished immediately, but the rice lasted long enough to raise the 1940 duck population to forty-five hundred birds.

Through the 1940s and 1950s, Kah Tai Lagoon provided the town with an unparalleled scenic entrance. Few people were left unmoved after seeing Port Townsend, the Cascades in the background, reflected in Kah Tai's waters. Of those unaffected by the lagoon's beauty, a substantial number were on the port commission. In 1963, lured by easy federal money and the legitimate need to expand the boat haven, the port commission, led by Colonel F. W. McIlroy approved a U.S. Army Corps of Engineers scheme to dispose of 231,000 yards of dredged sand into Kah Tai Lagoon. Faced with a public outcry against the fill, McIlroy's response was to turn off his hearing aid. Port manager Julian Oen took a more aggressive approach, stating, ''This so-called lagoon is just a swamp!'' For its part, the Corps of Engineers refused to consider other options for disposing of the material. The project would be done their way or not at all. When a lawsuit failed to halt the fill, opponents asked for a guarantee of a park on the site. Oen responded that a park ''was a waste of public money,'' but the port commission agreed to a three-year moratorium on development. Within a week after the salty fill had been dumped on either side of the highway, the stately poplars turned brown and died. By the end of 1964, eight acres of sand covered the southern lagoon.

Over the next thirteen years, the fill was left largely untouched as the lagoon began to regenerate. By 1976 the sands were covered with at least seventy varieties of grasses, trees, and shrubs, and the poplars were replanted. As the land recovered, pressure increased to develop it. That year a group of representatives from local government entities met to generate possible scenarios for the property; most involved commercial development. Simultaneously, a private landowner asked the city council to rezone twelve acres of the fill from public to commercial zoning. Despite substantial opposition, the request was quickly approved. Within months it was announced that Safeway would build a forty-thousand-square-foot store on the site. Thus encouraged, the port commission brought forward its own plan – a twenty-three-acre motel and retail complex in a nautical motif, accentuated by waterways cut in from the lagoon. A narrow circumference park and an interpretive center were offered to subdue the anticipated opposition.

The opposition wasn't satisfied. A broad-based coalition, called the Kah Tai Alliance, was formed to fight the development. Citing the negative social and economic impact of the project on the historic district, as well as the direct impact on the lagoon's environment, the Alliance filed lawsuits against both developments. Reams of petitions and letters, both in opposition and support, were entered into the port and council minutes each month. While Safeway eventually won its suit in the state supreme court (and then offered the city $25,000 for park development), the port had to abandon its project when it failed to clear the city's environmental review.

When the dust settled, the planning commission conducted a survey. They found that 79 percent of the population favored a municipal park at Kah Tai. Additionally, in 1980 the U.S. Fish and Wildlife Service named Kah Tai Lagoon as one of the ten most important wildlife habitats in the state. With this information, the city was able to obtain a $236,000 federal acquisition grant to purchase eighty acres of the privately held land surrounding the lagoon. On completion of the acquisition process, an additional $57,000 development grant was awarded. In August 1985, twenty-one years after it was filled, volunteers and city officials held a ground-breaking ceremony at Kah Tai Lagoon, Port Townsend's newest park.   [M.W]

A promontory on the western shores of Port Townsend Bay formed by sediment from Chimacum Creek, Kala Point was first known as the site of Joe Kuhn's periodic CLAMBAKES on KUHN SPIT which extends from this point. Since the 1970s, the point has become better known as a high-priced residential development that attracts mostly urbanites seeking refuge from the perils of the city. The development includes condominiums, tennis courts, a clubhouse with a swimming pool, and a remote-controlled gate at the entrance that seems to be inoperative much of the time. Kala is an Indian word meaning "bird;" the point was also called Kula or "goose." **KALA POINT**

Because of its oceanfront resort, Kalaloch is the better known of the two communities in Jefferson County's WEST END, the other being Clearwater. Although it is only 139 miles west and south of Port Townsend on Highway 101, the trip is a three-hour drive over narrow and curvy roads. The name derives from the Quinault Indians, roughly translating as "sheltered landing." Travelers in dugout canoes stopped at the mouth of Kalaloch Creek for fresh water while en route to and from the HOH RIVER. Settled in the late 1890s by Samuel Castile and Tom Lander, who built a clam cannery there, its first white population totaled seventeen when the post office was established as Castile. In 1925, Charles W. Becker, Sr., acquired forty acres immediately south of the creek and established a lodge with cabins. When the Olympic Loop Highway, since referred to as Highway 101, was completed in 1931, Becker expanded his operation into one of the most successful destination resorts on the peninsula. The Olympic National Park purchased the property in 1978, leasing it to a concessionaire. **KALALOCH**

Port Townsend merchant Israel Katz (1851–1917) became one of the first Jewish mayors in the western United States in 1915, when he was elected to head Port **KATZ, ISRAEL**

Townsend's city government. Two years later, Katz was the subject of great speculation when he disappeared without a trace (see *Disappearance of Israel Katz*).

KEY CITY The first of several "boosterisms" used by Port Townsend enthusiasts to psychologically secure the town's prominence. (See also *New York of the West*.) "Key City of Puget Sound" had at least some basis in fact. In 1854, the port of entry for Puget Sound was removed from Olympia to Port Townsend, thus requiring all foreign ships to stop at the Key City before venturing farther into United States waters. The name is still used by merchants and organizations.

KEYSTONE A ferry terminal at the north shore of Admiralty Inlet, Keystone serves as the eastern landing for the Port Townsend – Whidbey Island run of the Washington State Ferry System. The name was chosen when a town at the same site called New Chicago failed in the panic of 1893. Keystone was to have been the western terminus of the Chicago and Skagit Valley Railroad. The eastern terminus was to have been Sedro Woolley, Washington, some fifty miles distant.

KILISUT HARBOR The official name for SCOW BAY, which separates INDIAN and MARROWSTONE ISLANDS.

KILSID INDIANS A band of the TWANA INDIAN tribe anglicized as QUILCENE INDIANS.

KING GEORGE'S MEN Indians called traders for the HUDSON'S BAY COMPANY King George's Men and respected them more than Americans, whom they called BOSTON MEN.

KITSAP COUNTY Hood Canal both joins and separates Kitsap and Jefferson Counties. Though no land borders are shared, the two counties form the east and western shores of Hood Canal and are connected by the Hood Canal Bridge. Kitsap County, however, is decidedly suburban. With 161,600 people, it has the seventh largest population in the state, and its population density is 411 people per square mile, second only to King County. Its economy is secured with military bases; 57.3 percent of its jobs are government-funded. Kitsap County is the home of the West Coast base of the

Trident nuclear submarine fleet and, according to recently published though unofficial reports, is host to two of the state's five repositories for nuclear warheads.

The Klallam Indians who lived in the area from Port Townsend west along the southern shore of the Strait of Juan de Fuca were the most formidable of the area's Indians. Explorer/ethnologist George Gibbs, on an expedition through Washington Territory in 1854, gave their population estimate as "1,500 fighting men," a surprisingly high figure, but the Klallam had not yet been drastically reduced by small pox as had the MAKAH in Neah Bay. In the 1850s many Klallam were known to have moved to Lummi territory, settled, and intermarried there. Whatever the pattern of dispersement and depletion, the Port Townsend census of 1881 showed only twelve Klallam in Port Townsend. One hundred years later, Klallam live in the JAMESTOWN and lower Elwah areas, but hardly any Native Americans in the Port Townsend area trace Klallam ancestry. CHET-ZE-MOKA, a chief of the Klallam in the 1800s when Port Townsend was being settled, was dubbed the DUKE OF YORK by white settlers. His son Lah-ka-nim was called Prince of Wales. From this name came the Prince families of SEQUIM, who carry their Klallam ancestry to the present.

The Klallam were rarely praised for their life-style, morality, or art. An early informant suggested that the Klallam did not care about pretty things – they just wanted to have enough food and to be ready for war. GEORGE VANCOUVER reported his abhorrence of the Klallam's attempt to trade children for goods that he was carrying. The Klallam called themselves "strong people," indicating that their image of themselves was less as a refined society interested in art and decorative craft work – a description that characterized so many of their neighbors to the north – than as a people who could hold their own in battle and trade. Still, much is overlooked and ignored in this easy dismissal of Klallam artistry. Although their material artifacts generally lacked the finish and decoration of northern tribes, they did make many utilitarian items, including a variety of baskets, boxes, and canoes.

Like many tribes of the Northwest, the Klallam practiced head-flattening on babies as a mark of social standing; they thought that people with round heads looked like rocks. Their treatment of children contradicts many of the stereotypes of Klallam as a lazy and dirty people. Children were disciplined to rise early and run on the beach, to swim, to keep their teeth clean with a duck's quill, and to wash out their mouths before bed. Encouraged to respect animals, children often had small seals as pets.

Interestingly, the dog had an important role in this area long before the white settlers came. Not only did the Klallam breed a special long-haired dog for a wool that they wove into garments, but dogs also figured squarely into a Klallam origin myth. Though the details vary in different accounts, the story is one in which a tribal maiden gives birth to severals pups. Because of these unusual offspring, she is ostracized from the village and goes off to live alone with her dog-children. Soon the dogs start shedding their skins and acting like humans. Their mother catches them and burns their discarded skins. Exposed as humans, the brothers declare their destinies: one to be a whaler; another to kill sea mammals such as smaller whales, porpoises, and seals; one to be a fisherman; one to be a canoe maker; and one to be a hunter in the woods. The Klallam people are thus created with varying skills necessary for their society. The mother becomes rich and is accepted back into her society. In some versions the dogs are wolves, and by implication all Klallam are given a special affinity with these creatures.

The Klallam were a trading people; mostly they exchanged perishable food and skins. They developed considerable trade with Indians on Vancouver Island and with the Makah Indians of Neah Bay, exchanging their goods for blankets, canoes, hats, baskets, and other essentials. Their way of drying dogfish and clams was highly regarded; Indians as far inland as the Yakima sought Klallam dried clams.

All flora and fauna were an integral part of Klallam life. CEDAR was prized for building, both for single and group family dwellings and for the potlach houses, which could measure up to fifty feet by two hundred feet. Nettles were used to make ropes and nets that were strung between high poles to trap ducks as they flew up from nearby water refuges on foggy days. Cat-tail reeds were woven into mats used in every dwelling and served as building material for temporary houses while traveling. The flora that still grows along paths in and near Port Townsed provided a staple food and medicinal supply for the Klallam, notably gooseberry, wild strawberry, blackberry, salmon berry, and salal. They also ate fern roots (which some ethnographers called a "bread replacement"), tiger lily bulbs, wild carrot, wild onion, horsetail sprouts, and acorns. They made tea from leaves of cranberry, blackberry, and hemlock. For medicinal purposes they used cedar gum for toothaches, laurel leaves, and licorice root for colds; elderberry bark for diarrhea; fir pitch for deep cuts; gooseberry bark mixed with a woman's milk for sore eyes; and a variety of other plants for a variety of other ailments – especially for skin problems, which were common. These remedies included gray moss, alder steminate, or pistolate cones of cedar chewed and spit upon the sore; leaves of yarrow; thistle roots, especially for morning sickness; roots of skunk cabbage; snowberries, mashed; squaw plum leaf; rose haws; buds of cottonwood; and blackberry roots. The Klallam could generally find these items close to shore, which helped to keep them a shoreline people; they seldom ventured more than a few miles inland.

Port Townsend settlers who experienced the frequent chill throughout the year were surprised, not to mention distressed, to observe the Klallam often wearing no clothes. Some reports state that the Klallam bathed and swam in Port Townsend Bay in midwinter.

A village might have one hunter who would go off into the woods for deer or elk, but most of the harvesting was from the water or very near to it. The Klallam migrated every August to Hood Canal for dog salmon runs and grouped at the mouth of the Skokomish River and Hamma Hamma rivers and at Brinnon, with shorter migrations occurring constantly. Men would fish with weir traps made of fir interlaced with twined cedar limbs, with nets made out of nettle, or with spears at night. They also trolled from their canoes with lines of kelp and hooks of elk bone. Their fishing included all kinds of salmon, halibut, ling cod, flounder, herring, smelt, and candlefish.

While the men were fishing, women would gather roots, berries, and seafood that did not require fishing. Children and slaves helped gather the mussels, clams, fish, sea gull eggs, and various roots and berries. Although much has been made over the fact that the Klallam kept slaves – usually women and children captured from neighboring tribes – there is no indication that the slaves were expected to do any work that regular tribal members did not do.

149

Among the popular sports were various forms of gambling, including the bone and disk games (see *Indian Games*), which involved accomplished sleight of hand and which gave rise to professional gamblers whose art was reading opponents' expressions. They also played their own brand of field hockey and a hoop and pole game that involved rolling a hoop on the beach while someone tried to throw a pole through the moving hoop. Tug-of-war and target shooting with bows and arrows, using a kelp bulb as a target, were also favorite pastimes.

Their religion centered around a guardian spirit. The only deity they prayed to was the Earth (a woman) and then only in a time of great need. Pubescent children were sent out to seek a vision and acquire a guardian spirit; they would return to reveal the spirit in song or at a potlatch. Although shamans existed, they were not of high social rank; their primary function was to deal with illness. (See *Alder, Basketry, Cedar, Chet-ze-moka, Chimakum Indians, Duke of York, Kah Tai, Potlatch, James G. Swan, Tamanous, Tamanous Rock,* and *Wool Dogs*.)　　　　　　　　　[J.H.]

KLONDIKE GOLD RUSH　As the steamer *Portland* neared Cape Flattery on July 17, 1897, *Seattle Post-Intelligencer* reporters had assembled at the offices of the Puget Sound Tug Boat Company in Port Townsend. Rumor had it that the steamship was carrying gold-laden miners from the Klondike region in the Canadian Yukon. The enterprising reporters wished to charter a tug to intercept the *Portland* before it reached Seattle. Assigned the tug *Sea Lion*, they headed out the strait to Cape Flattery, where they met the steamer and got their story, one of the major scoops of the century. On board the *Portland* were sixty-eight miners with $964,000 worth of gold dust and nuggets, estimated at one and a half tons of gold. "A TON OF GOLD!" the *Seattle Post-Intelligencer* bannered in understatement, but a nation and a world were nevertheless electrified by the news and the Klondike promise.

The Port Townsend *Leader* chose, however, to ignore the event, noting only that "the tug *Sea Lion* went to the Cape yesterday;" they featured a story two days later, headlined "MOUNTAIN OF GOLD," about the purported gold find of three Port Townsend men at the headwaters of the Big Quilcene River in the

Olympics. "We have a Klondyke [an early spelling] of our own right here at our door," Dr. J. C. House proclaimed. Mayor Daniel C. Hill, House's partner, concurred. Acknowledging the stampede that was gathering throughout Puget Sound for passage to the Yukon, House repeated, "For mine, I will take my Klondyke in the Olympics and won't have to travel 2,500 miles to get there either." As it turned out, chances were better in the Klondike. House estimated that his find was valued at "thousands, if not millions," but nothing came of it. But the economy of Puget Sound, moribund since the depression of 1893, surged into prosperity with the rush to gold.

Port Townsend men were among the first to schedule trips north. Among them was William J. Jones, who founded the *Leader* but sold it to become a U.S. commissioner stationed at the Alaska-Yukon border. His concern for gold was secondary. Representing the U.S. government in the affairs of its citizens taking gold out of Canada, Jones also turned his newspaper background into a side enterprise when he contracted as special correspondent with twenty-one newspapers, including *Frank Leslie's Weekly*, the *New York World*, and the *New York Herald*, but not the *Leader*. He received fifteen dollars from Frank Leslie for a one-thousand-word article, and eight dollars to ten dollars per column from other periodicals. His early reports, reprinted by the *Leader* from other papers, told of the trials of the ill-prepared miners during that first year of scramble after gold.

Port Townsend merchants did their best to make certain that no one was undersupplied. "Last on, first off" was the marketing slogan local outfitters used to attract the hordes of stampeders. Nearly all Klondikers en route to Skagway stopped in Port Townsend, their last U.S. stop before Alaska and the rugged Chilkoot Pass. Local merchants advertised in Klondike promotional publications, noting that the gold-seekers' supplies would be stowed on top of those manifested in Seattle and would therefore be unloaded first, giving Port Townsend passengers an edge in the mad dash to Dawson before the snows closed access to the Yukon for the winter. The Port Townsend Board of Trade claimed that outfits could be bought in Port Townsend for 5 to 20 percent less than any other city on Puget Sound, and they even found miners to testify to that fact. Whatever the truth behind the hype, most gold seekers chose Seattle, and the booming business in the Queen City settled any lingering arguments about which town would be the primary metropolis of the Northwest. All Port Townsend got for its effort was an enduring though unsubstantiated legend concerning JACK LONDON. [P.S]

KORSAKOV, U.S.S.R.   A fishing community on the southern tip of Sakhalin Island off the Soviet Union's eastern seaboard, immediately north of Japan, Korsakov has twice been proposed as a sister city to Port Townsend. Many of its fishermen are engaged in a joint project with U.S. fishermen, including David Fraser and Jim Prince of Port Townsend, owners of the trawler MUIR MILACH. The sister city relationship was first proposed in 1983, but the project was abandoned after the Soviets shot down Korean Air Lines Flight 007, which crashed not far from Korsakov killing three hundred people, including a U.S. congressman. Just prior to the November 1985 U.S.–U.S.S.R. summit conference in Geneva, the commander of the Soviet fishing fleet suggested that Fraser and Prince obtain another letter from Port Townsend officials, which he agreed to deliver to the mayor of Korsakov. If the sister city relationship is established, citizens from the two cities will be unable to visit one another. Because of nearby military installations, both cities have been declared off-limits to citizens of hostile nations. (See *Jalapa, Nicaragua*.)

KUHN SPIT   As mayor of Port Townsend, Joe Kuhn took an active interest in the spiritual life of his constituency. When the tempo of downtown slowed beyond what he thought fitting, Mayor Kuhn would grab some musically inclined friends and hit the streets. Marching in and out of stores, through alleys and side streets, the *ad hoc* parade would gather momentum. Before long, bored shopkeepers, thrill-hungry children, and soiled doves would all be stepping down Water Street to Joe Kuhn's drum.

In 1866, after six years of freighting covered wagons across the plains of the Midwest, Joe Kuhn arrived in Port Townsend. He had come to visit his brother Louis, a local physician. Sensing opportunity, he stayed, supporting himself as a photographer while he studied law. After his admission to the bar in 1870, his ambition and entrepreneurial spirit led him to a series of careers and businesses. Besides mayor, he also served as a state legislator, probate judge, and commissioner of immigration, as well as school board and city council member. Kuhn was president of the Commercial Bank and a member of the "Big Five Syndicate". He participated in the organization of the star-crossed Port Townsend Southern Railroad and most of the city's major economic developments of the late 1800s. Over the years, whatever his activities, he never forgot his duties as social director. Every summer he would load the citizenry aboard a boat and head to Kuhn Spit, near Chimacum Creek. There they would eat clams, drink whiskey, make music, and debauch until dawn. (See *Clambake, Charles Eisenbeis*.)

Joe Kuhn

An eight-mile-long, crescent-shaped lake that is seventeen miles west of Port Angeles, Lake Crescent forms the northern boundary of Olympic National Park and of the Olympic Mountains. Its alpine setting is said to resemble Bavaria. In 1937, President Franklin D. Roosevelt visited the peninsula on a fact-finding tour that led to the establishment of the OLYMPIC NATIONAL PARK. Roosevelt and his party stopped at Singers' Tavern, now known as Lake Crescent Lodge, one of only four overnight facilities within park boundaries.

LAKE CRESCENT

Previously known as Lake Hooker, Lake LELAND was once a major glacial tributary.

LAKE LELAND

Lake Ozette, the third largest lake in the state, was known by Indians simply as "lahouk," or large lake. It is located three miles east of the Pacific shore and south of the MAKAH Indian nation. White settlers, mostly Scandinavian, began settling the lake area in the late 1880s. Settlement stopped in 1897 with the creation of the Olympic Forest Reserve, which caused many to leave. Ten years later, timber interests influenced Congress to redesignate half of the Olympic Forest Reserve as agricultural land. Instead of farmers purchasing new lands, however, the timber companies bought it all and still hold it. Settlers have long since left Lake Ozette; today it serves as access to CAPE ALAVA and the OZETTE DIG.

LAKE OZETTE

LANDES HOUSE   (*1034 Franklin Street*) A prime example of folk Victorian architecture in which a simple house is enlarged several times incorporating various styles as each addition is made, the Henry Landes house was first built circa 1871 as a basic rectangular structure not unlike the FOWLER and ROTHSCHILD HOUSES. Colonel Henry C. Landes purchased the residence in 1882, moved it to its present location and built a cross-gabled wing of similar size. In 1887, he added the two-story gabled bay, two one-story bays on the west wall, and the front porch, borrowing details of the Queen Anne style, filling flat surfaces with shingles, window surrounds, brackets, and spindle work. Later changes extended the porch across the front bay, but the recent restoration returned it to its original dimensions.

Landes was as imposing as his house. At six feet and 220 pounds, he towered over most of his contemporaries. German born, he came to the United States with his parents in 1847 at the age of four. At eighteen he enlisted in a Kentucky regiment to fight with Union forces during the Civil War. After the war, he moved west, first to California, then to British Columbian goldfields. In 1873 he took on the management of a trading post at Neah Bay, then three years later moved to Port Townsend. In 1879, he opened a financial service on Water Street in which he cashed drafts, sold exchange, and loaned money on good security – the first banking service of any kind in Port Townsend. By 1883, he had developed sufficient local and San Francisco capital to establish the First National Bank of Port Townsend with assets of fifty thousand dollars. It was the first of six banks that opened by 1890 and the only one to survive. Landes became active in local development activities and was a founding member and treasurer of the Port Townsend Southern Railroad. Leaving Port Townsend in 1905, Landes moved to Seattle, where he died twenty-one years later.

LA PUSH   The town of La Push is located on the west coast of the Olympic Peninsula, approximately 107 miles from Port Townsend. The area is noted for some of the most beautiful beaches on the Washington coast; within a few miles of coastline, both gradual sandy beaches and areas of wild surf, sheer cliffs and outcroppings can be found. La Push is home to the QUILEUTE Indian tribe and carries on its tides the history of one of the West

Coast's most accomplished whaling and sealing people. The name is Chinook Jargon and means "river mouth," an adaptation of the French *la bouche* (mouth), so named by early French fur traders.

The longest occupant of this historic building, the Port Townsend *Leader* has become closely associated with what is formally known as the FOWLER BUILDING.

LEADER BUILDING

A twelve-mile-long valley created by glaciers at the foothills of the Olympic Mountains between the head of Discovery Bay and Quilcene, the Leland Valley was settled by three families in the early 1880s. When in 1881 a post office was created, it was decided to name the community for its first woman resident. The word "land" was added to the initials of Laura E. Andrews, forming the name Lealand. Because the name was similar to Sealand in Pacific County, post office officials dropped the "a" and Leland it became. Through common usage, Leland eventually became the name of the nearby lake, previously known as Lake Hooker. During the last glacial period, twelve thousand years ago, the Leland Valley served as a spillway for melting waters between the Strait of Juan de Fuca and the southern reaches of Puget Sound.

LELAND

After the failure of the Clarendon Hotel, which was the original occupant of the FOWLER-CAINES BUILDING, Fred Lewis purchased the structure and renamed it for himself.

LEWIS BUILDING

(*1220 Lawrence Street*) "Port Townsend ought to have a public library. Steps to this end cannot be taken too soon in view of the rapid increase in population and the demand for an institution that will be a constant source of entertainment and educational benefits." This plea by the *Leader* in 1890 was answered eight years later when the ladies of Port Townsend met on May 19, 1898, in the home of Mrs. George Starrett and formed the Library Association.

Although women could not vote in general elections prior to 1920, they could vote in library and school board elections. In keeping with this division of authority, the ladies saw to it that the constitution and bylaws of the Library Association stipulated that man-

LIBRARY, CARNEGIE

agement "be in the hands of the ladies." No man served on the library board until 1945.

The ladies each paid a membership fee to participate in the association, and they set out to build up a nest egg in order to establish a lending library. They hosted an ice cream social that brought in $27.95; the Young Ladies' Reading Club Ball netted $10.00, which they generously donated; the Port Townsend Mercantile Company donated the $20.00 it had won for a float in the Fourth of July parade. With these funds they recruited some gentlemen to calcimine the walls of a room at Central School, to erect shelves, and install furnishings. The grand opening on July 26, 1898, netted an additional $29.25, mostly in small coin deposited on a silver receptacle. The first annual meeting on June 2, 1899, revealed the library had 681 books (almost all from donations), a circulation of 1,922, and a membership of 107 persons. The part-time librarian was paid $5.00 per month.

The ladies of the Library Association devoted most of their energies to fund-raising; through balls, rummage sales, and various entertainments, they raised sufficient monies to purchase in 1905 two lots on a "sightly location on Lawrence Street" for $900. From then on they strove to amass enough money for a building. Negotiations for Carnegie funding began in 1911, and the library was finally opened on October 14, 1913. Carnegie Foundation donated $12,500 for the building and required the city to support the venture with at least $1,250 per year.

In the summer of 1913, it was reported that the building was almost complete except for a "few finishing touches which will be looked after by the ladies of the Library Association, who will also have charge of the arrangements for the electric lighting of the building .... The beautifying of the grounds will also be taken care of by the ladies, guaranteeing that the surroundings of the new library will be attractive and artistic." The *Leader* reported on opening day that "the library stands as a monument to women who devoted their time and energies to its upbuilding, and the institution will now compare very favorably with those maintained by many towns of much more population than Port Townsend." Mrs. Hill, the president of the Library Association, in acceptance of the key to the front door made a "neat and well-worded address," and Mayor Klocker proclaimed, "It is right-fully said of woman [that] she is always forward in all good works . . . ."

The southeastern point of Marrowstone Island, Lip Lip is a Chinook word meaning "boiling" or "the sound of boiling," referring to the bubbling waters of RIPTIDES in the area.

LIP LIP POINT

A former ferry landing five miles south of the east side of the Hood Canal Bridge, Lofall was named for an early settler.

LOFALL

Legend has it that the Puget Sound lumber business got its start when two San Franciscans sent a vessel to Puget Sound to get a load of ice, which they reasoned must clog the northern waterways. When the schooner arrived in the Puget Sound's moderate climate, the captain, afraid to return empty-handed, ordered the crew to fill the boat with the easily harvested timber that lined the shore. However and whenever it began, the timber industry was a natural for the region. A vessel could anchor near shore almost anywhere to load timber. Ownership of the trees was not questioned; like the fish in the sea, timber's abundance led people to believe there was enough for everybody – forever.

LOGGING

The area's first sawmill was constructed at Port Ludlow in 1852. In 1858, a sawmill was erected on the west shore of Discovery Bay. (In 1792 George Vancouver and his men are reported to have carved their names in a rock on the shore of the bay; legend has it that this rock was broken up to use in the foundation of the mill.) In 1859, a small sawmill and gristmill were constructed at the mouth of Chimacum Creek. In its early years, logging was confined to waterfront stands. The Puget Mill Company, owned by POPE AND TALBOT, and still operating at PORT GAMBLE, used a rustic steam-driven saw to slice a mere two thousand board feet per day when the mill opened. Before long it had thirty-eight saws in operation, and by 1857 it cut eight million board feet per year, enough to fill a ship every week. Puget Sound timber stands produced five times more timber per acre than eastern forests, which until the Civil War were the United States' primary source of lumber.

"Trees are all monarchs, to whom all worshipful men inevitably lift their hats. To see one fall under the blows of steel . . . it is to experience a pang of sorrow." – Northern Pacific Railroad business agent on visit to Puget Sound, 1869.

To ensure a supply of timber, mills established logging camps or contracted with locals to supply logs, or sometimes employed both methods. Life in a logging camp was hard. Loggers worked up to sixteen hours a day at their perilous occupation and returned to the cookhouse for three "squares" (meals), which the "gut robber" (cook) constructed around salt pork, lard, flour, and cornmeal. It was not uncommon to find the sinewy old ox, that had broken its leg on the skid road, gracing the table the next day. The bunkhouse and cookhouse were large, crowded tents. The wooden bunks had mattresses of straw thick with vermin. There were no bathing or laundry facilities. The perils of the trade are well documented. Men were often crushed under a falling tree, mangled by a snapped cable, crippled by a fall, or maimed by a poorly aimed ax. Life in the sawmills was also dangerous with huge, circular blades slicing off anything in their path. (Even with modern safety precautions and equipment, death and injury make logging a high-risk business.)

The virgin Northwest forest's Douglas fir provided ideal lumber. The trees are thick-trunked, straight, and tough-fibered. They are sought by home-builders, shipbuilders, and bridge-builders alike. But the long-term spread of Douglas fir was inhibited by at least one natural factor. To germinate and grow well, it needs more sunlight than it can get in the shadow of other firs; so over the years, shade-tolerant hemlocks and spruces and the ever-present alder take over. Despite warnings at the turn of the century, it was not until after World War II that the logging industry realized that the key to the future of logging was tree farming. With much of the logged land given over to cultivation and urbanization, timber interests were forced to strive for high-yield cultivation to ensure a future supply. In 1900 there were approximately 31.6 billion board feet of standing timber in Jefferson County; by 1978 that number had been reduced to 4 billion, but the forest products industry was still the biggest employer on the North Olympic Peninsula. Pope and Talbot and Crown Zellerbach are two of the largest timber holders in Jefferson County and practice technologically advanced methods of tree farming.

Because Port Townsend was surrounded by more saltwater than timber, it developed primarily as a seaport rather than a logging community. Its part in the wood products industry has been the manufacture of paper and pulp. The MILL was built in 1928 and for nearly sixty years has remained the town's link with the economic heritage that first developed on her shores. [R.B.]

On July 25, 1897, twenty-one-year-old John Griffith London, struggling out of poverty and ignorance, set sail from San Francisco with an older relative on the steamship *Umatilla* from San Francisco with one of the first loads of gold stampeders bound for Canada's KLONDIKE region. The discovery of gold had been telegraphed only a week before to an astonished world and a depressed nation eager for riches. Never one to miss an opportunity, London booked passage immediately. Three days later, London disembarked at Port Townsend's Union Wharf, anticipating connecting passage to Dyea that evening on the *City of Topeka*. Delays prevented the steamship from departing until noon the next day, leaving London with a night to kill in Port Townsend. Whatever he did that evening has not been recorded (or discovered), but a legend developed and has persisted that he spent it in the basement jail of the Port Townsend City Hall.

Jack London was an unknown in 1897. His year in the Yukon provided him with experiences on which he built a career and fame, but he was just one of hundreds of strangers in Port Townsend that summer night. Certainly there were diversions on Water Street that could lead a careless man into trouble with the law, but with his half-sister's elderly and ailing husband as his partner it is questionable that he chose to pursue such pleasures. More likely, they took a cheap hotel or slept on the beach and simply waited out the twenty-four hours. In later years London was quoted as saying, "I never realized a cent up there [in the Klondike]. Still, I have been managing to pen out a living ever since on the strength of the trip." Much the same could be said for Port Townsend about the benefits it gained from his overnight stay. And generations later the legend served to release some family ghosts developed by London's great-granddaughter who moved to Port Townsend in the late 1970s. Burdened with expectations she felt of having to maintain family propriety, London's granddaughter, on hearing of the

159

Port Townsend legend, said to herself, "Well, if he could spend a night in jail and still succeed, I guess I can do as I please." It was, she recalls, a liberating moment.

LOWER HADLOCK   Originally known as Port Hadlock, the half-dozen or so remaining wood-frame buildings were part of a thriving lumber-based community. Hadlock was founded in 1870 on the southwestern shores of Port Townsend Bay by Samuel Hadlock, who established the Western Mill and Lumber Company there, but was unable to make it a viable operation. In the late 1880s, the Washington Mill Company at Seabeck in Kitsap County burned, and its San Francisco-based owner, W. J. Adams, chose to purchase Hadlock's concern and relocate there. At its peak, the Washington Mill Company could produce 150,000 board feet of lumber a day. It employed 125 men at a daily wage of $1.25 plus board. Its docks could accommodate seven ships at a time. The largest timber milled was 24 inches square by 120 feet long. It was run on rollers from the mill to the ship. The mill supplied all the lumber for buildings at Forts Casey, Flagler, and Worden. When the mill closed in 1907, it was sold to California concerns that operated it for a year before closing it; it burned in 1913. W. J. Adams extended his investments in the area in 1911 with the development of Classen Chemical Company's ALCOHOL PLANT, but that was an even shorter-lived project. (Adams's ultimate legacy was not his contribution to nineteenth-century industrialism but rather to twentieth-century artistic expression. His grandson Ansel became one of the nation's foremost landscape photographers.)

Recent archaeological discoveries suggest that Lower Hadlock may be the oldest continually inhabited site in Washington State. Artifacts have been found that show residence by Chimakum and Klallam Indians and, in the latter part of the nineteenth century, by Chinese laborers.

MADRONE   (*Arbutus menziesii*) The only evergreen tree on the Pacific Northwest Coast not of the coniferous family, the madrone, or madrona, is noted for its paperlike reddish-brown bark that peels annually to reveal a pale green layer underneath. Smooth, supple limbs suggest human form. It grows only where the soil is rocky and, according to Victoria folklorist and ballad singer Paddy Hernan, only where sea breezes blow. Common also to Ireland, where it is called arbutus, the tree is the subject of a touching legend. Told by Hernan, who learned the song from Paddy Grover's mother in Tipperary, the "Legend of the Arbutus" is the ballad of an Irish king with "a daughter fair, Arbutus was her name." The king has gone "a soldiering for the court of the King of Spain." Told of "her gentle grace, of her beauty and her fame," the Spanish king declares his love and begs that "she might share his name. Her lovely eyes, they filled with tears and her cheeks grew scarlet red" as she told her father that she loved another and " 'in truth, would rather be dead. I'll not leave my own true love for the hand of the King of Spain.'" Her father commands his daughter obey: " 'I swore you were a virgin fair and my chiefs did all agree; cast off your gown that we might examine thee.'" " 'Oh father, dear,'" Arbutus cried " 'don't shame me so. I would rather you see me dead before you'd let your noble chiefs search for my maidenhead.' 'Cast off, cast off that berry brown gown,'" he demanded, " 'the truth, it must be known.'" The gown she let fall free, but "ere its hem did touch the ground, she changed into a tree. Her love became that gentle sea breeze, through her branches did he play, and she has shed her soft brown bark until this very day."

An annual celebration the last full weekend in August, **MAKAH DAYS** Makah Days commemorate the raising of the U.S. flag at Neah Bay on August 26, 1913, and the granting of U.S. citizenship to Native Americans on June 1, 1924. Although a standard community festival in structure, the events are decidedly different: dugout canoe races, INDIAN GAMBLING known as bone games, Indian dances, and salmon bakes with fillets of fish butterflied on cedar stakes and smoke-cooked over alder.

Located at CAPE FLATTERY on the far northwest tip of **MAKAH INDIANS** the Olympic Peninsula, the Makah are historically a seafaring people, who seldom ventured more than a few miles inland. They were middlemen in the Indian trade that ran from the Columbia River to Nootka Sound. They began trading with whites in 1788, but because of their geographic isolation, they were not subjected to the typical onslaught of white colonization and were able to remain economically independent. As a tribe, the origin of the Makah is recent, the result of the organization of several tribes who lived in the Cape Flattery area. They received the name Makah in 1855 when they made their treaty with the U.S. government. The government interpreter was a KLALLAM, who gave them the Klallam name for the Cape Flattery people.

MAKAH MUSEUM   The Makah museum, or more accurately the Makah Cultural and Research Center, houses artifacts discovered at the Ozette archaeological site fifteen miles south of Neah Bay (see *Ozette Dig*). Displays of recovered items are enhanced by photomurals and arranged around seasonal themes, revealing various hunting and fishing activities of the Makah. Besides many food-gathering instruments, large numbers of games, children's toys, baskets, and ceremonial objects are displayed. One of the largest and most dramatic items displayed is a CEDAR carving of a whale fin inlaid with more than seven hundred otter teeth. The museum also displays several totem poles; replicas of fishing, whaling, and sealing canoes; and a complete cedar longhouse.

MANRESA CASTLE   One of two CASTLES in Port Townsend, Manresa was first a private residence for CHARLES EISENBEIS, then an educational retreat for Jesuit priests, and finally an inn for visitors to Port Townsend.

MARINE SCIENCE   Located on the dock at FORT WORDEN State Park, the
CENTER   Marine Science Center was established to increase public awareness of local marine life forms and their habitats and of the potential consequences of human activity on the marine environment. The marine center is bordered by both sandy and rocky beaches at the intersection of the Strait of Juan de Fuca and Puget Sound. The combination of strong currents and clean cold water has created an area rich with marine life.

Housed in an historic structure, the center has large open "wet tables," where visitors can handle such local sea creatures as starfish, sand dollars, sea cucumbers, tube worms, anemones, and snails. Glass aquariums provide viewing of many more of Puget Sound's underwater inhabitants: crabs, octopus, and a variety of fish. A laboratory is put to use for children's and adults' marine science classes.

The center's objectives are met through guided beach walks, classes in marine ecology for children and adults, fish printing sessions, seaweed workshops, evening slide shows, films, lectures, resource information for teachers, and marine programs for the schools. All the classes and programs focus on active forms of learning: pulling up a beach seine, looking through a microscope, or getting one's hands and feet into the sand and water.

The center was founded by a small group of local volunteers with a strong interest in marine biology and a desire to involve people in learning about the marine environment. They were aided by two small grants and by many donations and loans from individuals and local service groups.

MARMOTS

A relative to groundhogs, woodchucks, squirrels, and chipmunks, the marmot (*Marmota olympus*) is notable for its sharp whistle that can be heard at high altitudes in the Olympics, particularly at HURRICANE RIDGE and Deer Park. The marmot whistles when it becomes alerted, distressed, or frightened. A hibernator, the marmot doubles its weight in summer in preparation for a long, cold winter.

MARROWSTONE ISLAND

Forming the southern boundary of Port Townsend Bay, Marrowstone Island was first known as Craven's Peninsula, and later as Scow Peninsula. Eventually the name Craven fell into disuse, and Marrowstone – from the promontory that GEORGE VANCOUVER had named – was informally adopted. The island was homesteaded between 1865 and 1870 and was home to a colony of Norwegian immigrants, who farmed the land. Attempts to industrialize always failed, although Henry Morgan reportedly spent "large sums" in the 1890s to drill for coal (see *Morgan Hill*). Turkey farming was the island's principal business in the 1920s when fifteen farmers developed a national reputation for the quality of their birds, which were served, it is recalled, at the White House. Tourists, attracted by Fort Flagler State Park, and retirees provide the economic base for the island today.

MARROWSTONE POINT

At the southern tip of Port Townsend Bay, Marrowstone Point was named by George Vancouver for the cliff's pockmarked resemblance to bone marrow. Vancouver first thought the material, which surrounds the entire bay, to be fuller's earth, a clay common to western England used for stripping wool of its oiliness. The chalklike substance is, however, glacial till – dirt and rock deposited twelve thousand years ago by melting edges of the last ice age. Much of the Puget Sound landmass is composed of this till, a concern to cliff-dwelling homeowners, as the till erodes easily when exposed to water.

MASTODON   Twelve thousand years before the OLYMPIC GAME FARM began its animal preserve, the Sequim Prairie was home to mastodon and woolly mammoth. In 1977, Emanuel Manis was digging a farm pond on his property one mile south of Sequim, when he uncovered what appeared to be elephant tusks. Archaeologists from the OZETTE DIG were contacted, and identification was made: a mastodon. Subsequent digs revealed additional bones as well as weapons used to kill the beasts, which reportedly is the first evidence of man hunting mastodon on the North American continent.

MATS MATS BAY   Mats Mats Bay is a small body of water between Port Ludlow and Oak Bay that is reached by a narrow channel off the western shores of Admiralty Inlet. The Klallam name meaning "opened and closed" referred to the available access to the bay that was affected by the tides. The channel has since been dredged to allow continuous passage. The eastern shore of the bay is the site of a basalt quarry formed forty to fifty million years ago when the oceanic crust was forced upward as it collided head-on with the North American continental crust. The green-black, tight-grained volcanic rock is used throughout the area for fireplaces, rock gardens, and – in a finely crushed grade – as gravel for private driveways.

MAYNARD   One of several communities around the head of Discovery Bay, Maynard was established during the height of the bay's timber boom in the later half of the nineteenth century. Other communities include Eaglemont, Fairmont, East Uncas, and West Uncas. In Maynard, the colorful Henrietta "Ma" Maynard operated a popular hotel in the 1890s. The name has been eliminated from all but the most local maps. Until the early 1980s, Greyhound used the Discovery Bay Tavern as its transfer point for Port Townsend on the Seattle-Port Angeles run, but it has since abandoned the stop and now uses CENTER as its transfer station.

(633 *Van Buren*) Begun as a simple folk house in the early 1870s, the Captain James McIntyre House gained its embellishments as the town grew into a small Victorian city in the 1880s and 1890s. (Subsequent additions, which include the mansard wing, were constructed in the 1960s when the house was purchased by easterner Ralph Raphael, a flamboyant personality who always wore a captain's hat but whose history and means were never quite clear.)

MCINTYRE HOUSE

Captain McIntyre was one of many sea captains who chose Port Townsend as home port. A native of Scotland, he first sailed into the region in 1854. He sailed and traded throughout the Pacific for a number of years before his marriage in 1867 to Sarah Pettygrove, daughter of one of the three founding Port Townsend families. He remained active until his death at age seventy in 1902, when the ship under his command, the steamer *Bristol*, was wrecked on an island off the Alaskan coast. The captain and six men went down with the ship, but twenty survived; suspicions of less than honorable seamanship were voiced, but charges were never pressed. The captain of the rescue ship said upon arrival in Port Townsend that he was of the "opinion that Captain McIntyre was practically deserted to his fate by the other men of the ship." He noted that no two of the surviving men told the same story, and "not even one of them told the same story twice." Reconstructing the event, the captain said it appeared that as soon as the steamer struck the island, the majority of the crew abandoned ship without instruction, leaving only two boats on deck, one a little skiff that could hold only two men and the other a big lifeboat so firmly lashed that it could not be cut loose in time to be of service. Later exploration of the wreckage found little evidence, but reports were confirmed by Indians that the bodies of the dead had washed ashore, where they were eaten by wolves.

A year and a half later, in October of 1903, Captain McIntyre's eldest son, John, also the captain of a steamer, was shipwrecked off the Oregon coast, but in this case the circumstances were reversed. The young Captain McIntyre survived, but thirty of his crew and passengers did not. Early reports questioned the captain's judgment, although most of the seven survivors held to a story that the ship was dead in the water when his order to abandon was given. The chief engineer, who had been caught below but who struggled to the deck before the ship sank, contradicted the captain's and the others' testimony. He swore that the steamer was underway from the time she struck until the last raft was launched and that all could have been saved had the ship been stopped and an effort been made. Under cross-examination during the official investigation in San Francisco, Captain McIntyre admitted that he had lied, that the ship was indeed in motion when he and his fellow survivors had left it. Nevertheless, he denied any wrongdoing, and before his license was revoked, he bitterly predicted: "I suppose they will take my ticket away from me, although I did everything there was to be done.... There have been seven ships totally lost along this coast. What was said of them? The simple statement that they went down at sea with all on board. We had a terrifying struggle and are censured for coming home alive." Though his life was spared, his fate was likely worse than his father's.

[P.S.]

MIDDLEPOINT

Middlepoint is on the STRAIT OF JUAN DE FUCA halfway between POINT WILSON and CAPE GEORGE. In recent years, its name was formally changed to McCurdy Point in honor of the late James G. McCurdy, Port Townsend historian, banker, and civic leader, but the designation has not taken hold.

MILITARY
FORTIFICATIONS

When Congress approved its treaty with England in 1846 fixing the forty-ninth parallel as the border between Canada and the United States, the question of defending the inland waters was first addressed. Charged by President James Polk to designate military sites at San Diego and Puget Sound, the joint army-navy commission recommended that no fortifications be established in Puget Sound because construction would cost more than the wealth protected. Not until the Indian Wars of 1855 did the issue resurface. After the Ebey Massacre, two forts were established, one in Bellingham and another south of Port Townsend (see *Fort Townsend*), to join Fort Steilacoom near Olympia for protection of white settlements.

By the late 1880s artillery had so improved that cannons sixteen inches in diameter offered a ten-mile range of protection; forts in strategic locations could suddenly defend regions, not just settlements. With navy ships increasing in size and requiring larger dry docks, a new yard was established at Port Orchard, south of Port Townsend, in 1896. In the same year, the Puget Sound region was found worthy of an elaborate harbor defense. Three major sites were selected: FORT WORDEN at Port Townsend, FORT FLAGLER across the bay at Marrowstone Point, and FORT CASEY across Admiralty Inlet on WHIDBEY ISLAND. Approved by Congress with a budget of seven million dollars, the actual cost for the three forts was almost ten million dollars. More than thirty batteries trained 107 cannons at the entrance to Puget Sound awaiting a foreign invader. None came, and within twenty-five years, the defense system was rendered useless by the advent of submarines and military aircraft that could penetrate Puget Sound without even being seen from the three forts. The forts became primarily training installations; all were deactivated by the early 1950s and eventually turned into state parks.

After being jilted at the church door again and again, Port Townsend finally made it to the altar in 1927. After a sometimes stormy marriage of more than half a century with the Crown Zellerbach pulp and paper mill, even the pessimists must admit it became a "workable relationship," if not exactly a marriage made in heaven. But heaven is where Port Townsend thought she was when "go-getter" Ed Sims ("the best man around a table in the state of Washington") came home from San Francisco with the news that Zellerbach Corporation was ready to erect a kraft paper mill in Port Townsend. The corporation sank seven million dollars into its construction and in cooperation with the people of Port Townsend, financed a new water system that the city badly needed; half of it to be piped to the mill, half to the city. Port Townsend approved a bond issue of six hundred thousand dollars (its contribution to the agreement) by a vote of 879 to 5. The mill construction put hundreds of men to work. At Glen

MILL

Cove, south of the city, Albert Briggs's homestead was plowed under, and the willows from NAPOLEON'S TOMB that had sheltered Port Townsend's summering society folks were pulled down. Nary a tear was shed. At last Port Townsend was beginning to fulfill her destiny. In 1928, the Zellerbach Corporation joined with Crown Paper to create Crown Zellerbach Corporation, which dominated the spirit of Port Townsend for more than fifty years.

Perhaps fearing that "Crown Z" might be just one more bubble destined to burst, many residents did not respond to the company's call to build houses for mill employees. The *Leader* and community boosters also exhorted residents to start building small homes for mill employees and to open their own homes as boarding houses, and a *Leader* editorial that year urged Port Townsend housewives to show support of the venture by buying paper products manufactured by Crown Zellerbach mills. The corporation was gratified. "In view of the splendid co-operation on the part of Port Townsend citizens in fulfilling their promises to provide proper housing facilities for our employees, and in other ways, [Crown Zellerbach] directors have decided, to double the size of the original plans."

In 1928, 275 employees went to work at the mill for $4.50 a day. Although there were cutbacks and brief stoppages, the mill did not close during the depression as did much of the nation's other industry; for this the people of Port Townsend were grateful. In 1933, under provisions of the National Recovery Act, the mill went on four six-hour shifts and hired seventy-five more men. The average hourly wage was fifty-nine cents. In those days before the union, there were no pensions, no holidays, no paid vacation, and no health and welfare plan. Twelve workers unionized in 1934, and by Christmas, representatives of the International Brotherhood of Pulp, Sulfite, and Paper Workers and the International Brotherhood of Paper Makers had negotiated for a forty-hour work week and a 15 percent salary increase for men ($1.50 per hour) and a 10 percent increase for women ($.88½ per hour). By 1951, about one-quarter of the workers had joined the union and won numerous wage and safety benefits. Although an "open shop" under the current owners, most permanent employees were protected by the union in 1980. In 1946, there were 520 employees at the mill. By 1949, the number had increased to 630 with an annual payroll of $2,200,000, a 200 percent increase in fifteen years. In 1951, 175 women worked at the mill (or 22 percent) most of them in the bag factory which opened in 1948 and which provided "a good opportunity for employment of women in assembling, gluing, stitching, and binding...."

The community's attitude toward the mill was summed up by local businessman T. H. Baker, Jr., in an ad he ran in the 1953 issue of the *Leader* that celebrated the mill's first quarter-century in Port Townsend. Baker said that the basic American freedoms were thought, speech, and worship, plus "freedom of financial stability and security that keeps their constituents from the freedom of worry .... I cannot help but sense the inherent fact that the great firm of Crown Zellerbach has made all these freedoms ... available to all its employees.... as a pygmy would look to a giant, we in our humble manner would like to take this opportunity to thank Crown Zellerbach." Paper Mill City was how the community billed itself that year. Eight hundred of its citizens were working at the mill. According to the *Leader*, twenty-five hundred people in Port Townsend depended on Crown Zellerbach wages.

In the summer of 1960, Crown Zellerbach reminded the community that "paper is the key" in Port Townsend, and that the mill was the "Key Industry of the Key City." (See *Key City*.) Twenty-six percent of Jefferson County's taxes were paid by the mill. But the honeymoon was effectively over by the 1960s, largely because of the community's increasing awareness of the pollution produced by the plant. The company announced early in 1960 that it would spend $786,000 to "lessen chemical losses and decrease pollution." But it wasn't enough. Seattle *Argus* publisher Philip Bailey, who owned property on Discovery Bay complained in a 1966 column about the " ... blanket of foul smelling smoke that settles down over the lovely countryside, effectively contaminating the otherwise sparkling air. When mixed with moisture, this evil odor which could well be mixed by the demons in Hades, lies close to the ground, blanketing Chimacum Valley or befouling the summer homes that dot the inlet and beaches of the surrounding area. Crown Zellerbach, as the dispenser of most of the payroll checks that sup-

The mill's operation cooks five-eighths-inch chips in an alkaline solution under high pressure in a digestor until they become pulp. Chemicals are removed from the pulp, and the result is pressed into heavy paper. The pollution of air and water is caused by the by-products of this process: particulate matter, carbon monoxide, nitrogen, and sulfur dioxide.

port the economy and as a practitioner of feudal management concepts, wants no mention made of the problem. The weekly newspaper in Port Townsend has no editorial section; no local radio or TV station, so all criticism is effectively muted. In any event, talking against the mill is viewed in the same light as embracing communism.''

In a company brochure of the time, Crown Zellerbach reminded the community that it generated a $3.5 million-per-year payroll at its Port Townsend kraft mill, that kraft meant strong, and that Crown Zellerbach ''provides economic stability'' for the community. And most of Port Townsend, particularly mill workers, agreed and shrugged off the outside criticism by regarding the smoke as ''the bread-and-butter smell.'' In the late 1960s, the mill submitted to U.S. Department of Energy requirements and announced installation of a new kraft system with the ''most advanced pollution control devices'' at a cost of $12.5 million. A new ten-story recovery boiler and a new clarifier basin to improve the quality of water dumped into the bay were installed. The company reminded Port Townsend, ''No additional earnings potential results from large expenditures being made for these modifications, and in fact, these expenditures came during a period when the Company and the industry generally were caught in the cost-price squeeze.'' But in 1969, Crown Zellerbach announced in San Francisco that its assets topped one billion dollars.

By then, old-timers who remembered the bust years of the 1890s were gone, and those who remembered the lean years before the mill opened were no longer the movers and the shakers they once had been – they had been supplanted by new settlers, oftentimes refugees from urban areas of California or the East, who did not depend on the mill for livelihood, who valued clean air and water, and who supported the establishment of nonpolluting industry. The loyalty the workers had once held for the mill had eroded by the 1970s. It was ''just a job'' to many of the younger workers; it no longer represented a way of life. The *Leader* no longer featured a column about mill activities (originally entitled ''Fumes from the Mill''), and although it continued to print photographs of retiring workers, the impact of the industry on the community in general was apparently lessening. There were rumors of marijuana smoking on the swing and graveyard shifts, although supervisors hastened to reassure the community in a *Leader* report that mill workers were not a "hippy crowd."

In 1980, Crown Zellerbach instituted a gain-sharing plan as an employee incentive, eliminated some jobs, and made improvements, as the mill scrambled to retain a piece of the dwindling market. By 1983, 460 employees were producing 440 tons of kraft paper per day, the same amount as had been produced by 850 employees in 1956. Despite rumors to the contrary, a Crown Zellerbach official announced in 1982 that the Port Townsend "mill is definitely not for sale," although it was generally known that the mill manager was receiving foreign nationals who were seeking U.S. properties. In the summer of 1983, Crown Zellerbach announced the sale of the Port Townsend mill to the twenty-five-year-old West German paper-making company, the Haindl Corporation. A Haindl spokesman hastened to reassure the workers that " ... we'll still have the union." The mill changed hands at the beginning of 1984. The Haindl subsidiary, Port Townsend Paper Corporation with its headquarters on Bainbridge Island, was the new operator.

According to the county assessor, the value of the mill was $35 million – Haindl bought it for $24.5 million. Haindl wanted $10 million in loans for improvements, $5.2 million of which was issued in tax-exempt revenue bonds by the Industrial Development Corporation of the Port of Port Townsend. The expansion created more pollution, and in four of five standards, the Port Townsend Paper Corporation greatly exceeded Crown Zellerbach's emissions, though they still fell below federal requirements most days of the year. Two hundred and thirty-five of 365 employees were rehired by the new company. In January 1984, charges of discrimination and unfair labor practices were filed and ultimately dropped by the ninety-eight persons not retained. The ire of local residents was also raised when the Port Townsend Paper Corporation contracted with out-of-state firms for the modernization of the mill. As with many marriages, a certain distance came to characterize the relationship. [R.B.]

The only man ever to be elected mayor of both Port Townsend and Seattle, Thomas Minor (1844–1889)

MINOR, THOMAS T.

came to Port Townsend in 1868 after graduating from Yale University Medical School and serving a year's internship among the Winnebago Indians in Nebraska. He was twenty-three years old. Joining the practice of Dr. George V. Calhoun, who owned the Marine Hospital, he later bought out Calhoun's interest. Minor installed the town's first telephone in 1878 when he ran a line from his office on Water Street to the hospital on the hill. An orator and politician who had been a delegate to two national Republican conventions, Minor was elected mayor of Port Townsend upon his return from the Chicago convention in 1876, where he had supported James G. Blaine in an unsuccessful bid for the nomination won by Rutherford B. Hayes (see *Presidents*).

Though largely an ornamental position, the office of mayor of Port Townsend gave Minor continued exposure throughout Puget Sound. In 1882 he was selected to be the orator at the Fourth of July celebration in Seattle. Several thousand attended, and the *Seattle Post-Intelligencer* reported that Minor's oration on issues of statehood to be "ably prepared." The next year he sold his Port Townsend holdings and moved his practice to Seattle. Noting the shift, the *Seattle Post-Intelligencer* called him "one of the most experienced and skillful physicians on the Sound, and his immediate entry upon a large and lucrative practice cannot be doubted." Minor's success was indeed quick. Within two years he became part owner of the *Seattle Post-Intelligencer*, an interest he sold a few months later to a promising publisher, who distressed the conservative Minor by supporting women's suffrage in his first issue.

In 1887, Minor ran for mayor of Seattle and won handily. Many, including the ever friendly *Seattle Post-Intelligencer*, thought he would soon become governor, but on November 29, 1889 – just days after Washington became the forty-second state in the union – Thomas Minor, along with his former Port Townsend friend Morris Haller (see *Haller Fountain*) and Haller's brother-in-law, drowned while duck hunting near Whidbey Island. Minor was forty-five years old.

MORGAN HILL   One of two distinct hills in Port Townsend, Morgan Hill was named by and for Captain Henry E. Morgan, a quixotic developer during the town's boom years. A native of Connecticut, Morgan came west as a forty-niner. He reached Puget Sound in 1858, settling first on Whidbey Island, then relocating to Port Townsend two years later. He was engaged in many development schemes, most of which failed. He twice bought and sold PROTECTION ISLAND, drilled nine hundred feet on the shores of SCOW BAY in a futile search for coal, and helped establish a teachers' college – a three-story structure on the west side of Morgan Hill called the Northwest Normal School, which attracted only seventy-five students, who within two years had to find another institution in which to finish their education.

Earlier, in 1885, he platted Morgan Hill, rising behind Port Townsend's UPTOWN BUSINESS DISTRICT, and began the construction of a three-story hotel in the center of the tract. He named it The Mountain View in celebration of the Cascade and Olympic ranges that could be seen from its many rooms. As usual with a Morgan project, funds ran out before the job was done. Morgan sold the uncompleted hotel to local speculators at the height of the boom. Still unfinished, the hotel was then sold to D. T. Denny of Seattle. Never completed, the hotel's tower collapsed with a mighty bang in a windstorm in 1916. Later the site became Sather Park, named in honor of the mayor in office at the time of the acquisition. The area excavated for the hotel's foundation remains as a grassy courtyard among the tall firs of the park.

MOUNT BAKER

At 10,778 feet, Mount Baker is the third highest peak in the Cascade chain and is the northernmost active volcano in the United States. Though reports of eruptions were made as early as 1843, it was not until Mount Baker was first ascended in 1868 that its volcanic origin was verified. The Lummi Indian name for the mountain, Kulshan, or "shot at the point," suggests, however, that indigenous populations needed no such proof of its volatile nature. In 1790, Spanish explorer MANUEL QUIMPER sighted the peak and named it La Montana de Carmelo or "great white watcher." A far less romantic GEORGE VANCOUVER two years later renamed it for his officer, Lieutenant Joseph Baker, the first Englishman to see the mountain. Vancouver's choice prevailed.

Recent study has discovered evidence of four eruptions in the past ten thousand years, at least two lava flows, one volcanic avalanche, and numerous mudflows. In 1843, explorer/ethnologist George Gibbs reported that both Mount Baker and Mount St. Helens "broke out simultaneously and covered the whole country with ashes," but there were only fur traders – no settlers – in the area at the time, and the truth of the report remained in doubt. In 1868, in a party led by E. T. Coleman, Thomas Stratton, a mining geologist from Port Townsend, discovered three extinct craters. Before his ascent, the ladies of the town presented Stratton with a silk flag, which he promised "to plant ... on the top most crag ... or leave [his] bones as a warning to those who might thereafter attempt the feat." Until the Mount St. Helens' blow in 1980, Mount Baker was the most active of the Cascade volcano chain that extends from California to British Columbia. In March 1975 sufficient steam and ash spewed from its craters to make it the second worst polluter in the Pacific Northwest, right behind a since-closed copper smelter in Tacoma. Volcano expert Stephen L. Harris states that it is too early to tell whether Mount Baker is preparing for a major eruption or just changing its "internal plumbing."

MOUNT BAKER BLOCK (*Water and Tyler Streets*) Originally planned by Charles Eisenbeis as a five-story, ninety-six-room hotel, the office building he called the Mount Baker Block was scaled back to four stories when he joined another "first class" hotel development at the other end of town. The Mount Baker Block, together with the Hastings Building diagonally across the intersection, serve as cornerstones to Port Townsend's downtown commercial core.

Designed by Port Townsend architects Whiteway and Schroeder in the Richardson Romanesque style (see *Architecture*), the building was nearing its completion when the town's economy began to collapse. By November of 1890, the Oregon Improvement Company, which was laying RAILROAD track to Portland, had gone into receivership with only thirty miles completed. The reconstruction of Water Street from false-front wood-frame structures into a modern commercial center of masonry came to a halt. Eisenbeis suspended interior work on the Mount Baker Block. The top two floors were never more than framed.

Nevertheless, the building has a definite impact on the cityscape. Architectural historian Allen T. Denison notes that "the very bulk of the Mount Baker Block [has] a stabilizing effect on the community. Approaching the center of the city, there is a crescendo effect of increasingly large scale structures which culminate at (that) corner . . . . With the centrifugal energy that this core establishes, Port Townsend still maintains the cohesive, cosmopolitan quality of a city of importance."

Indians called her "Takkobad," one of two wives of DOSEWALLIPS, the legendary man who turned into a mountain in those days when inanimate objects of the earth were living things. Takkobad was jealous of Dosewallip's second wife and crossed to the west side of Puget Sound, where she gathered fire to throw at her competitor. The fire burned the trees off the head of the second wife, now known as MOUNT RAINIER. Takkobad settled in the Olympics and became known as Mount Constance when George Davidson of the U.S. Coast and Geodetic Survey visited in 1856 and promptly named several Olympic peaks for members of his fiancée's family. Constance Fauntleroy, Davidson's future sister-in-law, was a composer and writer, and founded the first permanent women's club in the country.

MOUNT CONSTANCE

At 7,743 feet, Mount Constance is the third highest of the Olympic peaks and the highest visible from Puget Sound. The climb is considered formidable. Mountaineer Robert Wood describes the two approaches as the "Terrible Traverse," which involves the crossing of a precipitous, exposed snowfield, and "Fingertip Traverse," a crablike climb along a narrow rock ledge.

The first geographical feature in Washington State to be named by explorers, Mount Olympus at 7,965 feet is the highest peak among the OLYMPIC MOUNTAINS. Spanish explorer Juan Perez first sighted the peak in 1774 and named it for Saint Rosalia, a hermit of the twelfth century, but four years later British Captain John Meares gave it the ancient Greek name for the "home of the gods." Of Washington mountains, only Mount Baker and Mount Rainier have more glaciers, and unlike most mountains, Olympus has few mead-

MOUNT OLYMPUS

owlands between its forests and ice.

Mountaineer Robert Wood calls a night on Five Finger Peak the "supreme Olympic experience. As evening progresses, the changing vistas are incredibly beautiful. When the sun disappears over the Pacific, the alpenglow is striking. The snowy peaks change quickly from white to rosy pink, then red, and finally lavender and purple as the shadows creep up from the deep canyons. With the coming of darkness, the stars appear, the lights of Victoria flicker faintly, and one can see the beacon lights along the coast. The day breaks bright, clear and cold, with fog in the low valleys, clouds in the distance."

MOUNT RAINIER

In 1792, the United States was three years into its newest institution, the presidency, having struggled for sixteen years to find a workable system of government. On May 7 of that year, GEORGE VANCOUVER sailed into what he named Port Townshend. He toured the bay, circling round to the high cliffs of glacial till that he named MARROWSTONE POINT. There his party went ashore to eat. "The weather was serene and pleasant [he wrote in his journal], and the country continued to exhibit, between us and the eastern snowy range, the same luxuriant appearance." To the north he could see Mount Baker, which he had named days before while sailing up the STRAIT OF JUAN DE FUCA, and to the south he sighted – the first European to do so – "a round snowy mountain," which he named in honor of his friend Rear Admiral Peter Rainier, best known for his victory over an American privateer during the War for Independence. At 14,410 feet, Mount Rainier is the tallest peak in the continental United States. Though its ninety-mile distance from Port Townsend makes it less imposing than the closer Mount Baker, most residents nevertheless mean Rainier when they refer to "the mountain."

MOUNT TOWNSEND

The crest of Mount Townsend (6,280 feet) is a ridge of two summits rather than a single peak. A well-marked trail begins in fir and hemlock with a dense undergrowth of rhododendrons, some thirty feet high. The high country is composed of meadows and subalpine trees. The view from the summit is among the best in the Olympics. To the west the interior range is in full view, and to the east sprawls all of Puget Sound and its suburbs. The skyscrapers of downtown Seattle are easily seen.

Halfway between Brinnon and Quilcene on Highway 101, Mount Walker is a mere foothill (2,730 feet) to its Olympic brethren to the east, but it is four times higher than Seattle's skyline, which, on a clear day, is the primary object of the view. Resembling a developer's model, Seattle and Elliott Bay appear as though seen from the wrong end of a telescope. At twilight Puget Sound's urban sprawl glows like an encrusted jewel. On a clear day, Canada's dog-toothed Cascades loom in the northern distance. The five-mile drive to the top is paved but steep, tough on radiators going up and on brakes coming down. A hiking trail makes the ascent in two miles for those with a good pair of lungs and sturdy quadriceps. In winter the road is barricaded, leaving the glorious view to just a few hikers.
MOUNT WALKER

An 86-foot Port Townsend fishing trawler, the *Muir Milach* has participated since 1979 in an annual joint venture with fishermen from the Soviet Union. When the U.S. established an offshore limit of two hundred miles in the 1970s, fishermen from the U.S.S.R. and other Pacific Rim nations were prohibited from harvesting in waters they traditionally fished. Because the fish of interest to the Soviets – hake, pollack, yellow-finned sole – are not commercially caught for the U.S. market, the *Muir Milach* (Gaelic for ''sea full of fish'') became one among a fleet of thirty-five U.S. ships to catch the fish, then sell them to the Soviets. Over the years, close friendships have developed among the U.S. and Soviet crews, and a sister city designation between Port Townsend and KORSAKOV has twice been proposed.
MUIR MILACH

(640 *Taylor*) Though typically Queen Anne style – hipped roof with cross gables, detailed sunbursts, no flat surfaces, wraparound porch with spindle work – the Mutty house is unique for the ornamental iron cresting on the roof and porch, a feature not commonly used in Port Townsend. Built in 1891 by Peter Mutty, a hotel manager at Discovery Bay, who later joined Clarence Wanamaker in the hay and feed business, the house was assessed by the county at a rate higher than the larger DE LION and STARRETT
MUTTY HOUSE

HOUSES, which were only a block away but were in styles no longer so fashionable.

MYSTERY BAY A small inlet off SCOW BAY between MARROWSTONE and INDIAN Islands, Mystery Bay is so situated that boats can easily slip in or out without detection. The bay was first called Nicholls Bay after James Nicholls, who established a farm on its shores in 1871. For many years, Nicholls Bay was noted for fishing; in the 1890s it was not uncommon to gather five hundred pounds of herring in one catch. In 1892 the name Mystery Bay first appeared on U.S. Coast and Geodetic Survey charts, but it was not until Prohibition that it gained common usage. Local bootlegging smugglers used the bay to escape detection by revenuers unfamiliar with the area.

NAPOLEON'S TOMB Local legend holds that a sailing vessel bound for the Pacific Northwest from Europe circa 1852 anchored in distress at St. Helena, site of Napoleon's tomb. Although Napoleon's remains had been removed to Paris more than a decade before, the captain visited the empty tomb and took with him several shoots from a willow tree at the site. Upon arrival in Port Townsend, the captain presented two of the cuttings to the deputy collector of customs, Albert Briggs, who had crossed the plains with Loren B. Hastings in 1847. The cuttings proliferated at Briggs's GLEN COVE home, and within years his residence became known as The Willows. In 1928 the Briggs's homestead became the site of the MILL; his house was torn down, and the willows uprooted. Other willows in the Glen Cove area may or may not be offshoots.

NEAH BAY Ancestral home and primary village of the MAKAH Indian nation, Neah Bay was named by English explorer Captain Henry Kellett in 1847 after a Makah chief, Dee-ah. In 1792 Spanish explorers established in this location the first known European post in what is now the state of Washington, but abandoned it after pressure was applied by Englishman GEORGE VANCOUVER, who sought to enforce the provisions of the Nootka Convention.

NEW YORK OF THE WEST When the *Albany Argus* (New York) reported in November 1889 that Port Townsend was "second only to New York City in the marine crafts reported and cleared in the whole United States," Port Townsend promoters coined a new appellation for the bustling seaport: New York of the West. The future in 1889 was full of promise. But the failure to secure a railroad terminus, the depression of 1893, and, twenty years later, the removal of the port of entry to Seattle shattered such dreams of glory.

Port Townsend's first newspaper was established in 1859, eight years after the city's founding, but it was not until 1870 that one found a large enough audience to survive. The *Puget Sound Argus*, established by Al Pettygrove, son of one of the town's FOUNDERS, started as a weekly and became a daily as the town's fortunes began to shine. A rival daily, *Cyclops*, was established and claimed that its legendary single eye could see far more than the *Argus* with its one hundred eyes. The boast was greater than the promise: almost as fast as an eye can blink, *Cyclops* ceased publication. The *Argus* lasted until 1890, when its plant and valuable files were burned; it never reopened. NEWSPAPERS

Five years earlier, in 1885, the *Port Townsend Call* was established as a Democratic paper with daily and weekly editions; it continued until 1910, by which time Port Townsend had become a minor factor in Puget Sound's economy. In October 1889, the *Port Townsend Morning Leader* began publication, declaring itself an independent daily, although its political opinions were always the opposite of the declared Democratic *Call*. The *Leader* still publishes. From time to time competitors emerge, but they are driven more by enthusiasm than by capital; in most cases their musings are printed with mimeograph machines or by quick-print operations. They last a few months and then are gone.

"Nootka" is a misnomer for the Indian people of the west coast of Vancouver Island and the northwest coast of the Olympic Peninsula. "Nootka" and its adjectival form "Nootkan" derived from Captain James Cook's misunderstanding of Indian descriptions of the sound he visited in 1778. "Notka" means "to circle about." The Indians may have been describing the geography of the sound or suggesting that Cook turn around and go back where he came from. A more appropriate name for the Indians is one adopted NOOTKA by the tribal council in 1980: "nuu-chah-nulth," freely translated meaning "all along the mountains." Through contact with whites, the population of Nootkan tribes decreased from about fifteen thousand when Cook visited to about two thousand in the 1930s. By the 1970s the number had risen to over four thousand. Existing Nootkan tribes in the Olympic Peninsula are the Ozette and MAKAH. (See *George Vancouver*.)

NORDLAND   A small community on Marrowstone Island, Nordland was established in 1892 by Peter Norby, one of three brothers who emigrated from Norway via Minnesota and South Dakota. Peter never lived there, but his younger brother Ole did, giving the town that now consists of a grocery store and a post office some identification with its founder.

NORTH BEACH   A residential area on the Strait of Juan de Fuca west of Fort Worden near the Jefferson County fair grounds, North Beach refers to the northern shore of KAH TAI Valley across which coastal Indians used to portage canoes to Port Townsend Bay. Settlers originally called it West Beach, perhaps because it was west as well as north of the early town site.

NORWEGIAN MEMORIAL   In January 1902 a Norwegian vessel named *Prince Arthur* apparently mistook the lights of settler Ivan Birkestol's cabin between La Push and Cape Alava for Cape Flattery and steered into what he thought was the Strait of Juan de Fuca. Instead, the vessel ran into the rock-strewn coastline, broke in two, and set the crew of twenty awash. Only two survived. A small memorial was established near the beach. (See also *Beach of the Dead, Shipwrecks*.)

NURSE LOGS   Dying conifers that fall to the floor of the RAIN FOREST come to rest above the dense undergrowth, providing a crested bed for evergreen seedlings. Roots of the new trees embrace the logs in search of the earth's nourishment. As the old tree rots, the root systems of the new growth are exposed and appear to be clutching an invisible log.

OAK BAY   South of Port Townsend Bay, to which it is connected by Portage Canal, Oak Bay was named by George Vancouver for several oak trees that he observed onshore.

Filmed in 1982 in Port Townsend, *An Officer and a Gentleman* is a 1940s-style romance updated with sex and strong language. The plot concerns local girls – known as Puget Sound Debs – who trick naval officer candidates into marrying them to escape a dreary future. The movie was directed by Taylor Hackford and featured Richard Gere, Debra Winger, and Lou Gossett, Jr., who won an Oscar as best supporting actor for his role in the film. (See *Hollywood*.)

OFFICER AND A
GENTLEMAN, AN
★ ★ ½

A platted town (population 0) at the mouth of the Hoh River in western Jefferson County, Oil City was established in 1920 to capitalize on oil exploration of that time. The $329 recording fee for the town site proved to benefit only the county coffers; oil was never found, and no one ever moved to Oil City, although a road still leads to it and dreams of oil persist.

OIL CITY

A promontory north of Mats Mats Bay named in 1841 by American naval officer and explorer Charles Wilkes, for an Indian word meaning "berry."

OLELLE POINT

Secessionist residents in western Clallam and Jefferson Counties often claim that the county seats in Port Angeles and Port Townsend are too far removed and their officials too indifferent. A proposal to establish Olympic County languished in two sessions of the state legislature in the early 1980s. Opponents were concerned that the tax base of the new jurisdiction would be insufficient and that the loss of revenue to Clallam and Jefferson Counties from which Olympic County was to be carved would be crippling. Proponents remained determined but the issue did not resurface in the 1986 legislature. In an earlier effort, a WEST END county called Quillayute was created in 1868 but was disbanded a year later when the sparse population could not muster enough candidates for the elected offices.

OLYMPIC COUNTY

Home base for dozens of animal movie stars, the Olympic Game Farm north of Sequim has provided four-legged actors for many Walt Disney films and television movies, among them *Never Cry Wolf*, *The Incredible Journey*, and the "Grizzly Adams" series. Sequences have often been shot at the farm, but when the script calls for a more exotic background, the animals are sent on location. Begun in the 1950s by Disney

OLYMPIC GAME FARM

photographer Lloyd Beebe, the farm features black and grizzly bears, bison, guanaco, yak, elk, deer, sheep, a white rhinoceros, and peacocks. Visitors may take drive-through tours (keeping the windows up), feed and pet the animals, inspect movie sets, and watch film clips of the stock at work.

OLYMPIC MOUNTAINS   With peaks averaging between fifty-five hundred and seven thousand feet in an area of only three thousand square miles, the Olympic Mountain range is not notable for its height or mass, yet it holds a number of contrasting distinctions. The Olympic Mountain range is the wettest spot in the continental United States with nearly two hundred inches of rain recorded on the western slopes. Yet forty miles east at Sequim less than seventeen inches fall annually, making the northern slope of the range the driest coastal region north of southern California. In winter, temperate coastal regions – at latitudes higher than Maine – have average temperatures in the mid-40s (degrees Fahrenheit), yet with year-round snow at six thousand feet, the Olympics have the lowest snow line in the continental United States.

Unlike the Cascades, which were built in part by volcanic action, the Olympic Mountains were created in a slow collision of oceanic and continental plates. Diving below the more stationary continent, the top of the oceanic crust was scraped off and thrust upward, a process that began thirty million years ago and continued for eighteen million years more. Repeated glaciation – the most recent just twelve thousand years ago – created a radial pattern of ridges and valleys that drain eighteen major rivers, all still fed by glaciers. Constant erosion has created a relief in which mountains rise five thousand feet and more in a stretch of just three miles. (See *Mount Constance, Mount Olympus, Mount Townsend*, and *Mount Walker*.)

OLYMPIC MUSIC   An annual summer event, the Olympic Music Festival
FESTIVAL   features the Seattle-based Philadelphia String Quartet and takes place on a forty-acre farm near Center, a few miles north of Quilcene and nearly twenty miles south of Port Townsend. The original farm buildings included a dairy barn that was converted into a 250 –seat performance hall. An adjoining milk shed was turned into a multipurpose hall used for art exhibits

and social gatherings. Student musicians are housed in cabins and given chores of slopping hogs, feeding cows, and ushering at concerts, in addition to their musical work. Although students come from all over the country, priority is given to the best young musicians from the Northwest. The festival includes performances by students, the quartet, and guest artists.

One of three national parks in Washington State, Olympic National Park records more visitors each year than both Mount Rainier and the Northern Cascades, even though few roads penetrate its boundaries and none traverse it. Favored auto stops include Hurricane Ridge, sixteen miles into the park from its headquarters in Port Angeles, Lake Crescent, the Hoh River Rain Forest, Lake Ozette, Pacific beaches, and Lake Quinault. With only two year-round and two seasonal resorts, the park is a backpackers' paradise.

OLYMPIC NATIONAL PARK

An idea first suggested in 1889, a forest reserve of more than 3,000 square miles was created by President Grover Cleveland in 1897. Four years later it was reduced to two-thirds that size. In 1904, nearly 625 square miles were proposed as Elk National Park, but Congress refused to pass the bill. In 1909, President Theodore Roosevelt established 954 square miles as Mount Olympus National Monument, primarily as a refuge for ROOSEVELT ELK. Six years later, President Woodrow Wilson reduced that number by half amidst claims that World War I allies needed timber (especially spruce for airplane construction). More than twenty years passed before President Franklin D. Roosevelt visited Lake Crescent in 1937 to discuss park boundaries. The next year Congress established the park with nearly 1,000 square miles. Two years later, Roosevelt expanded it with an additional 300 square miles. In 1953 President Harry S. Truman added 75 square miles to include a 40–mile coastal strip from the Quinault to the OZETTE Indian Reservations.

The art of demonstrating that one has less, uses less, needs less, and is less than the next person. Antonym: *one-upsmanship*

ONE-DOWNSMANSHIP

Port Townsend one-downsmanship has its roots in the counter-cultural politics of the 1970s, which regarded the consumerist bent of the American economy with profound suspicion. As the years passed, however, this resistance to a system that equates self-worth with material well-being, developed into aggressive humility – a parody of the one-upsmanship it sought to displace.

Certainly, not all Port Townsend residents practice one-downsmanship, and few are truly adept at the art. For those without means, one-downsmanship comes naturally, but many of the town's more well-to-do residents choose to drive old pickup trucks and wear faded flannel shirts and blue jeans downtown. The disproportionate number of secondhand stores in Port Townsend attests to the economic value of this state of mind.

However, in its purest form, one-downsmanship skirts the mainstream economic system altogether and becomes a subtle kind of verbal jousting. "What a lovely sweater," someone might remark in innocent admiration. "Where did you buy it?" "Buy?" the one-downer would reply with an arched eyebrow, "I couldn't afford to *buy* something like this. I knitted it. My neighbor has a sheep and gave me the wool in exchange for cedar shakes I split." Then follows a discussion of dyes from native plants, homemade needles, and hand-built looms.   [J.H.]

OZETTE   In 1970 a tidal erosion exposed a group of Ozette homes that had been buried and perfectly preserved in an ancient mud slide for five hundred years. The thousands of artifacts subsequently recovered proved to be one of the greatest archaeological discoveries in North America. Ozette was the southernmost of five Makah Indian villages and had been occupied for at least several thousand years. Located about fifteen miles south of Neah Bay, it is approximately a three-hour drive from Port Townsend.

Because of its proximity to rich sea life, Ozette was the principal sea-mammal hunting village along the Washington coast. The resident population increased each spring when other families moved into the area to hunt seals and whales. As a consequence, the houses contained a large number of artifacts related to the society's seafaring work. The site is considered significant for the completeness of its cultural record. Because of the nature of the dense gray mud, whole households of material were preserved intact, including vegetal and other materials that would normally have decayed within a few years. For example, a wooden bowl containing seal oil was found with the scent of the oil still fragrant. Digging was suspended in 1981 for lack of funding, but artifacts recovered up to that point are the basis of a collection at the MAKAH MUSEUM in Neah Bay.

Early in 1981 a group of peace demonstrators assembled in front of the main gate of the Indian Island military base, across the bay from Port Townsend. At issue was whether or not nuclear weapons were being stored at the ammunition depot. Leaders of the demonstration had asked for a meeting with the base commander. When he did not appear, one of the demonstrators stepped across the gate and thereby trespassed. The ensuing arrest led to the formation of the Peace Coalition to raise money for the court defense of the trespasser. The group then became active in a variety of peace issues including a freeze on nuclear testing and production.

PEACE COALITION

Later in 1981 members conceived of blockading the first TRIDENT submarine as it approached its home port of Bangor on the Kitsap Peninsula, where it was to be armed with nuclear warheads. The coalition served as a support team for all groups active in the blockade, which consisted of a string of small home-made rowboats tied together. In 1983 members became involved in Central American issues by helping relief efforts for El Salvadoran refugees in Seattle. By 1984 their attention was focused on Nicaragua, though they remained active in a variety of educational forums and films about the arms race. (See *Jalapa, Nicaragua.*)

Two species of beetles – true powder-post (*Lyctus* sp.) and false powder-post (*Typopitys* sp.) – thrive in the damp climate of the Puget Sound region. The distinction between the two beetles is their size; in their quest for cellulose, either can reduce support beams to sawdust in ten years' time. Along with carpenter ants (*Camponotus* sp.), subterranean termites (*Reticulitermes hesperus*), and DRY ROT, the powderpost beetle is a major though surmountable obstacle to easy RESTORATION of historic buildings in Port Townsend.

PESTS, STRUCTURAL

Petroglyphs are shallow indentations in hard sand-stone with stylistic representations of human and ani-

PETROGLYPHS

185

mal forms. Although debate continues over their significance – whether they had religious significance or were simply directional guides or casual artistic expression – early white informants reported that Indians showed respect, if not fear, for many of the petroglyphs. Although six hundred petroglyphs exist in the Northwest, only a few have been found on the Olympic Peninsula. Along with the archaeological discoveries at the OZETTE DIG at Cape Alava were several petroglyphs, depicting human figures, boats, whales, and perhaps a female fertility symbol. Other petroglyph sites include Agate Passage; Enetai on the Twana reservation, where a figure of the mythical THUNDERBIRD has since been lost; Eld Inlet, which yielded a carved boulder now in the State Capitol Building in Olympia; Otter Point, where a fish petroglyph rests high on flat vertical sandstone above basalt rock; and Point No Point, where a petroglyph depicts a whale and fish.

PETTYGROVE HOUSE   (*1000 G Street*) Francis W. Pettygrove, Jr., son of a founder of PORTLAND, Oregon, and of Port Townsend and the first white child born in Portland, built the Pettygrove House in 1889. With cross gables, a lack of flat surfaces, and a wraparound porch that has since been enclosed, the house is structurally of the Queen Anne style. But the incorporation of the tower into the main body of the house, the multipaned windows, and the shingles without interruption at the corners point to the emerging shingle style (see *Architecture*). Due to the collapse of the Port Townsend economy in the 1890s, the style – which was popular in New England – never took hold.

PHOTOGRAPHY   On a sunny day, the quality of the light in the Pacific Northwest presents certain technical difficulties to the photographer wishing to capture the unique colors and spectacular vistas in and around Port Townsend. Because the air is pollution-free, light is not diffused but strikes objects directly, and because of the northern latitude, the sun is at a strong angle, causing sharp shadows. Thus, photos tend to offer black shadows without distinguishing features. A blue sky in combination with the profusion of green foliage and blue water sets a scene of cool tones, while most film is calibrated more toward warmer tones. It is easier to capture the feel of the region when it is cloudy and gray than when the sun is bright. Under blue skies, warming filters should be used along with a faster-speed film (ASA 200 is preferable to ASA 100). Individualized rather than computerized printing is suggested.

(*1012 Water Street*) Unique among Port Townsend commercial buildings for its common facade and central stairway that serves two separate buildings, the Pioneer Block was the joint venture of Francis W. Pettygrove, Jr., (see *Pettygrove House*) and the State Bank of Washington. Designed in 1889 by Port Townsend architects Whiteway and Schroeder, the building displays round arches on the third floor, segmental arches on the second floor, and flat lintels on the first floor with separating bands between each, features borrowed from the Richardson Romanesque style (see *Architecture*). PIONEER BLOCK

An appropriate misprint appeared in a Seattle newspaper a few years ago when, referring to Port Townsend, it printed "Poet Townsend." The works of Port Townsend poets have appeared in the nation's most prestigious magazines and have won some of the most enviable writing awards offered in this country. Publications by Port Townsend poets would fill several bookshelves. Local restaurants and bars are frequently the scene of scheduled or open-microphone poetry readings. The Town Tavern has hosted a variety of poets, from the unknown local bards to Pulitzer-Prize winner Gary Snyder. POETRY

Poets tend to migrate. There are many who make Port Townsend their home, even if it is a kind of KAH TAI, that is, a portage or place to pass through and to replenish oneself. Port Townsend's attractiveness to poets no doubt includes its natural beauty and relative seclusion from city life. Poets here, as everywhere, must turn to other pursuits besides writing for a livelihood, but Port Townsend's openness to alternative life-styles has made the burden of survival less heavy for many. Several have built their own homes in the woods, some engage in seasonal work, and several travel elsewhere for short engagements that allow them to return to Port Townsend and write. Port Townsend is also attractive because of its many presses, and the CENTRUM FOUNDATION, which sponsors several annual programs for poets and writers. (See *Publishers*.) [J.H.]

POINT HUDSON   For years beyond number, nomadic Indians made a temporary home on the cape of Port Townsend Bay, a place known to white men as Point Hudson. The INDIANS migrated there to take advantage of the shellfish and other seafood that flourished in the area. Although the point could not sustain them year-round, the Indians would come and go, unquestioningly accepting what the sea and shore offered – not trying to gain from the swampy spit more than partial and temporary sustenance.

Much of mid-nineteenth-century Point Hudson was a tidal lagoon, and the white interlopers who appropriated the meager marsh have, since their arrival in 1851, striven to alter and show dominion over it, that it might be a consequential element in a permanent settlement. One of the white men's first contributions to the point was the construction of ramshackle saloons on the beach beyond the Indian settlement. These establishments, known as mad houses or gin mills, had the worst reputation in town. Beyond the saloons, beneath and just past the CROW'S NEST, was a "squaw dance house" that featured the "pleasures of Indian women and blue ruin whiskey." In 1859, Father Rossi built St. Anthony's Mission on the edge of the lagoon, which served the Catholic community until 1880. A shipyard was operating by 1868, and a small sawmill and icehouse soon thereafter. In 1881, Port Townsend boosters raised twenty-thousand dollars to establish a larger sawmill at the point. The mill languished under community direction and was finally turned over to a private owner, who successfully operated it for a number of years.

By then the Indians had adopted a more sedentary life, and from a small, permanent colony at Point Hudson, they sold fish, shellfish, baskets, and weaving door-to-door. But in an attempt to lure investment dollars, city fathers sought to rid the point of its "blight" and replace it with the blossom of commerce. The *Leader* reported in 1889 that the Indians of Point Hudson were almost all gone; "just a few tents and canoes" remained. Several years later, after the last of the Klallam had left, Makah, on their way to the hop fields in Puyallup, would stop at Point Hudson to sell baskets, mats, and other curios. By this time, the Indians were considered a picturesque attraction, and in 1914 *The Leader* lamented the dwindling number of Makah traders.

In the 1889 boom, two enterprising proprietors of the Point Hudson Ice Works announced they would "shortly construct a heated salt water natatorium . . . 30 x 60 feet, sufficiently deep for swimming." The plan came to naught, and the icehouse was closed for several years, then sold in 1901 for back taxes. A dry dock constructed at Point Hudson in 1893 was shipped away before it ever operated. In 1913, Point Hudson was proposed as a railroad terminus. The railroad never came. In 1917, Union Timber proposed yet another shipyard. It was never built. Ground was broken in 1929 for an airport on the point. It was not constructed. In 1934 a "thoroughly modern quarantine station" was erected by the federal government: the lagoon was dredged, a dock was constructed, and eleven buildings raised. Not one patient was treated there.

In 1939, the Coast Guard took title to the property to train recruits. The National Youth Administration appropriated some buildings for a vocational school, and the navy established an onshore patrol base that operated throughout World War II. The site was abandoned after the war until the army acquired it in 1947 as an auxiliary institution during the occupation of Korea. The property was declared surplus in 1953, and a convention center was proposed; nothing came of it. In 1960, a "boatel" was suggested, and a panel discussed the development of the site; it was just talk. The idea of a heated swimming pool was resurrected; the pool was built elsewhere.

Since 1962, the property has been leased to private interests. The first lessee dredged the marina but made few other improvements and, in debt, sold out in 1968. For a while, Point Hudson was a local arts and recreation headquarters. Classes were offered in dance, drama, painting, and sailing. Victor Steinbrueck, Seattle architect and preservationist, remodeled the detention barracks into a theatre, with a professional company led by his wife Marjorie Nelson in seasonal residence. In 1970, the lease changed hands again. The quarantine hospital was converted into a motel, the mess hall into a restaurant and store. Improvements were made on the marina. The beach front was turned

Port Townsend's first and only gallows was hastily erected at Point Hudson in 1859 to string up an Indian condemned by a lynch mob for the murder of a white mail-carrier. The intervention of Fort Townsend soldiers was necessary to quell the angry horde of whites. The Indian was later found innocent.

into a trailer court. Then in 1985, another conference center was proposed for the site. And once again Point Hudson's future was pondered as rounds of negotiations began. The Klallam, who for countless years reaped the bounty and treasured the beauty of the point must look down from their home in the sky and shake their heads at the white man's inability to know true wealth when he sees it.   [R.B.]

POINT NO POINT TREATY   The Point No Point Treaty was signed on January 26, 1855, between the territory of Washington and KLAL-LAM, CHIMAKUM, and TWANA Indians. Only four days earlier, the famous Chief Seattle (or Sealth) and western Washington Indians from Puyallup to the Canadian border had met with territorial governor Isaac Stevens at Mukilteo in a one-day council. After remarks by Stevens, the Indians had sung Catholic canticles and recited prayers. The next day the Indians had been given gifts, Chief Seattle responding, "We are the friends of the Americans. All the Indians are of the same mind. We look upon you as our father. We will never change our minds."

The council at Point No Point was not so simple. About twelve hundred Indians gathered on the northern tip of the Kitsap Peninsula to meet with Stevens

Point No Point was named by Charles Wilkes in 1841 because it appeared to be less of a point up close than it did from a distance. Indians called it "long nose."

and his party. The treaty, which had been prepared in advance, was read and explained to the assembled Indians. It had the usual surrender of lands to the United States (in this case, for sixty-thousand dollars over a period of years), the specifications for reservation territory, the outlawing of liquor on reservations, the outlawing of slavery, and so forth. The Twana had several objections. Largely because of their experience with whites, they had learned about the commercial value of land. One chief said, "Formerly, the Indians slept, but the whites came along and woke them up, and we now know the lands are worth much." Some were worried about living among the more numerous Klallam. Another chief objected to having to leave traditional food-gathering sites.

It is not clear how much Port Townsend Klallam chief CHET-ZE-MOKA had to do with pacifying the Twanas, but on the following day, January 26, they joined him in approaching Governor Stevens. As was the case with Chief Seattle's people on January 22, the Indians presented the governor with white flags, which were probably intended to be more an expression of friendship than surrender. They told Governor Stevens that their "hearts had become white." And they signed. All the represented chiefs signed with an X. Their Indian names were given as well as the names the white had given them – a list, ironically, of prestigious historical and literary figures. Among them were the DUKE OF YORK, Daniel Webster, Lord Jim, General Harrison, General Taylor, General Lane, and General Lane, Jr.

Instead of settling on the Skokomish Reservation as stipulated in the Point No Point Treaty, most of the Klallam integrated into surrounding white communities. Only the JAMESTOWN, Port Gamble, and Lower Elwha bands remained on their traditional sites. [J.H.]

POINT OF THE ARCHES

The most ancient of all geology on the Olympic Peninsula, the rocks and sea stacks between Cape Alava and the Makah Indian nation known as the Point of the Arches have been dated as 144 million years old. Since the Olympic Mountains were formed only sixty million years ago when the top of the oceanic plate was scraped upward as it dove under the continental plate, it is not certain how the Point of the Arches, some eighty million years older, either remained in place or became exposed. Indian legend says that the rocks are the abandoned children of DESTRUCTION ISLAND and Tatoosh Island. The awesome seascape was the destination of frequent ecological hiking trips in the 1950s and 1960s led by the late Supreme Court justice William O. Douglas.

POINT WHITNEY

The southern point that demarks Quilcene Bay from Dabob Bay and Hood Canal, Point Whitney was named for Robert S. Whitney, a Nova Scotian who was the first logger in the area. The Washington State Department of Fisheries operates a shellfish laboratory at the point, conducting various studies of artificial propagation of crustaceans for commercial use.

POINT WILSON

A promontory on Port Townsend's northeastern reach, Point Wilson marks the eastern end of the STRAIT OF JUAN DE FUCA and the beginning of ADMIRALTY INLET. It was named by GEORGE VANCOUVER for his "esteemed friend" Captain George

Wilson of the British navy. Extending from Fort Worden State Park, this point has become a popular recreation area for campers, fisherman, beachcombers, and viewers of Mount Baker.

POPE AND TALBOT

In 1775, the grandfathers of Andrew Jackson Pope and William C. Talbot raised guns to the whites of British eyes at Lexington to end an empire's hold on a new nation. Less than a century later, Andrew Pope and William Talbot used ships and saws to carve a new economic empire from the timber on the shores of Puget Sound. The history of Pope and Talbot Incorporated began in SAN FRANCISCO in 1850 with four farsighted immigrants from East Machias, Maine. They recognized that the anticipated building boom in San Francisco and other young western cities would be far more profitably served by the abundant timber of the Pacific Northwest than by eastern lumber, which required shipping on long, treacherous, expensive journeys around Cape Horn. In 1853, the company opened its first mill at PORT GAMBLE. By 1855 the mill was operating around the clock, and three years later it was the largest on Puget Sound. Lumber from Port Gamble was shipped to the Hawaiian Islands, Australia, Hong Kong, Tahiti, and South America.

Other companies paid their workers in script, redeemable only at the company store, but Pope and Talbot men paid up with four-bit pieces, honored anywhere. Two major decisions in these early years revealed a business acumen that was to serve Pope and Talbot for more than a century. The company acquired a shipping company so it could control its own transportation costs, and it amassed hundreds of thousands of acres of timberland – but did not log it. The company bought logs for its sawmills, saving its valuable timber for the future. By 1875, Pope and Talbot was the largest holder of timberland in the Territory of Washington and had enough board feet to maintain its output for at least seventy-five more years. Most of its landholdings were not more than a mile from saltwater, so ox-team logging would offer optimum profit.

In 1856, mill workers at Port Gamble took time out for two days to join the U.S. Navy in "parley and rather desultory fighting" with northern Indians who were in the area stirring up trouble. The only white casualty in the skirmish won the distinction of being the first U.S. navy man to die in the Pacific.

Over the years Pope and Talbot became involved in a variety of enterprises, venturing into trading, mercantile, log towing, tree farming, and real estate. The real-estate arm of the company served originally as a liquidating agency, selling off timberlands as they became more useful for other purposes. Many of Seattle's northern suburbs were built on Pope and Talbot holdings. The policy was reoriented in 1958 when the company began to acquire logged shorefront properties purely for speculation, development, and sale. Expansion and diversification culminated in a record year in 1973 when company revenue topped $100 million. The net income that year was $16.4 million, more than double the previous year's profit. But in 1974, inflation and high interest rates drove down the number of housing starts, marking the end of an era for the timber industry. As businesses go, however, eras are generally of short duration, and Pope and Talbot has seen many of them. It is likely to see many more. (See *Port Ludlow*.)

In 1980 when Pope John Paul II gave his signet ring to the poor in Brazil, a group of Seattle residents, inspired by the gesture, attempted to purchase the ring and return it to the pontiff. Unable to do so, they established a fund for the poor in the slums of Rio de Janeiro and commissioned Port Townsend jeweler Heiner Tamme (b.1922) to make a new ring for the pope. A refugee from Estonia, Tamme had come to the United States in 1948 by way of Finland and Sweden, where he had studied both painting and metal engraving. Tamme came to Port Townsend in 1977 and established a custom jewelry and engraving studio called the Baltic Gallery. For his papal commission, he adapted the Catholic pontiff's crest as the design for the new eighteen-carat gold signet ring, and for Buzz Aldrin, he engraved a medallion that the astronaut wore to the moon.

POPE JOHN PAUL II

Port Angeles has been described in the Seattle *Weekly* as "a town that makes Bremerton look like Paris . . . ." Port Angeles is a mill town, no doubt about that, but few care to hide the fact except perhaps the chamber of commerce, which attempts to divert the inattentive with festive banners downtown. Its setting is genuinely beautiful, particularly looking to the OLYMPIC MOUNTAINS from EDIZ HOOK. Its mill does not have the cabbage-sour fragrance of Port Townsend's, but rather the sweet odor of processed cedar and fir. Its harbor is active with cargo container ships, and serves as a gateway to the Olympics and to Victoria, British

PORT ANGELES

Columbia. And while Port Angeles's neighborhoods may lack charm and elegance, the city's collection of craftsman style, or bungalow, houses of the early twentieth century is impressive and totally unrecognized, and its history holds fascination (see *Insurrections* and *Utopias*).

With a population of seventeen thousand, it is the largest city on the North Olympic Peninsula, making it a regional center and giving it the distinction of housing the area's only junior college, airport with scheduled service, and franchise fast-food outlets. It lacks Port Townsend's diversity both culturally and demographically, but only Port Townsend seems to notice or to care. Reached by European explorers a year before they got to Port Townsend, Port Angeles was named Porto de Nuestra Señora de Los Angeles (Port of Our Lady of the Angels) in 1791 by Spanish captain Francisco Eliza. Less romantic English explorers shortened it to Port Angeles.

PORT DISCOVERY   The name given by GEORGE VANCOUVER to what is now known as DISCOVERY BAY.

PORT GAMBLE   Unique among Puget Sound towns, Port Gamble, thirty miles south of Port Townsend, was built by POPE AND TALBOT in 1853 as a mill town, and it retains that status 135 years later. Port Gamble is the only one of at least a dozen company towns created in the nineteenth century that still operates as one. Extraordinary maintenance by Pope and Talbot gives it a museumlike appearance.

PORT HADLOCK   The earliest name for what is now called HADLOCK and LOWER HADLOCK.

PORT LUDLOW   In 1852 on a bay called Paradise, west of the entrance to HOOD CANAL, W. F. Sayward build a sawmill on his 318-acre timber claim. "Timber – timber till you can't sleep!" one early visitor was moved to remark when beholding the forest as thick as a jungle. But the huge firs have long since fallen and the wild woodland that surrounded Sayward's sawmill has been brought to heel under a 3,000–acre resort complex, convention center, and planned community. Sayward sold his holdings in 1858, and his fellow "State of Mainers" Andrew Pope and William Talbot acquired the mill and properties in 1879. The Hall Brothers started a shipyard at Port Ludlow in 1874, and in 1880 the company built fifteen vessels, including two- and three-masted schooners, steamers, yachts, and barkentines. In these years, the port was known as a marine community, not a mill town.

By October 1883, POPE AND TALBOT had remodeled the mill and manned it with a crew of 120, who, with their families, accounted for almost the entire population of Port Ludlow. As a sign of its commitment to permanence, the company established a school for twenty youngsters. From 1880, an influential force in Port Ludlow was the manager of Pope and Talbot's mills in Port Gamble and Port Ludlow, Cyrus Walker. Stories abound about him. He had been with the company for years before he became manager and had been responsible for the land acquisitions policy that led to Pope and Talbot's resilience in years when the timber industry was depressed. He worked at everything from designing sawmills to piloting company tugs. On Sundays he could be found straightening bent nails. He chipped mortar from used bricks so that they might be reused. He was a stern, conservative manager reluctant to employ "new-fangled devices" in his mills.

Walker's home in Port Gamble burned in 1885, and he decided to "build the biggest damn cabin on the Sound" in Port Ludlow. When completed, the mansion lent the air of a kingdom to the western sawmill town. For a few halcyon years, life at Port Ludlow was as luxurious and cosmopolitan as Port Townsend or Seattle. Walker's "palace" was guarded by a cannon that fired salute to visiting dignitaries. The house was constructed of the finest lumber, which Walker himself had handpicked from his mills; the furnishings were handmade of mahogany and black walnut. It was a massive two-story building with more than a dozen bedrooms. Elevators operated from the basement to the pantry and cold storage. Walker entertained in a style that would have done credit to any San Franciscan host of the day. White-coated Chinese boys served from the well-stocked pantry fare that included local meats, fish, and fowl, as well as imported delicacies. Although Walker himself was a teetotaler, he boasted the finest wine cellar in the region.

As Walker's home was his castle, likewise were the homes of the mill employees: each was built in tradi-

The Leader *reported a closure of the mill at Port Ludlow as the result of a strike in which the workers walked out because of the "poor cooking of a heathen Chinese" in the mess tent.*

tional New England style with no stinting of timber. (Modern Port Gamble still features such homes, since restored.) Their homes were the center of their lives. Many an evening was spent gathered around the parlor organ (a not uncommon fixture) singing with friends. Whist, five hundred, and hearts occupied those lacking musical inclination. A group was formed for the serious study of Shakespeare. Members of the community staged dramatic productions. Dances in the club social hall featured orchestras from Seattle or Port Townsend. The mill sponsored a baseball team, which competed with other mill teams in the area. Competition was so keen that the mills vied for the employ of a good pitcher.

Life was more comfortable, of course, for the family of a foreman or executive than for laborers' families, and for white people than for Chinese (Indians working at the mills usually maintained a separate village). But the mill saw to it that all its employees and families were sheltered, clothed, and fed. A transient population of (usually) single men made up about one-third of the workers at Port Ludlow, and their pastimes were more boisterous than those of the permanent familymen. They headquartered at the hotel (one of the few businesses not owned by the company), where liquor flowed freely, serious gamblers found their way to the back room, and other entertainment could be had upstairs. Steamers dropped anchor daily at Ludlow on the way from Seattle and Olympia to Port Townsend.

The depression of 1891 marked the beginning of years of off-again on-again operation at the mill. It was shut down that year, and many of the employees rowed to Port Gamble on Sunday afternoon, worked six ten-hour days, and rowed back on Sunday morning. With the Klondike gold rush of 1897, business picked up, but shutdowns were never again unusual.

When Cyrus Walker retired, his home was converted into the Admiralty Hotel, and a bid was made for tourist trade. Publicity stressed the separation of public dining and "company dining," and prospective guests were assured that workers would enter the hotel at the rear and go directly to the washrooms "without disturbing the guests." The community struggled to preserve its identity as a genteel, cosmopolitan town. In 1915, the school accepted a donation from Mrs. Cyrus Walker (whose own son was educated at home under the tutelage of a Rhodes scholar) of a substantial library, piano, and a Victrola. The latter permitted the students to hear "Caruso, Melba, Tetrazzini, Johanna Gadski, Alma Gluck and many others.... It is the policy of the school board not to buy any of the cheap rag time records," according to the *Leader*.

Things looked up during World War I. The demand was great for spruce for military airplanes, and the mill at Ludlow was given preference because it could cut large logs. During that time, the Spruce Division of the U.S. Army, seventy-five men strong, was stationed at Ludlow. After the Great War, a county road was completed between Port Townsend and Port Ludlow, and some Port Townsend residents worked at the mill in the good years. After the paper MILL was built in Port Townsend, the commuter traffic often flowed the other way.

Pope and Talbot was sold to Charles McCormick Lumber Company in 1925, and two years later the mill was running at capacity, employing four hundred men. Ultimately, however, the mill fared badly under McCormick and in December 1935 was permanently shut down. The hotel was closed in 1936, and Port Ludlow began to resemble a ghost town. But hope dies hard; ferries from Edmonds and Ballard still docked several times a day. Finally, the mill was dismantled and sold for scrap. What was left burned in January 1940. That same year, the hotel was demolished. When World War II created a demand for housing, the houses that had been so loving constructed sixty-five years before were unceremoniously loaded onto barges and towed away. Pope and Talbot had regained control of the property in 1938 when it bought back its holdings in a public auction, but the town became a sleepy retirement and vacation community; the hum of commerce was silenced.

In the late 1960s, the sounds of construction broke the stillness as Pope and Talbot Development Company converted its acreage into a family resort complex and residential community. By 1975, the complex boasted a fully equipped marina, the Admiralty Inn Restaurant (on the site of Cyrus Walker's Admiralty Hall), a conference center, a beach club, a teen center, a game room, condominiums, and a regionally acclaimed golf course. For years the resort won Mobil Oil's coveted four-star rating of excellence.

Cyrus Walker reportedly acquired the first automobile in Jefferson County in June 1902 – an Oldsmobile.

A failing economy and the sinking of the Hood Canal Bridge in 1979 forced Pope and Talbot to halt development in the early 1980s. In 1982, the resort holdings and 2,700 undeveloped acres were put on the market for $16.5 million. In 1984 and 1985, Pope and Talbot closed the resort for the winter while embroiled in allegations that the residential development was responsible for increasing pollution in Paradise Bay. The resort is one of the largest employers in Jefferson County. Homes, land, and condominiums continue to be bought and sold. Talk of incorporating as a municipal government surfaces from time to time. It would seem the complex is here to stay, but one hundred years ago, residents said the same thing about the new sawmill and Cyrus Walker's splendid home.

[R.B.]

PORT TOWNSEND
MINIATURE

A thirty-six-foot-square plaster of paris and papier-mâché relief sculpture depicting Port Townsend and environs "in every way original and grand" was constructed by artists E. T. Callan and A. G. Patrick for entry in the Spokane Falls Industrial Exposition in October 1891. The impressive work was the brainchild of James G. Swan and Callan (who had made a similar model of Central Park in New York City) and was constructed in six six-foot squares. The artists' workshop was on the corner of Monroe and Washington Streets. They worked two months, using old issues of the *Call* and the *Leader* as the base for the papier-mâché. Every street and building of Port Townsend was represented as was timber and foliage, "just exactly as it is in reality." According to the *Leader*, the artists duplicated the "work of the Almighty by constructing in miniature the finest piece of land and water in the great state of Washington." The representation of the waterfront was perhaps the most striking feature of the piece. Every wharf and pier was shown with perfect models of frequently calling steamers, schooners, and full-rigged barks all in the harbor filled with real water with live fish swimming about.

After its successful debut at the exposition, the piece languished in a warehouse until early spring 1893, when Swan had it installed in a large room under the chamber of commerce. In a letter to the editor of the *Leader*, Swan encouraged citizens to view the piece and leave a cash token of appreciation, which would be used to pay for sending the work to the Chicago World's Fair. Swan's enthusiasm was apparently not matched by the citizenry, for though some smaller works of local art were sent to Chicago, the Port Townsend miniature did not make it. Sadly, the fate of this unique three-dimensional advertisement for Port Townsend is not known. [R.B.]

PORT TOWNSHEND PORT TOWNSEND's original name, given by GEORGE VANCOUVER in honor of his friend, "the noble" MARQUIS OF TOWNSHEND.

PORTLAND Oregon's largest city is something of a half sister to Port Townsend as they were both cofounded by Francis Pettygrove (1818–1887). With a good friend from New England, Pettygrove established the Oregon settlement in 1844. Pettygrove wished to name the new city for the capital of his native state of Maine, while his partner wanted to call it Boston. They flipped a coin, and Pettygrove won. In 1851, Pettygrove sold his Oregon holdings and joined Loren B. Hastings, who had come across the Oregon Trail in 1847, to settle farther north in Port Townsend. (See *Founders*.)

PORTUGEE HILL A residential section of the northwest hillside of Kah Tai Valley, Portugee Hill was so called when twenty Portuguese immigrant families who knew no English settled together in 1884 after a two-year voyage from Madeira. Several families later resettled at Discovery Bay and in Blyn. Although many descendants remain, they are scattered throughout the peninsula. The name Portugee Hill has thus fallen into disuse except by old-timers.

POST OFFICE The colloquial name for the CUSTOMS HOUSE AND POST OFFICE.

POTLACH "Potlatch" is taken from CHINOOK JARGON, meaning "to give." As practiced by the Northwest Indians, the potlatch was an occasion for gift-giving, but the various implications in the giving often made it more than a simple celebration of generosity. Generally speaking, the potlatch was a festive gathering of people who were ceremoniously and often individually invited to observe and share in the demonstration of a family prerogative. The host summoned guests from neighboring tribes and bands to whom he gave large quantities of goods and to whom he expounded the claims of his family in matters of property, economic rights, and family position. The event was marked by feasting, dancing, singing, canoe racing, gambling, and other games.

The occasions for particular potlatches varied. They may have been given as a simple gathering for the naming of children, or as a way of celebrating one's good fortune, or as a means of establishing one's status against the challenges of the upwardly mobile. The Indians in the Port Townsend area probably used the potlatch for more noble reasons than did the tribes farther north. Among the Kwakiutl, for example, the potlatch was often a way of putting down a rival by overwhelming him with so many gifts that he could never hope to repay them through a reciprocal potlatch. It became a way of maintaining a cold war between parties and was even known to lead to suicide by the humiliated recipient of gifts. In the Port Townsend area, however, the potlatch may have been a spontaneous social welfare system in which the fortunate redistributed the wealth through their generosity. Whaling often brought considerable riches, and wealth was associated with power of the guardian spirit or spirits. The person who showed wealth in potlatching was therefore thought to have great spiritual powers. The recipients might still lose social status if they did not at some future date sponsor their own potlatch, but the giver of the potlatch rose in social standing through the perception of this goodness rather than through the power of his intimidation. [J.H.]

PREHISTORIC TIMES Recent digs on the OZETTE Reservation at Cape Alava, at the HOKO River near Sekiu, and at the MASTODON site in Sequim have obscured other archaeological finds on the Olympic Peninsula. Though not spectacular as singular finds, they collectively offer enough material to provide a sketch of prehistoric man on these shores.

Glaciers covered much of the land that is now exposed, and as they receded they gouged out various channels, among them HOOD CANAL, Port Townsend Bay, and the STRAIT OF JUAN DE FUCA. During this late Pleistocene age, the first men and women arrived, probably from the south, following the glacial recession. Some experts hypothesize that the glaciers isolated civilization on the Olympic Peninsula from Eurasian influences. The first people developed unsophisticated technology: Chipped basalt was used to butcher animals and to scrape hides for clothing. They traveled in groups of twenty-five to thirty, some in clusters of only two families. Their type of shelter is not known.

Between 4,000 and 1,000 B.C. (when classical Greece was beginning to flower), Olympic Peninsula man began to shift from hunting to gathering of tidal foods. With the development of the dugout canoe, fish became an important food source. Stonework was refined with projectile points, and stone was ground, rather than chipped, into six-inch knives. Shells were used for blades, antlers for wedges.

The last prehistoric age (extending roughly from Greece's zenith in 1,000 B.C. to the Norman invasion of Britain in 1066 A.D.) brought a much more complex society with more complex tools and instruments, such as harpoons and clubs adorned with decorative handles.

Overlapping that period was the era of early maritimers, who abandoned many of their hunting tools for a highly developed offshore and river fishery. This transition may have been enhanced by the availability of iron from ship wreckage brought by the Japanese current and washed ashore. (Early explorers noted that the native populations had metal tools but no raw materials from which they could have been forged.) The HOKO DIG reveals evidence of CEDAR plank houses and a growing population. By the arrival of early explorers in the eighteenth century, delineated societies had formed, multiseasonal villages were established, stylized art forms had evolved, social status was differentiated, and a specialized economic base had developed. The prehistoric era on the Olympic Peninsula ended in 1775 with the landing at the Hoh River of a party of Spanish sailors, who were immediately killed by native populations.

(*Franklin and Polk Streets*) In 1889, at the peak of Port Townsend's economic boom, the seventeen-year-old congregation of the First United Presbyterian Church decided to build anew, as its original church building

PRESBYTERIAN CHURCH, FIRST UNITED

– the first house of worship north of the Columbia River to be built of stone – was too small to accommodate its growing numbers. As proposed by Port Townsend's major architectural firm, Whiteway and Schroeder, the stone structure was dismantled and used as foundation material for a far larger wooden structure that incorporated three styles of the period: Gothic, Queen Anne, and stick. Its steeply pitched roof and the pointed arches of its windows are characteristic of the Gothic style. Overhanging eaves, horizontal boards, and the use of shingles on the bell tower signify the stick style. The asymmetrical gabled wing and the avoidance of smooth walls are typical of the Queen Anne approach.

The church is remarkable more for its pipe organ than any other feature. Built by Whalley and Genung of Oakland, California, its 692 pipes range from two inches to sixteen inches in length, and its exterior is covered with eastern walnut. It cost $2,500, a princely sum in 1890. It is the oldest organ in Washington still in its original location. Ceiling frescoes, as they were called – though in reality they were only paint over plaster – were executed by George Chapman, who reached his zenith in Port Townsend with his work at the Starrett House. (The paintings were removed along with the plaster in the 1970s when it had deteriorated beyond repair.) The church was dedicated on March 16, 1890, having cost the congregation $19,748. The hawthorne trees in the parking strips were planted by the Reverend James Crawford, who brought them back from a visit to his birthplace in Northern Ireland.

PRESIDENTS   In 1880 Port Townsend was a prominent enough force in Puget Sound economics and politics that visiting dignitaries always made a stop. In September of that year, Rutherford B. Hayes became the first and only U.S. president in office to visit the Key City. Met at Union Wharf by a brass band, President Hayes disembarked and mounted the balcony of the Central Hotel at the corner of Water and Taylor Streets to address a throng of townspeople and school children who had been dismissed for the occasion. He admonished them to do well in their schooling. Four years later, U.S. senator Benjamin Harrison and his wife came to Port Townsend to visit his boyhood friend Albert Bash. Five years later, as president, Harrison was helpful influencing Congress to ultimately appropriate funds for Fort Worden, Fort Casey, and Fort Flagler.

By the mid-1970s, Port Townsend had to go to the president in order to gain his attention. During visits to Seattle in 1975 and in 1976, President Gerald Ford agreed to pose for publicity pictures with TREES FOR PORT TOWNSEND representatives because Mrs. Ford had been impressed by the organization's QUILTS used for fundraising.

By the late 1880s, only a few pockets of wilderness remained to be probed in America. One of the largest of these lay within the interior of the OLYMPIC MOUNTAINS. Over the years, the thick underbrush and steep approaches had dissuaded the most ardent white explorers. Strangely, even the peninsula's Indian population lacked any substantive knowledge of the interior. One popular myth held that each year the ancient tribes of the Olympic Peninsula entered the mountains to gather in a high valley. There, on neutral territory, they would temporarily abandon tribal conflicts while they competed in games of strength and skill. At one such gathering, according to the legend, something occurred to anger Seatco, chief of all evil spirits. In his wrath, he caused the earth to swallow the assembled tribes, allowing only a few to survive and spread word that they had been banished from the mountains forever.

Territorial governor Eugene Semple, fascinated by the mystery and mythology that surrounded the Olympics, campaigned to encourage exploration. His cause was carried on by his successor Elisha Ferry. Regional newspapers, hungry for new adventure to entice their readers, picked up the cry. One of the most vocal was the Seattle *Press*, which in 1889, compared Olympic exploration to Sir Henry Morton Stanley's journeys in Africa, and invited "hardy citizens of the Sound to acquire fame by unveiling the mystery." Hyperbole aside, there were practical reasons for exploration. In 1885 Second Lieutenant Joseph P. O'Neil, who had become enamored of the mountains while in command of Fort Townsend, conducted the first of his two expeditions to inventory the area's resources for the military. Crossing the foothills from Port Townsend to Port Angeles, O'Neil then turned his party south following Ennis Creek to its headwaters. After exploring the area around Mount Angeles and Hurricane Ridge, O'Neil was called back for duty in Kansas. His second, more extensive journey into the Olympics would not occur until the summer of 1890. By the fall of 1889, interest in Olympic explorations was at its zenith. Several expeditions, including O'Neil's, were in the planning stages for the following summer. The *Press*'s call had been answered by a thirty-five-year-old Scottish adventurer named James Helbold Christie. Recognizing that a summer expedition would leave his party just a face in the crowd, Christie was determined to take the lead and begin his exploration immediately. With the *Press*'s support, Christie assembled a six-man team to attempt a north-south crossing beginning at the Elwha River and exiting from the Quinault. The expedition, equipped with fifteen hundred pounds of supplies, four dogs, and two mules, departed Port Angeles in December of 1889. An unusually harsh winter and an unfortunate but persistent idea that the Elwha was navigable by flatboat impeded their progress. The first three months of travel found them only twelve miles from Port Angeles. As spring arrived, their progress improved. They reached Lillian Creek by April 1890 and passed into the low divide during the first week in May. They emerged from the Quinault Valley on May 20, achieving the first documented crossing of the Olympics. [M.W.]

PROSTITUTION   Uptown society in Port Townsend's early years had a saying that "sin flourishes at sea level." Those who dwelt on The Hill shopped on The Hill, and established their schools and churches on The Hill, in the rarefied air of assumed purity, away from the soiled quarters of the other element downtown. Port Townsend was both landfall and haven for thousands of sailors over the years, as well as a fair number of loggers and soldiers, many of whom were likely to be young, single, and adventuresome. For their entertainment, saloons and whorehouses were established. At the height of the maritime years, saloons outnumbered all other types of businesses in Port Townsend. Initially, the sailors' whorehouses, staffed mostly by half-breeds with a few white women, were located near POINT HUDSON. Captains and mates had their own brothels (of all white women) up against the hill in the vicinity

of today's Memorial Field. The houses were identified on maps of the day as "female boardings" and were shoulder to shoulder with the Chinese residences and businesses; together they were the untouchables of the frontier society.

An account of the early days is recorded from the reminiscences of an old sailor who visited Port Townsend as a young man: "In the evenings we went down to Water Street and visited the bars. And we would sit for a while in the honkey-tonk and order a few beers. Now and then a half-breed woman would come out on the platform and try to sing, and we would clap and jeer. Up on the sides of the big room were chicken coops the management called 'boxes.' Painted old whores sat in these boxes, pretending to enjoy the show, and trying to coax sailors to sit with them . . . . After the honkey-tonk we would visit the whore houses and finish off the evening at the Salvation Army." One of the early gin mills was located below the CROW'S NEST, between Point Hudson and Point Wilson. In a *Leader* account after the turn of the century, the editor gave an aura of romance to the place where romance was not the primary commodity: "All was a blaze of glory insofar as coal oil lamps could make it and the quietness of the daytime was transformed into wild and weird sounds of revelry. It was the evening resort for all classes of humanity. The merchant, the tailor, the shoemaker, the sailor, the logger, the soldier, and in fact nearly all classes would assemble to while away a weary hour. Upon their arrival they would be greeted with the smiles of . . . the pigeon-toed squaw, the wild-eyed halfbreed, and the cigarette-smoking white fairy with a scant wardrobe. Some were pale and lean, others were fat and greasy . . . . To the uninitiated the sight was disgusting. The room filled with tobacco smoke and the fumes of smoked salmon, whisky and beer, tinged with a faint odor of the most delicate perfumery. At the conclusion of each dance, the gentlemen would treat their partners at the bar and immediately after which another dance would be announced and the guests were treated to a continual round of pleasure until daylight would begin to dawn, when the revelry would cease, and the quietness would again reign supreme, save the soft murmur of the gentle sea breeze."

The life of a prostitute often began when a young

girl ran away from home. Pearl Roff was reportedly "enticed" from her parents' home in Shelton in 1886 when she was thirteen years old. In 1889 she was discovered in "one of the lowest resorts" in Port Townsend. Known among associates as the Astoria Tramp (she had gone first to Astoria from Shelton), "she sank steadily downward and reached the lowest level of her calling" and, discovered by her father, "returned to her home in a state of moral and physical ruin," according to the *Leader*. Prostitutes seldom stayed long in one place, being driven from town to town by the vagaries of business and the whims of law enforcement agencies, who sporadically "rounded-up" the "denizens of the tenderloin" and shipped them out of town or fined them. The *Leader* reported, just after the New Year 1900 that Port Townsend was hosting prostitutes driven out of Seattle. Léon Richardson "of the contingent of colored women that the police of Seattle have been ridding that place of" was picked up by the Port Townsend police and told to "get off the earth or in other words leave Port Townsend." Said the *Leader*: "Léon Richardson sounds like fiction but is a great big black reality."

Police did come to the aid of the "soiled doves" when summoned, but it was usually the prostitutes themselves the police arrested. If there were too many in town, or if there was a popular movement to "clean up the streets," the police forced them out. More often they simply exacted fines: "The City yesterday received a contribution to its funds from the frail and unfortunate women who inhabit the tenderloin district as a result of a round-up of those creatures .... The handsome ones who were more prosperous than the others paid $15 while the homely ones paid $10. Thirteen in all contributed to the city."

The prostitutes as a group were something of an economic force. The houses were extended credit by local businesses and though proprietors were rarely disappointed in quality or quantity of payment, there were some defaulters. Frankie Williams, a "bird of plumage" who "had been for sometime an inmate of a restricted district resort," visited a mercantile "near close of business one day ... and presented a demand for credit on the strength of a verbal order from the proprietress of the place where she lived. The favor was granted ... ." And Miss Williams hopped the next

steamer for Seattle with $14 worth of kid gloves and finery.

The sometimes cozy relationship between city officers and prostitutes occasionally became too much for respectable citizens to bear. When a person of "good family" was implicated in the business, it was a sign for increased vigilance. One such man took his life when spurned by Violet Wade, "the assumed name of a dancehall girl with whom he was smitten," in a home rented by a local landlord who claimed to have "no inkling to the kind of tenants he was harboring." The chief of police stepped in by ordering a roundup of people in town "who might be living together without the legal ties existing which both society and the laws demand." Reported the *Leader*: "As a result of the warnings which have been issued by the Chief there are familiar faces missing from the streets and terror has been struck to many hearts which have been or are guilty of the condition intimated."

But when it was a prostitute who died or was killed, the "small tragedy" if recorded was in a short, sometimes poignant obituary: "Mona Hervey is dead . . . . She has been a woman of the town for the past eight or ten years and as an accompaniment for such a life she became addicted to the use of liquor to such an extent that physically she was a complete wreck and life had almost become a burden to her. Nothing is known of her antecedents beyond the fact that she was an English woman by birth. She will be given a decent burial and all will bear in mind that at one time she was her mother's darling, but in later years she was led astray and her death ends a life of shame." [R.B.]

PROTECTION ISLAND

"We gathered some gooseberries and roses," recorded George Vancouver during his springtime 1792 journey to the manta-ray-shaped island at the head of DIS-COVERY BAY. He named the island Protection because it protected the bay from northwest winds and could protect the bay's future settlers "against all attacks of an enemy when properly fortified." Struck as he was with its propitious placement, it was the island's splendid scenery upon which he waxed most eloquently: "a landscape as enchantingly beautiful as the most elegantly finished pleasure grounds of Europe."

Protection Island may not always have been surrounded by water. In some age long past, it might have been a part of the mainland; mastodon bones and teeth have been revealed in the strata of the two-hundred-foot cliffs on the west side of the island, slowly exposed after time and tide have worn away the shelter of ancient soil.

On their journeys through the Strait of Juan de Fuca, Indians used the island as a way station, perhaps browsing on wild cherries, salal berries, or currants, which flourished on the nearly four-hundred-acre island. But the Indians wisely recognized that the seemingly ceaseless winds pummeling the island and a lack of potable water rendered it inhospitable for permanent habitation. Mostly free of dense timber and therefore promising to the eyes of an inexperienced farmer, Protection Island was not immune to the settlement fever that was epidemic in the area after the middle of the nineteenth century. Some whites tried to put down roots there in 1857, but their fervent conviction in manifest destiny wavered in the face of threatened raids by hostile northern Indians; the neophyte pioneers abandoned their claims for the relative security of the nearby mainland shore.

Parceled out by the government, the island was consolidated under the ownership of Captain Henry E. Morgan in the mid-1860s. He never lived there. He sold it to John Power, Sr., whose wife, Mary, and children moved to the empty island in 1875. Mr. Power was working in Port Townsend, and so his daily commute was a twenty-mile pull by rowboat – ten miles each way – often in heavy seas and, because of the shifting direction of the prevailing winds, with a head wind each way. The eccentric Mrs. Power and her children eked out an existence for more than ten years, storing rainwater in cisterns or hauling water from the mainland, while slaking their livestock's thirst on brackish marshwater. The rigors of island living took their toll on Mrs. Power, who after thirteen years retired to the mainland, announced she was not long for this world, took to her bed, and stayed there until she died, fifty-two years later. Power sold the island in 1887.

Under the new owners, a few tenants struggled with the elements and the soil. The Portland Gun Club cultivated pheasants, which thrived with no predators save for gun club members. Once Prohibition began, smugglers in swift, darkened cutters would put in to hide on the island and trade some of their booty for pheasants. If the tenants refused the offer of liquor, the hootch-carriers helped themselves to dinner anyway. Although residents recorded that the bootleggers behaved as "perfect gentlemen," the islanders were always relieved when the sleek sailcraft slipped away.

From 1937 to 1943, Arthur Einarsen, a wildlife management biologist, conducted studies of the island's ring-necked pheasant population and in 1940 urged the government to acquire the island as a permanent wildlife sanctuary. With a different end in mind, the government did take over the island in the early 1940s; living up to its name, Protection became a part of the HARBOR DEFENSE SYSTEM, property of the U.S. Navy. In August 1946, a fire ignited by a careless camper burned in thirty-two hours virtually all of the uninhabited island. Developers bought the property for twenty thousand dollars in 1953, intending to carve out a hunters' and sportsmen's paradise. Eventually the island was parceled out into eight hundred lots among five hundred owners; major development was continually thwarted by lack of water.

The island's final chapter may have been written by two inspired women, Zella Schultz and Eleanor Stopps. Until her death in 1974, artist Schultz had spent twenty-five years banding and studying the island's glaucous-winged gulls – the largest population of the birds in the state – for the U.S. Fish and Wildlife Service. Upon her death, her friend Stopps initiated a process that after years of struggle resulted in the declaration of the island as a permanent wildlife sanctuary. Seventy-five percent of the birds that breed and nest in the inland waters of the strait and Puget Sound do so on Protection Island. The island's last residents will be allowed to live out their lives there, but no new development or settlement will be permitted. The island is off-limits to picnickers and boaters. Eventually only caretakers and an occasional scientist will share the land with its feathered natives and families of harbor seal. So this island that Captain Vancouver envisioned protecting people and that white men have been trying to subdue for more than a century is to be returned to solitude and the comings and goings of its tufted puffins, pigeon guillmots, pelagic cormorants, rhinoceros auklets, nighthawks, owls, bald eagles, and black oystercatchers.   [R.B.]

PUBLISHERS   Port Townsend boasts at least one book publisher for every 850 citizens. The ratio would be even lower if the smallest of the presses – those that publish only occasional titles – were counted. In 1984 when the National Endowment for the Arts announced its monetary awards to noncommercial literary presses, only New York City had more recipients than Port Townsend. In the minds of many people in the literary world, Port Townsend has become synonymous with quality publishing. Copper Canyon is the oldest of Port Townsend's literary presses, with a backlist of more than one hundred volumes of poetry. Dragon Gate Press and Graywolf Press developed their reputations in Port Townsend and have since split off editorial functions to larger cities, where fund-raising is easier. (Graywolf's Scott Walker was chosen for *Esquire* magazine's 1985 register of "men and women under forty who are changing the nation.") Empty Bowl Press focuses on political, social, and environmental issues (see *Cooperatives*). Lockhart Press dedicates its efforts to dream-related work (see *Jungians*). The Port Townsend Publishing Company offers books on local history. Bay Press publishes critical essays and books about the Northwest.

PUGET SOUND   Named by GEORGE VANCOUVER in 1792 for his officer Peter Puget, who was the first European to explore the area, Puget Sound was located south of the Tacoma Narrows on original charts. Subsequent usage has expanded its boundaries to include all the water south of Admiralty Inlet and Whidbey Island. Geologically, the Puget Sound lowland was formed by the weight of glaciers that covered the entire region as recently as twelve thousand years ago and was then further sculpted by the carving advances and retreats of ice floes. During high tide on the sound, the water's surface covers 1,016 square miles; at low tide, 899 square miles. The major transportation route for INDIANS until the advent of the highway system of the 1930s, the waters of Puget Sound were known to them as "Wuldge".

PYSHT   Named after a river in the WEST END of Clallam County where a community of homesteaders began settling in the late 1870s, the town of Pysht included a store, a hotel, and a post office. Now there is only a

tree farm. The name derives from the CHINOOK JAR-
GON meaning "fish."

A village of the QUINAULT Indians.

Like most Pacific Northwest small towns with a century or more of accumulated history, Quilcene once
had great dreams of success. Hampden Cottle arrived
from Maine in 1860 and settled near the mouth of
Quilcene Bay. Others followed, and logging became
the driving force of the economy. During the transcontinental RAILROAD craze of the 1880s and 1890s,
Quilcene became the first major stop on the Port
Townsend Southern Railroad's route to the Union
Pacific rail line in Portland. Said the *Quilcene Queen*:
" ... our fine harbor will be lined with oceangoing
ships carrying the products of factories that will be
established here . . . ." But Quilcene was not just the
first major stop, it was also the final stop because the
railroad never extended beyond that point. During the
first decade of the twentieth century, Quilcene turned
to Klondikean dreams with the development of the
Tubal Cain Copper and Manganese Mining Company
on nearby Iron Mountain. But inaccessibility (one
route required fifty-seven crossings of the same river),
harsh weather, and, fatally, the lack of a major payload
brought the effort to a halt around 1920.

Today, Quilcene's economic base includes a ranger
station for the Olympic National Forest, a fish hatchery, some logging, and brush picking, which provides
salal, ferns, and huckleberry greens for florist shops.
Quilcene is probably best known, however, for its
oysters which are appreciated internationally. The
most noted grower is Canterbury Oyster Farm, which
carries on the tradition established by Ray Canterbury
in 1934 when he planted Japanese oyster seed, the first
species to be successfully introduced to the shallow,
cool waters of Quilcene Bay. (See *Aquaculture*.)

The Quilcene Indians were located at Quilcene Bay
and were known also as the Kilsid, or Kol-ceed-o-
bish (their pronunciation). They were a band of the
TWANA Indians that occupied the shorelines of HOOD
CANAL. Through wars and intermarriages, the tribe
lost its identity and little is known of its history. In the
1870s, Myron Eels recorded some oral history of young

tribe members who told of conflicts and wars with neighboring tribes. Popular oral history in the early twentieth century suggested that the Quilcene population was dealt a severe blow by raiding QUINAULT. As the story goes, the Quinault were invited to a Quilcene potlatch, lost many goods through gambling, and returned later in revenge to kill many of the Quilcene.

QUILEUTE INDIANS   Located in and near the coastal resort town of LA PUSH, the Quileute Indians in the 1980s number about 350. Although geographically sandwiched between the Salish people (the QUINAULT) to the south and the Nootkan groups (OZETTE and MAKAH) to the north, the only tribes known to be close to them linguistically were the Hoh on the HOH RIVER and the CHIMAKUM across the peninsula near Port Townsend. Together they constituted the Chimakuan linguistic stock. The origin-legend that the Quileute share with the Chimakum concerns a great flood: The people got into their large ocean canoes and tied them together so that they would not separate, but when the waters subsided, some drifted toward Chimakum while the others came down the river to La Push. These were the Quileute.

The depth of shell deposits at La Push suggests that the Quileute may have been living in the area for a long time. Evidence from place names suggests that the entire northern Olympic Peninsula may once have been controlled by people related to the Quileute, giving rise to speculation that theirs was a small empire spoiled by the arrival of the Makah and Klallam, who forced or wiped them out. Accounts of their first contact with white people indicate that the early Quileute on the Hoh River were not receptive to outsiders. Landing parties from both the Spanish in 1775 and the British in 1778 were massacred. (See *Destruction Island*). In the mid nineteenth century the Quileute resisted being moved to a reservation outside their own territory and in 1889 were given their own reservation at La Push.

Culturally, the Quileute share many characteristics of the northern tribes, which extend as far as the Alaskan panhandle. They were skilled artisans, excelling in the engineering masterworks of the dugout canoe as well as CEDAR-bark clothing and watertight baskets. Throughout their history the Quileute have been seafarers. They continue to fish for a living, their rivers being rich with steelhead, salmon, and smelt. Although they no longer are the great whale and seal hunters they once were, the stories and myths of those days are still preserved by a few of their elders. They have not forgotten the days when the Quileute were regarded as the best sealers on the coast.

In late spring 1974, quilt fever came to Port Townsend by way of Orcas Island. The carrier was an Orcas artist who mentioned to Donna Daubenberger that the islanders had raised a fair amount of money for their library fund by making and raffling a quilt depicting their old homes. Daubenberger, who had restored one of the city's more interesting Victorian residences, the FRANK HASTINGS HOUSE, saw the possibilities, and in six weeks Port Townsend had a quilt, the first of a series that came to be called Heritage Quilts. By the end of the year, the first quilt had raised more than twenty-seven hundred dollars for the Port Townsend High School Scholarship Foundation, and three more quilts were under way. Enthusiasm was briefly dampened when the first quilt was not won by a local resident, but a local couple purchased the quilt from the winner and donated it to the Jefferson County Historical Society Museum, where it has safely rested ever since. The second quilt was completed as a benefit for TREES FOR PORT TOWNSEND. In 1975 and 1976, President Gerald Ford posed with two quilts and project volunteers in Seattle. All in all, thirteen quilts were such successful fund-raisers (one year raffle tickets brought in seventy-five hundred dollars) that various groups in the area took up the idea, and soon the novelty was gone. Quilting, however, has become a major craft in the area. **QUILTS**

Sent to secure Spanish holdings in the Pacific Northwest in 1790, Manuel Quimper became the first European to explore the length of the STRAIT OF JUAN DE FUCA. In the process he named much local geography, including the Haro Strait (Canal de Haro). His voyage took him as far east as DISCOVERY BAY, which borders the peninsula that now bears his name. **QUIMPER, MANUEL**

A thumb of land between Discovery Bay and Admiralty Inlet on which Port Townsend is sited, Quimper **QUIMPER PENINSULA**

Peninsula is one of the few Spanish names to survive English cartography. The peninsula honors explorer MANUEL QUIMPER, who visited the western shores of the peninsula in 1790, two full years before GEORGE VANCOUVER, who renamed most of the earlier Spanish sightings. Ironically, the name Quimper Peninsula was reaffirmed in 1846 by the British explorer Henry Kellett, who disregarded an earlier American attempt to rename it for a U.S. secretary of the navy.

QUINAULT INDIANS   In 1805, explorers Lewis and Clark estimated a census of about eight hundred Quinault Indians. In a 1939 census of the Quinault Reservation, that number had increased to twelve hundred, after having been as low as ninety-five in 1888, due probably to a smallpox epidemic. The Quinaults are still located on their homeland, south of the QUILEUTE Reservation at LA PUSH. Community villages are located at Queets at the mouth of the Queets River and at Tahola at the mouth of the Quinault. Lake Quinault is a popular resort area, and the tribe retains jurisdiction over it. In an effort to protect the environment, the Quinault tribe has made its ocean beaches on the reservation off-limits to non-Native Americans. Historically, the Quinaults are of the Salish stock, and early historians recorded them as prosperous and comparatively peaceful. Still, an early attack on Spanish explorers may have been by Quinaults or by their neighbors, the Hoh. (See *Destruction Island*.)

RAILROAD   When the golden spike that symbolized the uniting of the country by rail was driven into the ground in 1869, it struck a nerve in Port Townsend, and the city began scheming to realize a bit of railroad gold herself. Port Townsend was considered a likely terminus because of her fortuitous location and deep-water port and, not incidentally, because of the fine job her boosters had done spreading this information throughout the railroad community. When Northern Pacific wanted to extend a line northward from Portland–Seattle, Tacoma, and Port Townsend vied for the honor. JAMES G. SWAN, a Northern Pacific agent, set out to procure signatures (and promises of financial support) for a proposal to build the extension to Port Townsend. The scent of railroad in the air, however distant, set local and out-of-town real estate hounds into a buying frenzy that precipitated an intense flurry of speculation. Tacoma was awarded the terminus in 1873, and Port Townsend retreated, licking her wounds. A brief depression hit the town as prices plummeted and people abandoned the KEY CITY.

In 1887 a cluster of diligent developers incorporated as Port Townsend Southern Railroad to build a line south along Hood Canal to Olympia in the hope that a railroad company would snatch up the track as its northern extension. Nothing happened for two years; then in 1889 a wave of speculation spawned by ever-present dreams and rumor hit Port Townsend. Local residents had convinced themselves (and some outside investors) that Port Townsend was the preeminent city of the inland waters and that it was certain to have a railroad terminus in a matter of months. The boom had begun. Although no railroad stepped forward to develop the right-of-way Port Townsend Southern had acquired, the speculation boom made it easier for the corporation to raise money, so it took bids for construction of six miles of track. After one mile was built, funds were depleted and work stopped.

Also in 1889, the transcontinental Union Pacific had purchased the Oregon Railroad and Navigation Company lines and announced Port Townsend would be its northwest terminus. The *Leader* said: "This day means a great deal more to us than we are aware of at present. It means that Port Townsend will be made the shipping point and supply station of a vast fleet that will bring to it the commerce of ... the world .... Port Townsend will now get its share of the wealth and commerce of Europe that annually finds its way hither and has heretofore passed us by. It means the development of our latent resources and the advancement of our people." Within weeks, Port Townsend Southern officials negotiated to transfer its franchise and considerable real-estate holdings plus an additional $100,000 to a Union Pacific subsidiary, the Oregon Improvement Company.

Virtually the whole town turned out for the ground-breaking on October 2, 1889, on the Briggs's farm, two miles west of town. The speaker that day, The Reverend D. T. Carnahan, said the project had been started in such a way "that there would be no such word as fail." He drew parallels with Napoleon: "... When he was starting on his great campaign one of his lieutenants called attention to what had apparently escaped the mind of Bonaparte, that the insurmountable Alps were between him and the country he wished to go to. 'Sir,' said Napoleon Bonaparte, 'there shall be no Alps!'" On Valentine's Day, 1890, the Oregon Improvement Company promised to have twenty-five miles of road built, equipped, and running by September 1. The estimated cost of the first twenty miles was $550,000. The *Leader* rejoiced: "Within two years it is a conservative estimate that Port Townsend will have a population of twenty thousand people. The Key City is the center of the commercial kingdom of the northwest."

The stock of the Port Townsend Southern was transferred to the Oregon Improvement Company on the ides of March; the contract for the track from Port Townsend was awarded on April Fools' Day. Sixty thousand ties had been delivered. Newspapers advertised openings for one thousand two-dollar-a-day laborers. A steamer from upsound brought eighty horses. Tools accumulated in the eighteen construction camps. Sixty tons of provisions packed the stores and warehouses in town. By June two thousand men and six hundred horses were working on the railroad. On June 4, grading on the first ten-mile stretch was complete, and work on the second stretch began. On June 17, two hundred tons of steel rail arrived.

During the summer, part of the KAH TAI Lagoon was filled, and work began on a depot, roundhouse, and yards. When completed in August, the *Leader* reported: "The terminal grounds of the Port Townsend Southern Railroad consists of depot, supply offices, roundhouse, warehouse, and turntable. The depot is of the Queen Anne and Eastlake designs, and presents an exceedingly pretty appearance. The building is 52 by 26 feet, two stories.... The interior of the building is finished in hard finish and cedar, with gas and electrical appliances. Taken in all, it is one of the finest finished depots in Washington."

By September 12, trains ran daily between Port Townsend and Lake Leland. On that day, the *Leader* reported on the excursion. "At a few minutes past 3 o'clock ... a train load of smiling, happy-faced Port Townsendites were whirled rapidly over twenty miles of as smooth a track as one could wish.... The run to Lake Hooker [LELAND] was made in a short time, when the entire party left the train and crossed over to the farm of Mr. Nicols where the party regaled themselves with pure water, milk . . . . About 5:30 P.M. the train started for home, and the run to this city was made in 55 minutes."

But construction had slowed. Throughout the Northwest, the blush was off the rose. There simply was not enough railroad money to go around. Port Townsend was flooded with depressing railroad rumors. The once blooming economy was fading. It appeared that Oregon Improvement Company officials were more intent upon real-estate speculation than in building railroads. Union Pacific, too, suffered losses and lost the confidence of its supporters. But the city desperately grasped at its dreams. The *Leader*'s editor wrote in September 1890: "When I look on the maps the surroundings of Port Townsend look very much like Manhattan Island, and I cannot help comparing the Port Townsend of the future with New York of today . . . We have every confidence that what has been so successfully commenced will be as successfully carried forward to completion."

Eight months later the *Leader*'s cheer squad shouted the familiar refrain yet again, "It is inevitable that the Union Pacific must and will come here and it is no good to contend with the inevitable, Port Townsend forever, 'rah." The chamber of commerce picked up the refrain and in a settlers' information pamphlet of the time announced: "During the present year it is expected the Port Townsend Southern railroad will be completed . . . . it cannot be doubted that Port Townsend . . . must eventually become the great wheat-shipping depot of the Puget Sound country."

In December 1897, when Great Northern and the Northern Pacific Railroads established ticket agencies in Port Townsend, it was assumed by many that the next inevitable step would be completion of the Portland–Port Townsend connection. Indeed, with every year came new hopes and rumors. In 1901 a line from Portland to a northern terminus was rumored yet again when Union Pacific announced a petition for condemnation of lands along the old right-of-way for the Oregon Improvement Company. Although Union Pacific declined to identify the northern terminus, Port Townsend boosters asserted, "Evidence is fast accumulating which tends to show that the Union

Pacific is determined to reach the largest and best harbor on the coast, which of course, means Port Townsend Bay.''

Putting a happy end to some rumors, Northern Pacific acquired the Port Townsend Southern but undertook no further development. In February 1904, the railroad announced it would "make general repairs along the line of the Port Townsend Southern during the coming summer, but the plan of uniting the two branches of the road will not be carried out this year.'' But by November 1904, the *Leader* was grasping at straws. "The Railroad Coming Next Year Sure" it declared (though the strength of the declaration was somewhat modified by the fact that it appeared on page seven). In 1907 the city was still willing, desperate even, to believe any good railroad news. "The *Leader* is in a position to announce on the authority of a well-known former resident who received his information direct from high railroad officials in Tacoma recently . . .''

Although the longed-for union with Portland was never consummated, trains continued to run the track to Quilcene. But nobody was able to make the railroad pay. In a brisk succession of owners and lessees during the opening decades of the twentieth century, the short line moved a bit of freight and furnished excursions along the twenty-five-mile track. For a while, a regular gas-powered bus especially equipped with train wheels ferried sightseers to Quilcene. The line became somewhat more profitable in the 1920s when Milwaukee Railroad bought a spur connecting Port Angeles with the Port Townsend Southern at Discovery Bay. For a few years, before the automobile became king of the road, travelers to Port Angeles regularly "rode the cars.'' The twelve-mile stretch to Discovery Bay became the primary route of the Port Townsend Southern, although the Quilcene portion was used as a logging railroad until 1951, when it was torn up and its rails sold. The line, operated exclusively as a freight line, serviced mills and small industry on the north Olympic Peninsula, shipping from its Port Townsend spur onto barges bound for Seattle and other ports.

Milwaukee lost its rail subsidy in 1976 and just before Christmas in 1977 filed for aid under the federal bankruptcy act. In December 1978 Milwaukee gave notice of its intention to abandon the line. If Milwaukee was to stay afloat as a national railroad, it had to cut loose its money-losing routes, and its northern Olympic route was a big loser. Although the courts forced Milwaukee to maintain the route, its service declined considerably, sometimes necessitating shutdowns for safety reasons. Though more costly than rail service, the twelve shippers on the fifty-eight-mile line trucked their goods when Milwaukee could not or would not run.

An alliance of manufacturers, port commissioners, county planners, and countless state and federal bureaucrats campaigned for renewal of adequate rail service. Seattle and North Coast Railroad won a lease from Milwaukee and began operation in the spring of 1980. Shippers said service "improved 110%" when the new operator took over. They had "all new equipment, plenty of cars, and no delays," all of which was a big change from the previous years with Milwaukee. Seattle and North Coast invested $250,000 on the most basic repairs, just to lift the Federal Railroad Administration's safety restrictions. And then the local economy bottomed out. North Coast ran a twenty-five-car train over the line twice weekly. The two hundred cars it had leased sat idle. Seattle and North Coast was losing money. And its customers desperately wanted it to stay. The shippers feared they would price themselves out of the market if they had to switch to trucking their goods. By summer 1981, Seattle and North Coast was shipping eighty cars per week from the peninsula, but had to put another $150,000 into repairs. It could never seem to get its head above water. In June 1984, it filed for reorganization under chapter 11 of the bankruptcy laws. Trains stopped running. The following month it defaulted on its lease-purchase agreement with Milwaukee.

The little railroad line, which is reputed to have changed hands more often than any other in the nation, was orphaned. Various authorities have considered resurrection of the line, but, as before, nothing definitive has been offered. It is interesting to follow the one-hundred year-old path, trying to visualize the thousands of men who at one time or another pickaxed and pounded, cut and graded, sweated and wallowed knee-deep in mud to lay the tracks now rotting, undercut by winter rains and choked by summer weeds.

[R.B.]

RAIN Rain is legendary on the Olympic Peninsula. Moisture collecting over the Pacific Ocean condenses into clouds that collide with the OLYMPIC MOUNTAINS and dump some of the heaviest rainfall recorded on earth. Rainfall at the mouth of the HOH RIVER averages 90 inches per year. At the junction of Hoh Road and Highway 101, it increases to 100 inches. Nineteen miles east at the Hoh Ranger Station at the RAIN FOREST, the annual count is up to 142 inches, and on the upper Hoh on Mount Olympus, it reaches 200 inches – all within the span of less than fifty miles. Spent, the clouds lift, and within another forty miles at Sequim and Port Townsend, the rainfall is only sixteen to eighteen inches per year, making the area the driest coast north of southern California. The MAKAH INDIANS believed that the heavy rains from the southern reaches of the vast sea had other origins. JAMES G. SWAN recounts the story of Kwartseedie, the south wind that is prevalent in winter. "Once upon a time the Mouse, the Flounder, the Cuttlefish, the Skate, with several other fishes and some land animals, resolved to visit Kwartseedie and see how he lived. After a journey of many days they found him asleep in his house, and thought they would frighten him; so the Cuttlefish got under the bed, the Flounder and Skate lay flat on the floor, and the other visitors disposed themselves as they thought best. The Mouse then jumped on the bed and bit Kwartseedie's nose, which suddenly awakened him; as he stepped out of bed he slipped down by treading on the Flounder and Skate, while the Cuttlefish, twining around his legs held him fast. This so enraged him that he began to blow with such force that the perspiration rolled down from his forehead in drops and formed rain. He finally blew all his tormentors home again; but he never has forgotten the insult, and comes at intervals to annoy his enemies, for the land animals at such times are very uncomfortable, and the fish are driven from their feeding grounds on the shoals by the great breakers, which also often times throw vast numbers of them on the shore to perish."

RAIN FORESTS Canopies of Sitka spruce and western hemlock reaching two hundred feet, understories of big leaf maple and other deciduous trees, and draperies of club moss and ferns – these layers of vegetation have created rain forests in the OLYMPIC MOUNTAINS unique among forest wetlands in the world. Unlike tropical rain forests, the temperate climate of the western Olympic Peninsula river valleys has created forest floors that are essentially free of tangled vines. Despite 140 inches of annual rainfall, the forests are neither dark nor gloomy. Instead, overcast skies offer a reflective shield to diffuse light throughout the stately spruce, hemlock, fir, and CEDAR. Of the three major rain forests, the Hoh River Rain Forest is easily the most spectacular and most accessible.

RAIN SHADOW

A climatological phenomenon created by prevailing winds and the OLYMPIC MOUNTAINS, the rain shadow benefits Sequim and Port Townsend with a significantly lower annual rainfall than the rest of Puget Sound. STORMS generally approach the Washington coast from a southwesterly direction. As the storm air moves upward into the mountains, it cools and condenses into rain and snow. Areas in the WEST END of the peninsula receive between 90 and 200 inches of rain per year. By the time those clouds reach the northeasterly communities of Port Townsend and Sequim, the clouds have become a sponge wrung dry. Annual rainfall in Sequim is 16.8 inches, in Port Townsend, 18.3 inches, while nearby Port Angeles attracts 25 inches and Quilcene is double that at 51 inches. The rain shadow extends its triangular mercy north to the San Juan Islands and east to parts of Whidbey Island.

RAINBOW DECALS

Port Townsend does not have proprietary rights to rainbow decals, but in number they may be third only to dogs and morning glories. The presence of rainbow decals in such abundant numbers even produced controversy, at least in some circles. Some people see the decal as a symbol of a satanic cult or conspiracy, or, at the least, a symbol whose connotations invaded their own spiritual territory.

The most notable biblical reference to the rainbow is, of course, in the story of Noah. When the floods receded and Noah landed the ark on Mount Ararat, the Lord promised He would not send such a flood again, and to prove it, ''I set my bow in the cloud'' (Gen. 9:13). Many children like to draw and color rainbows because doing so gives them a chance to use lots of different colors out of their crayon boxes and because the arches are relatively easy to draw with some accuracy. For them the rainbow becomes an early symbol of personal success and beauty, and most displays of children's art in Port Townsend have a large representation of rainbows.

Some Northwest Indians refer to the rainbow as "spider snare." The reasons for this are not clear, though there is at least one Canadian Indian legend in which a spider lives in the sky. Other Northwest Indians thought the rainbow to be "thunderbird's snare," at the end of which could be found plentiful game. This story may, of course, remind us of the pagan story, common among Christians as well, of the pot of gold at the end of the rainbow (which was actually another form of the Celts' Holy Grail, a womb symbol related to the pots where Mother Moon [Mana] kept the souls of the dead in her western paradise). Another story in Northwest Indian mythology tells how a rainbow once acted as a magnetic force, pulling all the people in the village up into the sky. The implied moral is that one should never try to touch a rainbow. In another Indian story, a rainbow appeared as a beautiful woman wearing rose branches and dentalia shells. In yet another story, a rainbow gave special powers to an orphan and was equated with God (or Jesus after missionaries had visited the tribe). Other Northwest Indians believed that God put the rainbow in the sky as a line on which people could place their wishes or prayers.

So many stories from so many different traditions converge in so many different ways that one would need a spiritual vision more powerful than a prism to differentiate them. Even the advertising departments of companies manufacturing the decals are attuned to the symbolic energy. The back of one package of decals reads: "A bridge for our aspirations to travel on, to journey on, thru light and color to a place beyond." Another reads: "Ancient sign of harmony and good fortune to all peoples of the earth, they lift our hearts with wonder and awe." [J.H.]

RED TIDE The common name for the marine infestation causing paralytic shellfish poisoning, red tide is a potentially fatal condition that occurs when shellfish consume certain types of plankton. The ingested plankton, usually dinoflagellates, (*Gonyaulax catenalla*), produces a neural toxin one thousand times more lethal than sodium cyanide. While the waters around the infected tidelands often show a red hue, uncolored waters cannot be taken as a sign that shellfish are safe to eat. Toxins remain in some shellfish for several months after infection.

In the 1890s when Port Townsend's building boom was derailed by the failure of the Oregon Improvement Company (see *Railroad*) and the national depression of 1893 stopped even thoughts of continued expansion, the town nonetheless looked prosperous. Hundreds of residences on the bluff and virtually every brick commercial building on WATER STREET had been built in the previous five years.

But when national recovery skipped Port Townsend, arriving in Seattle and Tacoma instead, deterioration began to set in. The once proud and hopeful community began to look weathered as paint faded and peeled and rust grew like red mold on sheet-metal cornices downtown. Spindle work and brackets began to loosen and fall. Few building owners had the money for maintenance, others seemed not to care. Fashions changed. The craftsman or bungalow look, with its pared-down, simpler manifestations, prevailed. But few were built in Port Townsend; money was no more available for new construction than it was for repair of old. Folks made do. Some took in boarders, others converted once-grand mansions into apartments.

By 1928 when the MILL opened, a new spirit had taken over the community. Port Townsend was no longer the home of nineteenth-century capitalists in search of grandeur; it had become a working man's town with sensible men and women wanting to establish secure lives and homes, a place to raise children without fear of want. The outsized Victorian dwellings were unwelcome symbols of an earlier generation's desire, and they were drafty and hard to heat. Homeowners began to remodel: Ceilings were lowered, and linoleum was placed over fir floorboards that had begun to separate; brackets were removed, window surrounds stripped and simplified; double hung windows were replaced by single panes; and porches were removed, or enclosed, or torn off and begun again in a new style. In the early 1950s, clapboard siding had so weathered and shrunk with age and neglect that

223

asbestos siding was sold as the best method for "tightening" a house. Probably one-fourth of Port Townsend's homeowners agreed, and they obligingly covered the original siding, tearing off even more gingerbread and trim in the process.

The return to an appreciation of the Victorian styles began in 1958 when the BARTLETT HOUSE was purchased by Harry and Mary Johnson, a Tacoma dentist and his artistic wife. The Johnsons, serving as a model, encouraged and exhorted others to follow their lead (see *Architecture*). Some did, most of them out-of-towners whose appreciation for Victorian high style had not been mellowed by broken dreams or practical considerations. During the early 1970s, when all of Puget Sound was suffering under the Boeing Company's great depression, real estate prices were so low as to be considered "a steal" by Californians and others seeking the good life away from urban centers. Restoration became fashionable. Ceilings were returned to original heights, decorative molding was refashioned, foundations were restructured, roofs reshingled, and asbestos siding torn off with grim satisfaction.

Though one who was not involved could easily marvel at the transformation, restoration was no easy sleight of hand. To restore, one became acquainted with DRY ROT and powder-post beetles (see *Pests, Structural*) and with plaster dust everywhere, no matter how many layers of wet sheets were hung over doors. The houses had settled after eighty years, making the floors so uneven that it became possible to locate any mislaid round object by looking only in corners. Walls were no longer plumb, making the fitting of plasterboard and, worse, wallpaper, a tricky and curse-producing maneuver. The houses may have been cheap, but restoration was not. Before plastic decorative molding was generally available, one early restorationist had special steel knives cut in Kansas City so that the cornices of his living and dining rooms could be reproduced in redwood at a local mill; there were no craftsmen who could reproduce it in the original plaster.

Some would-be restorationists, those holders of a timid dream, quit their partial efforts in full disgust and sold to others who were certain they could make it to the end. For most, restoration is a onetime event, something one is glad to have experienced, the joy not in the doing but in the having done. Still, others thrive and take on one house after another, finding pursuit more thrilling than attainment. For Joe Calabrese, a restorationist who has devoted his life to the cause, purchasing another house is based solely on whether or not "I can restore it faster than the powder-post beetles can eat it."   [P.S.]

From the outset, Port Townsend's populace has been mercurial in its choices of occupations, and these changing roles have been reflected in the local retail community. Original settlers were pioneers, adventurous souls who made their way to the QUIMPER PENINSULA in canoes and schooners, across hundreds of miles of open ocean or endless prairie and who gave little thought to material or creature comforts. They lived for years in their new town without a dependable source of retail goods, relying instead on their own labor and invention, on the bounty and generosity of passing ships' captains, and on an occasional trip to supply depots in Portland, or in Victoria, British Columbia.

Seven years after the settling of Port Townsend, D.C.H. Rothschild opened the town's first general mercantile business, The Kentucky Store. Shortly thereafter, Solomon Katz and Sigmund Waterman opened a similar store, which as a ship chandlery also carried supplies for the fleet of vessels that anchored in Port Townsend's harbor. Most retail business in the early years was geared to the needs of ships' crews, loggers, and frontier settlers – there were few niceties on display amongst the tools, dried beans, linsey-woolsey, and harness.

By 1880, a regional business directory described Port Townsend as a port of entry with a "healthy trade," listing among the community's retail offerings five general merchandise stores, one grocery, hardware, meat market, bookstore, stove and tinware shop, and by then, one store offering "fancy goods." Port Townsend had grown to 1,500 in 1886, before the speculation boom, and according to the Polk Directory, had four tobacco stands, three general stores, grocers, and outlets offering "Chinese merchandise," two each purveying meat, notions, dry goods, drugs, and hardware, and single storefronts for millinery, secondhand merchandise, bakery goods, boots and shoes,

RETAIL BUSINESS

liquor, jewelry, crockery and glassware, and men's furnishings. There were, in that year, at least seventeen saloons to satisfy other needs.

During the years of the boom, followed suddenly and sadly by the bust, retail outlets came and went with a flurry unknown until recent years. The KLONDIKE GOLD RUSH of 1897 produced another outburst of retail activity, as outfitters opened shops for the duration. The overall retail community during the nineteenth century was geared to transients, for with an average population of less than 1,000, the visiting sailors, loggers, and miscellaneous adventurers provided a constant source of new money.

By the turn of the century, though, after the heyday of speculation, after the passing of the era of tall ships, when roving sailors permanently put down anchor, when boisterous loggers settled into domestic tillers of the soil, the focus of the retail community shifted to its resident audience. The residents' needs had not been met by Port Townsend's shops, so they acquired merchandise from out-of-town sources, either through mail order or on trips to Seattle and to Victoria, British Columbia, or even Portland and San Francisco. So by 1901, local retailers had to struggle to capture a greater share of the resident commerce. This year marked the end of an era in more ways than one, for on February 2, retail businesses were shuttered for two hours for the funeral of Queen Victoria. The modern world had begun.

By 1903, the community had lost almost half the saloons it had sported at its zenith, and its retail inventory had come to include five CHINESE merchants, four grocers, three purveyors each of notions and tobacco, two hardware stores, jewelers, clothing stores, shoe stores, and drugstores, and a single fish market, meat market, furniture store, general mercantile store, dry goods store, second-hand store, and bicycle shop. While business districts today are burgeoning with gift shops, the community was void of such enterprises until October 1913 when Mrs. Calhoun and Mrs. Rene Heath opened Port Townsend's first such store.

After the paper MILL opened in 1928, the community's optimism was reflected in new retail stores, including grocery, appliance, furniture, and clothing outlets. J. C. Penney opened in April 1929, featuring

"Marvelite fixtures which come more nearly than any other light to simulating actual daylight" and a "rest room for women, and comfortable settees for those wishing to spend spare time." When the local forts were occupied, particularly during the wars, the number of business catering to "the boys" increased: laundries, eateries, and purveyors of spirits to name a few. When the forts closed permanently in 1953, some of these businesses, too, shut their doors forever.

The next new development in the retail community occurred in 1966 with the opening of a shopping plaza on WATER STREET, the forerunner of the omnipresent mall that has claimed so much of the nation's retail community. Safeway, which first opened its doors in Port Townsend in 1937, anchored the new plaza. Safeway created a stir in 1977 when it announced its plan to pull out of the downtown business core and construct a new store – four times larger – on undeveloped property near KAH TAI LAGOON PARK. According to a *Leader* article in 1977, a Safeway spokesman tried to forestall objections by saying that the corporation was "aware of the sensitivity to construction and design" and promising that the building would be "designed and landscaped so as to be compatible with the Key City's Victorian architecture." After extended legal battles that engaged the state supreme court, Safeway prevailed.

By the mid-1960s, Port Townsend began to market its Victoriana to lure visitors in much the same way it earlier sought the visiting maritime trade, though the merchandise was decidedly different. And townspeople still journey to larger communities in neighboring counties to shop, attracted by discount merchandise and greater variety, and hometown businesses continue to exhort them to shop locally.

A community celebration in Port Townsend, the Rhododendron (or Rhody) Festival has been held annually since 1935 during the third weekend in May. The usual activities of parades (pet, kids, and grand), coronation ceremonies, carnival, arts and crafts booths, high school musical production, and the like have become routine over the years, and one of the Northwest's best road RUNNING events, the Rhody Run, highlights the celebration. The festival honors the delicate pink bloom of the Washington state flower (*Rhododendron*

RHODODENDRON
FESTIVAL

macrophyllum), which drapes the roadsides on the east side and north end of the Olympic Peninsula from late May to mid-June.

RIPTIDE (*Also called tide rip.*) A phenomenon of currents in collision caused when tidal flows are deflected into each other as water careens off shorelines, riptides are visible as churning surface water that resembles a slow boil. In a rip, waves often appear to be dancing in place, although this can also occur when waves meet such obstacles as rock cliffs or the HOOD CANAL BRIDGE. (See *Lip Lip Point, Point Wilson.*)

RIVERS Along with once-extensive glaciers, rivers have been the dominant force in shaping the OLYMPIC MOUNTAINS. Eighteen rivers are fed by melting snow or rain brought year-round by storms from the Pacific. The river system has created a radial drainage pattern by eroding soft shale and sandstone, leaving basalt from the ancient ocean floor in bold relief. The river systems directly reflect the weather pattern of the peninsula. Seven of the rivers are located on the western side of the Olympics, where as much as two hundred inches of rainfall per year have been recorded. The damp but somewhat drier southern and eastern slopes host four and five rivers, respectively. In the north where the Olympic RAIN SHADOW keeps local residents drier than any Pacific coastal inhabitants north of Los Angeles, only two rivers descend from the Olympics.

All but one of the rivers retain Indian names. On the west, the Quillayute ("river with no head") is the shortest at only six miles, but it carries the combined volume of the Soleduck ("clear, sparkling water"), the Bogachiel (" muddy waters"), and the Calawah (" middle river"), which meet at various junctures to form the Quillayute west of Forks. The HOH ("fast white water" or "snow water") begins its course to the Pacific from the northern and eastern slopes of MOUNT OLYMPUS, snaking west and south to share with the Quinault River ("lake on the river," among other definitions) the distinction of being the longest rivers on the peninsula. Between them lies the Queets, named for its indigenous people, who still reside along its shores. To the south, in Grays Harbor County, the Humptulips ("chilly region"), the Hoquiam ("hungry for wood," referring to driftwood found at its mouth), the Wynoochee ("shifty," for its meandering course), and the Satsop ("on a stream") all are tributaries of the Chehalis River, which drains from the Cascades, the only combination of waters from the two mountain ranges. Generally the shortest descents are on the west side, where the Skokomish, the HAMMA HAMMA, the DUCKABUSH, the DOSEWALLIPS, and the Quilcene rivers supply fresh water to HOOD CANAL. On the northern slope, the DUNGENESS (the only Anglicized name of the eighteen rivers) and the Elwha ("elk") are the only rivers of major import.

ROAD WARRIORS

A group of generally responsible Port Townsend residents spawned from the Australian Mad Max movies about postholocaust barbarians, the Road Warriors first surfaced at the 1983 Kinetic Sculpture Race. The initial small brood included such *noms de théâtre* as Moisthamper and Major Burnout, who designed the Karl Marx/Oscar Levant Road Warrior Special kinetic sculpture that navigated a course consisting of road, bog, sand, and water, cheered on by The Whip, Captain Arnold, and The Lord Hugh Mongous, all clad in black and metal and various kitchen utensils. Floating behind, on a two-ton flatbed truck, was the Max Planck Heavy Metal Rock Band.

Through subsequent appearances at RHODODENDRON FESTIVAL parades, Kinetic Sculpture Races (in 1984 they started and finished but skipped the middle), and out-of-town parades ("I thought Port Townsend was a quiet little place," one announcer complained), their breed increased. Their appearances came to include beautiful young women (the Strumpettes and the Mutettes), dressed in leopard skins and chains, and a drill team of ten- to twelve-year-old girls who marched in vague formation, carrying electric drills and looking somewhat bewildered. Attempting at all times to be bad, the Warriors never quite seemed to pull it off. How frightening, after all, is a face mask made from a food colander? (See *Halloween*.)

ROTHCHILD HOUSE

(*Jefferson and Tyler Streets*) A pristine example of the national folk architectural style, the Rothschild House was built in 1868 overlooking Port Townsend Bay. Its gabled front borrows elements from the Greek revival style – wide bands of trim in the cornices, square doric columns on the porch with oversized, nonfunctional adaptations at the corners of the walls, and a full transom with side panel windows surrounding the front door. David Charles Henry Rothschild (1824 –1886) was born in Bavaria, immigrating in 1843 to Kentucky where he opened a store. He was engaged in merchant and mining activities in San Francisco, China, and the East Indies before moving to Port Townsend in 1858, where he established a mercantile business he named The Kentucky Store. Called "the Baron" by Port Townsend residents, Rothschild is reported to have said he was related to the European banking family enough "to get the name, but not the money." For ten years he and his wife Dorette lived over the store. In 1868 he contracted with A. H. Tucker to build a home on the bluff (see *Architecture*), which remained in the family until 1958, when Rothschild's daughter Emilie died. His surviving son, Eugene, donated the house and grounds to Washington State Parks, which, with strong community support, has since maintained it as a museum. Most of the furnishings belonged to the family. The family business, which evolved from retail to shipping, still exists as the Jones Washington Stevedoring Company, but – like the house – it is no longer held by Rothschilds.

D.C.H. Rothschild House, built in the national folk style

RUNNING

In 1896, the resumption of the Olympic Games focused the eyes of the world on athletics. At the turn of the century, in what must have resembled the recent fitness craze of the 1970s, sedentary Americans turned into athletes. Not to be outdone, Port Townsend erected a velodrome for cycling enthusiasts and then in 1902, on the same site, a running track, used by the high school track team (boys only) as well as by visiting runners, who presented exhibitions for prizes. One such exhibition was the "75–yard fat man's race" during the annual fair of 1905. The winner took home $7.50, but the identity of the first fat man to cross the finish line is lost to history.

Running events were part of the "races and stunts" program on community holidays such as Flag Day and Independence Day, but these were generally just good-natured competitions for the youngsters. Port Townsend's Earl Sturrock gained fame throughout the country as a foot racer. When he retired from the circuit, he returned home, where he occasionally pulled the hose cart for the fire department, being able to grab the heavy cart and run short distances more quickly than it took to hitch the horse and get to the blaze. The community's first big running event was a race to Port Angeles cosponsored by the *Port Angeles Evening News* and the *Leader* in May of 1929. The race was open to any resident, and on race day eleven men and one woman set off from Water Street along the fifty-two-mile course, cheered on by large crowds and festive music. Nine hours and twenty-two minutes later, John Gehrke of Port Angeles crossed the finish line, two toenails lighter and one hundred dollars richer.

The 1976 Olympic Games sparked a national running craze, and Port Townsend followed suit. Bill Burmester, after outstanding showings in national masters' competitions, introduced weekly fun runs in 1977. That year Port Townsend High School student Irene Griffith won the women's division at Trail's End, Oregon, with a time that placed her among the top women in the country. She went on to set several national records. In 1978 Dr. William Scheyer began a column in the *Leader* offering advice and encouragement to joggers and runners. He served as physician for the U.S. women's track and field team in the 1984 Olympics and founded the Port Townsend Marathon Association, which introduced Port Townsend's premier running event, the twelve-kilometer Rhody Run.

Among Port Townsend's running legions, Gary Wall spends each birthday running his age in miles. Starting the annual event at age thirty-four while living in Colorado, ten years later he ran forty-four, out from Port Townsend twenty-two miles and back, with an average pace of seven and a half minutes per mile, for a total time of five and one-half hours.

ST. MARY'S STAR OF THE SEA CATHOLIC CHURCH

(*1335 Blaine Street*) The first church to establish a house of worship in Port Townsend was Roman Catholic. On May 30, 1859 – eight years after the town was founded – a contract was let to build St. Anthony's on Water Street near Point Hudson. In 1880, the church built anew uptown in the residential area. Under the stewardship of Father Regis Maniloux, the church was renamed St. Mary's Star of the Sea. The congregation was not a wealthy one, and when it decided to expand the church, Father Maniloux borrowed from his family in France to finance the construction. After his death in 1919, Father Maniloux's congregation was unable to meet payments, and the Maniloux family repossessed the building and rectory. The congregation found another wood-frame church for worship, which it used until 1958 when it built its present red brick complex near the high school campus.

ST. PAUL'S EPISCOPAL
CHURCH

(*1020 Jefferson Street*) The oldest church in the Olympia Diocese and probably the oldest standing structure in Port Townsend, St. Paul's was built sometime between 1863 and 1865 at a cost of between fifteen hundred and two thousand dollars. The builder was A. Horace Tucker (see *Architecture*), a member of the congregation. The original location, near the present LUCINDA HASTINGS HOUSE, was donated by Loren B. Hastings. The church was moved in 1883 when the Jefferson Street grade was cut to allow easier access from downtown to the residential area on the bluff. Placed on logs and pulled by horses and windlass to its new location, the church suffered structural damage; the bishop's committee had iron tie-rods installed, which are still in place.

The first rector was the Reverend Peter Edward Hylund (1829–1909), born in Ireland and forced by that nation's potato famine to emigrate to New York. Attending a lecture that encouraged clergy to come to Oregon and to Washington Territory, Hylund and his brother heeded the call. Serving in Portland from 1860 to 1865, the Reverend Hylund was then assigned to Olympia, from where he served congregations in Port Townsend and other parts of Puget Sound. Upon seeing the church that the congregation had built, Hylund wrote ''this is a wonderful work for so few people.'' In 1866 he became St. Paul's first rector, but he was still required to serve congregations in PORT LUDLOW, PORT GAMBLE, PORT DISCOVERY, Seabeck, CHIMACUM, Steilacoom, and DUNGENESS.

Though the church was handsome evidence of the congregation's faith, the wherewithal provided Reverend Hylund and his family was scant; unlike Episcopal parishes in other communities, St. Paul's has never been a wealthy congregation. Since its founding, it has always been placed in mission status, which means – among other things – that its expenses are subsidized to some extent by the diocese. In 1962 the Reverend Benjamin T. Spinks – the seventeenth son of a seventeenth son – painted the doors on the Gothic church a bright red "to signify the blood of Christ and the financial condition of the church." (See *Foghorns*.)

(*Gaultheria shallon*) The ubiquitous shrub of the western forest, salal is distinguished by leathery oval leaves that end in a point. An evergreen, it bears fruit in midsummer that resembles the huckleberry. It was much prized by Indians, who dried the berries in cakes for winter use. Ethnologist Erna Gunther reports that the Quileute would pick an entire branch of the berries, dip it in whale oil, then pull it through their teeth to eat the fruit. The Klallam and Quileute chewed the leaves as medicine, and the Makah mixed it with kinnikinnick to smoke.

Among the Indians of Puget Sound, it was a common belief that salmon were people who lived beneath the sea. There were five villages of salmon people beyond the horizon. At certain times each year, the salmon people would change into fish and, led by their chief, would ascend the rivers. If the first salmon caught was not treated with respect, others would not follow.

Traveling under a confusion of aliases, the five species of salmon (*Oncorhynchus*) continue to pass Port Townsend on their way to and from their spawning grounds. The Chinook (king, Quinault, tyee, blackmouth, Sacramento) is the largest and least common of the Pacific salmon. Prized for its size as much as its flavor, one remarkable specimen taken in Alaska weighed in at just over 126 pounds. The average size for a returning Chinook is a more modest 20 pounds. The Chinook spends the first year of its life in fresh water before migrating to the Pacific. After reaching sexual maturity two to seven years later, the adult salmon returns to the parent stream to spawn and die.

Although it is fourth in abundance among Pacific salmon, the coho (silver, hoopid, kisutch, skowitz, white salmon, Pacific salmon, arctic trout) accounts for the majority of fish caught by sports fishermen. Due to its similar features, it is often mistaken for a Chinook. Unlike the Chinook, however, the coho has white gums on the lower jaw. It is also a considerably smaller fish with a life cycle of only two to three years. The coho is a resilient fish that does well in a hatchery environment.

The pink salmon (humpback, humpie, haddo,

Indians frequently used a weir to catch salmon in rivers.

holia) is the most abundant salmon. It is also the smallest and shortest-lived. The pink's fixed two-year life span gives it a regularity unknown among other salmon. Native runs return to Puget Sound on odd numbered years. The pink's spawning behavior is similar to other salmon species. On returning to the parent stream, the ripe female digs a narrow trench called a redd, in a riffle, usually below a pond. Waiting nearby will be several male fish. When the female inserts her anal fin into the redd, the dominant male will swim to her side and quiver, stimulating the release of eggs. The other males will then move in and join the spawn. The female moves immediately upstream and digs another trench, covering the initial trench in the process. The rite is repeated until all the eggs have been laid.

The sockeye (blueback, saweye, silver trout, nerka, sukkegh) differs from the other salmon in that it requires a lake environment for one to two years of its life cycle. Some populations of sockeye, called kokanee, spend their entire life in fresh water. In both its fresh and saltwater existence, the sockeye feeds primarily on plankton and shrimp. Consequently, it is rarely taken as a sports fish. Spawning adults develop a distinctive green head and bright red body.

Similar to the sockeye in appearance, the chum (dog) was an important fish to the area's Indian population. In the north it provided food for sled dogs, hence the title dog salmon. The female chum is known for its aggressive behavior toward other females during spawning. In some instances they will expend so much effort defending their redd that they will die before completing the spawn. Mature chum have spent six months to four years at sea. On return they average nine pounds with a length of twenty-five inches.

SAN FRANCISCO   California's city by the Golden Gate was in the midst of its gold rush boom in 1851 when Port Townsend was settled, and for twenty years it offered the only consistent economic base for Port Townsend and all of Puget Sound. San Francisco's response to the forty-niners was to build to the miners' needs, and even California's redwoods could not supply all the timber required to meet the demand. Trees for piling, for ships' knees, and for squared building timbers were felled and shipped south. San Francisco capital and entrepreneurs POPE AND TALBOT journeyed north to establish a mill at PORT LUDLOW, as did W. J. Adams at Port HADLOCK. Salted salmon from Puget Sound and oysters from Shoalwater Bay were served in San Francisco restaurants.

In 1852 Klallam chief CHET-ZE-MOKA journeyed to San Francisco, where he met JAMES G. SWAN whom he invited to visit Port Townsend. Their friendship lasted until Chet-ze-moka's death in 1888. Chet-ze-moka observed in San Francisco the size and scope of resources available to the white man, who was just beginning to populate the Puget Sound area, and he used this information to discourage violent responses from Indians to claims being made by whites.

Legend would have it that San Francisco and Port Townsend each received a TREE OF HEAVEN as a gift from a Chinese emperor. And from 1928 to 1982, San Francisco was the headquarters for the Crown Zellerbach MILL that anchored Port Townsend's economy for more than half of the twentieth century.

SAN JUAN ISLANDS

A group of islands north of Port Townsend, the San Juans were discovered in 1790 by Lopez Gonzales de Haro who was under the command of Francisco Eliza. Eliza named them Isla y Archipelago de San Juan, and though anglicized, the name survived later English explorations, most of which attempted to rename nearly every Spanish designation. Although a treaty in 1846 between the United States and England established the forty-ninth parallel as the border between Washington State and Canada, confusion remained about the ownership of the San Juans. Both the United States and England claimed them, and each established military camps at opposite ends of San Juan Island in 1859. The dispute continued for years and was settled finally in 1872 when German kaiser Wilhelm I, asked to arbitrate, found in favor of the United States.

SAND DOLLAR

(*Dendraster excentricus*) So named because it is similar in size to the silver dollar, this hard-shelled member of the family Echinodermata and close relative of the sea urchin has developed one of the most curious migratory techniques in the animal kingdom. Covered with hairlike tube feet, the deep purple sand dollar propels itself over the seafloor by moving its velvety spines in waving unison. As it travels, a small mouth on its underside probes the sands for the minute particles of organic matter on which it feeds. When it dies it washes into shallow intertidal areas, where, invariably, it is picked up by a beachcomber who throws it back out to sea. Its two- to three-inch diameter, four-ounce weight, and flat undersides make it irresistible for skipping across placid waters. Even for a neophyte, tosses of fifteen to twenty skips are not uncommon.

SAPPHO

A small WEST END community on Highway 101 (at the junction of Burnt Mountain Road, which leads to CLALLAM BAY), Sappho was established in 1895 by Frank M. Ackerley. It was named by a logger of Greek descent for the ancient Greek poet from the Isle of Lesbos. As to why he chose that name, no one seems to know or is willing to tell.

SAUNDERS HOUSE

(902 *Sims Way, also known as Holly Manor*) Designed by Port Townsend architect Edward Batwell in 1891 for Collector of Customs James C. Saunders, the house is a blend of two styles: Queen Anne and shingle. The Queen Anne features include a steeply pitched hipped roof with gables, a wraparound porch with a pediment roof over the entrance, and a distinct tower with an S-shaped roof. The shingle-style elements include a roof and wall covered by cedar shingles that are uninterrupted at the corners and that curve into a recessed porch and window about the entrance. The dormer with a broken-arch pediment borrows from the Georgian style, not often used in Port Townsend. Though typical of no particular style, the fireplace with a window in the middle of the chimney, just above the mantel, is an unusual feature. What also is unusual is that the exterior of the house has not been altered over the years. The Queen Anne porch remains as open today as when it was built, giving the house a sense of solidity without bulk.

SCOTCH BROOM

Like much of the flora around Puget Sound, Scotch broom (*Cytisus scoparius*) came from someplace else, but now its roots are deep and strong, and as if heeding a heavenly admonition, it is fruitful and multiplies. As its name implies, it is indigenous to Scotland as well as other parts of northern Europe. "Broom" is from the Old English word for "bramble" and is used to identify any one of several related low, spreading shrubs, the branches of which were cut, bound, and used for sweeping. Robert Burns and other bards and romantics have composed odes to the "glory of the broom," while gardeners and farmers are inclined to lose their composure contending with its prodigious peskiness. Where it flourishes on rocky, steep slopes, its roots are trusty hand- and footholds for climbers.

It is a member of the pea family (Fabaceae) and has many small branches of perennial foliage that range from a fresh medium green in spring to a dusty, pallid "canned pea" green in autumn. It may grow to a height of ten feet and thrives along open roadsides, sparse woods, and fields. Small animals seek shelter in its friendly density; deer may carve trails into the haven of the heart of a broom clump. It can be seen in its glory in the months of April, May, and June, arrayed in profuse, bright-yellow "pea flowers"; on some bushes, each blossom is highlighted with a vivid splash of scarlet. An inedible pod is formed, and in late summer, long after the bloom has faded and fallen, the slender green pods turn brown. On hot days, when the peas have ripened, the pods snap open to release the seeds with a sound like raindrops spatting on asphalt.

Scotch broom ranges from northern California to British Columbia, where it was likely introduced to the continent. An excellent place to observe it in Port Townsend is on the southeast half of ARTILLERY HILL at FORT WORDEN. When the fort was constructed at the turn of the century, the native cover was stripped; the eager broom has since sprawled over the hillside so thickly that in spring it seems the sun has scattered bits of itself from the sky, and they settled here, soughing in the breeze. [R.B.]

SCOW BAY

Scow Bay is officially called Kilisut Harbor, an Indian word meaning "protected waters," but the more inelegant name persists. This long stretch of shallow water separating MARROWSTONE and INDIAN ISLANDS was named by Albert Briggs as a memorial to the primitive craft which brought him, floating with the tide, from Tumwater to Port Townsend in 1852. The flat-bottomed boat, thirteen by fifty-two feet with square ends, carried his possessions and thirteen cows to GLEN COVE, where he established his homestead. The bay has also been called Long Harbor. (See *Napoleon's Tomb*.)

SEA GALLEY On January 24, 1935, an advertisement in the *Leader*
announced the opening of the Palms restaurant on
Union Wharf in the location of the old Europe Cafe.
The new "high class house" owned and operated by a
former police chief featured "wines: for those who
want to reduce!" and "beer: for those who don't
care." During World War II, the Palms patriotically
observed meatless Tuesdays. Full-course dinners
"from 11:30 A.M." were sixty-five cents in 1945. On a
typical Sunday, the meal would begin with chicken
noodle soup and bread sticks, followed by chicken fric-
assee with egg noodles or roast leg of pork with
applesauce or grilled pork chops or the standard roast
sirloin of beef with brown gravy. Hot rolls and butter
and a pineapple salad would accompany the meal, and
topping it off would be rice pudding with whipped
cream and coffee. "Workingmen's lunches" could be
had for fifty cents and included "two sandwiches, pie,
and fruit to go." And, boasted the management, "To
make your lunches more interesting we change them
daily."

In the late 1970s, this spot – where city politicos for
years met unofficially in its "smoke-filled rooms,"
– became the first restaurant of the Sea Galley chain.
Known for its zany television commercials that star
singing and dancing human crabs, the Sea Galley's Port
Townsend outlet is the only one of the chain located
on water.

SEALS AND SEA LIONS (family *Phocidae*, family *Otrariidae*) Of the marine
mammals found in Puget Sound, none are more read-
ily observable than seals. It is difficult to spend much
time on the water or around the shorelines without
coming under the quiet scrutiny of the harbor seal
(*Phoca vitulina*). The most common local seal, it is also
the smallest, with a length of only four to six feet and a
weight ranging from 100 to 230 pounds. It is easily
identifiable by its softly rounded head, gray mottled
coat, and large dark eyes. Shy and awkward on land,
the harbor seal becomes curious and graceful upon
entering the water. A fast and powerful swimmer, it
can dive to three hundred feet and remain under water
for more than twenty minutes. In the 1940s the state
population of harbor seals was estimated between six
thousand and ten thousand. At that time it was
believed that salmon runs were being damaged by the

seal, and a bounty was placed on it. From 1947 until the bounty was removed in 1960, some seventeen thousand seals were killed. Recent studies have shown, however, that salmon plays only a minor role in the diet of the harbor seal, which eats mainly Pacific herring, flounder, hake, and sculpin. A 1978 census put the total state population of harbor seals at twenty-six hundred.

The elephant seal (*Mirounga angustirostris*) is an infrequent but notable visitor to Puget Sound. In the late 1800s, it formed the basis of a lucrative, if short-lived, sealing industry. Hunted almost to extinction, it now numbers thirty thousand over its North Pacific range. The largest seal to visit Puget Sound, the adult male may reach sixteen feet in length and weigh over two tons. The seals are generally encountered dozing on the surface by boaters, who mistake them for large deadheads or odd misplaced buoys.

During the winter months, Puget Sound is home to two species of sea lions: the northern, or Steller's (*Eumetopias jubatas*), and the smaller, less common California sea lion (*Zalophus californianus*). Much larger than the harbor seal (the northern sea lion male may weigh 2000 pounds, the female 600 pounds), the sea lion differs from the seal in several respects. Its hind flippers, unlike those of the true seal, can be rotated forward, allowing it to walk on all fours. Also, once in the water, it uses its fore flippers as a motive force and its hind flippers as a rudder. The most striking difference, however, is its voice. On a calm day the cacophony of barking emitted from a sea lion rookery, such as on Protection Island, can be heard for miles. To a knowledgeable boater, a sea lion can be almost as effective as a foghorn as an aid to navigation. [M.W.]

SEA STACKS

Narrow pillars of earth along the Pacific coast and western reaches of the Strait of Juan de Fuca, sea stacks are formed by surf as it works into weak spots on cliffs. Continued wave action creates caves, which erode into arches that are left standing alone. Eventually, the tops of the arches collapse to form sea stacks. Ultimately sea stacks – unless made of rock – are washed away by the same force that created them.

SEATTLE

An early Port Townsend rival for supremacy on Puget Sound, Seattle was founded in late 1852, six months after the KEY CITY. The competition between the two began early, and until 1880 the contest was a fairly even one. Port Townsend was the port of entry for all of Puget Sound, which required that ships stop, register cargo, and perhaps take on supplies and crews there. Seattle, however, was centrally located on the inland waters and was better able to respond to upsound and downsound needs, particularly as steamship schedules became increasingly reliable. By 1880, Seattle had pulled ahead, both in population and in economic diversity.

The choice of Tacoma as the terminus for the Northern Pacific railroad switched commercial attention to those cross-sound cities, but Port Townsend kept trying. In 1889 when the Oregon Improvement Company, a subsidiary of the Union Pacific, agreed to purchase the Port Townsend Southern RAILROAD and to build a track to PORTLAND giving the Key City a transcontinental railroad terminus to match its port of entry, Port Townsend believed it was not only back in the race but also the obvious winner. The elation was good for only thirty miles of track, however, and by the fall of 1890, the Oregon Improvement Company was in receivership.

The rivalry was over, although Port Townsend tried again during the KLONDIKE GOLD RUSH. By the turn of the century, Seattle was so far ahead of Port Townsend that only the *Seattle Post-Intelligencer* and the *Leader* kept the rivalry going with baiting headlines. In 1908, in an argument with a Queen City proposal to the state legislature on tax assessments, a *Leader* headline pronounced: "Seattle Again Showing All-Hog Spirit," and the *Seattle Post-Intelligencer* responded on another issue by referring to Port Townsend as "that little town on the rocks down Sound." By 1911 even the shouting was over. The port of entry, Port Townsend's plum since 1853, was moved to Seattle.

SEAWEED   No discussion of the marine life of Puget Sound would be complete without the salad course, the red, green, and brown algae called seaweed. Exploring the tidelands around Port Townsend, one's first encounter with seaweed is likely to be with bull kelp (*Nereocystis luetkeana*), so named because of its obvious resemblance to a bullwhip. It is a similarity that children throughout history have been quick to exploit. Growing in large beds in the rocky areas beyond the lower tide line, bull kelp will often reach thirty feet in length. With the first winter storms, much of the bed will tear loose, covering the beaches in a tangled mess.

Other than the flogging of children, Indians had many innovative and valuable uses for this aquatic plant. The bulb and long hollow stem were used as a bottle to store oil rendered from CANDLEFISH and as a vessel in which to steam wood for bent-wood fish-hooks. It was also used as a head for dolls. The long tough stalk, or holdfast, which attaches the kelp to the bottom, was dried, tied in lengths, and used as halibut line. The beds themselves were used as natural anchors while fishing and were sometimes selectively pruned to serve as weirs for harpooning fish. On a more basic level, many of the local seaweeds were valued for their culinary qualities: dulse (*Rhodymenia palmata*) and red laver (*Porphyra perforata*), called nori in Japan, were dried and eaten as a condiment or cooked fresh with fish and shellfish. (See *Aquaculture*.)

SEKIU

An Indian word meaning "calm water," Sekiu was so named in 1907 to better distinguish it from neighboring CLALLAM BAY; previously the two towns had been called West Clallam and East Clallam. Sekiu was the first WEST END town founded on an economic base other than timber. In 1870, a Seattle canning company established an outpost to can salmon closer to their source. In recent years, most of the residents of Sekiu have depended on commercial and sports fishing for their livelihood.

SEQUIM

One of three incorporated towns in CLALLAM COUNTY, Sequim (pronounced "Skwim") is thirty-five miles west of Port Townsend on Highway 101. Its name is an Indian word meaning "quiet water." Though its population is only 3,013, its business community serves three times that number. Homesteaded in 1854 by John Bell, a Scotsman, Sequim Prairie – as it came to be known – was unique among peninsula settlements for its lack of trees and underbrush. With a scant seventeen inches of rain per year, the prairie was host to grasshoppers and a type of cactus. As the settlement grew, farms required more water than the skies could provide, so in 1895 irrigation canals were dug to divert water from the DUNGENESS RIVER. Eventually, twenty-five thousand acres came under cultivation, and Sequim thrived as the commercial center. Though it retains a sizable dairy and farming industry, agriculture has become less important to the economy in recent years. Sequim is now better known as a retirement community. During the 1960s, Sequim's low rainfall, its small population and reasonable real-estate prices attracted retirees from around the country. In 1960 the population in the corporate limits was 1,164. By 1970 it had increased 33 percent. By 1980 the population had grown to 3,013, a 159 percent increase in two decades. The median age in Sequim is 60.2 years (the highest in the state, which in 1980 had a median age of 29 years), and 42 percent of its population is over the age of 65. Sequim has been described as "a town made up of old people and their parents."

SHANGHAIING   Max Levy was a merchant. Although ostensibly a clothier, his real commodity was the flesh beneath the fabric. With partner Ed Sims, Levy owned a seamen's boarding house, a place where sailors could stay between voyages, where their needs would be met. They were given a bed, food, and even pocket money for tobacco and liquor. All on the cuff. When the bill came due, as it always did, it was "on the tide." When a ship needed a crew, its master would contact Levy or one of the other "crimps" that worked Port Townsend's waterfront. For a fee of thirty dollars per head, plus up to three months advance on each sailor's wages, Levy would fill the ship's complement with the indebted bodies from his hotel. Those who balked were met by Levy's "runners," specialists whose job it was to render sailors compliant. The ship then sailed out on the next tide. When business was slow, Levy worked the other side of the fence, running crews off ships so that the master would be forced to buy another. He once took three complete crews off the ship *America* before it was able to clear the harbor. Until the practice was banned after the turn of the century, operations like Levy's were routine, an accepted part of life in every major seaport.

What was also routine, but considerably less legitimate, was shanghaiing. When not enough men were available through legal means to fill out a ship's crew,

Levy or his competitors Tom Saunders and Limey Dirk would dispatch their runners to the brothels, called cribs, and bars that bordered the waterfront. The next morning a few hapless farmhands and loggers would probably catch their first view of Cape Flattery's west face. Their victims were carefully picked: Professional sailors were always the first choice, soldiers next, local residents and Indians were almost always avoided. The method might be as subtle as a few free drinks or as vulgar as back-alley sapping.

In recent years, a popular misconception evolved that shanghai victims were carried to the beach and a waiting dory by way of a series of underground passages. The shanghai tunnels, as they were called, were said to have been built expressly for the trade. In reality they were no more than vaulted sidewalks, added to facilitate access to the basements of the downtown buildings. As romantic as the notion is, it seems unlikely that more than incidental use was made of them. Generally, there was no need for such contrivances. The greased palm has always been less capital-intensive than underground construction, and it involves far less organization. By most accounts, shanghaiing usually took place in one of the seventeen saloons or dozen brothels that lined the waterfront. Most of them had direct water access through their back entrances. A few, built on docks, had trapdoors for the disposal of garbage. Through them an unconscious man could easily be lowered to a waiting skiff.

The sailors did not always take the abuse and manipulation lying down. A particularly nasty operation was being run by Limey Dirk at the Pacific Bar on Union Wharf. Dirk was a notorious bully and shanghaier, besides which his food was bad. The Sailors' Union of the Pacific organized a boycott and, when that was not enough, followed it with a campaign of stone throwing. Every night, under cover of darkness, the sailors would gather near the brothels across the street from Limey's and lob rocks through his windows. Each night Dirk would charge outside, a pistol in each hand, shooting at anything that moved. Fortunately, he was a lousy shot and did not hit anyone. After several days of this guerrilla war, one of the stones hit Dirk on the head, knocking him unconscious. The sailors thought they had killed him, but the next day he was back at work. [M.W.]

Two stories are told about the origins of Shine, a small residential community near the west end of the Hood Canal Bridge. One says that original residents wished to name their town Sunshine, but postal officials refused, accepting the diminutive instead. A second story says that the town was first called Squamish, a derivation of Suquamish, a tribe from across Hood Canal. Postmaster Robert A. Slyter had wanted to change the town's name to Cheyenne and submitted this to postal officials, who obliged. Unfortunately, Slyter was not a good speller, and the result was Shine. The community became a favorite with subscribers to the *Leader* in the 1960s when Peggy Stark wrote a column entitled, "Gleanings from Shine." With idiosyncratic syntax, wayward pronouns, and homespun homilies, Mrs. Stark offered her weekly observations of goings-on in Shine and in her home:

"Alvin Stark had a lung removed recently and is trying to put a garden in."

"I rescued a large baby robin with an injured wing and fed it, but very unwillingly by it. I wondered if it was worth bothering with and got food down, but it acted very upset and fearful and the second day it died. That solved the problem."

"I haven't been able to keep up with events or the strength and courage to cope fully with them. But a busy mind is a happier mind, and that is where our happiness is, actually."

"A patrol car with its red lights flashing went 'screaming' by Wednesday evening and stopped a car half up the hill and curiosity made me wonder if he was tending to a violation or just speaking to a fellow worker as the first car seemed to have red lights also. We have many cars that stop in front and along here but they struggle over the steep hill from the ferry and then give out, down here. Flat tires, lack of water, gas or parts, even needing to use our phone and most always charged on the other end, thankfully. Even a patrolman came in one day for water, to help a lady motorist, and another while my mother was here, and I was down to my brother's while he was in a Seattle hospital, picking his vegetables, and the fellow borrowed a bucket and took water and never knocked when he returned the bucket and she fretted, needlessly."

Within fifty miles of Port Townsend there have been at least seventy-five shipwrecks of vessels over fifty tons since 1835. The loss of life from these disasters will never be fully known but certainly it is in excess of two hundred persons. These figures do not reflect the hundreds of tragedies involving smaller vessels: the fishing, sailing, and pleasure craft that have been lost with their crews beneath the waters of Puget Sound.

Perhaps the worst disaster befell the steamer *Clallam*. Less than one year old, the *Clallam* left Port Townsend for Victoria, British Columbia, with more than ninety passengers and crew shortly after noon on Friday, January 8, 1904. A heavy southwest gale was building, but Captain George Roberts, a seasoned veteran of the coastal trade, had made the crossing under similar circumstances many times. At about 2:30, just off Trial Island, and about one-half hour out of Victoria, a seam opened in the ship's hull. The *Clallam* began to settle by the bow. A headlight had been knocked out on a trip some weeks previously, and, although reported to the company, had gone unrepaired. As the rising waters reached the exposed port the situation rapidly deteriorated. Shortly, the *Clallam* had lost all way and was being carried northeast by the wind and current. The crew set a small foresail to give the craft some helm as it ran before the storm.

A company official in Victoria spotted the vessel, but assumed that because no flares had been fired, the problem was minor. The *Clallam* had been having some mechanical difficulties during the previous voyage, and the observer presumed an encore. What he could not know was that the *Clallam*, through company neglect, carried no flares. Nevertheless he sought a tug to lend assistance. Aboard ship the crew worked frantically. Efforts were made to plug the gaps in the hull and to start the pumps, but it was quickly discovered that the pumps not only were inoperative, but also allowed even more water to enter the stricken steamer. In desperation, crew and passengers formed a bucket brigade.

Shortly after 3 P.M. the *Clallam* entered a large riptide. Fed by the storm, huge seas pounded the ship. Captain Roberts, fearing the ship could founder at any moment, ordered the women and children to the lifeboats. The first boat, overloaded with passengers, failed to even clear the ship as a wave shattered it against the side of the hull. Women and children spilled into the heavy seas. The second fared little better; as it pulled away from the *Clallam*, a panicked male passenger leapt screaming from the hurricane deck. The force of his landing overturned the small craft. A woman, dumped from the lifeboat, swept past the hull desperately holding her baby aloft. A crewman attempted to grab the pair, but they slipped through his hands and perished. The last boat made about fifty yards before it too vanished beneath the sea. All the women and children and the crew sent to keep them from harm's way had been lost. The remaining survivors kept bailing, and within a short time the *Clallam* had drifted clear of the rip and imminent danger of sinking.

Finally, the tug *Holyoke* arrived on the scene followed closely by the tug *Sea Lion*. An attempt was made to tow the *Clallam* to Port Townsend. The exhausted survivors were left on board the *Clallam* as the sea conditions made a transfer risky. As the *Clallam* was pulled across Hein Bank, it capsized, and crew and passengers were forced to swim for the tugs. Hawsers were cut, and the two rescue vessels combed the dark sea for survivors. In all fifty-one lives were lost, mostly women and children. Captain Roberts faced charges of manslaughter in Canada but was never prosecuted. A board of inquiry ultimately revoked his papers for a year. The Black Ball Line, of which Captain Roberts was co-owner, received a severe fine. The incident forever altered the inspection and regulation of passenger-carrying vessels on the sound.

The loss of the *Clallam* sent waves of grief through Port Townsend, which had just recovered from the shock of losing the passengers and crew of another well-known vessel the previous year. The *Discovery*, a small packet-steamer owned by L. B. Hastings and intended for inland waters, had been pressed into service on the Inside Passage route to Nome. Crewed by local men, the ship had left Nome in October 1903, with more than forty persons on board. After brief stops in Valdez and Yakutat, it began racing the season back to Puget Sound. It never arrived. For more than a year, rumors and speculation abounded as to the ship's fate; not so much as to what happened as to where and how. Little hope was given for the survival of the occupants through the dismal Alaskan winter. Finally, after many false reports, word was received that a chief of the Littuya Bay tribe had seen the *Discovery* founder and sink during a severe storm ninety-three miles south of Yakutat on the afternoon of November 2, 1903. As expected, there were no survivors, and the *Discovery* became another grim statistic for the waters of the Gulf of Alaska.

Not all local maritime disasters were the result of bad weather. The collision between the *West Heartland* and the *Governor* occurred on a calm night under clear, starlit skies. The *Governor*, built in 1907 and operated by the Pacific Steamship Company, was registered at 5,474 gross tons and was 392 feet long. At one time the Seattle press had proclaimed her and a sister ship, the *President*, the only safe vessels on the coastal routes. In 1913 her triple expansion engines had driven her from San Francisco to Seattle in a record forty-nine hours.

But the *Governor* was not seeking a record as it steamed toward Seattle shortly after midnight, April 1, 1921. It was the end of the coast run from San Pedro, and a few passengers had just disembarked at Victoria. The *Governor's* pilot spotted the glow of the Marrowstone Lighthouse as he rounded Point Wilson. From the entrance to Port Townsend Bay, he could see the range lights of a freighter departing the harbor. It was the *West Heartland*, under charter to the *Governor's* owners, heading out to sea after dropping its pilot. The freighter had the right of way, but to the *Governor's* pilot, there seemed to be ample clearance and no cause for concern. Moments later five staccato blasts from the *West Heartland's* whistle played a terrifying dirge to his judgment. The bow of the *West Heartland* drove deep into the side of the *Governor*, nearly cutting it in half.

From the moment of impact, there was no doubt as to the fate of the stricken liner. The *West Heartland* hull now formed the only impediment that kept the *Governor* from the waters of the sound, and the *Heartland's* captain kept the bow wedged there as long as he reasonably could. Many of the frightened passengers were thus able to climb to safety over the freighter's bow, while others fled via the *Governor's* lifeboats. Despite the efforts of both crews, ten persons died. Some went bravely, others foolishly. The mother of two young girls trapped in their berths by the collision elected to remain with her daughters rather than save herself, while two older women who had refused to appear on deck in their nightgowns drowned for their modesty.

Today, all commercial traffic through the Strait of Juan de Fuca, San Juan Islands, and Puget Sound is controlled by a federal agency. Operating much like an air traffic control center, the movements of every vessel in the system are monitored by radar at a central location in Seattle. In the years since the *Governor's* sinking, advances in technology and marine safety have helped the commercial traffic on Puget Sound to establish an enviable record.   [M.W.]

SHUBRICK   Built in Philadelphia in 1857, the brigantine-rigged *Shubrick* arrived in Puget Sound in 1859. While generally regarded as a revenue cutter, the 140-foot, side-wheel steamer also served as the first lighthouse tender on the Northwest Coast. In 1862, under the auspices of Treasury Agent Victor Smith, its three twelve-pound guns wielded enough authority to relieve Port Townsend of its port-of-entry status. (See *Insurrection.*) The *Shubrick* met its end in 1886 in San Francisco where it was sold as scrap for thirty-two hundred dollars.

SIMS WAY   The main arterial leading into Port Townsend was named for Ed Sims (1875–1945) who arrived on the peninsula in 1890. Bigger than life, Sims was only fifteen when he began his varied career. Like a character out of a Howard Fast novel, he was first a sawyer, then fisherman, seal hunter, gold miner, iron molder, shipbuilder, hotel keeper, canner, financier, globe-trotter, and lawmaker. In his early years, he was convicted of smuggling, a taint that never left him despite his legitimate endeavors. He was the first packer of fish to develop a European market for mild cured salmon. The Canadian-born Sims became the third largest fish canner in the United States, and he pioneered the floating cannery that moved with the catch, a concept still active in Alaska. As a state senator, he was so effective he was nicknamed The Legislature by the press. In 1926 the *Seattle Times* described him as ''big, successful and aggressive, a leader of men, two-fisted, ready at all times for a frolic or a fight, but nearly always battling.'' Sims was a believer in the potential of oil in western Jefferson County and invested much of his fortune in its development. It was one of his rare failures.

248

Two boys had been patching a derelict skiff for days,
picking up remnants of oakum from the boat yard and
stuffing them into the cracks and crevices that lined the
old hull. They were close to a launching but needed
some pitch to top the seams. They searched around
the many piers that dotted Port Townsend's waterfront in the 1920s, hoping to find some roofing tar
among the accumulated debris. At the tide line, near
UNION WHARF, one of them found a large, tightly
sealed can. On prying it open, they discovered a dark
sticky substance that appeared to be just right for the
job. They carried their find to the old boat and built a
fire. Before long they were covering the dinghy with a
hot goo. There was a familiarity to the odor that
drifted down the beach. By time the old sailors had
tracked it to its source, the boys were somewhere
beyond incoherent. They sat in a stupor contemplating
their labor, a worthless rowboat caulked with five
pounds of opium.

October was unusually cold in 1979. The cruising
season was two months gone, and except for commercial traffic, few boats ventured into the twisting channels that separate the San Juan Islands. Of those that
did, one was under special scrutiny. Drug Enforcement Agency (DEA) men had been watching a particular island for a long time. They had expected the boat
and knew why it had come. It was dark when the
agents went ashore. In the ensuing confusion, the boat
managed to slip its moorings and escape, heading
south. It was fast and powerful, a good match for the
Coast Guard cutter that pursued it. They followed by
radar as it cleared Cattle Point and headed across the
Strait of Juan de Fuca. By the time they reached Point
Wilson, it had vanished from their screens.

The morning after the unsuccessful DEA raid, a
Discovery Bay resident reported finding a large plastic
bag full of tightly wrapped plant material. Via citizens
band radio, word spread fast. While the Coast Guard
cutter *Point Bennett* raced around the eastern end of the
strait picking up bale after bale of "Thai stick," the
shore near North Beach was being scoured by interested citizens and local police. A local gillnetter
informed the Coast Guard by radio that he had picked
up several kilos and would deliver them to Seattle. In
all, more than two million dollars worth of marijuana
was recovered, much of it still on the smugglers' boat,

which was found abandoned off Whidbey Island. The helpful fisherman never arrived in Seattle. Twelve days later he put out a distress call. He was found drifting in his boat south of Smith Island. Due to lack of evidence, no charges were filed against him.

When the DEA made its raid in 1979, the boys who had caulked their boat with opium were more than sixty years old, but over the years the game had changed very little. Even the basic commodities remained the same. Smuggling on the Olympic Peninsula began as soon as there was a border to cross. At first it was done with relative impunity. In the early 1850s, the customs district headquarters were located in Olympia, a comfortable spot, but too far away from the action to be an effective deterrent. When the port of entry was moved to Port Townsend, the level of risk increased slightly, but important contraband flowed like water through a sieve.

Until Victor Smith took over customs duty in 1861, smuggling was a truly democratic institution, practiced by each according to want. Smith took the radical approach that even in the territories, laws were to be accorded a certain respect. His first act was to come down hard on the importation without taxation of Canadian whiskey. By increasing the level of difficulty, he also increased the degree of specialization necessary to overcome it. By the end of the Civil War, smuggling was a well-established trade in the Northwest.

With restrictions on CHINESE immigration and the inception of the Chinese Exclusion Acts, an element of grotesque cruelty was added to the scene. Chinese, desperate to get into the country, would sign on with unscrupulous smugglers. Herded on board ships like cattle, they were shackled on deck to an anchor chain. If the ship were approached by a customs boat, the anchor would be cut loose, sending the evidence to the bottom of the strait.

Like other outlaws of the time, a cult of personality surrounded the smugglers. They were both reviled and revered as Robin Hoods. While their deeds were often widely known or at least surmised, lack of sufficient evidence kept most from jail. Those that were apprehended generally received light sentences. The most notorious, men like James Jamieson and Larry Kelly, were a continual topic in Puget Sound newspapers. The blame for every unsolved crime in the region would invariably find its way to their doorstep. A few, like State Legislator Ed Sims, even managed to turn their notoriety to political advantage.

Since the turn of the century, smuggling on Puget Sound has waxed and waned with the fashions of law and society, its profitability increasing in proportion to the measures used to halt it. [M.W.]

Snow comes to Port Townsend only when an arctic front descends from Canada, which may occur up to four times a winter or not at all. A cold front depends upon high-pressure systems that hover above the snow slopes of British Columbia. When a low-pressure system moves in from the Pacific, cold British Columbia air is squeezed into the Puget Sound area. Temperatures from the cold front are usually below freezing, and when they mix with the moisture-laden low pressure system, snow results. Snow stays three to ten days before the rains return. Sustained snowfalls have been recorded in 1880, 1916, and 1968.

Old-timers still speak of the "winter of 1916." It began New Year's Eve, 1915, with the season's first measurable snowfall, enough at least for the eye to notice at the dawn of the New Year. Two days later, snow fell so thick that two passenger steamers went aground, fortunately neither to disastrous result. Four days later, six inches fell in the county; Port Townsend, being surrounded on three sides by water, was spared. Then the Canadian cold front came, first without snow but so cold that water pipes broke and concern was voiced for the town's water supply, which required above-freezing temperatures to keep the reservoir full. Ice skaters, however, had their first opportunity in years to practice their skill.

A week later, warmer temperatures ruined the fun, but the next day a fifty-mile-per-hour gale sent residents scrambling for their hats and other loose possessions. Snow came again, piling ten inches. As shops were closing on February 2, 1916, snow began to fall again and did not let up until 5 P.M. the next day, by which time nearly twenty-one additional inches had been deposited. Everything stopped. Automobiles were abandoned for sleds to haul fuel and supplies, railroad service to Quilcene and Port Angeles stopped cold at Tukey's Landing, all but emergency deliveries were halted, schools were closed, old roofs collapsed,

251

telephone and telegraph lines fell, and communities throughout Puget Sound became isolated from ready information.

After a couple of days of continued cold, temperatures warmed some, and fear of sudden thaws and resulting floods gripped the community. Then, the water supply stopped; not a drop came out of the main. Water-system worker Peter Norby found skis and headed for the reservoir, where he discovered that the main line had been clogged by debris. He freed the system and made the front pages of the *Leader*. Thaws continued, but the flood never materialized. Finally the winter of 1916 subsided, except in the memories of those who witnessed it.

SOUTH POINT The southern extreme of Squamish Bay below HOOD CANAL BRIDGE, South Point is best known as a ferry landing used prior to the construction of the bridge in 1961 and during its three-year closure when the western half sank during winter STORMS in 1979.

SPORTS Between 1893 and 1899, the Port Townsend Athletic Club and the University of Washington football teams met six times. Port Townsend won on three occasions and lost once, and the two teams tied twice. Then Port Townsend wisely retired from the competition. Not much in team sports has happened since, but at least four accomplished sportsmen have emerged from their experiences with Port Townsend area athletics.

When twenty-year-old San Franciscan Billy Lange came to the Key City in the early 1890s to join the semi-professional baseball team the Port Townsend Colts, it took little time for him to be discovered by major league scouts. Within two years he was playing center outfield for the Chicago Colts, and he became the first national hero of the sport. Lauded by sportswriters as "the premier flycatcher of all time," "the first exceptional gift to baseball," and, in later reference, "the Joe DiMaggio of his day," Lange was the National League's top hitter four years out of five between 1893 and 1898. Years later, Connie Mack said of him: "I have seen them all for fifty years and am still watching them. But I have yet to see an outfielder whose all around ability compares with Billy Lange in his prime."

Billy's prime lasted only nine years, which included his two in Port Townsend. Lange, whose six-foot two-inch, 215-pound frame earned him the accolade "the fastest big man who ever played baseball" and his teammates' nickname of "Little Eva," gave it all up to please his bride, who asked him to join her father's San Francisco business. It was a choice he had little difficulty making, but in a 1940s interview with sportswriter John Lardner, he recalled: "I had made up my mind [to retire] and given my promise [to his bride]. And right then – this was 1899 – the Boston club got in touch with me and started propositioning. They offered me $5000 to stay in the game and play with them. I turned it down. The offer went to $7500 and then $9000. They took a deep breath and said 'ten thousand,' and that's where I stopped them. 'Please don't talk like that any more,' I asked them. 'Get thee behind me, Satan. I promised to quit the game, and I'm going to quit it, and a little more of this kind of talk and we'll all go crazy.'" Lange went back to San Francisco as he had promised and developed a lucrative real estate and insurance business.

Chimacum's Tommy Yarr and Port Townsend's Art McLarney excited fans during their high school years and then went on to make their respective hometowns proud by their collegiate exploits. McLarney gave Washington State College its first All-American honor in baseball in 1932, then went on to be named to the All-Pacific Coast basketball team. He later coached at two Seattle high schools and then at the University of Washington, where he was coach of both the baseball and basketball squads, turning in championship teams. In 1981 Washington State University named McLarney to their Cougar Hall of Fame.

Thomas C. Yarr's exploits were more renowned because he was part of the "Fighting Irish" team at Notre Dame in 1930 during Knute Rockne's final year. Part Snohomish Indian and part Irishman, Yarr was called Yahoo by his teammates, including Frank Leahy who later said of him, "He came from a little town in the state of Washington with no reputation, but he fought his way to the top by his willingness to trade a lot of hard effort for success. He rates easily as one of the best centers in Notre Dame history." Yarr played professional football with the Chicago Cardinals for a few seasons, then went into business. He died of a heart attack in 1941 at the age of thirty-seven. In 1982 he was inducted into the American Indian Athletic Hall of Fame in Lawrence, Kansas.

Port Townsend high school graduate Chuck Robinson gained fame as a middleweight boxer of great promise before his untimely death. An all-round high school athlete, Robinson's special talent was in the ring. During his brief career he won 275 bouts, losing only twelve. In 1977, he won the bronze medal in the senior Golden Gloves championship and was invited to join Muhammad Ali's Boxing Club. While traveling with the National Amateur Athletic Union boxing team in 1980, Robinson's plane crashed shortly after takeoff in Warsaw, Poland, killing eighty-seven, including the twenty-two members of the boxing team. At services in Port Townsend, Muhammad Ali spoke to a grief-stricken crowd at the high school gymnasium: "There's a lot of weeping and grieving here and that shows he was a good man . . . . There are many good white fighters. Us [black] brothers rule fighting, but Robinson was a good one, and he would have been a top-notch professional." (See *Running*.)

SPRUCE BEER   Early explorers and sailors had little knowledge of the causes and prevention of scurvy. Often, men died needlessly in areas where plants containing vitamin C were abundant. Usually their suffering arose from ignorance, but in later years, it was all too often through the neglect of their commanding officers. Fortunately the late eighteenth century ushered in a new type of ship's officer. Men like Captains Cook and Vancouver were known for a relatively humane approach to their crews, going to great lengths to keep health and morale at a high level. One of the antiscorbutic techniques used by both officers was frequent and copious doses of spruce beer.

• CAPTAIN COOK'S SPRUCE BEER (recipe recorded by ship's botanist Anders Sparman): 10 gals of water, 6 lbs of molasses and 3 oz of bruised ginger boiled together for half an hour. Then 2 lbs of the outer sprigs of the spruce fir are added and boiled for 5 minutes. The whole is strained through a hair sieve, and, when milk-warm, put in a cask and a teacup of good yeast is stirred well into it. When it has fermented a day or two, it is bunged up and the next day bottled. It will be fit for use in a week.

A triangular-shaped bay south of the Hood Canal Bridge between Termination Point and South Point, Squamish Harbor was named for the Suquamish, an Indian tribe across the canal.

(*744 Clay Street*) The signature building of Port Townsend's Victorian ARCHITECTURE, the Starrett House was designed and built in 1889 by George E. Starrett (1855–1927) using a combination of remarkably well-integrated styles. The steeply pitched cross-gable roof and studious avoidance of smooth wall surfaces were taken from the Queen Anne style and added to decorative trusses, overhanging eaves, and horizontal and vertical bands from the stick style. Most unusual is the octagonal tower that pulls together the various and competing elements. Architectural historian Allen T. Denison calls the house "truly remarkable in the originality of its concept and the successful integration of diverse elements into an imposing and harmonious mass which make it – more than any other Port Townsend house – not only of local but of national significance."

The work was the crowning achievement of George Starrett who was the major residential builder in Port Townsend at the time of its 1889–1890 boom. Born in Maine, Starrett came to Port Townsend in his twenties, just as Port Townsend's hopes for preeminence in the Puget Sound economic sweepstakes were reemerging. In 1889 Starrett told the *Leader* that he had built an average of one house per week since his arrival in town, or more than 350 houses. Starrett was successful in most of his varied endeavors, which included undertaking, sawmill operation, and dry dock construction. He built the Starrett House as a six-thousand-dollar gift to his wife, the former Ann Van Bokkelen, daughter of a Port Townsend pioneer. The house gained local notoriety when Starrett had artist George Chapman paint his interpretation of the four seasons on the ceiling of the octagonal tower. Chapman's vision was a young woman dressed differently for each season, with winter's costume incongruously the most delicate. Local legend says the shivering creature shocked so many Port Townsend matrons that they either shunned Mrs. Starrett's soirées or left them in full gossip. [P.S.]

George E. Starrett House

Prevailing winds from the Pacific Ocean bless Port Townsend and the Northwest Coast with a year-round temperate climate unparalleled in the United States for the latitude. Port Townsend is as far north as Quebec's Gaspé Peninsula, yet its winter temperatures average well above freezing. But there is a hitch. The long stretch across the Pacific allows for the development of what have become known as superstorms, and at least once a decade they hit with such force that the region spends weeks cleaning up and years discussing it. Superstorms always come from the south and originate in the subtropics or tropics. Most dissipate in the Gulf of Alaska. Occurring between fall and spring, the storms often give little warning of their approach.

The Columbus Day storm of 1962 began as a small typhoon east of the Philippines. For nine days it wandered about the Pacific, moving toward Japan, veering, fading, switching toward the Aleutian Islands, then reversing course and aiming for Mexico. On the morning of October 12, the storm was twelve hundred miles due west of Los Angeles; by 8:15 P.M. it hit Port Townsend and the entire Oregon and Washington coast with hurricane winds, cutting a thousand-mile swath that killed, maimed, and destroyed. No injuries were sustained in Port Townsend, but seventy-foot trees were uprooted, and the roof of what is now the police department was lifted off and sent sailing one block before crashing into the entrance of Jefferson County Memorial Stadium. Marquees were ripped off buildings, windows blew in, loosened bricks fell down chimneys.

Seventeen years later, on February 13, 1979, another storm, originating in Hawaii, slammed against the coast, skipped over the Olympics, and in eastern Jefferson County blew down millions of board feet of timber, blocking highways and crushing homes. Sections of forest land appeared to have been cut with a scythe. Coupled with a high tide beginning to ebb and moving with the wind, the storm broke up the western half of the HOOD CANAL BRIDGE. The pontoons drifted northward and sank within ten minutes. It was three years before the bridge was returned to service.

STRAIT OF JUAN DE FUCA The eighty-mile-long Strait of Juan de Fuca separates the northwest coast of Washington State from the southwest coast of Vancouver Island, British Columbia. At its entrance off CAPE FLATTERY and as far east as Race Rocks near Victoria, British Columbia, the strait is about twelve miles wide. Eastward to WHIDBEY ISLAND, it broadens to approximately sixteen miles as it opens into ADMIRALTY INLET and PUGET SOUND to the south and into Rosario Strait and the SAN JUAN ISLANDS to the north. The Strait of Juan de Fuca provides the primary corridor for shipping from the Pacific Ocean to the major ports of Puget Sound and British Columbia.

Long before GEORGE VANCOUVER sailed into Puget Sound by way of the strait, its existence had been suggested by legend and postulated by a peculiar eighteenth-century science of "theoretical geography." Rumors originated from a sixteenth-century sailor's tale about the Northwest Passage. According to legend, a Portuguese ship journeyed across North America in 1540 to China and back, passing through a body of water called the Straits of Anian. The story was given additional credibility in 1625 with the publication of a book by Samuel Purchase. Purchase related the tale of one Apostolos Valerianos, who sailed under the name of Juan de Fuca. A Greek pilot in Spanish employ, he sailed from Acapulco, Mexico, in 1592 in search of the fabled passage. Somewhere between the zone from forty-eight to forty-nine degrees north latitude, he found an inlet into which he voyaged for twenty days until reaching the Atlantic. His mission successfully completed, he returned to Acapulco. While some record exists to indicate that Valerianos did sail the coasts of Mexico and California during that period, it is considered unlikely that his travels took him anywhere near the strait and pure fantasy that he sailed through it to the Atlantic. The legend, nevertheless, has persisted for almost four hundred years.

It was not until the late eighteenth century that any serious exploration of the Northwest Coast was to occur. During that period, Spanish, English, American, and a few Russian vessels began to venture into the area in search of new fur-trading sources. The strait may have been seen as early as 1774 by a Spaniard, Captain Estaban José Martinez. Later, while governor at Nootka in 1789, Martinez ordered a vessel to explore the opening. In March of 1778, Captain James Cook narrowly missed discovering the strait on his final voyage to the Pacific. Passing near and naming Cape Flattery, he noted, "it was in this very latitude . . . that the geographers have placed the pretended Strait of Juan de Fuca, but we saw nothing like it, nor is there the least probability that iver [sic] any such thing existed." Unfortunately for Cook, rain and haze obscured the strait, and forced him to tack his ship away from the shore. Ironically, serving as a midshipman on his consort vessel, the *Discovery*, was George Vancouver, who would perform the first accurate survey of the strait and Puget Sound fourteen years later.

Credit for the European discovery of the strait is generally given to Captain Charles Barkley, an English fur trader who noted the "long lost Strait" on his charts in July 1787. He was followed two years later by Captain Robert Gray of Boston, who sailed some fifty miles into the inlet before retracing his wake to the Pacific. After Gray, the Spanish took the lead in exploring the strait. MANUEL QUIMPER went as far as New Dungeness in 1790, taking possession of the Washington coastline for Spain. He was followed by Eliza in 1791. But it was not until Vancouver's survey in 1792 that the full dimensions of the area would be recorded. [M.W.]

STUMP RANCHER "A man in this country is like the one who went to see the city but could not see it on account of the houses. It is almost impossible to see the country here on account of the trees. The trees and underbrush are so thick, and the fallen timber so plentiful and interwoven together that it is with the greatest difficulty that a person can penetrate it, consequently the first and succeeding settlers usually selected the first partially open bottom land they could find on the outskirts and branded the whole of the rest in the interior as worthless. It is strange indeed if land that produces such a dense growth of timber will not produce grain, vegetables and fruit."

Strange perhaps, but true, despite the otherwise hopeful promise offered in the Immigration Aid Society Manual written in 1880 to attract newcomers. It was a truth learned the hard way by enthusiastic greenhorns who heeded propaganda from real estate agents, regional boosters, and timber companies stuck with acre upon acre of logged (i.e., useless) land. Thousands of families, heeding the call to the frontier, settled amongst snags, stumps, and debris. And they learned, said one settler, "as no other person ever learned, exactly how many huge trees had stood on an acre, exactly how big these trees had been, and how deep and tough and extensive had been their roots." And in time they learned that much of the cutover land of the region was good for nothing except growing timber. Many tried to remove the stumps when the vision of acres of golden grain was still vivid in their minds' eye, but as the vision faded many simply gave up and moved away. Some eked out a meager existence raising chickens and coaxing skimpy vegetables from the soil.

The most successful stump-ranchers were not ranchers at all, but timbermen who cut the stumps for firewood and shingles and made posts or poles or railroad ties from remnants of standing timber. The hand stump-puller and horse stump-puller gave way after World War I to more powerful gas stump-pullers. Ten million pounds of war-surplus explosives made available through county extension agents became popular for stump removal; danger increased with efficiency, and many a rancher was maimed or killed in a desperate attempt to blast the land into submission.

It may have been the hucksters' failure to market this logged land or the failure of the land itself as breadbasket soil that finally put timbermen to thinking about the efficacy of tree farming, which began on a major scale after World War II, one hundred years after the first trees had been felled. (See *Logging*.)   [R.B.]

Sufi dancing, also known as Dances of Universal Peace, is a form of group dancing that incorporates sacred phrases from many spiritual traditions into song and dance, mostly simple circle and partner dances. These dances were inspired by Murshid Samuel Lewis, also known as Sufi Sam, an American Sufi master, as a means for "experiencing joy and attunement with one's inner life as well as a way of knowing the divinity in each other and in one's self." Sufi dance classes have focused on particular themes such as joy in the winter, International Peace Day, or the solstice. Occasionally, Sufi dancers have gathered at Sather Park for their rounds or ventured onto Point Hudson at low tide in celebration of a universal spirit.

SUFI DANCING

SUQUAMISH INDIANS   The Suquamish were closely connected to the Duwamish, and the famous Chief Seattle was chief of both tribes. According to an 1857 report, they occupied the west side of Puget Sound from Applegate Cove to Gig Harbor, although one early informant said they lived south of Everett, near Mukilteo and on the islands opposite. In either case, their official numbers by U.S. Indian Office census in 1910 were 204. In 1937 there were 168 Suquamish. Intermarriage with neighboring tribes and with early white fishermen in the area was common, and some feel that at any point it would have been difficult to determine the exact number of actual Suquamish.

SWAN, JAMES G.   James Gilchrist Swan (1818–1900) should be Port Townsend's most famous citizen, but history is slow to recognize some of its giants, and there are still some people living in Port Townsend who would not recognize the name of this incredible and paradoxical man. Friend of the Puget Sound INDIANS, Swan is perhaps best remembered as a frontier scientist whose interest in Indian culture led him to collect many of the Smithsonian Institution's most valued artifacts from this area.

But Swan was not a person of single dimension. His occupations and preoccupations included anthropologist, student of nature and literature, promoter, historian, ethnographer, folklorist, naturalist, lawyer, legal legislator, doctor, cook, schoolteacher, musician, artist, journalist, boat-builder's helper, commission merchant, justice of the peace, diplomat, linguist, notary public, county school superintendent, railroad speculator, customs official, homesteader, and explorer. Swan was all of these, but as Ivan Doig notes in his book *Winter Brothers*, he was also an obsessive diarist, and left behind valuable material about his life and times. He was an indefatigable man who was driven by what Doig terms a "flywheel of curiosity."

Swan's life was filled with failed enterprises and false starts that led to personal confusion, crankiness, bouts of excessive drunkenness, and poverty. Still, it is hard not to love a man whose imaginative ambitions included a fantasy of making paper from Puget Sound seaweed. The same hindsight that notes his failures shows us a lifetime of continuous curiosity and dedication that provided a fund of knowledge and a collection of artifacts from Puget Sound Indians that simply would not have been preserved if he had not lived as he did. In 1857 he published his book *The Northwest Coast* about his experiences at Shoalwater Bay (now called Willapa Bay). His articles in newspapers were to appear for decades, and his diaries and notebooks provide the rest. Even the twentieth-century archaeologists at the OZETTE dig turn to his descriptions of MAKAH INDIAN implements for reference.

In 1851 in San Francisco, James Swan met Klallam chief CHET-ZE-MOKA from Port Townsend, who had been taken to San Francisco to visit. Swan showed Chet-ze-moka around the white man's world, a tour which was to impress Chet-ze-moka the rest of his life and which in part motivated Chet-ze-moka to mediate between the Indians and the whites, because he understood the strength of the white world. It was not until 1859, however, that Swan came to Port Townsend, where he renewed his friendship with the Klallam chief. Swan's express purpose in coming to Port Townsend was to start a whaling business, one of his many moneymaking schemes that made him precious little money but did allow him to digress into his real vocation – the study of Indian life. Swan spent much of his time on the water, meeting coastal Indians and gathering material for museums, studying their work and customs, and sketching pictures of what interested him. Many of his observations from these trips appeared in newspapers in Olympia and San Francisco.

In 1862 he went to teach the MAKAH in Neah Bay but never lost contact with Port Townsend, which was his home from 1867–1900, allowing, as was his style, for considerable time elsewhere. In Port Townsend he worked hard to achieve peaceful relations between Indians and whites, often advising Indians on how to deal with the white man's ways. In 1868 he was made notary public, in 1869 county school superintendent. In 1870 he was elected judge of the probate court of Jefferson County; in 1871 he took and passed the bar exam. All the while, he was also harboring a personal and perhaps selfish wish that the Northern Pacific Railroad would come to Port Townsend, but in 1873 the prize was given to Tacoma. This was another lost dream for Swan, but he stayed on. In 1874 he was

James Swan

appointed collector of the customs for Puget Sound District and in 1882 was elected justice of the peace.

Though Swan seems to have gained respectability in Port Townsend, he complained frequently of how his work was not appreciated. Judging from his continual poverty, this does seem to be the case, but there is also evidence that he often spent his money, when he had it, on gifts. He seemed to live a life of paradox. Imagine, for example, Swan among the Makah in Neah Bay when news of Lincoln's assassination reached the Olympic Peninsula, observing a day of fasting in the Great Emancipator's honor among Indians who still enslaved their own. Swan also lived with the irony of trying to stop the flow of liquor to Indians while having a drinking problem himself: On June 2, 1883, he made the court docket in "the matter of the habitual drunkenness of James G. Swan."

Swan died in abject poverty, having done more to promote scientific research than any other pioneer in Washington Territory, having written the first significant literary work from the new territory, having made invaluable contributions to the historical and ethnological knowledge of the Northwest, and having collected extensively for U.S. and European museums. When he died, his debts were greater than his assets, and his executor had trouble raising enough money for his gravestone.   [J.H.]

SWANSONVILLE   A small residential community on the ridge above PORT LUDLOW, Swansonville was named for Hans Swanson (1854–1946), a Norwegian native who came to the area in 1890. He was county treasurer for a number of years, a position assumed by his brother Arthur after his death.

SWELLS   Waves generated during storms over the Pacific Ocean funnel into the STRAIT OF JUAN DE FUCA, where they stretch into long troughs and heaving crests that cause one to develop sea legs, or, failing that, seasickness. Swells are most notable on board the MV *Coho* from Port Angeles to Victoria, British Columbia, and along the western shores of WHIDBEY ISLAND en route to and from the SAN JUAN ISLANDS.

SWIMMING   Brrrrrrr.

(Also tomanous, tomahnawos, tumanamus.) In con-
trast to the Great Spirit of some Indian people, the
"tamanous" of the Coastal Indians is a particular
guardian spirit for a specific individual. The tamanous
would reveal itself in either direct or symbolic man-
ifestation to young men and women in a ritual of fasting and isolated retreat from the tribe. It might take
many forms, such as the sun, a spider, or a wolf. Different tamanous figures had different powers, which
would be bestowed upon the recipient, who would be
protected by his or her tamanous through life. Any
form of worship or petition was made in private to
one's own tamanous. The term is also used to refer to a
ritual or ceremony. Thus a tamanous during a potlatch
would be only for the initiated, and whites would be
excluded as from a secret society meeting.   [J.H.]

Just northwest of Chimacum, over the hill from
Anderson Lake, is a large rock that appears to have
thrust itself out of the valley floor. Its face is nearly vertical, but it can be climbed, and the view encompasses
most of Chimacum Valley, Port Townsend, and the
San Juan Islands to the north. Some say that it was an
Indian lookout, a vantage point for spotting approaching enemy tribes, but others claim it was used as a lookout only by FORT TOWNSEND garrisons when the
army built their station in the 1850s. With the near
extinction of local Indian tribes, the rock began to lose
its mythical origins and in recent years has been
referred to as Big Rock. Still, at least four legends have
endured about the Indian's use of the rock, involving a
dragon, a flood, the vision quest, and fertility.

The late James G. McCurdy, in *By Juan de Fuca's
Strait,* tells of a creature "resembling a dragon, covered
with bright golden scales and its eyes emitting a
strange, unearthly light." The dragon lived in Anderson Lake and sunbathed on Tamanous Rock. The
Indians thought it was a devil. But when a young brave
named Quarlo did battle with the dragon and was
doomed to defeat, the dragon, instead of administering a fiery coup de grace, mildly licked Quarlo's face
and proceeded to be something of a fairy godmother
throughout his two-hundred-year life, providing him
with vast riches in pearls, seals, otters, and fish. After
Quarlo's burial, the disconsolate dragon lumbered off
into the sound and disappeared never to be seen again.

A story told by Marion Lambert and recorded in the *Leader* in the 1920s recalls a legend as originally told by Quyats, a chief of the KLALLAM. According to this story, a great rain fell for nearly fifty days. The biblical parallel is immediately apparent, and in many ways Tamanous Rock is the Indian's Mount Ararat. As the rains fell, the Klallam boarded their canoes and rose with the tide. As the water receded, a great fog came, and many canoes were separated. The ones who drifted west later became the Quinault, Queets, and Quilcene; the ones who drifted north became the Makah, Esquimalt, and Port Rupert tribes; the ones who drifted east became Lummi, Tulalip, and Snohomish tribes; the ones drifting south became the Puyallup, Skokomish, and Twana tribes – thus the creation of all Puget Sound tribes. One canoe containing a man, his wife, their son, and daughter-in-law was left high and dry on Tamanous Rock, where the canoe remained for generations. The Klallam held the rock in reverence, since the image of the canoe proved they were the first people of the land. Marion Lambert claimed that she saw the canoe when she was a child but was unable to find it years later when she returned.

A third legend involved a test of young braves' manhood. Young Indian men climbed the rock in pursuit of their vision, their tamanous or guardian spirit. They fasted for days through wind and cold until they saw a vision or symbol of their future.

A final story suggests that the phallic appearance of the rock caused Indians to regard it as a fertility symbol. Although there are other rocks in the Northwest whose appearance led to the symbolic association with human fertility, notably the huge Beacon Rock along the Columbia River, this story has the least authority and is possibly more related to early white men's fantasies than to Indian lore.   [J.H.]

TARBOO   The name of the lake, creek, and bay that lead to DABOB BAY in the southern end of Jefferson County near QUILCENE, Tarboo is an Indian word meaning "windy."

TERMINATION POINT   The northern terminus of HOOD CANAL was named by Captain Charles Wilkes in 1841. Termination Point is also the western terminus of the HOOD CANAL BRIDGE.

On the east side of the TOANDOS PENINSULA on HOOD CANAL, Thorndyke Bay was named for John R. Thorndyke, a San Franciscan who established a mill there in 1852.

THORNDYKE BAY

A legendary Indian bird that briefly inhabited the CROW'S NEST and gave tribal hunters the power to kill WHALES.

THUNDERBIRD

(*1004 Water Street*) What has become the Palace Hotel was built in 1889, designed in the Richardson Romanesque style by Port Townsend architects Whiteway and Schroeder, and financed by Henry L. Tibbals, Sr., (1829–1920). The three-story Tibbals Building is notable for its arched windows that appear to extend two stories, an impression created by the elongated Ionic columns that bracket them.

TIBBALS BUILDING

Had there been media heros in the nineteenth century, Captain Tibbals certainly would have been among them. Connecticut-born, Tibbals went to sea in 1839 at the age of ten, apprenticing for a decade under Captain "Billy" Thatcher out of New York. By the age of twenty, he had become a master seaman. His later voyages involved carrying a cargo of railway iron for the pre-canal railroad crossing of the isthmus of Panama and testing the first diving bell in the United States, which led him to Mexico, where he was granted the salvage rights to the Spanish ship *San Pedro* by Governor General Santa Anna. The frigate had blown up in Mexican waters in 1814 with a cargo containing three million dollars in silver. Using the diving bell, Tibbals dove in one hundred feet of water and retrieved sixty-eight thousand dollars before a change in the Mexican government halted the operation. He then traveled to Panama and Acapulco, where he dove for pearls.

In 1853 the twenty-five-year-old Tibbals came to Port Townsend, where his life became somewhat more sedate for a time. He built a hotel, served in the territorial legislature, and established Union Wharf with L. B. Hastings and another partner. He became the agent for a direct steamship route between Port Townsend and San Francisco, and over time served as sheriff, county commissioner, postmaster, and city council member. At age fifty-nine, his life turned melodramatic when he divorced his wife Caroline to marry a younger woman. The town's sympathy lay with the discarded Caroline, and Tibbals's new wife was shunned. She later returned the insult by abandoning him. Some years later, the young Mrs. Tibbals returned to Port Townsend with her father and brother-in-law and became engaged in a nasty altercation that saw Tibbals "assaulted, choked, and beat ... in an unmerciful fashion." He thereupon divorced her. Tibbals lived to age 92 and died penniless.

TOANDOS PENINSULA

A long, narrow peninsula between DABOB BAY and HOOD CANAL, the Toandos Peninsula resembles the shape of Italy without its boot. Its name is a phonetic adaptation of "tu-an-hu," meaning "portage," a word from the Twana Indians who inhabited the area.

TOWNSHEND, MARQUIS OF

A British nobleman for whom George Vancouver named a "safe and ... capacious harbor ... [with] good holding ground" that he discovered on May 7, 1792, neither George Townshend nor any of his descendants have ever seen the bay or town that bears their name. The name Port Townshend held for nearly fifty years while the bay was visited only by occasional fur traders from Hudson's Bay Company. With the arrival of American settlers in the 1850s, however, the name was deanglicized, causing historian Edmond S. Meany to remark some years later that this was one "case where the Americans, and not the English, drop[ped] an *h*."

George Townshend, a godson to King George I, was the first child of Charles and Ethelreda Townshend. Also known as Audrey, his mother was considered "one of the most beautiful [and] witty women ... in the eighteenth century." After four children, she and Charles decided they were incompatible. She removed to London where she became an "audacious woman of fashion"; Charles took to mistresses. Upon his majority, George began a military career. He was not one to quietly suffer foolish commanders, and more than once his ability as a caricaturist got him into difficult situations with his superiors. In 1759, he was appointed by King George II as brigadier general under the command of James Wolfe, whose battle on the Plains of Abraham – the plateau above the city of Quebec – brought an end to the French and Indian wars that lasted for seventy-five years. Wolfe was killed in the fierce battle; Townshend assumed command,

and four days later Quebec capitulated. Townshend was elevated to marquis and subsequently became Lord Lieutenant of Ireland, where his sympathy for the peasants and a revived interest in caricature got him recalled. He was nevertheless promoted to full general some years later.

George's younger brother, Charles, was responsible for the Colonial Importation Bill known as the Townshend Act, which imposed heavy duties on tea and other merchandise. This infamous piece of legislation resulted in the Boston Tea Party and helped to spark the American Revolution. The present and seventh Marquis of Townshend, also named George, was born in 1916. He has lived a less colorful life, but certainly an influential one. He is chair or member of the board of various British corporations, insurance companies, banks, and associations. In 1937, on the occasion of his twenty-first birthday, the city of Port Townsend invited him to visit. He graciously replied, promising a visit in the future, but he has yet to make good on it. Perhaps if the *h* were restored . . . . [P.S.]

TOWN TAVERN *(Water and Quincy Streets)* When a University of Oregon psychology professor was towed into Port Townsend in 1973 by the U.S. Coast Guard after an unsuccessful attempt to sail to Victoria, British Columbia, serendipitous seeds were sown for one of Port Townsend's more curious economic and social phenomena – The Town Tavern. What was to become a democratically run bar, a restaurant, and a home-for-the-wayward began as a theatre project. The professor returned to Eugene with pictures he had taken in Port Townsend. Two teaching assistants and their families returned with him to start what they would call Savoy Associates, after the Gilbert and Sullivan Savoy Hotel in London.

The building was bought in 1973 for fifty-three thousand dollars, and the project moved quickly from the theatre concept into a halfway house and commune. The N. D. HILL BUILDING was spacious, with fifteen thousand square feet of floor space and the potential of thirty-eight rooms in floors above the tavern. Some of the owners had backgrounds in psychology and counseling, and the group began to envision the Town Tavern as a place for people to drop out and assess their lives. The group had weekly "family meetings," when

A deputy jumped up on the stage and shouted: "State Police! This is a raid!"

workers would schedule the calendar of sixteen-hour tavern days divided into four-hour segments. Each was obliged to work twenty hours per week for room and board; they could work more for spending money. One early resident remembers that "We planned for everything except making money," but the Town Tavern did make money. Money from the pool table alone covered the monthly payments, and excess proceeds went into building restoration. When the Town Tavern opened, the building had not been used for fifteen years, and much time and money went into its restoration. Others who joined the project had electronic and carpentry skills to develop the tavern's sound system, wiring, stage, and bathrooms.

About 75 percent of the building's restoration was in exchange for room and board. As one of the owners puts it, "The Town Tavern has probably saved the taxpayers a lot of welfare money." Word soon spread that the Town was a haven for people who needed a home and who wanted to reassess their lives. Many were drifters who left in a few weeks, but others found what they wanted in Port Townsend and developed skills that allowed them to move out of the tavern and start their own businesses. Many early workers describe the "wonderful energy" that characterized the place. They remain amazed at how few people caused problems for the tavern or the town. When hostilities arose in the bar, either from workers or customers, the Town's policy was to smother the problem with nonviolence and when that did not work, to call the police.

Two major events mark the Town's relatively placid history – the Great Drug Bust of '79 and the Great Fire of '82. In July of 1979, the newly elected sheriff staged a drug raid on the Town Tavern. Three narcotics agents were hired to uncover drug traffic in Port Townsend and they focused their attention on the Town Tavern. A dozen deputies and policemen with search warrant in hand raided the tavern. A small amount of marijuana along with some pills that turned out to be caffeine were found. One tavern member was charged with selling marijuana, possession of phenobarbitol, mescaline, and morphine. The Port Townsend Chamber of Commerce went on record to congratulate the sheriff's department for its work, but by the time the smoke cleared, not one charge against Town Tavern residents or owners stuck.

In July of 1982, a fire started in an upstairs room, and before it was brought under control, major damage had been done to the structure. The owners carried no fire insurance, and many people thought the damage would spell the end of the Town Tavern. Most workers did leave, but donations of money, tools, labor, and moral support suddenly emerged from all quarters of the town. The *Leader's* letter-to-the-editor column printed numerous letters of thanks, and in many ways the Town Tavern had never seemed such an integral part of the community. The organization returned to some of its old ways but not all. It became the N. D. Hill Corporation, with one of the early owners in charge of operations, hiring and firing, and running the restoration project. The restaurant stayed closed, but seventeen rooms were rehabited by January of 1985, and most workers were still working for room – if not board – at the rate of eight hours per week. Within weeks after the fire, the tavern was open for business and the doors to the wayward thrown open again.   [J.H.]

On a spring afternoon in 1862, John Tukey, standing near his cabin on the east shore of Discovery Bay, saw an Indian canoe plying the waters toward his property, known as Tukey's Landing. After beaching the vessel, two Indians and a white man climbed out, lugging an apparently heavy chest, and disappeared into dense timber nearby.

TREASURE, BURIED

His curiosity sparked, Tukey watched for the men to return. Suddenly, the Indians emerged from the forest empty-handed and quickly, silently slipped into their canoe and paddled rapidly away. As the puzzled Tukey watched the Indians disappear, the white man abruptly appeared, empty-handed, from the forest. He brusquely requested a mount to Port Townsend, where he aimed to catch a steamer for Olympia. Tukey gave him the horse, and the man galloped furiously away. As trained, the stallion trotted back to Tukey's Landing, riderless. Armed with a shovel, Tukey tramped into the timber in search of the stash, but found no trace.

The stranger had reached Port Townsend in time to catch the steamer, but unfortunately for him, the sharp-eyed captain recognized him at once from "wanted" posters as a paymaster from Victoria who had relieved his employer of six thousand gold sovereigns worth thirty thousand dollars. After the thief retired to his stateroom, the captain turned the ship around and hastened to Victoria, British Columbia, where he surrendered the unwitting captive to Canadian authorities. Within a few days, Canadian officers arrived at Tukey's claim and spent several weeks digging, unearthing nothing with the glimmer of gold. The paymaster was tried, convicted, and sentenced to a long prison term. When released he went to Texas, where he lived modestly with a brother, apparently without the benefit of his booty.

Until his death, Tukey believed the treasure was buried on his land, and he could often be found puttering about his property with a shovel, digging here, digging there, hoping that one day his spade would strike that chest full of gold.   [R.B.]

TREE OF HEAVEN   In the 1860s, during the latter days of the expansionist Manchu dynasty, the son of an emperor of China visited San Francisco on a goodwill tour. Treated well by the new but flourishing society, the young royal returned to Peking. His father wished to thank the people of America with a gift of permanence and selected two young specimens of the tree of heaven (*Ailanthus glandulosa*). Carefully prepared for the cross-Pacific journey, the two saplings were placed aboard a vessel headed for SAN FRANCISCO.

Beset by continuously rough seas, the ship was blown wildly off course and came limping into the Strait of Juan de Fuca, its rigging badly damaged. It reached Port Townsend and here the ship was repaired and its crew treated well. In thanks, the captain presented one of the trees to the city, where it now grows on the hillside below Washington Street between Tyler and Taylor Streets. The other was taken to its original destination of San Francisco, where it was planted in Golden Gate Park. So says legend. No evidence has ever supported it. Recent attempts to verify the story with Golden Gate Park officials reveal no record of either the story or the tree. Most legends have a basis in fact; in this instance, that kernel eludes discovery.

TREES FOR PORT   The trees along Port Townsend's downtown streets
TOWNSEND   are not a replication of Victorian urban landscaping. An 1890 photograph of Water Street reveals utility

poles but no trees. A similar photograph in early 1973 would show the same. After all, downtown Port Townsend was constructed on fill-dirt quite unsuitable for trees, and most early residents were more interested in cutting than planting trees anyway. But in April of 1973, two Port Townsend residents, Marge Abraham and Donna Daubenberger, initiated a project called Trees for Port Townsend. What followed was a model program in small-town community spirit and effort, a project that bridged generations and nurtured friendships, with more than fifteen hundred volunteers assisting in the beautification program in the first seven years.

Funds were raised through grants, the historic homes tours, the annual sewing and then raffling of a Port Townsend historic quilt, and the sale of postcards picturing the QUILTS. As of January 1985, nearly all of a desired ten-thousand-dollar trust fund had been raised to maintain the project. More than five hundred trees and thousands of flowers were planted and maintained along business streets, near schools, at KAI TAI Lagoon, and at Jefferson County Memorial Field. The beautification goals of the project also produced a zig-zag stairway on Tyler Street that leads downtown and landscaping around the Bell Tower. The value of the project has been conservatively estimated at three hundred thousand dollars. In 1983 Trees for Port Townsend was nominated for the National Arbor Day Award.

The unincorporated communities of CHIMACUM, HADLOCK, and IRONDALE merged in the 1960s as a collective commercial consciousness known as Tri-Area. In the absense of county ordinances concentrating development, the business and industrial community spread willy-nilly along Tri-Area's more or less triangular arterials. "Alpine beauty huts" are cheek-by-jowl with building supply firms and junk car yards; at Hadlock's main intersection, Western-style, neo-Bavarian, and slapdash twentieth-century buildings clamor for attention. Once these towns were all visually distinct, but no longer. Yet, somehow, it works. Chimacum, with a large school campus and many farms, provides the educational and agricultural base of the Tri-Area; Hadlock is the primary retail core; and Irondale concentrates on residential development. The

TRI-AREA

Tri-Area is the epicenter of Jefferson County's population of eighteen thousand and is the focal point of a fierce rivalry with Port Townsend.

TRIDENT In a worst-case scenario, Defense Department planners estimate that in the aftermath of a first strike by the Soviet Union against this country at least four thousand deliverable nuclear warheads would remain. A large percentage of these, they believe, would be located on Trident submarines. Twenty miles south of Port Townsend, on the eastern shore of Hood Canal near Poulsbo, is a 12.5–square-mile naval submarine base at Bangor, Trident's North Pacific home. The brainchild of Admiral Hyman Rickover, the Trident was developed to strengthen the third prong of the nation's national defense triad based in the air, on the ground, and in the water. In theory, the Trident's ability to hide beneath millions of square miles of ocean makes it less vulnerable to Soviet detection and hence destruction.

The largest submarine ever built, the 560–foot long Trident is capable of cruising at least four hundred feet below the ocean surface at speeds of more than thirty knots. (For obvious reasons, the navy will not divulge exactly how deep or how fast the Trident can go, but some experts estimate maximum depth to exceed one thousand feet and its speed to be as high as forty-five knots.)

Statistically, Trident is the most powerful weapons system on earth. In the long bay behind the conning tower, twenty-four Trident missiles, each with multiple, independently targeted warheads, contain enough explosive force to equal one Hiroshima each second for thirty-four minutes. Its ninety-thousand-horsepower nuclear reactor contains ample fuel to power it for ten years. Through distillation and electrolysis, it produces its own fresh water and air. The major limit to staying submerged is its food supply and the effects of isolation on the crew.

Since its conception, the Trident has been the subject of continual controversy. Critics regard its size as one of the biggest flaws: By replacing ten Poseidon- and Polaris-class subs with one Trident, they argue, we effectively place our eggs in fewer baskets. Supporters counter that the greater range of the Trident missile (four thousand nautical miles, 60 percent farther than

Poseidon) along with more advanced soundproofing and other technical advantages give it a greater area in which to hide and less chance of detection. They point to the effectiveness of the craft's sophisticated inertial guidance system and to its ability to place a warhead within two hundred yards of its intended target. System opponents see that accuracy, if real, as a destabilizing force in the balance of terror. A "silo buster," they say, is a first-strike weapon and likely to make the Soviets quicker to press the big button.

Even before construction began on the Trident base in 1973, fierce local opposition developed. While much of Kitsap and Jefferson Counties welcomed the economic boost the base would bring, others were asking what effect an influx of perhaps seventy thousand new residents would have on the quality of life in the area. Some eighty million dollars in Trident impact funds were pumped into the communities most affected by the base. New roads, schools, and sewage treatment plants were built to shore up a fragile infrastructure.

Even with the money, local governments could not contend with the effects of growth. By 1979 armed robberies were up in Kitsap County by 300 percent over 1973. More murders occurred that year than in the previous ten. Yet, the ratio of law enforcement personnel to citizens was less than one-third the state average. When 100–mile-an-hour winds sank the Hood Canal Bridge in 1979, it created a mile-wide moat, temporarily insulating Jefferson County from the social effects of Trident. Had that not occurred, much of the county's southeastern corner would likely have become Bangor's bedroom.

In the summer of 1982, as the arrival of the first Trident neared, opposition reached its zenith. A broadly based coalition of groups spiritually and pragmatically opposed to the Trident began to gather in the Puget Sound region to express their dissent. Among their numbers were middle-class mill workers from Vancouver, Buddhist monks from Japan, and an eighty-year-old Washington State "Grandmother of the Year." Coordinated by Ground Zero, an antiwar organization, and the Seattle Religious Peace Action Coalition, they formed what became known as the Peace Blockade.

Their plan was to stage a series of nonviolent demonstrations and educational events throughout the summer, all designed to bring national attention to their cause. When the USS *Ohio* attempted to enter Hood Canal in late July or early August, they planned to use small boats to impede its progress. They would be assisted in these efforts by the *Pacific Peacemaker*, a fifty-four-foot ketch from Australia. Sponsored by the Society of Friends and the Australian Longshoremans' Union, the *Peacemaker* had brought its crew of twelve Australians and New Zealanders eleven thousand miles to participate in the protest.

As July drew to a close, the demonstrators established a base camp on the shores of Oak Bay, south of Port Townsend. With support from local groups, such as the Port Townsend Peace Coalition, they set up observation posts along the strait, and a phone tree that would signal the protest boats into action when the submarine was sighted. While they waited, they planned, meditated, and trained for their act of civil disobedience. For its part the government was also preparing itself. All locally available Coast Guard vessels had been brought to the northern sound. The FBI set up spotting scopes and acoustical monitors on Indian Island opposite the demonstrators. An edict was issued, citing the Waterways Safety Act, declaring a thousand-yard zone surrounding the USS *Ohio* as off-limits and closing an eighteen-mile stretch of Hood Canal to any nonmilitary vessel. Violations could mean ten years in jail and a fine of ten thousand dollars.

After weeks of waiting and numerous false alarms, word of the *Ohio's* arrival finally came in the morning hours of August 12, 1982. It had been decided earlier that only fifty of the demonstrators would violate the *Ohio's* security zone and risk arrest. The rest of the group would board "witness" boats and follow the events from a legal distance. Fog shrouded the sound, creating an eerie, surreal atmosphere and reducing visibility to about three-quarters of a mile. As the blockade boats rounded the southern tip of Marrowstone Island, the *Ohio's* entourage emerged from the haze. Flying low over the water, the sound of their rotors shattering the quiet, a half-dozen helicopters, most from Seattle television stations, cut through the mist toward the protestors. They were followed almost immediately by high-speed Zodiac inflatable boats containing orange-uniformed coastguardsmen. After them came the cutters, armed with machine guns and water cannons. In all, one hundred well-prepared government boats faced the demonstrators.

The *Peacemaker*, towing a string of smaller boats and dinghies, was one of the first to be halted. Crew members of the Coast Guard cutter *Point Glass* boarded the vessel and placed its crew under arrest. They were handcuffed to the lifelines; the armada of rowboats the *Peacemaker* towed was cut loose. Small naval gunboats were used to stop other members of the blockade and disable their boats. Those that tried evasive action were hit with the water cannons. Well away from the action, almost invisible in the fog, the dark form of the *Ohio* could be seen moving slowly past. One protest boat, the *James Jordan*, with a crew of one man and two women, managed to break through the lines. With government boats in hot pursuit, they were able to circle the huge submarine once before being captured. Their gas line was cut, and they were left to drift as the flotilla headed into Hood Canal.

In all, seventeen arrests were made, and three boats were taken under tow to Bangor. Eventually, all the protestors were released and their boats returned. Both sides claimed a modest victory. Today most of the demonstrations in protest of the Trident program center around the "white train" that delivers hydrogen bombs to the Olympic Peninsula. Sleek and sinister, Tridents come and go with unscheduled regularity, a grim reminder of how nations now defend their differences.   [M.W.]

TWANA INDIANS

The Twana Indians originally occupied both sides of HOOD CANAL. They were divided into three bands: the Du-hle-lips at the head of the canal; the Skokomish fifteen miles below; and the Kilsid (since anglicized as Quilcene) thirty miles further south at the mouth of the DOSEWALLIPS near Kilsid Bay. Skokomish, meaning "river people," is often given as the name of the entire tribe, but originally it referred to only one band. It has since become the name of the reservation. The Twana traded frequently with the KLALLAM and are known to have stopped in Port Townsend to buy gifts en route to a POTLATCH in the late 1800s. Intermarriage with neighboring tribes, and sometimes more distant tribes along the coast, was common among them.

UFO SIGHTINGS   It was 1947 when ex-army test pilot Kenneth Arnold sighted nine metallic disks flying in tight formation around Mount Rainier. He coined the phrase flying saucers to describe them, and over the next thirty-five years, the term and the phenomenon, became an integral, if suspect, part of American culture. A deluge of sightings and encounters were reported worldwide, peaking during the mid- to late 1950s, when political paranoia and technology collided in the ozone.

Port Townsend was not immune to the effect. On May 1, 1954, Jefferson County sheriff Peter J. Naughton observed six bright, yellow objects flying in echelon over Port Townsend. A call to the air force at Paine Field near Everett brought a surprising response: "Ground all planes at Port Townsend; interceptors are coming in with live ammunition." For at least two years previously, air force pilots had been issued a standing order not to fire on UFOs unless they showed hostile intent. Fortunately for all concerned, no commercial aircraft were in the vicinity to attempt landing on the thirty-two-hundred-foot runway at the county AIRPORT, and by the time the fighters arrived the saucers had vanished.

The incident received little publicity at the time, but later found its way into the files of the air force's Project Bluebook and from there into the script of a closed-circuit air force broadcast produced at Lackland Air Force Base. While the controversial Lackland program was ultimately scrapped, it is intriguing to note that at several points in the script it was stated that "All incidents in this program have been authenticated by the United States Air Force."

UNCAS   The small community of Uncas at the head of DIS-COVERY BAY was first known as Junction City and later as Junction. With the failure of the Port Townsend Southern Railroad, a postal official suggested changing the name to Cooper for Postmaster George R. Cooper. Cooper declined the offer and suggested instead that it be named for Uncas, chief of the Mohegan Indians in seventeenth-century Connecticut, made famous a century later in James Fenimore Cooper's *Last of the Mohicans*. It is not known whether a relationship existed between George and James Fenimore. Other than road signs, little is evident of the community.

(*Foot of Taylor Street*) Union Wharf was constructed in
1867 by the first incorporated company in Washington
Territory, the Union Dock Company, and was the
second dock to serve ships on Puget Sound. The
principal interest and operation of Union Wharf was
controlled by H. L. Tibbals, Sr. The wharf extended
342 feet into the harbor, and when a ship from SAN
FRANCISCO rounded Point Wilson, a muzzle-loading
cannon on the tip of the wharf boomed out a welcome
and announced the vessel's arrival – a tradition that
endured forty years. Ample enough to accommodate
three large ocean steamers, the dock was fifty-five feet
wide. It housed a corrugated-iron warehouse and
smaller wooden structures for maritime and other
commercial operations. Seafaring traffic determined
the nature of businesses that located along Taylor
Street at the wharf's head.

In the early years, the Blue Light Saloon and the
Eureka Saloon were popular watering holes on the
wharf, joined in a few years by the Gold Room Saloon.
Children were attracted to Union Wharf, and in 1877
the weekly *Puget Sound Argus* printed a letter from
James G. Swan deploring the actions of youthful
troublemakers on the dock. He said they constructed
"bombs or cartridges filled with giant powder, which
the boys frequently used to see their effect on the fish
around the piles at the end of the Wharf. The effect
was generally more than was contemplated . . . ." The
wharf was also home to retail business. B. S. Miller
Jewelry and Music Emporium found a home there in
the 1870s, as did the People's Market. The *Port Townsend Call* in 1903 paid homage to this twenty-five-year-
old business: " The [People's] Market butchers all its
own stock and kills nothing but prime stock, and in
addition to supplying a large local demand, ship in
large quantities to outside points, covering all of western Washington north of Seattle, and also Alaska . . . ."

But the wharf was first and foremost a place for ships
and the movement of freight and passengers. The
Pacific Coast Steamship Company, of which H. L.
Tibbals, Sr., and his son and namesake were agents,
put in at Union Wharf. Garfield's Launches was headquartered on the dock, "always ready for quick service
– long or short distance – day and night," according
to an ad in the *Port Townsend Call*. During the boom
years when activity on the wharf was at its peak, busi-

nesses were founded, bought, and sold overnight.

Activity at Union Wharf was doubtless slowed during the depression in the nineties. But the humdrum rhythm of commerce was broken on May 4, 1901, when a "genuine juvenile sea serpent" was caught off Union Dock. According to reports in the *Leader*, Mr. Cates of the Port Townsend Fish Market "was skinning salmon to sell as cod and haddock, when he heard a great lashing of the water under Union Wharf, near his place of business. Going to the spot he discovered a monster snake and four or five of her young. The eldest serpent was forty feet in length, and the young ones some three or four feet. The old serpent had evidently been feeding on tin fruit cans so plentiful in the bottom of the bay, and had become choked, as the waves she caused in her lashings nearly sank the gasoline launch *Cascade*, moored nearby. Hastily baiting a hook and line with a herring, and casting it alongside of the wharf, . . . Cates soon had the satisfaction of seeing one of the young reptiles fastened to his line. When he drew a snake from the water the old one was so angered she bit off several partially decayed piles."

Another notable incident in the life of the wharf was the arrival in June 1902 of the first automobile ever seen in Port Townsend. The *Leader* said the conveyance was of the "Oldsmobile variety, said to be one of the finest vehicles of that kind manufactured." A newsstand joined the businesses on the wharf in 1905, and Norby and With Hardware opened in January 1907. A canning factory was installed on the dock in 1911. During World War I, the Women's Christian Temperance Union opened its "Hostess House" amidst the saloons and wharf rats on Union Wharf. In 1925, Puget Sound Navigation Company installed ferry slips on Union Wharf for auto ferry service to Seattle, Port Angeles, and Victoria. Ferries to KEYSTONE also docked there.

In 1929 Tibbals dissolved the corporation, and the wharf was sold to Puget Sound Navigation, which also operated Black Ball ferries, forerunner of the Washington State Ferry System. Under Puget Sound Navigation, the wharf underwent a major overhaul. Buildings on the wharf were improved first: Greenwood Printery, Europe Cafe (see *Sea Galley*), and Jefferson Fish Market were all remodeled or refurbished. The Quality Fish Market opened. R. W. Martin of Port

Angeles Air Transport tied up at Union Wharf when he came to give weekly flying lessons. (See *Airport*.) Then the wharf itself underwent fifteen-thousand-dollar renovation with 550 new piles installed requiring five thousand pounds of spikes and bolts. Six buildings were removed. A seawall was constructed, and the whole wharf was raised two feet to accommodate automobile traffic. In 1936, Union Wharf was named an airway weather station and reported wind speed and direction three times daily to Boeing Field in Seattle.

The Union Wharf warehouse was completely destroyed by an arson fire in November 1940. Fanned by stiff winter winds, the conflagration sent sparks to the top of Morgan Hill. A new warehouse was begun in February 1941, and the wharf was in operation through World War II. In the summer of 1953, it was remodeled and renovated again. The Quincy Street ferry dock was completed in 1953, and passenger traffic left Union Wharf. Black Ball continued to use the dock for freight until 1973 when it was sold to Union Wharf Corporation for $13,500. Union Wharf was seen by millions of people in the 1973 film *Cinderella Liberty* starring James Caan and Marsha Mason, portions of which were filmed on the dock and on an abandoned Canadian minesweeper moored there for the film. A fish processing company used the dock in the mid-seventies. For a while millions of pounds of sea urchins were processed on Union Wharf, their gonads extracted for export to Japan, where they are considered a delicacy (see *Aquaculture*). The fish processors operated until 1981 when the approach to the dock collapsed under forty-thousand pounds of dogfish and sixteen thousand pounds of truck. According to the *Leader*, the city engineer had said in 1973 that the underbeams were weak with dry rot, but the dock had passed inspection in the summer of 1980.

The Internal Revenue Service seized the wharf in early 1983 for back taxes, and it was bought at auction by Service Activities Corporation for $3,000, the only bid. The company was unable to make the wharf productive. The county assessed the property at $192,000 in October 1984. The property was again on the blocks in a foreclosure sale in 1984, and it became the property of Jefferson County when no one bid the minimum amount. A Jefferson County planning commissioner was quoted, "We got it, we don't want it, but we're concerned not to let the thing die." And a county commissioner expressed an interest in selling the dock. Whatever its future, it is safe to say that Union Wharf's heydey was over when the state assumed a monopoly on ferry service, when people chose to travel and ship by car and truck instead of steamer, and when maritime commerce and travel ceased to be viable in small ports and passed into history.   [R.B.]

UPTOWN BUSINESS DISTRICT   A commercial area developed in the 1870s for genteel ladies and their daughters high on the bluff above the sailors, gamblers, prostitutes and other riffraff on WATER STREET.

UTOPIA   In the late nineteenth century, while Port Townsend was seeking to secure a reputation as a capitalist's paradise, a very different utopian ideal was gaining momentum east of Port Angeles. The Puget Sound Cooperative Colony, founded in 1887, was to become the vanguard of a widespread communalist movement in western Washington. The industrial age was pressing hard on the individual in post–Civil War America. Jobs were lost to machines and to recent emigrants willing to work for little pay. Workers felt disenfranchised and politically impotent. In Washington State these sentiments took expression in the anti-CHINESE riots of the 1880s. Groups such as the radical Knights of Labor and Seattle's Liberal League openly advocated violence against the Chinese. They manipulated workers' fears to promote their cause and increase their membership.

Some groups offered the promise of a model city, a cooperative utopia, where the security of the worker was paramount. The leader of one of those groups was George Venable Smith. As acting city attorney for Seattle, Smith had influence and connections to organize and coordinate the diverse factions necessary to create such a community. He drew many of the leaders of the local anti-Chinese movement to his cause. Together, in 1885, they began to develop plans and raise funds for the Puget Sound Cooperative Colony.

Within two years the Central Society, as they called their organization, claimed a thousand members, with branches in twelve states. A convention was held in Seattle in May 1887. Elected delegates chose to incorporate with a capital stock of one hundred thousand dollars. Shares were authorized with a par value of ten dollars each. Smith, just returned from a nationwide promotional tour, was elected the corporate president. The long-awaited announcement of the site for their utopian venture was made. Working quietly, leaders had secured twenty-five platted blocks at the mouth of Ennis Creek near Port Angeles from Norman R. Smith, son of the town's founder. Additionally, they also had purchased a two-hundred-acres stand of timber nearby. Some twenty members had been working at the town site since January. Lots were offered for sale at from twenty to two hundred dollars.

By the end of June, 229 colonists had arrived, including Smith and colony president John J. Knoff. The first efforts of the community were encouraging. A variety of necessary occupations were represented in the original colonists. A crude but effective sawmill was brought from Seattle, and by the end of summer, it had cut 250,000 board feet of lumber. A kiln on the beach produced usable brick; a blacksmith's shop and a wharf were planned. Houses were being built. But as the gray of fall moved into the gray of winter, the colony's weaknesses became apparent. The community was rapidly becoming top-heavy with dependents. Homes were not being built fast enough to house the original colonists, much less the many families that arrived daily. Eventually, a plea was issued to members not to come until called. Expenses ran more than expected, and less than a third of the money that had been pledged actually materialized. Dissension and disillusionment became common.

President Knoff resigned and returned to Seattle with a group of followers, denouncing the colony as a land speculation scheme by Smith. New officers were elected, but it was soon apparent that the democratic government promised by the founders was more pretense than fact. Power in all the most critical areas continued to be held by Smith and his associates. Ultimately, in February of 1888, dissatisfied laborers and foremen unseated Smith and his fellow trustees. The reorganized board was perceived by the general membership to be a victory of pragmatism over theory. Plans were made to cut deadwood from the labor force and refinance new building improvements.

During the next two years, while colony workers embarked on many generally unsuccessful cooperative ventures, the community's leadership became increasingly involved in land speculation. The colony's properties were floated on the capricious tides of the regional economy, and although they showed substantial growth during 1889, they were strictly paper assets. With the economic ebb of 1890, the colony foundered in its own accountancy. The last full meeting of the colony apparently took place in 1889 at the Fourth of July picnic. It was cut short by a freak snowstorm. (See *Cooperatives.*)   [M.W.]

VALENTINO, RUDOLPH   Whenever a Valentino film was booked into the Rose or Townsend Theatres in the 1920s, Port Townsend moviegoers had more than a casual reason to attend. They actually knew someone who knew the famous star of the silent screen. Margaret Neff had been a popular member of Port Townsend's younger set, but she sought a more glamorous life than Port Townsend offered following World War I. After a year at the University of Washington, she went to southern California in 1921, where she became secretary to a movie producer, then served the Russian-born star Nazimova. The height of her achievement came – and set Port Townsend agog – in 1923 when she was hired by Valentino to be his private secretary. *Photoplay* magazine ran a feature on the trials and tribulations of a movie star's secretary, including a picture of Peg Neff opening the large volume of Valentino's morning mail. The caption under her photo advised others seeking the Hollywood dream: "Being a private secretary to a star means hard work, but being a secretary to 'Rudy' means being a feminine Hercules."

VANCOUVER, GEORGE   Of all the people to have played a part in the history of the Pacific Northwest, none, for achievement or for omission, was more pivotal than George Vancouver (1757–1798). Few details remain of Vancouver's early life. He was born at King's Lynn, Norfolk, England the youngest of six children. His mother was of manorial lineage; his father held the lucrative and politically important post of deputy collector of customs. As was customary for the time, it was Vancouver's family connections that afforded him the opportunity of a career with the Royal Navy, which he began at age fifteen.

Fortunately for Vancouver, he was selected by Captain James Cook to serve his apprenticeship aboard

Cook's vessel, the *Resolution*. After two voyages to the
South Seas, exploring the coastline of New Zealand,
and probing the impenetrable ice floes of the Ant-
arctic, Cook returned to England in 1775 and within six
months was preparing for what was to be his final
voyage, an expedition to the northern Pacific Ocean in
search of the Northwest Passage. Vancouver joined
Cook again, this time as a midshipman on the consort
vessel *Discovery*. Another young officer, William Bligh,
who would achieve fame as the captain of the HMS
Bounty also shipped with Cook on this voyage.

The expedition departed Plymouth for the Pacific
Ocean in July of 1776, only days after the Declaration of
Independence had been signed. After several months
in the South Seas, the ships sailed north from Bora
Bora in December of 1777. A month later they became
the first Europeans to visit the Hawaiian Islands. After
hurried reprovisioning on Kauai, the vessels sailed on
to the mainland, arriving in March of 1778. The coastal
weather that spring was typically unstable, forcing
Cook to explore the shoreline via telescope, well clear
of potential hazards. Only the largest features made his
journals. As daylight faded on March 29, Cook sighted
a promontory which he called Cape Flattery, noting
incorrectly that it did not lead to the fabled STRAIT OF
JUAN DE FUCA. After pausing briefly to trade for furs
with Indians at NOOTKA Sound, the *Resolution* and
Discovery spent the next several months examining
much of what is now the Canadian and Alaskan
shoreline before returning to Hawaii. The natives
received the English visitors with a hospitality bordering on deification. Cook, as the leader, was the recipient of most of the adulation, but enough peripheral
benefits fell on the crew to make them view their
departure from the islands, the following month, with
considerable regret.

Their absence was to be short-lived. Encountering
heavy weather north of the islands, the *Resolution*
sprung a foremast, forcing them to return and effect
repairs. Their welcome was not what they had anticipated. The natives had turned inexplicably sullen and
resentful. Incidents of petty thievery, followed by
altercations, began to occur. The situation deteriorated rapidly. A chisel and blacksmith tongs were
stolen; one night the *Discovery*'s cutter was taken. The
following morning, Cook took a party of men ashore

to recover the boat. Cook, a peaceful man, underestimated the potential for violence. Ill-prepared, the Englishmen were overwhelmed by the angry islanders. Cook and four marines were killed.

After returning from the Cook expedition, Vancouver, then a lieutenant, was assigned first to a warship and later to a survey ship in the Caribbean. While Vancouver's career accelerated, events occurred in the Northwest that would determine the course of his remaining life. Fur trading with the Indians had escalated into a small but extremely lucrative East-West industry since Captain Cook's casual trading with the Indians at Nootka. Traders from several nations had begun to eye the Northwest with a certain avarice.

Among these entrepreneurs was an Englishman named John Meares, who had served Cook on his last voyage and was quick to recognize the potential profit at Nootka. Trade by the English in the Pacific was, at that time, exclusively controlled by two monopolistic companies: The South Sea Company held all rights to trade on the Northwest Coast, and the East India Company held jurisdiction over trade in China. An English vessel desiring to enter a pan-Pacific enterprise was required to have a license from both firms. Further, the trader had to submit his ship to the often capricious command of the East India Company. A trader found in noncompliance was considered a poacher and could have his vessel seized as a lawful prize.

In spite of the risks, John Meares took the outlaw path. His first efforts ended disastrously when twenty-three of his crew succumbed to scurvy while wintering in Prince William Sound. He was rescued by two legitimate vessels sent out from London, both captained by Cook alumni. Although they did not seize Meares's ship, they did require him to post a bond guaranteeing that he would no longer trade on the Northwest Coast. Meares traveled to Macao and took on a figurehead Portuguese partner, returning to the Northwest in 1788 with two ships, both ostensibly under the Portuguese flag. He encountered no difficulties that year and returned to Macao with enough financial clout to engineer a merger with a licensed English trading company. He planned to return to Nootka the following spring with four vessels.

In California, the Spanish were concerned about

British and American interest in territory they considered their domain. Since 1774 they had periodically sent expeditions up the coast charting and taking possession of lands as far north as Prince William Sound. In order to secure their claim, Captain Esteban José Martinez was commissioned to sail north from Mexico and establish a garrison at Nootka. When he arrived, Martinez found that Meares's ships and an American vessel had arrived two weeks earlier.

Suspicious of the Portuguese-British documentation of Meares's ships, Martinez seized one vessel, releasing it two weeks later because he could not spare the men to deliver it to Mexico. It left hastily on a trading cruise. Meares's second ship, which had been away trading with the Indians, returned only to be held by the Spanish as security against debts they claimed the first ship had accrued. A few days later, one of Meares's new ships arrived. Relations were cordial, and the English crew watched the Spanish formally take possession of the Nootka Sound. That evening the last of Meares's ships, under the command of Captain Colnett, sailed into port, bringing with it the components of a processing plant that Meares intended to erect at Nootka. Martinez told the captain that he would not allow the construction of an English factory on Spanish soil. The Englishman, in an act of sterling diplomacy, called Martinez "a God damned Spaniard."
He was immediately arrested and his ship seized, as was each of Meares's other vessels on their return to Nootka.

Silhouette of Captain Vancouver's flagship, HMS Discovery

At this time, the English were readying their own official expedition to Nootka, using Cook's voyage as justification for possession. Two vessels would take part. One would travel to Australia with a complement of convicts to be used as laborers and settlers. The *Discovery*, a new ship with the same name as Cook's consort vessel, commanded by Captain Roberts, would chart the Northwest Coast and take formal possession of Nootka. While Vancouver, as first lieutenant, readied the *Discovery* for the voyage, word of the Spanish action at Nootka reached England. Spain sent a demand that England henceforth keep its vessels out of Spanish territory. England responded that it did not recognize Spanish sovereignty in the Northwest and was itself planning a settlement at Nootka. They further demanded the return of Meares's ships and financial restitution. Spain did not immediately reply to the British, using the time to mobilize forces. Recognizing that giving in to Spain would mean the exclusion of British interests from the eastern Pacific, the English king ordered an armament and general impressment to match Spain's. The English expedition to Nootka was postponed.

England, pressing its case internationally, secured powerful allies in the Dutch and Prussian fleets. Faced with England's vastly superior position, Spain yielded and in November of 1790 accepted a negotiated settlement. The Nootka Convention secured for Britain the return of the lands and buildings taken at Nootka in 1789 and awarded payment for damages. It provided free access for settlement and trade to both countries in any territory north of the Spanish settlements that existed prior to the seizure at Nootka. In essence, it gave the British a territorial grasp on the Northwest without defining Spanish boundaries.

The idea for an English expedition to Nootka was immediately revived. Captain Roberts had accepted another command in the Caribbean, and consequently Vancouver was promoted to master and commander. The *Discovery* took only a month to activate. The *Chatham*, a 130–ton brig, was acquired as the consort vessel. On April 1, 1791, the expedition departed Falmouth for Nootka. In addition to taking possession of the lands at Nootka, Vancouver's prime responsibility was charting the coast from thirty to sixty degrees north latitude. While the Spanish had explored much of that area previously, none of their charts were published. To the English it was virgin territory. By the time they departed the South Seas for America, the crew had charted areas of Australia, New Zealand, Tahiti, and Hawaii.

Vancouver was meticulous. In the three weeks before making a landfall on the California coast, he had made eighty-five lunar observations to ensure the accuracy of his starting point. Coastal bearings were kept on an eight-column chart and updated each mile. Even so, he was to make a crucial omission. For all his care, Vancouver failed to notice the low-lying entrance to the Columbia River. Shortly thereafter he chanced upon the American vessel *Columbia* under Captain Robert Gray, who told Vancouver of the river's existence. Two weeks later Gray sailed into it. His exploration eventually gave the United States important leverage in Northwest boundary disputes with England. Vancouver continued up the coast and entered the Strait of Juan de Fuca in late April of 1792. For two days the ships worked through bad weather along the southern shore. As they prepared to anchor at New Dungeness, Lieutenant Baker first spotted through the dissipating overcast the mountain that bears his name.

The arduous journey had taken its toll on the ships. Vancouver spent the following two days locating an appropriate anchorage where they could refit and collect the astronomical data necessary for accurate surveying. On May 2 the *Discovery* and the *Chatham* anchored in a well-protected harbor Vancouver named PORT DISCOVERY in honor of his ship. While much of the crew set about building an observatory and collecting supplies, Vancouver took a party of three small boats under himself, Lieutenant Puget, and Mr. Johnstone of the *Chatham* to reconnoiter the waters ahead.

On May 7, 1792, the expedition spent the night on the shore near Point Hudson. Vancouver and several of his company walked the shoreline south to an abandoned Indian village at KAH TAI. Menzies, the ship's botanist, was impressed with the agricultural potential of the land, suggesting that European cattle might someday replace herons as the land's preeminent species. Before departing, Vancouver bestowed the name Port Townshend on the harbor in honor of the MARQUIS OF TOWNSHEND.

Using small boats and always following the right-hand shore, Vancouver mapped HOOD CANAL in eight days. Puget, assisted by Whidbey, took the next expedition, charting all of the upper sound in the same amount of time. For his effort Vancouver gave the name PUGET SOUND to the area from Restoration Point southward. In just over a month, the crew of the *Discovery* mapped virtually the entire shoreline of what is now known as ADMIRALTY INLET and PUGET SOUND. In the process they left their names indelibly on much of the area's topography.

From Puget Sound the *Discovery* and *Chatham* moved north into the SAN JUAN ISLANDS. While Vancouver continued his work through the Inside Passage, the Spanish waited anxiously for his arrival at Nootka. Revilla Gigedo, the Spanish viceroy in

Mexico, was a staunch opponent of the Nootka agreement. He had earlier been made aware of an English map that placed Spain's territorial boundary just north of San Francisco. To Gigedo this was proof of England's imperialist intentions. After conferring with Madrid, he ordered an armed garrison established at NEAH BAY. He then began to build a case against Meares's claim at Nootka, believing that if he could force a compromise with the English there, the case for setting Spain's boundary north of the Strait of Juan de Fuca would be stronger. To handle the delicate negotiations, he assigned Captain Juan Francisco de la Bodega y Quadra as governor at Nootka.

Vancouver, for his part, was under instruction to wait for Admiralty orders before entering into any discussions with the Spanish. As his survey cleared the northern tip of Vancouver Island, he received word that his orders had arrived. Vancouver sailed into Nootka on August 28. After the usual formalities, Vancouver and his men were entertained lavishly by the always charming and hospitable Quadra. Although neither Vancouver nor Quadra spoke the other's language, a solid friendship began to develop. Two days after their arrival, Quadra sent a letter outlining the Spanish position. In addition to a discussion of Spain's early explorations in the area, Quadra presented letters from two American captains as well as the captain of one of Meares's ships, discrediting Meares's claims to Nootka. Quadra indicated that in the interest of peace Spain was willing to cede Nootka to England, providing Vancouver would recognize Nootka as the northern border of Spain's territory and stay out of the Strait of Juan de Fuca.

Vancouver's instructions from England, prepared a year earlier, were woefully inadequate, directing him only to take possession of the properties at Nootka. He had no authority to reopen negotiations. The Admiralty had not even specified what Vancouver was to do with Nootka once he had taken possession of it. For two weeks Quadra pressed his case while Vancouver steadfastly refused to compromise. Ultimately they agreed to continue the status quo. Vancouver would not accept anything that could weaken the Nootka Convention, therefore Spain would not deliver the properties. Their decision in effect returned the issue to their respective governments, and both Quadra and

Vancouver retreated down the coast to enjoy Spanish hospitality at Monterey for the winter. Viceroy Gigedo, seeing this as a victory, abandoned the garrison at Neah Bay.

Over the next two summers, Vancouver continued his survey of the Northwest coast while awaiting word from England on Nootka. During this period he charted with extraordinary accuracy the continental coastline north of Vancouver Island to Kodiak Island. He also cultivated a relationship with Chief Kamehameha of Hawaii that led to the islands' cession to the British throne. Had England followed up on Vancouver's achievement, Hawaii would probably be British still. In 1795 Spain and England agreed to a mutual abandonment of Nootka. English colors would be flown then struck. Both countries would withdraw from the area and open it to use by any nation. Coupled with Gigedo's withdrawal from Neah Bay, this agreement once again left San Francisco as Spain's de facto northern boundary.

Vancouver did not return to Nootka for the finale. His survey complete, he was on his way home. After four and one-half years and sixty-five thousand miles at sea, the *Discovery* arrived in Deptford on October 20, 1795. Vancouver's voyage and his achievements went largely unnoticed by the general population. England was at war with France, and events of half a world away could be easily ignored. In failing health, Vancouver began to organize his journals for publication. On May 12, 1798, while working on the last of the six books that encompassed his journey, Vancouver died. He was buried in an obscure grave at St. Peter's Church in Petersham, Surrey.   [M.W.]

The bite: Used in "Where's the bite?" or "When's the bite?" referring to the place where fish are biting or the time, usually one hour before or after a slack tide.

The black buoy: Place reference, actually a green buoy (having been repainted) located at the west end of Protection Island.

Breath mints: Herring (also called Norwegian breath mints).

Chicken: A small halibut.

Dog salmon: Chum salmon.

Gillnetter: A fishing boat equipped with a vertically

suspended mesh net that entraps the heads of fish.

Green eyes: A dogfish.

High liner: A successful fisherman, recognized by having a broom on the mast of the boat signifying a "clean sweep."

Hippie beads: Round, fluorescent beads placed behind the hook.

Hippie chrome: Duct tape.

King salmon: Also called blackmouth, Chinook, springers, and tyee (a Canadian expression usually referring to salmon over thirty pounds).

Mid-channel: Mid-Channel Bank, an underwater shelf that extends north and west from Marrowstone Point for approximately one to one and one-half miles.

Mooching: A local method of fishing salmon, using herring, a lightweight sinker, and the tide or a small motor to provide just enough movement to keep the bait spinning.

The Point: Point Wilson. When fisherman talk of where the fish are biting near the point, they may be more specific by adding "close to the dock," "by the bathhouse," or "by the fence" (same as "by the hole").

Purse seine: A weighted net that closes at the bottom, trapping a school of fish.

Reef netting: A type of fishing practiced by Indians near Lummi Island, in some areas of the San Juans, and on the Hoh and Quilcene rivers. Nets that look like reefs are suspended between two anchored boats; fishermen standing on platforms watch for fish and pull in the nets (also called set-netting).

Scow: A large, flat-bottomed boat that hangs a large net vertically in the water (see purse seine).

Silvers: Coho salmon.

Slab: A big salmon, usually a king.

Squaw candy: Smoked salmon.

Strawberry: Fish bait made from salmon eggs wrapped in a tiny cheesecloth bag.

Tourist: Anyone unfamiliar with fishing.

Troller: A boat that trolls lines with hooks on them. Gill-netters, purse seiners, and trollers are three major types of Northwest commercial fishing boats.

Turkey bell: A small bell used by steelhead fishermen as an alarm when the fish strikes.

Barber chair: A tree that splits up the middle as it is cut down. A rare but potentially lethal occurrence; also refers to the remaining stump that was split, leaving a piece of the wood standing up.

Bonus: Getting more than one log on a single choker.

The brush: Any area where downed logs lie before being taken to the landing.

Caulks or calks: (Pronounced "corks") Loggers boots with metal spikes protruding from the soles to prevent slipping while walking on wet logs.

Choker: A cable that is wrapped around logs before they are hauled to the landing.

Cutter: One who fells trees, limbs them, and cuts them into logs for transport. (Also "busheler" or "faller.")

Fell: To cut a tree down.

Gyppo: A contract logger or owner of a small company that logs for large timber holders or buys timber to log from state or federal lands.

Hickory shirt: The blue and white pin-striped denim shirt that is common logger apparel (see *Forks Tuxedo*).

Pecker poles: Small trees.

Piss fir: Douglas fir.

Punkin': A big log.

School marm: A tree with a trunk that forks near the base, usually forming two logs.

Skid: To drag a log from its stump.

The breakwater: Formerly the downtown area where the Port Townsend Plaza Shopping Center was built; a onetime favorite hangout for teenagers after ball games and other evening activities.

Crutcher around: Milling around in cars. In the early 1940s, the Crutcher brothers were renowned car buffs and were forever cruising around in their cars.

Disco Bay: Discovery Bay.

The flats: Sims Way, along the swamp before the S-curve.

The Follower: The *Port Townsend Leader*

Gazelles: A great many; lots of anything. The term derives from a large pioneer Dungeness family named Lotzgesell.

Hilltop: Formerly a reference to the entire area above the S-curve to the Hilltop Tavern. The area is now known as "Castle Hill."

Mill rat: A young temporary employee hired by the paper mill as a summer replacement for vacationing regular employees, usually a college student or recent high school graduate. Also, to work at the paper mill in any unskilled capacity (as in response to the question, "What are you going to do this summer?" "Guess I'll mill rat.")

Mortgage Hill: Residential area of Morgan Hill.

The mountain is out: Mount Rainier is visible from Port Townsend.

The mountains are out: Mount Baker, Mount Rainier, the Cascade range, and the Olympic range are visible from Port Townsend.

Nammies: Vietnam vets.

No spray: Words often posted along roads by local landowners and tenants to request that county employees not spray herbicides in the ditches of that area.

P.A.: Port Angeles

P.T.: Port Townsend

Port Tacky: Port Townsend.

Only in Port Townsend: The phrase is generally appended to a local citizen's expressed amazement at discovering yet another way in which Port Townsend is a special, wonderful, or exasperating place, as in "Five thousand people at a chili feed? Only in Port Townsend!" or "Elect a jazz musician as mayor? Only in Port Townsend!"

Quil: Quilcene.

Quilbilly: Someone from Quilcene.

Ragtown: Formerly the houses below the mill in the Glen Cove area.

Rhody: Rhododendron.

Scow Bay raincoat: A condom.

See-quim: A deliberate mispronunciation of the town of Sequim (correctly pronounced "skwim").

The Sleeze: The Sea Galley Restaurant.

The swamp: Formerly the area of the current KAH TAI LAGOON PARK and surrounding lowlands.

Townie: Someone who lives at or frequents or is associated with the Town Tavern.

VICTORIAN CHAMBER CHOIR

Early in 1979 a group of people began to meet informally in the Ace of Cups Coffee House in the UPTOWN BUSINESS DISTRICT. The piano that stood against one wall was open for use for the personal pleasure and entertainment of the customers. It was around this old upright that the Victorian Chamber Choir was conceived and nurtured. Marilyn Spafford and Sydney Keegan, both with extensive backgrounds in singing, initiated the concept of a choir to perform chamber music, both a cappella and with instruments. Their rehearsal hall moved to St. Paul's Episcopal Church, and the choir began to focus on renaissance and baroque music, adding contemporary works to their repertoire through the years. Their range includes carols, English madrigals, songs by Bach, Brahms, Berlioz, and P.D.Q. Bach. They have performed exclusively in the Olympic Peninsula, with seasonal concerts in Port Townsend and impromptu performances on Washington State ferries.

The state of Washington has the second largest veteran population in the country. In 1983 an estimated seventy-five thousand Vietnam veterans lived in King County alone, but it was estimated that some nine thousand vets had left the Seattle-dominated county for more rural areas. Statistics about Vietnam veterans are chilling: They include higher rates of unemployment, divorce, alcoholism, and domestic violence. Many have sought refuge in Port Townsend and the woods of the Olympic Peninsula. Approximately five hundred Vietnam veterans registered to vote in Jefferson County in 1985, but some veterans think there may be as many as two thousand living in the area. A high percentage are unemployed; many live in the woods, some surviving on what they hunt or fish. "We're all survivors," said one former U.S. Navy Seal who saw violence in Vietnam, "and it's easier here: the seclusion, the possibility of survival." "The ocean is the mother," suggested a woman partner of one traumatized vet. "They can recover here; they can be nursed back to health psychologically by the healing presence of nature, especially the ocean." After one year of weekly meetings dealing with what has popularly been termed "posttraumatic stress disorder," only one vet of a group working on healing themselves was still drinking alcohol, and all had stopped using other heavy drugs. Several set about establishing a veterans' center in Port Townsend, believing that this is indeed an appropriate place for men to recover from the traumas of war.

VIETNAM VETERANS

VIOLET POINT   The southeast point of PROTECTION ISLAND, Violet
                    Point was named by American Captain Charles Wilkes
                    in 1841, probably for a profusion of violets that would
                    have been in bloom at the time of his landing.

WARENSKJOLD,   American soprano Dorothy Warenskjold experienced
DOROTHY   a first in her career while performing in Port Townsend
                    during a community concert tour in 1953. During an
                    aria requiring a sustained high note, she broke the
                    eyeglasses of a twelve-year-old listener. Later, Miss
                    Warenskjold said that the incident had been the first
                    time she had been able to shatter glass with her voice,
                    although she had tried many times unsuccessfully in
                    her own bathroom.

WARHAWK   Built in 1855 in Massachusetts, the square-rigged *War-
                    hawk* was originally designed for the Cape Horn and
                    China trade. At 1,067 tons, the 182–foot-long V-hulled
                    clipper ship was synonymous with speed, frequently
                    showing its wake to steam-powered vessels. In 1871
                    the *Warhawk* was sold to a San Francisco firm that en-
                    gaged her in the coastal lumber trade. The following
                    February the *Warhawk* set a record for the route,
                    traveling from SAN FRANCISCO to Port Discovery in
                    four days, loading 750,000 board feet of lumber in
                    fifteen days, and finishing the return trip four days
                    later.

                    The *Warhawk* remained on the coast routes until its
                    end on April 12, 1883. While tied along the dock at the
                    Discovery Bay mill, fire broke out on board. The crew,
                    enjoying themselves at a local saloon, heard the alarm
                    and returned to form a bucket brigade, but the fire was
                    out of control. Afraid that the flames would spread to
                    the mill, the master of the ship ordered mooring lines
                    cut. As the *Warhawk* drifted into the bay, a small
                    boarding party managed to open the vessel's sea cocks.
                    The men's stay on board was short-lived as heat from
                    the decks caused their shoes to smoke, and the flames
                    began to close rapidly around them. They watched
                    from shore as the *Warhawk*, engulfed in a plume of
                    steam, sank in the shallow waters of Discovery Bay.
                    The *Warhawk's* grave has since become an underwater
                    state park. As the only clipper ship to have sunk in
                    continental U.S. waters, it offers scuba divers a rare
                    view into another era.

As with every community in America, Port Townsend has provided its share of youth to be consumed in the fires of war. Ensconced in bronze and marble, the classic materials of ritualized grief, their names are all that publicly remain. A plaque at the Jefferson County Courthouse commemorates twelve county men that perished in the horrors of World War I. Memorial Field is dedicated to those men plus thirty-eight others who did not return from World War II. Fort Worden has its cemetery with orderly rows of white tombstones. Even the MILL commemorates the loss of its employees in war.

On SIMS WAY, overlooking Port Townsend Bay and on to Mount Rainier, is a monument honoring only one man, Marvin Shields. A heavy-equipment mechanic with the U.S. Navy Seabees, Shields was born in Port Townsend on December 30, 1939, and spent most of his life in eastern Jefferson County. After enlisting in the navy, Shields was assigned to a civilian defense group camp at Dong Xoai, fifty miles north of Saigon. On June 9, 1965, the camp came under attack by a well-armed Vietcong regiment. For three hours after he was wounded, Shields returned enemy fire and supplied his fellow troops with ammunition. During a massive, close-range Vietcong attack with hand grenades and flame throwers, he assisted in carrying a more seriously wounded man to safety. For four more hours under heavy fire, Shields held his gun position. When the Americans came under machine-gun fire from a heavily fortified enemy emplacement, he volunteered to accompany his commanding officer outside their defensive perimeter in an attempt to knock it out. Using a 3.5–inch rocket launcher, they were able to destroy the machine gun, but while returning to their lines, Shields was mortally wounded. He died four days later. Shields was posthumously awarded the Congressional Medal of Honor by President Lyndon Johnson on September 13, 1966; he was the first Seabee to receive that medal in Vietnam.

There are no surface streams and few springs on the northeasternmost part of the Quimper Peninsula where Port Townsend perches, surrounded on three sides by saltwater. Some early settlers relied on wells: shallow wells sufficed on the flats, and water could be reached at a depth of thirty or more feet uptown and on Morgan Hill. Some people relied on rainwater, which they captured in large casks. Some used cisterns to store water. So their homes could have running water, many residents erected storage tanks filled by windmills that pumped water from the wells.

Spring Valley Water Company supplied the town with water from wells in Spring Valley, where the municipal golf course was later established. A horse-drawn water-wagon transported water door-to-door. Eventually, a gravity system was installed whereby well water was forced to an uptown reservoir at the corner of Garfield and Harrison Streets, from where it was distributed. The *Key City Mirror* went on the record with its opinion of the quality of the well water from Spring Valley: "The water is pure and healthful, but until one gets used to its flavor he does not like it, and the stranger, not knowing that it contains medicinal qualities that recommend it to the initiated generally go away with the belief that the water is unfit to drink."

A new source was sought. According to the *Leader*, the Mount Olympus Water company proudly asserted in 1889 that "Port Townsend can easily be supplied with water for every purpose for centuries to come, with their millions of population, from a large river fed by the snowy alps of the Olympic Mountains." The company proposed piping water from the Little Quilcene River: "The quality of the water is unsurpassed." But money was hard to come by, and during the nineties, although several systems were proposed, the city continued to rely on its well water.

With the arrival of soldiers at Fort Worden, the city recognized that future development and expansion depended on a reliable, abundant supply of water. By 1902 Spring Valley Water Company was raising money for a pipeline from the Olympics to reservoirs on Morgan Hill, where water enough for twenty five thousand people could be stored. James G. Swan, in 1904, was convinced that the future of Port Townsend depended on its newly acquired Fort Worden (and neighboring Forts Casey and Flagler). But increasing the size of the forts, he said in the *Leader* "is absolutely conditional on securing an adequate water supply . . . . This is an open secret on which the mayor and city councilmen were fully advised. It is also known that the war department has for some time past been regarding the re-occupation of old Fort Townsend with favor, but here again, met with lack of water supply."

On September 20, 1904, the city signed a contract with the Spring Valley Water Company. But there were, inevitably, nay-sayers who put a chill in the hearts of promoters. A "former member of the Water Company" wrote anonymously to the *Leader* that the water Spring Valley planned to use was not pure. He suggested that the city council should, before signing final contracts, "investigate, not only the supply from, but also the sources of what makes up the so-called 'Snow Creek.'" He said that Snow Creek was found "entirely inadequate as to quantity and extremely faulty as to quality, draining, as it does, a plateau of 'skunk cabbage.'" He continued, "the water is a decided red color." But the system was built at last, and water was on its way. The *Leader* gleefully announced on August 10, 1905, that water would reach the city on the 13th "and by the end of next week the people of Port Townsend should be reveling in the knowledge that the city has a supply of water surpassed for purity nowhere on earth." The *Leader* urged residents to go to the flats where the water would be coming and witness "the dawn of another and better era in the history of Port Townsend. It means more than the most sanguine anticipate."

And its arrival certainly did lift the spirits of the little town. Although delays were had in serving the city, water continued to flow to an outfall in Spring Valley, where the curious traipsed to sample the water. Finding not the slightest tinge of red or aroma of skunk cabbage, many experimented. The *Leader* reported, "Mrs. Schnath, living out in the valley, claims to be the first person to try the water of the new system as a medium for cleansing linen . . . . She tested its merits thoroughly, so she claims, and found it the best ever. In fact, linen upon which this water is used needs little elbow grease . . . . Its application to dirt eradicates that article with a celerity that is truly amazing and should bring the price of laundry work to away below Chinese prices . . . . People of Port Townsend . . . have been used to water so hard that it has driven many a man to hard drink and brought the price of a liquor license down to $300 per . . . according to engineers, . . . it has been known to rust the boiler tubes of an alimentary canal and has made appendicitis an unfashionable disease in this community. The change is appreciated." The first child christened with Snow Creek water was blessed on September 3, 1905, though his godfather had to walk two blocks for it. Later that month, the mayor said, according to the *Leader*, there was "enough water to provide for a city of 100,000 people."

After a breaking-in period, when water tended to burst out of the line here and there, the system served passably, with summer shortages, until the twenties. On August 10, 1927, the city-county health officer announced it would be "an excellent precaution to boil all drinking water." Tests show "nothing alarming but sudden rains have sent grass and leaves into the reservoir." In a timely move, Zellerbach Corporation announced its plans to assist the city in constructing a new water system in conjunction with Zellerbach's plans for a pulp MILL in Port Townsend. The city passed a bond issue for its portion of the agreement by a vote of 879 to 5. The plan to dam and pump water from the Big Quilcene and Little Quilcene rivers to Port Townsend was described as one of the largest water projects in the Northwest.

Construction on the $850,000 system was well underway in February 1928. The pipeline took eight months to complete. When water finally filled the pipes, it was directed to an outfall into Port Townsend Bay until the unpalatable flavor of creosote (that permeated the wooden pipes) had weathered away, a process which took almost two months. Although the wood pipes have since been replaced with asbestos-cement, essentially the same system supplies water to Port Townsend today. More than nineteen million gallons per day are drawn from the Big Quilcene or from Lord's Lake and channeled to the Port Townsend Paper Corporation mill and Port Townsend, with some diverted to Chimacum, Hadlock, Irondale, and Indian Island. Excess flows into the Admiralty Inlet through a picturesque cobblestone brook in Chetzemoka Park.   [R.B.]

WATER STREET   Port Townsend's main street extends one mile from SIMS WAY through the downtown commercial strip to POINT HUDSON. Until the removal of the port of entry from Port Townsend to Seattle in 1914, Water

Street was a rough-and-tumble, down-and-out thoroughfare catering to sailors, crimps, prostitutes, gamblers, and other unsavory characters. Because local businessmen were discomfited by their mothers, wives, and daughters having to shop amidst the lowlife and riffraff of Water Street, the town's only commercial core in the late nineteenth century, they encouraged the development of an uptown business district on the bluff, where shopping could be conducted in a more genteel milieu. Although Water Street was tame by World War I, it was not until 1981 that alcoholic beverages could either be purchased or consumed uptown.

An isolated western portion of the Olympic Peninsula, the West End has been described as "not quite the end of the world, but you can see it from there." The 1,200 –square-mile area is characterized by lonely Pacific beaches, tall timber, wild rivers, pounding surf and heavy and insistent rainfall that annually averages one hundred inches (more in some places), with nights as dark as the inside of a whale. Human activity is observed in the form of logging trucks, television dish antennae, Indian villages, and the town of FORKS. Though something of an endangered species, loggers and other workers in the timber industry are readily visible and easily identifiable – outsized in hickory shirts, wide suspenders, and spiked boots called caulks (pronounced "corks"), and frequently with a finger or part of a hand missing.

WEST END

The most highly held values of West Enders are a fierce sense of independence and the freedom to do what they want without outside assistance, which is seen as interference. Though established in 1937, Olympic National Park is still considered by many to be a violation of their right to use the land. Their frontier values have been maintained by their isolation.

Before 1921, the West End was reached by beaching on the ocean at Ozette or anchoring at Neah Bay and hiking inland. From Seattle the trip took seventeen hours by steamer to Clallam Bay, where a five-passenger, two-horse buckboard left at 7:30 A.M. and arrived in Forks at 5 P.M., three times a week. With the construction of the road around LAKE CRESCENT in 1921, the trip was drastically shortened, but the ten miles of harrowing curves that still lead an occasional unwary motorist to a watery grave continue the psychological isolation of the West End.

WHALES When the Makah Indians were still whalers, it took eight men to harpoon a thirty-foot, ten-ton minke whale (*Balaenoptera acutorostrata*): one man in the bow to harpoon, another in the stern to steer, and six to paddle. Towed to shore, the whale was hauled high onto the beach, and as the tide receded the crew began to carve with precision. Blubber was cut into two-foot squares that were either boiled for oil or hung out to dry. Tougher than pork, the fat was described by James G. Swan as sweet with "none of the nauseous taste which whites attribute to it." The choicest portions, near the dorsal fin, were reserved for the harpoonist, and all other cuts were distributed according to a mutually accepted ranking system.

The whale was as useful to the Indians as the CEDAR tree. Its flesh was a major source of food, and its sinews were turned into rope, cords, and bowstrings. The stomach and intestines were inflated and dried, then used as containers for the oil which was used in the same manner as butter was by whites. Swan said that "when fresh, it is by no means unpalatable." The whale was also the primary food of the Thunderbird, who was believed to be a giant MAKAH living in the high mountains. When hungry, the Thunderbird would don a bird's head, enormous wings, and feathers, then fly over the ocean to hunt whales, which he carried to his aerie to eat. It was the Thunderbird's wings that caused thunder and lightning, and when storms occurred, the Makah searched for a bird feather or carcass, which would endow them with great power, including the ability to kill whales. Swan told of an occasion in Port Townsend during the 1860s when fireworks were lighted and "a number of rockets upon bursting displayed fiery serpents. The Indians believed they were Ha-hek-to-ak, or thunderbird, and for a long time made application to the gentleman who gave the display for the pieces of the animal for which they offered fabulous prices ($200)."

Makah painting of the Thunderbird and the Whale

In the late twentieth century, four species of whale can be seen in inland waters. The minke favored by the Makah were difficult for white whalers to catch. Spared commercial exploitation until recent years, they are fairly abundant; at ten tons they are the smallest of the species. The Humpback whales (*Megaptera novaeangliae*) were nearly extinguished because of their accessibility from shorelines and inland waters; the largest of the species, the humpback gained protected status in 1966. California gray whales (*Eschrichtius robustus*) migrate from the Bering Sea in summer to Baja, Mexico, in winter and visit local waters in late fall and late spring, passing by Port Townsend on their way to the mud bays of Bellingham and southern Puget Sound. The orca or killer whale (*Orcinus orca*) is the most abundant, with eighty whales in three pods known to reside in Puget Sound. Shiny black with a stark white belly, the orca is actually a dolphin. It impresses with its six-foot-high by three-foot-wide dorsal fin. It is an extraordinarily intelligent animal with a brain larger than man's. It has a complex social organization and highly refined linguistic skills. As the only cetacean to prey on warm-blooded animals as well as cold, the orca occupies a position in the hierarchy of the sea equivalent to man's position on the land. It seldom is threatening to boaters or divers, and those who encounter an orca are often so awestruck by the experience that they become advocates for the whales' protection.

WHIDBEY ISLAND

A 172-square-mile island east of Port Townsend that extends from PUGET SOUND to the STRAIT OF JUAN DE FUCA, Whidbey Island is the largest island surrounded by saltwater in the continental United States. (New York's Long Island is nearly ten times larger, but a recent U.S. Supreme Court ruling declared it a peninsula.) The southern and central portions of the island are essentially rural in character. The northern reaches of the island, however, are congested by the impact of seven thousand military personnel attached to the Whidbey Island Naval Air Station, which is one of the state's five repositories for nuclear weapons. The island's population of forty-five thousand is expected to nearly double by the year 2000.

WHITNEY GARDENS

A seven-acre showcase of the Washington State flower – the rhododendron, Whitney Gardens on the HOOD CANAL at BRINNON features twenty-five hundred display plants of more than seventy species, which begin blooming in February and continue into July, with the peak season around Mother's Day. William E. Whitney began the gardens in 1956, and his interest in hybridizing was continued by his successor, Anne Sather. More than twenty-five thousand plants are for sale, giving the gardens one of the largest selections of rhododendrons in the state.

WINERIES Though largely dependent upon other areas in the state for vinifera grapes, three wineries nevertheless are established on the peninsula. The largest and best known is the prizewinning Neuharth Winery in Sequim, which features both white and red table wines. Californians Gene and Maria Neuharth began their Sequim operation in 1979 and soon started experiments in the local propagation of several varieties, which they bottle under the generic name Dungeness. More recently, the Lone Mountain Winery was established on the west side of Sequim, and the Hoodsport Winery on Hood Canal has developed a prizewinning rhubarb wine.

WOODEN BOAT FESTIVAL Celebrating the renaissance of the art of wooden boat building in Port Townsend, the Wooden Boat Festival has been held annually since 1977. The festival comprises three days of demonstrations and workshops and a Sunday afternoon regatta that harks back nearly a century to when Port Townsend Bay was filled daily with wooden boats. (See *Boat Building*.)

WOOL DOGS Indians along the Strait of Juan de Fuca once kept and bred a peculiar long-haired dog and used its wool to make blankets and other garments. Because dog wool was highly prized, any woman possessing a large number of these dogs had special status. To shear the animals, Indians tied the dogs' forelegs together and cut the wool with a stone knife. The color of the fur was light, though not as white as the mountain goat's. The Indians were known to beat the dogs' wool with a white diatomaceous earth to remove some of the grease, a process which also bleached the wool somewhat. Sometimes the wool was dyed pink with hemlock or alder bark. According to George Vancouver, the wool was so thick and tight that a whole piece could be picked up by one corner and would not fall apart. It was often mixed with other materials such as cedar bark, fireweed cotton, geese or duck down, or cattail rush.

The wool dog is an odd historical phenomenon since Indians did not typically control and domesticate animals as they did the wool dog. They even kept the animals on separate islands to guard against interbreeding. The history of the breed is also a mystery. It disappeared in the latter part of the nineteenth century when Indians began using fragments of HUDSON'S BAY COMPANY blankets and weaving them into their own to make more colorful and complex designs, and began allowing their dogs to interbreed. Few reports remain of its behavior or appearance. Early explorers noted that it howled instead of barked. Vancouver said the dog resembled the Pomeranian, but the Pomeranian of Vancouver's day may not been the same Pomeranian lapdog of later centuries. Another explorer also used the Pomeranian reference but reported that the Indian breed was much larger.

These descriptions still do not offer a history of the breed, but they do give grounds for speculation. The Pomeranian is a member of the spitz family and was once a large dog, like the German wolfspitz. Known to Europe for several centuries, it was common in the 1800s when it was called loup-loup, a name that acknowledged the wolflike side of its ancestry. Some have speculated that the breed wandered across Asia with nomadic German tribes, established itself, and joined other tribes that eventually made their way onto the North Pacific coast of America. Although plausible, it does not explain why wool dogs were found almost exclusively in the Puget Sound area and not farther north.

XENOPHOBIA

A story goes that when asked by an anthropologist what his people called America before the white man came, an Indian replied, "Ours." That is how many non-Indian natives have felt about Port Townsend since *their* arrival. It is theirs. And heaven help the newcomer who does not figure this out. The question is not simply one of territory or ancestry, although acceptance does come sooner if at least one parent was born in Port Townsend. Rather, it is mostly about time. Old-timers judge newcomers on a lot of things, but durability and "the good sense to stay out of things that aren't any of their business" are major criteria.

Dues are paid in Port Townsend by putting in time, settling down, and waiting one's turn to have a say. The town is known for its hospitality to visitors and tourists, but that is because they are just passing through; all new residents are thought to be transient for their first twenty or thirty years. Acceptance of this norm is easily observed when those who have put in two, five, or ten years can be seen to roll their eyes and sigh knowingly at the uninvited suggestions of the even more recent arrivals.

It was ever so. From its earliest days, Jefferson County residents have been unenthusiastic about newcomers. At the first meeting of Indians and Europeans, hostility was evident (see *Destruction Island*), and once white settlers took hold of the land, the hostility reversed (see *Indians*). Although treated better in Port Townsend than in other Puget Sound towns, CHINESE laborers fell victim to xenophobic prejudices in the 1880s.

At the opening of World War II, Japanese families became the victims. In April 1941, the *Leader* reported that high school senior George Nakano was the third member of his family to be valedictorian of his Port Townsend high school class. One year and one day later, the *Leader* headlined: "Japanese Farmers Dispose of Property." Some sold, others rented, some let the land go fallow. In all, five Japanese families and the Japanese wife and child of a white resident were relocated. The *Leader* made no mention of threat from or to the departing group; neither was mention made of any local objections to their removal. On June 4, 1942, the *Leader* said that "many of the Japanese appeared sad at having to leave their homes. Most of them, children of several established county families, were American born." The last Nakano child, Evangeline, finished her schooling in an internment camp.

The Vietnam War brought another rash of xenophobic fever when several Democrats, some old-timers but mostly newcomers, began in the early 1970s to protest the country's involvement in Southeast Asia. Political meetings grew rancorous. As in the rest of America, opposition to the war was often associated with "hippies," an all-inclusive designation that conjured up images of unkempt, long-haired youth wearing beads, beards, ankle bracelets, dirty T-shirts and blue jeans; smoking marijuana and hashish; and having sex wherever and with whomever they pleased. Drug raids were held, usually with minor success – a half-smoked joint, a stray amphetamine.

The increase of counter-cultural residents in the 1970s brought speculation as to their source – it was as if Haight-Ashbury had moved north. Some claimed issues of the *Berkeley Barb* contained stories and advertisements extolling Jefferson County as a place for easy welfare benefits. The suggestion that Port Townsend was an easier touch than elsewhere had no basis, but the rumor persisted. One summer the county commissioners took complaints from a constituent that his neighborhood was "devaluating and degrading" because hippies had rented the property next door. Although none had actually moved in yet, he wanted to know if the property could be condemned. He was, he said, afraid to leave his own property, even for a few days, for fear what the hippies might do. To their credit, the commissioners declined to interfere directly, although they did agree to notify the property owners that a neighbor had complained about their choice of tenants.

When newcomers in the 1970s challenged commercial development plans for Kah Tai Lagoon, filing lawsuits that reached the state supreme court, many old-timers were outraged, calling them "professional dissenters." "What it's all about," says Bob DeWeese, one of those so labeled, "is getting people to think about these things ... you have to operate on the premise that knowledge is better than ignorance." In 1976 – the nation's bicentennial – the Town Hall Forum was established. For the first time – outside local coffee shops and other watering holes – a public forum was available for the discussion of public issues. It helped. Old-timers met and argued with newcomers about everything under the sun.

One longtime observer says that Port Townsend is an either/or town, boom or bust, us versus them, a take-it-or-leave-it sort of place. There exists – something almost encourages – a clash among people: a territoriality, a view of others as competitors – the enemy. It is not, he observes, a town of team players, but rather of solo acts, and it attracts more of the same.

Those who come want to be the last ones in the gate. They agree with an old-timer who puts a nice reverse on the booster's maxim, observing that Port Townsend needs only two roads: a dirt road in, and a paved road out!

The yearning to keep things the way they never were, to go back to the good old days, made public appearance in Port Townsend as long ago as 1890. A front-page letter to the editor opined: "Can you tell me where I can get a claim five miles away from the nearest settler? I came to Quilcene 25 years ago, and for 20 years I ate my clams and tended my potatoes in peace; but now everything is changed. Newcomers object to my way of life, saying I am in the way. They build roads across my ranch, levy taxes for schools and are now in a fare way to cut me in two with a railroad .... Now, 'twixt the ringing of the bells and blowing of whistles I reckon I shall go plum crazy. So send me down a chap with the cash and he kin take my cabin and 'tater patch, and I'll take the road again...."

One hundred years later, hardly a week goes by that some newcomer doesn't write the *Leader* with one or more of the same complaints, threatening to leave the minute the town changes by admitting even one more newcomer. Newcomers often are miffed at being labeled as such, quizzing local residents about how long it takes before people stop referring to them as new. The answer is, it depends. As a general rule, if the person the newcomer is talking to can remember when the newcomer moved to Port Townsend, then the newcomer is still new. Old-timers especially like to devil newcomers of only twenty or thirty years residence, maneuvering them into an exchange that is the secret delight of all old and new members of the club: "Have you lived here all your life?"

"Not yet."

YOUTH HOSTELS   More than two thousand travelers a year, nearly one-third of international origin, stay at the American Youth Hostel at FORT WORDEN. In addition to the year-round facilities at Fort Worden, a hostel at FORT FLAGLER State Park is open from April to October. The hostels operate on the European model: Users bring their own bedding and food, sleep in bunk-style dormitories for men and women (although Fort

Worden has two family rooms), cook their own meals in the hostel's kitchen, and socialize with other travelers in the common room.

(*Greater Harmony Company*) Owned by the Ng family, the Zee Tai Company was the earliest (established in 1879), and the most prosperous of the CHINESE mercantile houses in Port Townsend. In 1890 it was the largest grossing business in the city, clearing more than one hundred thousand dollars. Unlike many Chinese businesses, established primarily to bypass the Chinese Exclusion Acts, the Zee Tai Company was a vigorous and active concern, with at least three branches in the Northwest. As with the smaller Wing Sing and Yee Sing Wo Kee companies, Zee Tai concerned itself primarily with importing Chinese goods such as rice, china, tea, and opium. For the latter, they provided smoking facilities in the basement of the store. Zee Tai Company was also a labor contractor, providing much of the Chinese labor used in the Northwest. Contrary to popular belief, most Chinese labor contractors made their profit not from garnishing a percentage of the laborer's wages, but from contracting with companies to supply board for the workers they provided. The company closed its doors in the 1930s.

Charlie Tze Hong, an agent for the Zee Tai Company

A summer squash that grows in incredible profusion in the cool climate of Puget Sound, the zucchini is shared more frequently than any other vegetable. By the end of summer, residents are known to not answer their doors when they spy a neighbor gardener arrive with a cardboard box; invariably it is filled with a gift of zucchini. In SEQUIM, an annual international zucchini festival is held in September as the season is ending. The best of the crop is put on display with exhibits and recipe contests, carvings (such as a working flute made of zucchini), and a look-alike contest. The largest vegetable to date was recorded at twenty-three and one-half pounds. The Zucchini Olympics concludes the daylong celebration: The vegetable is hurled as a discus, passed as a baton, thrust as a lance, and tossed as a basketball in a hoop-shoot contest. Said a visiting Briton at a recent festival, "We have them in England, although we call them 'marrows,' ... but I don't think we would have a festival like this." (See *Abundant Life Seed Foundation*.)

OLYMPIC PENINSULA

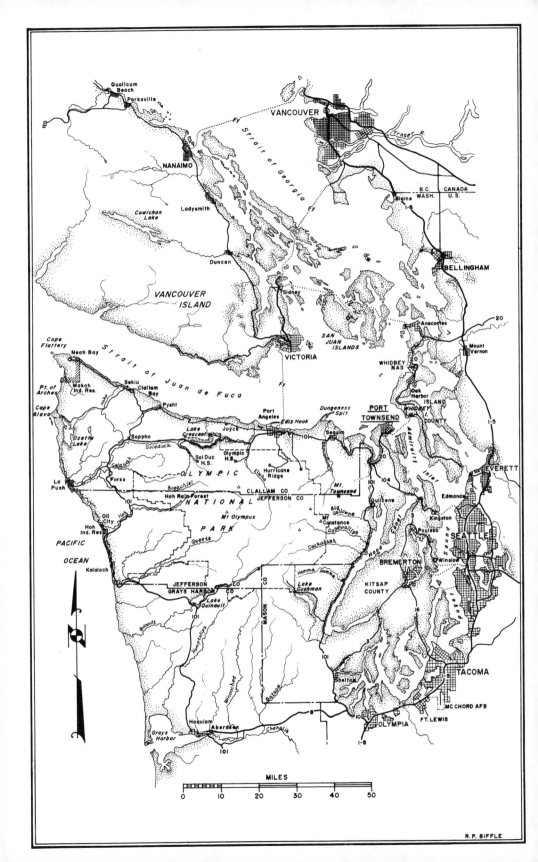

MILES

0   10   20   30   40   50

R.P. BIFFLE

EASTERN JEFFERSON COUNTY

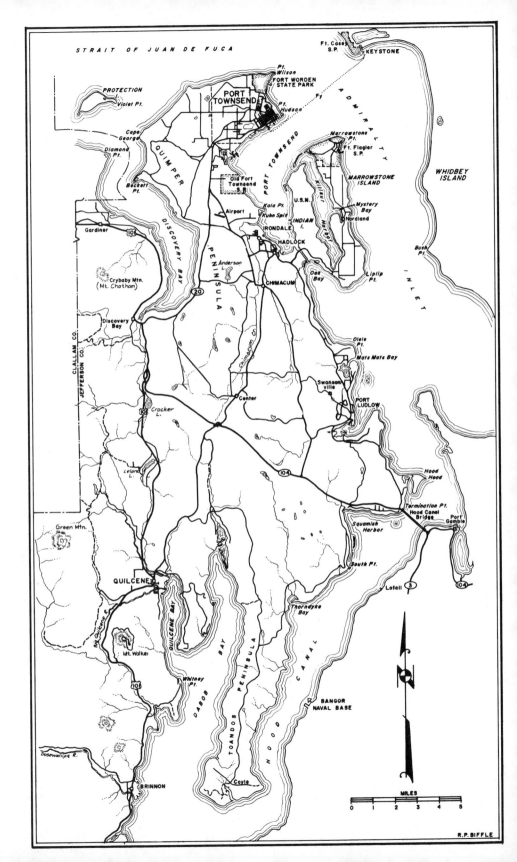

CITY OF PORT TOWNSEND

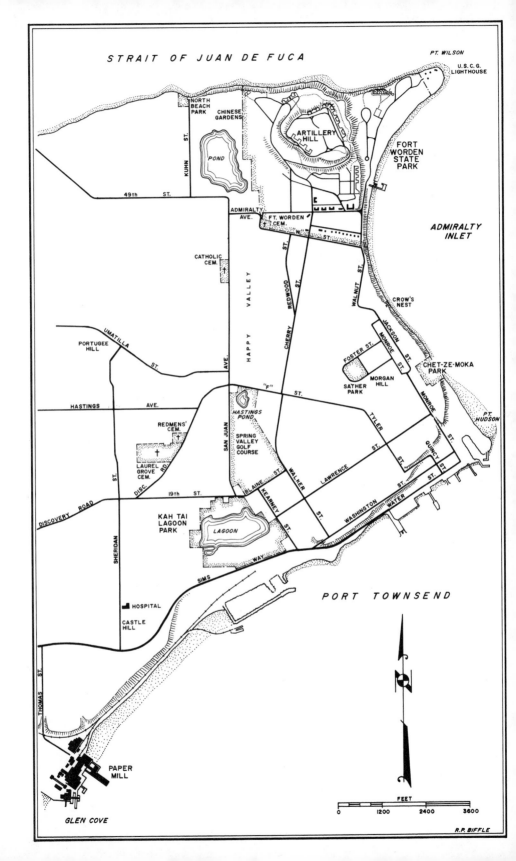

PORT TOWNSEND CITY CENTER

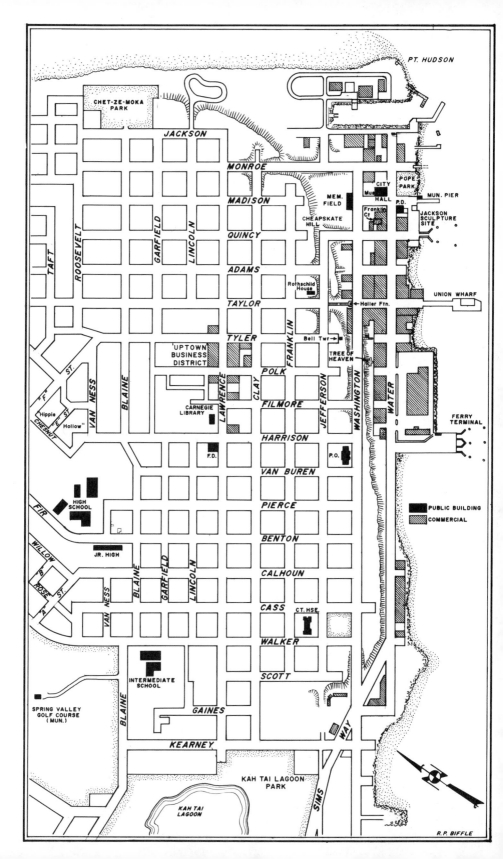

Bibliography

ADAMS, W. CLAUDE. *History of Papermaking in the Pacific North-* BOOKS
west. Portland, Ore.: Binfords & Mort, 1951.

ALT, DAVID D. and Hyndman, Donald W. *Roadside Geology of Washington*. Missoula, Mont.: Mountain Press, 1984.

ANDERSON, BERN. *Surveyor of the Sea: The Life and Voyages of Captain George Vancouver*. Seattle: University of Washington Press, 1960.

ANGELL, TONY, and Balcomb, Kenneth C. III. *Marine Birds and Mammals of Puget Sound*. Seattle: Puget Sound Books, 1982.

ANDREWS, RALPH W. *Indian Primitive: Northwest Coast Indians of the Former Days*. New York: Bonanza Books, 1960.

ARIMA, E.Y. *The West Coast (Nootka) People*. Victoria, B.C.: British Columbia Provincial Museum, 1983.

BAGLEY, CLARENCE B. *Indian Myths of the Northwest*. Seattle: Lowman & Hanford, 1930.

BEAGLEHOLE, J.C. *The Life of Captain James Cook*. Stanford: Stanford University Press, 1974.

BECKETT, ADELLE S. *Relative Speaking*. Santa Monica: Castle Press, 1981.

BERMAN, BRUCE D. *Encyclopedia of American Shipwrecks*. Boston: Mariners Press, 1972.

BINNS, ARCHIE. *Sea in the Forest*. Garden City: Doubleday, 1953.

BERGLAND, ERIC. *Summary Prehistory and Ethnography of Olympic National Park, Washington*. Seattle: National Park Service, 1983.

BISH, ROBERT L. *Governing Puget Sound*. Seattle: Puget Sound Books, 1982.

BLAU, S. FORREST. *Exploring the Olympic Seashore*. Washington, D.C.: Government Printing Office, 1980.

BROWN, BRUCE, *Mountain in the Clouds: A Search for the Wild Salmon*. New York: Simon and Schuster, 1982.

BURNS, ROBERT. *The Shape and Form of Puget Sound*. Seattle: Puget Sound Books, 1985.

CAMPBELL, PATRICIA. *A History of the North Olympic Peninsula*. Port Angeles, Wash.: The Daily News, 1977. Reprint Port Angeles, Wash.: Peninsula Publications, 1979.

CHASAN, DANIEL JACK. *The Water Link: A History of Puget Sound as a Resource*. Seattle: Puget Sound Books, 1981.

CLUTESI, GEORGE. *Potlatch*. Sidney: Gray's Publishing, 1969.

COLE, DOUGLAS. *Captured Heritage: The Scramble for Northwest Coast Artifacts*. Seattle: University of Washington Press, 1985.

COLSON, ELIZABETH. *The Makah Indians: A Study of an Indian in Modern Society*. Minneapolis: University of Minnesota Press, 1953. Reprint Westport, Conn.: Greenwood Press, 1974.

COMAN, EDWIN JR., and Gibbs, Helen M. *Time, Tide and Timber: Over a Century of Pope and Talbot*. Stanford: Stanford University Press, 1949.

COUSTEAU, JACQUES YVES. *Costeau Almanac*. Garden City: Doubleday, 1981.

COSTELLO, J.A. *The Siwash: Their Life, Legends, and Tales*. Seattle: The Calvert Company, 1895. Reprint Seattle: The Shorey Book Store, 1967.

CROWN ZELLERBACH CORP. *Neah Bay, Washington: A Brief Historical Sketch*. San Francisco: Crown Zellerbach Corp., 1964.

DENISON, ALLEN T. and Huntington, Wallace K. *Victorian Architecture of Port Townsend, Washington*. Saanichton, B.C. and Seattle: Hancock House, 1978.

DOIG, IVAN. *Winter Brothers: A Season at the Edge of America*. New York: Harcourt Brace Jovanovich, 1980.

DOWNING, JOHN. *The Coast of Puget Sound: Its Processes and Development*. Seattle: Puget Sound Books, 1983.

DRUCKER, PHILIP. *Indians of the Northwest Coast*. Garden City: The Natural History Press, 1955.

EELLS, REV. MYRON. *The Twana, Chemakum, and Klallam Tribes of Washington Territory*. Washington, D. C.: Smithsonian Annual Report, 1897. Reprint Seattle: The Shorey Book Store, 1971.

EVANS, GAIL. *Historic Resource Study, Olympic National Park*. Seattle: National Park Service, 1983.

FISH, HARRIET U. *Tracks, Trails and Tales in Clallam County*. Carlsborg, Wash: Harriet U. Fish, 1983.

FLETCHER, ELIZABETH HUELSDONK. *The Iron Man of the Hoh: The Man, Not the Myth*. Port Angeles, Wash.: Creative Communications, 1979.

GARRAND, LIVINGSTON. *Traditions of the Quinault Indians*. New York: American Museum of Natural History, vol. 4, 1902. Reprint Seattle: The Shorey Book Store, 1973.

FITCH, JAMES MARSTON. *American Building: The Forces That Shape It*. Boston: Houghton Mifflin, 1948.

FITCH, JAMES MARSTON. *American Building: The Environmental Forces That Shape It*. Boston: Houghton Mifflin, 1972.

GIBBS, GEORGE. *Indian Tribes of Washington Territory*. Washington, D.C.: report to U.S. House of Representatives, 1854. Reprint Fairfield, Wash.: Ye Galleon Press, 1967.

GREGORY, V.J. *Keepers at the Gate*. Port Townsend, Wash.: Port Townsend Publishing Co., 1976.

GREGORY, V.J., McCurdy, Richard F., and Davis, Zilpha B., eds. *With Pride in Heritage: History of Jefferson County*. Port Townsend, Wash.: Jefferson County Historical Society, 1966.

GUBERLET, MURIEL LEWIN. *Animals of the Seashore*. Portland, Ore.: Binfords & Mort, 1962.

GUNTHER, ERNA. *Ethnobotany of Western Washington: The Knowledge and Use of Indigenous Plants by Native Americans*. Seattle: University of Washington Press, 1940.

GUNTER, ERNA. *Indian Life on the Northwest Coast of North America*. Chicago: University of Chicago Press, 1972.

GUNTHER, ERNA. *Klallam Ethnography*. Publications in Anthropology vol. 1, no. 5. Seattle: University of Washington, 1927.

GUNTHER, ERNA, and Haaeberlin, Hermann. *The Indians of Puget Sound*. Seattle: University of Washington Press, 1930.

HANIFY, MARY LOU, and Blencowe, Craig. *Guide to the Hoh Rain Forest*. Seattle: Superior Publishing Co., 1974.

HILSON, STEPHEN. *Exploring Puget Sound and British Columbia*. Holland, Mich.: Van Winkle Publishing Co., 1975.

HOLBROOK, STEWART. "The Epic of Timber." In *Northwest Harvest: Regional Stock-Taking*, edited by V.L.O. Chittick, pp. 83–100. New York: McMillan, 1948.

HUNT, HERBERT, and Kaylor, Floyd C. *Washington West of the Cascades*. Chicago: S.J. Clarke, 1917.

JOHNSON, THOMAS H., with Wish, Harvey. *The Oxford Companion to American History*. New York: Oxford University Press, 1966.

JULYAN, ROBERT HIXSON. *Mountain Names*. Seattle: The Mountaineers, 1984.

KAUNE, ROBERT W, JR. *Indian Village Nature Trail*. Rev. ed. Port Angeles, Wash.: Olympic Natural History Assn., 1973.

KEYHOE, DONALD. *Flying Saucers: Top Secret*. New York: G.P. Putnam's Sons, 1960.

KIRK, RUTH. *The Olympic Seashore*. Port Angeles, Wash.: Olympic Natural History Association, 1962.

KOZLOFF, EUGENE. *Plants and Animals of the Pacific Northwest*. Seattle: University of Washington Press, 1976.

KOZLOFF, EUGENE. *Seashore Life of the North Pacific Coast*. Seattle: University of Washington Press, 1973.

LeWARNE, CHARLES PIERCE. *Utopias on Puget Sound, 1835–1915*. Seattle: University of Washington Press, 1975.

LILLY, KENNETH E. *Marine Weather of Western Washington*. Seattle: Starpath, 1983.

LUCIA, ELLIS. *The Big Woods: Logging and Lumbering – from Bull Teams to Helicopters – in the Pacific Northwest*. Garden City: Doubleday, 1975.

MACDONALD, BETTY. *The Egg and I*. Philadelphia: J.B. Lippincott, 1945.

MAKAH NATION, in cooperation with Washington State University, National Park Service, National Science Foundation and Bureau of Indian Affairs. *The Ozette Archaeological Expedition*. Undated.

McALESTER, VIRGINIA AND LEE. *A Field Guide to American Houses*. New York: Alfred A. Knopf, 1984.

McCURDY, H.W., with Newell, Gordon. *Don't Leave Any Holidays*. Portland, Ore.: Graphic Arts Center, 1967.

McCURDY, JAMES G. *By Juan de Fuca's Strait*. Seattle: Metropolitan Press, 1937. Reprint Portland, Ore.: Binfords & Mort, 1951.

McCURDY, JAMES G. *Indian Days at Neah Bay*. Seattle: Superior Publishing Co., 1961.

McDONALD, LUCILE. *Swan Among the Indians*. Portland: Binfords & Mort, 1972.

McINTYRE, JOAN. *Mind in the Waters*. New York and San Francisco: Charles Scribner's Sons, 1974.

MIDDLETON, LYNN. *Place Names of the Pacific Northwest*. Seattle: Superior Publishing Company, 1969.

MILES, JOHN N. *Koma Kulshan: The Story of Mount Baker*. Seattle: The Mountaineers, 1984.

MORGAN, MURRAY. *The Last Wilderness*. Seattle: University of Washington Press, 1955.

MORGAN, MURRAY. *Puget's Sound: A Narrative of Early Tacoma and the Southern Sound*. Seattle: University of Washington Press, 1979.

MUSEUM OF HISTORY AND INDUSTRY. *Puget Sound Pioneer Artists: 1870–1915*. Seattle: Museum of History and Industry, 1984.

NEWELL, GORDON, ed. *The H.W. McCurdy Marine History of the Pacific Northwest, 1895–1965*. Seattle: Superior Publishing, 1966.

NEWELL, GORDON, and McCurdy, H.W., *Duty, Honor, Country: The Biography of George H. McManus, Brigadier General, United States Army*. Vancouver, Wash.: Evergreen Press, 1974.

NEWELL, GORDON. *Pacific Coastal Liners*. New York: Bonanza Books, undated.

NEWMAN, COLEMAN C. *Roosevelt Elk of Olympic National Park*. Port Angeles, Wash.; Olympic Natural History Association, 1958.

NICHOLSON, IAN. *Surveying Small Craft*. Camden, Maine: International Marine Publishing, 1974.

NIEBAUER, JAMES. *Port Townsend's Victorian Homes*. Palo Alto, Calif.: Southgate Press, 1984.

OLYMPIC MOUNTAIN RESCUE AND THE MOUNTAINEERS. *Climber's Guide to the Olympic Mountains*. 2nd ed. Seattle: The Mountaineers, 1972.

PARRATT, SMITTY. *Gods and Goblins: A Field Guide to Place Names of Olympic National Park*. Port Angeles, Wash.: CP Publications, 1984.

PELLY, T.M. *Dr. Minor*. Seattle: Loman & Hanford, 1933.

PETER, LAURENCE J. *Peter's Quotations: Ideas for Our Time*. 2nd ed. New York: Bantam Books, 1980.

PETHICK, DERECK. *First Approaches to the Northwest Coast*. Vancouver, B.C.: Douglas & McIntyre, 1976.

PHILLIPS, JAMES W. *Washington State Place Names*. Seattle: University of Washington Press, 1971.

POPPELIERS, JOHN C., Chambers, S. Allen Jr., and Schwartz, Nancy B. *What Style Is It? A Guide to American Architecture*. Washington, D.C.: Preservation Press, 1983.

POWELL, JAY, and Jensen, Vickie. *Quileute: An Introduction to the Indians of LaPush*. Seattle: University of Washington Press, 1976.

RICHARDSON, DAVID. *Pig War Islands*. Eastsound, Wash.: Orcas Publishing Company, 1971.

ROCHLIN, HARRIET AND FRED. *Pioneer Jews: A New Life in the Far West*. Boston: Houghton Mifflin Company, 1984.

RUBY, ROBERT H., and Brown, John A. *Myron Eells and the Puget Sound Indians*. Seattle: Superior Publishing Co., 1976.

RUE, WALTER. *Weather of the Pacific Coast*. Mercer Island, Wash.: The Writing Works, and Vancouver, B.C.: Gordon Soules Book Publishers, 1978.

RUSSELL, KAREN, and Bean, Jeanne. *Marrowstone*. Port Townsend, Wash.: Port Townsend Publishing Co., 1978.

SALE, ROGER. *Seattle: Past to Present*. Seattle: University of Washington, 1976. Reprint with corrections, 1978.

SHERSON, ERROLL. *The Lively Lady Townshend and Her Friends*. London: William Heinemann Ltd., 1936.

SIMPSON, PETER, and Hermanson, James. *Port Townsend: Years That Are Gone*. Port Townsend, Wash.: Port Townsend Publishing Co., Quimper Press, 1979.

SNOWDON, CLINTON A. *History of Washington: The Rise and Progress of an American State*. Vols. 1–4. New York: The Century History Company, 1909.

STERLING, E.M. *Trips and Trails, 2: Family Camps, Short Hikes, and View Roads in the Olympics, Mt. Rainier, and South Cascades*. Seattle: The Mountaineers, 1968.

STEWART, HILARY. *Indian Fishing: Early Methods on the Northwest Coast*. Seattle: University of Washington Press, 1977.

STEWART, HILARY. *Cedar: Tree of Life to the Northwest Coast Indians*. Vancouver, B.C.: Douglas and McIntyre, and Seattle: University of Washington Press, 1984.

SWAN, JAMES G. *Almost Out of this World: Scenes from Washington Territory*. Introduction by William A, Katz, Tacoma, Wash.: Washington State Historical Society, 1971.

SWAN, JAMES G. *The Indians of Cape Flattery*. Washington, D.C.: Smithsonian Institution, 1869. Reprinted Seattle: Shorey Publications, 1964.

SWAN, JAMES G. *The Northwest Coast, or Three Years' Residence in Washington Territory*. New York: Harper & Bros., 1874. Reprinted Seattle: University of Washington Press, 1972.

SWANTON, JOHN R. *Indian Tribes of the Pacific Northwest*. Extract from Smithsonian Institution Bureau of Ethnology, Bulletin 45. Reprint Seattle: The Shorey Book Store, 1973.

TABOR, ROWLAND, W. *Guide to the Geology of Olympic National Park*. Seattle: University of Washington Press, 1975.

THOMAS, EDWARD HARPER. *Chinook: A History and Dictionary of the Northwest Coast Trade Jargon*. 2nd ed. Portland, Ore.: Binfords & Mort, 1935.

TOWNSHEND, LT. COLONEL C.V.F. *The Military Life of Field-Marshall George First Marquess Townshend, 1724-1807*. London: John Murray, 1901.

UDVARDY, MIKLOS. *The Audubon Society Field Guide to North American Birds*. New York: Alfred A. Knopf, 1977.

UNDERHILL, R. *Indians of the Pacific Northwest*. Indian Life and Customs, vol. 5. Washington, D.C.: Education Division of U.S. Office of Indian Affairs, 1944.

WALKER, STUART H.M.D. *Wind and Strategy*. New York: W.W. Norton, 1973.

WEIR, ALLEN, ed. *North-Western Washington*. Port Townsend, Wash.: Immigration Aid Society of North-Western Washington, 1880. Reprint Seattle: The Shorey Book Store, 1967.

WORKS PROGRESS ADMINISTRATION. *Washington: A Guide to the Evergreen State*. Portland, Ore.: Binfords & Mort, 1941.

WHITNEY, STEPHEN R. *A Field Guide to the Cascades and Olympics*. Seattle: The Mountaineers, 1983.

WILHELM, EUGENE L. JR., *Common Birds of the Olympic National Park*. Port Angeles, Wash.: Olympic Natural History Association, 1961.

WINTHROP, THEODORE. *The Canoe and The Saddle: Adventures Among the Northwestern Rivers and Forests*. Boston: Ticknor & Fields, 1863.

WOOD, ROBERT. *Across the Olympic Mountains: The Press Expedition, 1889-90*. Seattle: University of Washington Press, 1967.

WRIGHT, E.W., ed. *Lewis and Dryden's Marine History of the Pacific Northwest*. 1895. Reprint New York: Antiquarian Press, 1961.

WYDOSKI, RICHARD S., and Whitney, Richard R. *Inland Fishes of Washington*. Seattle: University of Washington Press, 1979.

PERIODICALS   CARSON, ROB. "Port Townsend Revisited." *Pacific Northwest*, April 1984.

GEDOSCH, THOMAS F. "A Note on the Dogfish Oil Industry of Washington Territory." *Pacific Northwest Quarterly*, vol. 59, no. 2 (1968), 100–102.

GOGOL, J.M. "Nootka, Makah Twined Fancy Basket." *American Indian Basketry*, 4 (1981), 4 ff.

GUNTHER, ERNA. "Vancouver and the Indians of Puget Sound." *Pacific Northwest Quarterly*, vol 51, no. 1 (1960), 1–12.

HUSSEY, JOHN A. "Fort Casey – Garrison for Puget Sound." *Pacific Northwest Quarterly*, vol. 47, no. 2 (1956), 33–43.

KERR, WILLIAM T. JR., "The Progressives of Washington, 1910 –1912." *Pacific Northwest Quarterly*, vol. 55, no. 1 (1964), 16–27.

WILSON, MARGARET and McDonald, Jeffery. "Racial Tension at Port Townsend and Bellingham Bay, 1870–1886." *The Annals of the Chinese Historical Society of the Pacific Northwest*, 1983.

THESES AND UNPUBLISHED MANUSCRIPTS   PARKS, MARION. "A Man for his Season: Victor Smith, 1826 –1865," Master's thesis, University of Washington, 1981.

POWER, EDWARD ALLEN. "Washington Pioneers: The John and Mary (Bartlett) Power Family." Jefferson County Historical Society, undated.

POWER, EDWARD ALLEN. "Protection Island and the Power Family." Jefferson County Historical Society, 1976.

SMITH, MAY B. "Picturesque Port Townsend." Original manuscript. University of Washington, 1929. Copy in Jefferson County Historical Society research library.

NEWSPAPERS   *Port Angeles* (Wash.) *Daily News*
Port Angeles (Wash.) *Evening News*
Port Townsend (Wash.) *Call*
Port Townsend (Wash.) *Leader*
Port Townsend (Wash.) *Morning Leader*
Port Townsend (Wash.) *Weekly Leader*
Puget Sound (Wash.) *Argus*
Seattle Post-Intelligencer
Seattle Times

INTERVIEWS   B.G. Brown, Paul Boyer, Bob De Weese, David Etheridge, Steve Hayden, Anne Hirondelle, Tom Johnson, Lainie Johnson, Linda Okazaki, Liz Smith, Wendy Sternshein, Mrs. Heiner Tamme, Thomas T. Wilson.

LETTERS   Nelsa M. Buckingham to Jerry Gorsline, June 19, 1985.

ROBERT BIFFLE is a native of Montana. He moved to
Port Townsend in 1977 where he operates a drafting
studio.

ROBIN BIFFLE has Montana in her blood but has been
a Washington resident off and on since her graduation
from Whitman College in 1974. She is a writer who has
lived in Port Townsend since 1982 and hopes one day to
qualify for old-timer status in the community.

JIM HEYNEN moved to Port Townsend with his wife
Carol Bangs and their children in 1976. For several years
he was employed by Centrum Foundation as their literature and gifted education program coordinator.
Since then he has traveled extensively, giving readings
of his own work and teaching workshops in creative
writing and gifted education. In 1985 he was a recipient
of the National Endowment for the Arts Fellowship in
fiction. He is the author of several collections of poetry
and short stories, among them, *The Man Who Kept
Cigars in His Cap* (stories, 1979), *A Suitable Church*
(poems, 1981), and *You Know What is Right* (stories,
1985).

NORA PORTER is an army brat whose father was stationed at Fort Worden; she is also the daughter of a
native daughter, wife and mother of native sons, and
related to "nearly half the town." A Washington State
University graduate in radio and television communications, she is co-founder of the Port Townsend
High School Scholarship Foundation, the Key City
Players, and the summer theater of the Port Townsend
Summer School of the Arts. A former teacher and
retail merchant, Porter is a civic and arts activist, politician, and feminist whose previously published writing was confined to letters to the editor.

PETER SIMPSON first came to Port Townsend with his wife in 1959, three years out of college. In 1968 he moved his family to the Washington D.C. area. Ten years later they returned. With interest in local and regional history, he is active in the Jefferson County Historical Society and is a member of the board of curators of the Washington State Historical Society. Simpson is author of two previous works on Port Townsend, a chapbook (1961) about the city's Victorian architecture, and an illustrated history (1979).

MARK WELCH is the great grandson of Port Townsend's first mayor, Charles Eisenbeis. A graduate in film and television production from Washington State University, he has pursued a sequence of eclectic careers including meat taster, photographer, and construction worker. He currently owns and operates several small Port Townsend businesses, and is a member of the city parks commission and a trustee for the Jefferson County Historical Society. He and his wife live in a house built on the site of his great-grandfather's brewery.

Index

Abraham, Marge, 271
Adams, Ansel, 160
Adams, W.J.
    development of alcohol plant, 12
    purchase of Washington Mill, 160,235
Ah Tom, 11
Anderson, Guy, 23
Andrews, Laura E., 155
Andrews, Richard, 134
Antonakos, Stephen, 133
Arnold, Kenneth, 276
Aldrich, Ben, 13
Aldrich, Clark Jr., 14
Aldrich, Clark Sr., 13
Aldrich, Fred, 14
Aldrin, Buzz, 193
Alexander, John B., 14
    builds castle at Fort Worden, 39,91
Ali, Muhammad, 254

Bachelder, Charles, 97–98
Bailey, Philip, 169
Baker, Joseph, 173,287
Baker, T.H., Jr., 169
Balch, James, 137
Balch, Lafayette, 97
Ballinger, Richard A., 58
Barkley, Charles, 27
    at Destruction Island, 69
    identification of Strait of Juan de Fuca,
        39,258
Barkley, Francis Hornby, 27
Bartlett, Charles C., 28
Bartlett, Frank, 28
Bartlett, Josiah, 28
Batwell, Edward A., 53,236
Bash, Albert, 64,202
    biography, 29
Bash, Clementine
Beard, James, 29
Becker, Charles W. Sr., 145
Beebe, Lloyd, 182
Beecher, Henry Ward, 22
Beecher, Harriet Foster, 22
Beecher, Herbert Foote, 22
Bell, John, 241
Birkenstol, Ivan, 180
Bishop, William
    farming in Chimacum, 10,49
    at Hastings Pond, 108
Blaine, James B., 172
Bligh, William, 283

Blyn, Marshall, 33
Bodega y Quadra, Juan Francisco de la
    Discovery Bay named for him, 72
    at Destruction Island, 68–69
    as governor at Nootica, 288–289
Boldt, Judge George, 124
Boyle, Kay, 5
Briggs, Albert
    home at Glen Cove, 103,178
    homestead as site of Mill, 168
    names Scow Bay, 237
Brinnon, Elwell P., 37
Brown, Joan, 134
Buckingham, Nelsa M., 87
Bugge, William A., 116,118
Burmester, Bill, 231
Burns, Capt. John E., 35
Burns, Robert, 237

Caan, James, 279
Caines, Robert, 101
Calabrese, Joe, 225
Calahan, Kenneth, 26
Calhoun, George V., 172
Calhoun, Mrs. (first gift shop owner), 226
Callan, E.T., 198
Canterbury, Ray, 211
Carnahan, D.T., 215
Carson, Rob, 5
Castile, Samuel, 145
Cates, Mr. (of Port Townsend Fish Market), 278
Chapman, George, 202,255
Charles II (King of England), 119
Chase, Mary, 46–47
Chase, Salmon P., 125–126,128
Chet-ze-moka (Chief of the Klallam),
        37,62,87,120,138,147
    biography, 44
    park named in his honor, 45
    role in Chimakum massacre, 50
    likeness on Post Office column capitals, 65
    known as Duke of York, 44,76
    meets James G. Swan in San Francisco,
        44,235,261
    placard at Spring Valley Golf Club at Point
        No Point Treaty, 190–191
Chill'lil (wife of Chet-ze-moka), 65
Christie, James Helbold, 204
Clapp, Cyrus F., 56
Cleveland, Grover, 183
Clise, John, 14
Colbert, Claudette, 83

325

Coleman, E.T., 174
Collins, James, 125
Colnett (Meares' commander), 285
Conner, Harriet, 47
Connor, Sam, 36–37
Cook, James
    at Cape Flattery, 39
    misunderstanding of Nootka, 179–180
    recipe for Spruce beer, 254
    misses Strait of Juan de Fuca, 257–258
    exploration of the Northwest Coast, 282–284
Cooper, George R., 276
Cooper, James Fenimore, 276
Costello, J.C., 50
Cottle, Hampden, 211
Coyle, George, 61
Crawford, James, 202

Daubenberger, Donna, 212,271
Davidson, George, 175
Dean, B.F., 33
Dean, Orville, 33
Dee-ah (Chief of the Makah), 178
deKooning, Elaine, 26
DeLeo, Carl, 66
DeLeo, James, 66
DeLeo, Michael (son), 66
DeLeo, Michael (father), 31
DeLion, Rudolph W., 67
Denison, Alan T., 56,105,108,255
Denny, D.T., 173
Devoe, Elias, 68
DeWeese, Bob, 305
Dieguito (Flamenco dancer), 86
Dirk, Limey, 243
Dodd, Charles, 78
Doig, Ivan, 260
Douglas, William O., 191
Downs, George W., 74
Duddenhausen, August, 108
Duke of York (see Chet-ze-moka)

Earles, Michael, 118
Ebey, Emily, 78
Ebey, Isaac N., 77–78
Edbrook, N.E., 64
Eels, Myron, 211
Einarsen, Arthur, 209
Eisenbeis, Charles, 20,162
    biography, 83–84
    brick factory near Fort Worden, 91
    builds castle-like residence, 40
    builds Mount Baker Block, 174–175
Eisenhower, Dwight D., 84–85
Eldridge, William
    farming at Chimacum, 10,49
    at Hastings Pond, 108
Eliza, Francisco, 194,235
Etheridge, David, 15

Fahlen, Charles, 134,135
Fauntleroy, Constance, 175
Ferry, Elisha, 203
Fisher, Elmer H., 20
    designs Hastings Building, 107
    designs N.D. Hill Building, 109
Focke, Anne, 134
Foo, Charley
Ford, Gerald, 203,212
Ford, Mrs. Gerald, 203
Ford, Luther, 90
Ford, Ollie, 90
Foster, Jean, 84–85
Fraser, David, 152
Fowler, Enoch S.
    builds Fowler Building, 100
    builds Fowler House, 101
Fowler, Mary Caines, 101

Gardner, Herbert, 103
Gehrke, John, 231
George I (king of England), 266
George II (king of England), 266
Gere, Richard, 181
Gibbs, George, 147,174
Gigedo, Revilla, 287–289
Gonzales de Haro, Lopez, 235
Gossett, Lou, Jr., 114,181
Grady, A.C., 116
Grant, Lizzie, 104
Grant, Capt. Thomas, 104
Graves, Morris, 23
Gray, Robert, 258,286–287
Greeley, Horace, 124
Green, Joshua, 89
Greening, Charles, 134
Griffith, Irene, 231
Gritt, Peter, 27
Grover, Paddy, 161
Gunther, Erna, 233

Hackett, Regina, 132
Hackford, Taylor, 181
Hadlock, Samuel, 160
Haight, Dennis, 120
Haight, Suzannah, 120
Haller, G. Morris, 104,172
Haller, Granville O., 104
Haller, Theodore N., 104
Hamrol, Lloyd, 134
Harris, Stephen L., 174
Harrison, Benjamin
    assistance with Customs House
        construction, 64
    visits Albert Bash, 29,202
    influences Congress to fund Fort
        construction, 203
Hasse, Carol, 36
Hastings, Frank W., 107

Hastings, Loren B., 107,133,138,178
  as boat builder, 35
  purchase of tugboat *Mastic*, 35
  as founder of Port Townsend, 96–100,199
  at Happy Valley, 106
  at Hastings Pond, 108
  donates site for St. Paul's Church, 232
  sinking of his ship *Discovery*, 246
  partnership with Henry L. Tibbals, Sr., 265
Hastings, Lucinda (Bingham)
  as founder of Port Townsend, 96–98
  builds James-Hastings Building, 107
  builds house, 108
Hastings, Oregon Columbus, 96,97
Hayes, Gary, 86
Hayes, Rutherford B., 171
  visits Port Townsend, 202
Heath, Rene, 226
Henry, Anson, 129
Herbert, Frank, 109
Hernan, Paddy, 161
Herstrom, Walt, 65
Hervey, Mona, 207
Heskett, Bob, 83
Hill, Daniel C., 151
Hill, Nathaniel D., 110
Hill, Robert C., 84
Hill, Sallie, 99
Hill, Mrs. (president of the Library
    Association), 156
Hirondelle, Anne, 134
Hollis, Doug, 134,135
Hood, Lord Samuel, 115
Hop Yuen, 10
Horiuchi, Paul, 23
House, Dr. J.C., 151
Huelsdonk, John, 110–111,130
Hylund, Peter E.
  biography, 232
  rings church bell on foggy days, 88

Ickes, Harold, 130

Jackman, Thomas, 84
Jackson, Ruth Seavey, 132–135
Jacobsen, Andrew, 118
James, Francis W.
  builds James-Hastings Building, 107
  builds James House, 136
Jamieson, James, 250
Jarman, William, 136
John Paul II (pope), 193
Johnson, Harry, 24,29,56,101,224
Johnson, Lainie, 101
Johnson, Lyndon B., 295
Johnson, Mary P.
  as arts leader, 24,25–26
  restoration of Bartlett House, 29
  restores Cyrus F. Clapp Building, 56

  restores Fowler-Caines Building, 101
  encourages restoration, 224
Johnson, Tom, 101
Johnstone (Vancouver's commander), 287
Jolles, Arnold, 134
Jones, Nard, 6
Jones, William J., 151
Joyce, J.M., 141
Juan de Fuca, 142
Jung, Carol, 142

Kamehameha (Hawaiian chief), 289
Katz, Adele (Maas), 70–72
Katz, Edwin, 72
Katz, Israel, 145–146
  disappearance, 69–72
Katz, Solomon, 69,225
Keegan, Sydney, 292
Kellett, Capt. Henry, 31,39,178,214
Kelly, Larry, 250
Kern, Marybell, 37
Klocker, Mayor, 156
Knoff, John J., 281
Kuhn, J.A., 84
  biography, 152–153
  clambakes, 54–55,145
  tricks Chet-ze-moka, 50
Kuhn, Louis, 152

Lah-ka-Nim (Chet-ze-moka's son), 62,120,147
Lambert, Marion, 264
Lander, Tom, 145
Landes, Col. Henry C., 84
  biography, 154
Lange, Billy, 252–253
Lardner, John, 253
Leahy, Frank, 253
Lerner, Alan Jay, 105
Lewis, Fred, 155
Levy, Max, 242–243
Lincoln, Abraham, 127,129
Lockhart, Russell, 142
London, Jack, 159–160
Lowe, Frederick, 105

Maas, Louis, 70
McCool, H.J., Sr., 36
McCormick, Adeline, 22
McCormick, Charles, 197
McCurdy, James G., 52,137,166
  tale of dragon at Tamanous Rock, 263
  tale of Thunderbird at Crows' Nest, 62–63
MacDonald, Betty, 83
McIlroy, F.W., 143
McIntyre, James, 165
McIntyre, John, 165–166
Mack, Connie, 252
McLarney, Art, 253

MacMurray, Fred, 83
Magnuson, Sen. Warren G., 94
Maniloux, Fr. Regis, 231–232
Manis, Emanuel, 164
Manuel de Alava, José, 39
Martin, R.W., 278
Martinez, Capt. Estaban José, 257,285
Mason, Marsha, 279
Mastick, S.B., 72
Maynard, Henrietta, 164
Meares, Capt. John
    recovery of Destruction Island relic, 69
    names Mount Olympus, 175
    trading on Northwest Coast, 284–285
Menzies (Vancouver's botanist), 287
Mercer, Asa, 21
Merriman, J.H., 127–128
Miles, Nelson, 92
Milholland, Doug, 136
Milholland, Nancy, 136
Millar, Herbert, 71
Minor, Thomas T., 104
    biography, 171–172
Miss, Mary, 134
Moody, Dwight L., 88
Moore, James A., 131
Morca, Teo, 86
Morgan, Henry
    purchase of tugboat *Mastic*, 35
    biography, 172–173
    buys and sells Protection Island, 208
    drills for coal on Marrowstone Island, 163
Morris, Carl, 26
Mutty, Peter, 177

Nakano, Evangeline, 303
Nakano, George, 303
Naughton, Peter J., 276
Neff, Margaret, 282
Nelson, Marjorie
    establishes Port Townsend Festival
        Theatre, 104
    leads professional theatre at Point
        Hudson, 189
Neuharth, Gene, 302
Neuharth, Maria, 302
Ng (owner of Zee Tai Co.), 307
Nicholls, James, 178
Norby, Peter, 180,252

Oen, Julian, 143
Okazaki, Linda
    marginalia, 135
Oliveira, Nathan, 26
Olson, C.A., 107
O'Neil, Joseph P., 203–204
On Tai, 42

Palmer, J. Frederick, 39
Patrick, Andrew G., 53,198
Pershing, Gen. John, 93
Petrich, Nora, 36
Pettygrove, Al, 179
Pettygrove, Francis William
    as founder of Port Townsend, 96–98,199
    as founder of Portland, 199
Pettygrove, Francis William, Jr., 186–187
Pettygrove, Sophia, 98,108
Pickering (Territorial Governor), 128
Pierce, Franklin
Pinchot, Gifford, 58
Plummer, A.A.
    as founder of Port Townsend, 97–100
Plummer, Ann, 98
Polk, James, 166
Pope, Andrew Jackson
    establishes logging enterprise, 192–193
    at Port Ludlow, 194–198,235
Power, John Sr., 208
Power, Mary, 208
Prince, Jim, 152
Prince of Wales (see Lah-ka-nim)
Prothero, Robert, 37
Puget, Peter, 210,287
Purchase, Samuel, 257

Quadra (see Bodega y Quadra)
Quimper, Manuel, 39
    first entry into Discovery Bay, 72,213–214,258
    names Mount Baker, 173

Rainier, Peter, 176
Raphael, Ralph, 165
Rauschenberg, Robert, 25,29
Ray, Dixy Lee, 117
Redford, Grant, 22–23
Reposa, Joe, 48
Rhinehard, Chris, 136
Richardson, Henry Hobson
    influence on design of Customs House and
        Post Office, 64
    influence on design of Jefferson County
        Courthouse, 140
    influence on Port Townsend architecture, 19
Richardson, Léon, 206
Rickover, Adm. Hyman, 272
Ritchie, Willis A., 139–140
Roberts, George, 245–246
Roberts (English explorer), 285,286
Robinson, Chuck, 254
Robinson, Reuben S., 49
Rockefeller, Jeannette, 26
Rockefeller, Winthrop, 26
Rockne, Knute, 253
Roff, Pearl, 206

Rogers, Caroline (Mrs. Victor Smith), 126
Roosevelt, Franklin D., 153,183
Roosevelt, Theodore, 58,86,183
Rosellini, Albert, 29,116
Rossi, Fr. (Catholic priest), 188
Rothschild, D.C.H., 20,225
    biography, 230
    opens Kentucky Store, 78
Rothschild, Dorette, 230
Rothschild, Emilie, 230
Rothschild, Eugene, 230

Sankey, Ira D., 88
Sappho (Greek poet), 236
Saunders, James C., 236
Saunders, Tom, 243
Sayward, W.F., 194
Scheyer, Dr. William, 23
Schmidt, Howard, 118
Schmidt, Juanita, 118
Schnath, Mrs. (valley resident), 297
Schroeder, Julius C., 20,101,174,187,202,265
Schultz, Zella, 209
Seattle (Chief of the Suquamish), 190–191,260
Seavey, James
    marginalia, 133
See-hem-itza (wife of Chet-ze-moka), 65
Seldon, J.W., 88
Semple, Eugene, 203
Serra, Richard, 133
S'Hai-ak, 138
    likeness on Customs House capital, 65
    at conference with founders of Port
        Townsend, 97
Shaw, George Bernard, 105
Sherman, William Tecumseh, 91
Shields, Marvin, 295
Shirley, Brent S., 136
Shomer, Forest, 9
Simpson, Buster, 134
Sims, Ed, 66,167,242,251
    biography, 248
Slyter, Robert A., 244
Smith, George Venable, 280
Smith, May, 27
Smith, Norman R., 281
Smith, Victor, 125–129,248,250
Snyder, Gary, 187
Snyder, Tim, 37
Sokol, Vilem, 23,91
Spafford, Marilyn, 292
Spafford, Michael, 133
Spinks, Benjamin T., 232–233
Spielberg, Stephen, 114
Spinks, Benjamin
Stanley, Henry Morton, 203
Starrett, George E.
    biography, 255
    as major contractor in Port Townsend

Starrett, Mrs. George (Ann Van Bokelen), 155,255
Stark, Peggy, 244
Steinbrueck, Victor
    influence on Port Townsend preservation,
        24,114
    remodels building at Point Hudson as
        theatre, 189
    restores Thomas Grant House, 104
Sternshein, Wendy, 27
Steve, Joe, 27
Stevens, Governor, 191
Stopps, Eleanor, 209
Stowe, Harriet Beecher, 22
Stratton, Thomas, 174
Sturrock, Earl, 230
Swan, James G.
    attempts at aquaculture, 15
    meets Chet-ze-moka in San Francisco, 44,235
    agent for Northern Pacific Railroad, 79,214
    role in passage of military fortification bill, 80
    comment on gun sales to Indians, 119
    attitude toward Indians, 124
    develops model of Port Townsend, 198–199
    tale about Kwartseedie, the southwind, 220
    biography, 260–263
    complains of youthful troublemakers, 277
    support of new water system, 296
    describes taste of whale meat, 300
Swaney, Homer H., 131
Swanson, Arthur, 262
Swanson, Hans, 262

Taft, William, 58
Talbot, William C.
    establishes logging enterprise, 191–192
    at Port Ludlow, 194–198,235
Tamme, Heiner, 193
Thomas, George, 134
Thorndyke, John R., 265
Tibbals, Caroline, 265–266
Tibbals, Henry L., Sr.
    biography, 265–266
    ownership of Union Wharf, 277–278
Tobey, Mark, 23
Townshend, Charles, 266
Townshend, Charles (son), 267
Townshend, Ethelreda (Audrey), 266
Townshend, George (Marquis), 266–267
Townshend, George (7th Marquis), 267
Tucker, A. Horace
    early contractor, 20
    builds St. Paul's Episcopal Church, 232
    builds Rothschild House
Tuey, Charley, 10
Tukey, John
    builds Chevy Chase, 46
    buried treasure, 269–270
Tworkov, Jack, 26
Tze Hong, Charley, 307(M)

Valerianos, Apostolos, 257
Vancouver, George, 39,61,142,194,214,256
   naming of Admiralty Inlet, 9
   trading with Indians, 27
   naming of Cape Flattery, 39
   observes evidence of small pox among
      Indians, 50
   names Dungeness, 76
   names Discovery Bay, 72
   sails HMS *Discovery*, 73
   names Hood Canal, 115
   sights Mount Rainier, 176
   Klallam attempt to trade children, 147
   crew carves names on rock at Discovery, 157
   names Marrowstone Point, 163–164
   names Mount Baker, 173
   influences Spanish to leave Neah Bay, 178
   names Oak Bay, 188
   names Point Wilson, 191
   at Protection Island, 207,209
   names Puget Sound, 210
   treatment of crew, 254
   names Port Townsend Bay, 266
   biography, 282,289
   exploration of Northwest Coast, 282–289
   describes wool dogs, 302
Vanderlip, Dianne, 134,135
Valentino, Rudolph, 282
Victoria (queen of England), 40

Wade, Violet, 207
Walker, Cyrus, 194–198
Walker, Scott, 210

Wall, Gary, 231
Wanamaker, Clarence, 177
Warenskjold, Dorothy, 294
Waterman, Sigmund, 69,225
Watt, James, 58
Whistler, Garland N., 95
Whistler, James McNeil, 95
Whiteway, A.S., 40
Whiteway, William T., 20,101,174,187,202,265
Whitney, Robert S., 191
Whitney, William E., 301–302
Wilhelm I (kaiser of Germany), 235
Wilkes, Charles, 181,190,264,294
Williams, Frankie, 206
Willoughby, Charles, 21
Willoughby, Sarah (ne Cheney), 21
Wilson (commander of Shubrick), 128
Wilson, Capt. George, 191–192
Wilson, Tom, 25,26
Wilson, Woodrow, 183
Wing Sing, 307
Winger, Debra, 181
Winston, Patrick Henry, 6
Wolfe, James, 266
Wood, Robert, 175,176

Yarr, Tommy, 253–254
Yee Sing Wo Kee, 307
Yip Suey, 10

Zamora, Robert, 86

CITY OF DREAMS

Designed by Tree Swenson
Galliard text and titles composed by Type Gallery, Seattle
Additional Galliard titles composed by Walker & Swenson, Port Townsend
Printed by Arcata Graphics, Fairfield